Monte Verità Proceedings of the Centro Stefano Franscini Ascona

Edited by K. Osterwalder, ETH Zürich

Programming Environments for Massively Parallel Distributed Systems

Working Conference of the
IFIP WG 10.3, April 25–29, 1994

Edited by
K. M. Decker
R. M. Rehmann

1994

Springer Basel AG

Editors:

PD Dr. Karsten M. Decker
Director of Research and Development
Swiss Scientific Computing Center
CSCS ETH-Zürich
Via Cantonale
CH-6928 Manno

e-mail: decker@cscs.ch

Dr. René M. Rehmann
Research Scientist
Swiss Scientific Computing Center
CSCS ETH-Zürich
Via Cantonale
CH-6928 Manno

e-mail: rehmann@cscs.ch

A CIP catalogue redord for this book is available from the Library of Congress, Washington D.C., USA

Deutsche Bibliothek Cataloging-in-Publication Data

Programming environments for massively parallel distributed systems : working conference of the IFIP WG 10.3, April 25 – 29, 1994 / ed. by K. M. Decker ; R. M. Rehmann. – Basel ; Boston ; Berlin : Birkhäuser, 1994
(Monte verità)

NE: Decker, Karsten [Hrsg.]; International Federation for Information Processing / Working Group on Software Hardware Interrelation

ISBN 978-3-0348-9668-9 ISBN 978-3-0348-8534-8 (eBook)
DOI 10.1007/978-3-0348-8534-8

Originally published by Birkhäuser Verlag Basel, Switzerland in 1994

Camera-ready copy prepared by the editors.
Printed on acid-free paper produced from chlorine-free pulp.

9 8 7 6 5 4 3 2 1

Preface

The 1994 working conference on *Programming Environments for Massively Parallel Systems* was the latest event of the working group WG 10.3 of the *International Federation for Information Processing* (IFIP). It succeeded the 1992 conference in Edinburgh on *Programming Environments for Parallel Computing.*

The purpose of the conference was to bring together researchers who are working on ways how to help programmers exploit the full potential of massively parallel systems, and to discuss the state-of-the-art of software for massively parallel systems with special attention to programming tools and environments.

The conference was held from April 25 to April 29, 1994, at *Centro Stefano Franscini* (CSF), Monte Verità, located in the hills above Ascona on the banks of Lago Maggiore, in the southern part of Switzerland. It was jointly organized by the Swiss Scientific Computing Center *Centro Svizzero di Calcolo Scientifico* (CSCS) and CSF. The more than 60 participants at this conference came from both academia and industry in Europe, USA and Japan. The conference was sponsored by the Swiss Federal Institute of Technology Zurich (ETHZ), the Swiss National Science Foundation (SNF), NEC Corporation, and Sun Microsystems, Switzerland.

During the five days of the conference, more than 40 scientific papers were presented in 14 sessions on topics covering all aspects of software for massively parallel systems. During a demonstration session, the audience was able to get the 'touch and feel' of several different recently developed tool environments. The technical program was supplemented by a public talk in Italian by Prof. Marco Vanneschi, University of Pisa, Italy.

Each day of the conference was devoted to a specific theme in programming of massively parallel systems. Two sessions in the morning and one in the afternoon consisted of in-depth technical presentations. The remaining time was organized in an innovative fashion to serve the purpose of a working conference. First, one of the participants gave a critical review of the state-of-the-art of the day's theme and summarized open questions. After that small working groups were formed, each focusing on one of the most pressing problems of that day's theme. An assessment of possible solutions to that problem was made and the findings presented informally in the late afternoon. Both, the review and the working groups were generally considered useful by the participants. This forum not only brought the participants closer together to discuss matters informally, but also led to the presentation of interesting perspectives.

Last, but surely not least, I want to express my gratitude to René Rehmann and Klara Mafli (CSCS), Katia Bastianelli (CSF/ETHZ), and the other staff of SeRD–CSCS and CSF who all did an exceptional job in organizing the conference. Through their dedicated work, they ensured that the conference ran smoothly and created a very pleasant and stimulating atmosphere at Monte Verità. Thanks to them, the conference will surely remain an unforgettable experience to all of us.

Manno, May 18, 1994 Karsten M. Decker

Table of Contents

Programming Environments for Massively Parallel Distributed Systems, Monte Verità, Switzerland

Introduction

Karsten M. Decker

The promise of scalable computation and storage space provided by Massively Parallel Systems (MPSs) is becoming more and more important for high-performance computing. Growing acceptance of MPSs in academia is clearly visible now. In spite of this fact and the widespread view that MPSs represent an important technology for progress in science and engineering, and, more generally, for commercial competitiveness, the usage of MPSs in industry is still minimal. One obstacle to higher usage is the fact that the programming of MPSs is still a complex task. Alleviating this software problem is sometimes referred to as one of the biggest challenges of the 1990's.

The strategic importance of MPSs for the progress of high-performance computing is recognized in national and international information technology programs in Europe, USA and Japan. While previous activities in Europe focused on the development of the methodical foundations of massively parallel computing, there is now a strong orientation towards porting real applications to MPSs. In the USA, there is a concentration on the so-called *Grand Challenges* of science. Japan's recently launched *Real World Computing* program has a wider scope and investigates the general application of massively parallel systems to soft information processing.

The acceptance of MPSs on the application user level has grown significantly. But, in spite of all the efforts and achievements, their usage still lags far behind expectations. This is especially true for the pragmatic industrial users. From their perspective, ease of MPS use has not yet been achieved even for applications believed to be well-suited for these architectures.

Analyzing the current situation, one of the major reasons for this failure is the still insufficient level of abstraction provided for programming MPSs. In particular, still missing are *high-level* programming methods and corresponding tools supporting the demanding design phase of parallel applications. Most of the available programming tools still do *not* operate on a sufficiently high level of abstraction; often they provide inadequate means to handle the natural level of granularity of an application. Standard high-level programming languages with language extensions or run-time libraries supporting programming of the distributed address space of MPSs require considerable effort and experience to develop efficient programs. To a lesser extent, the latter is also true for higher-level application-oriented programming languages like High Performance Fortran (HPF). Although the underlying programming paradigm of HPF frees the user of programming the detailed inter-process communications, the ambiguities involved in the required data decomposition and distribution demand decisions which cannot be treated safely by the average scientific programmer. Moreover, the data decomposition and distribution strategy may vary significantly from one system to the other, putting severe constraints on portability. Interactive assistance in this complex programming task would be most desirable, but does not yet exist.

Another criticism is that the syntax required in the programming process is still far too convoluted to be mastered easily by application users. While MPS programming is still based on the concepts underlying high-level programming languages, it is loaded with numerous additional notions unfamiliar to even the experienced programmer of conventional systems.

Finally, the portability issue is still addressed insufficiently. The recently finalized Message-Passing Interface (MPI) standard, which soon will provide a common, low-level virtual machine interface to all commercially available parallel computer systems, ensures only purely formal portability. Similarly, the HPF standard also contributes to increased portability, at least for data parallel problems. Parallel efficiency, however, is generally not assured across different hardware platforms, even though this requirement is of utmost importance to application users concerned about the protection of their software development efforts.

The research and development work presented at this conference addresses the entire spectrum of problems identified above and thus reflects recent progress in software development for MPSs. Significant progress was achieved in a variety of fields, from *virtual machines* which are less cumbersome to program, to more convenient *programming models*, advanced *programming languages*, as well as to more sophisticated *programming tools*.

Only a short time ago, the basic *programming model* underlying the majority of all programming efforts for MPSs was based on message-passing providing only a low degree of abstraction from the hardware. Although conceptually clean, it is general considered too difficult for scientific programmers to deal with — the programmer must assume full responsibility for the management of the distributed address space.

In the last two years, efforts were undertaken for higher levels of abstractions. For example, in data parallel problems, a more advanced programming model providing a single thread of control, a global name space, and loosely synchronous parallel computation gained acceptance. Using programming languages based on this model, the programmer specifies the data decomposition and distribution with the help of program annotations or language extensions, and the actual generation of communications, i.e., the management of the distributed address space, is shifted to the language level and performed at compile time. This model adds considerable programming comfort and is probably well-suited for highly structured problems. However, unstructured problems requiring run-time analysis, cannot be appropriately treated. A further step with respect to hardware abstraction goes the physically distributed, single address space programming model. Here, the management of the distributed address space is shifted to the operating system level. There also exist parallel machines which provide hardware support for this programming model. The suitability of both of these models for programming real applications in the data parallel regime is currently under practical evaluation.

Research in *Programming languages* has also been rampant in the last few years. Analogous to the evolution of programming models, recent developments indicate a trend toward higher levels of abstractions. Numerous activities in research laboratories resulted in a rich spectrum of new languages which can be classified according to the organization of the address space, and the level of abstraction which they offer to the programmer. Languages exist with distributed address space, further classified according to the utilized communication mechanisms, and languages with single or shared address space, further classified according to programming language type or organization of the data structures. Proposed parallel languages offer also different levels of abstraction. Furthermore there are standard high-level languages (C, C++, Fortran), extended by language constructs or supplemented by run-time libraries.

Probably the most important development for the scientific programmers' community is HPF, a high-level, application-oriented language which uses code annotations for parallel distribution of code and data. HPF's development is remarkable because of its user- and vendor-driven definition which led to quick and unconventional standardization in a bottom-up approach. The usefulness and range of applicability of HPF is currently under practical evaluation. One of the deficiencies of HPF is that it does not support the important class of unstructured grid problems.

Major advances in public and vendor research and development laboratories were made in developing *programming tools*. As a result, all MPS vendors now offer a parallel debugger and a performance analyzer supporting at least a low-level, message-passing based programming paradigm. The horizontal integration of these tools into integrated environments, resulting in improved tool interaction, is now under way. Other recent developments aim for improved support of higher-levels of abstractions such as global data views, hierarchical performance analysis and optimization, as well as support for changing the level of abstraction, i.e., zooming into critical program regions in increasing detail on the one hand, and abstracting from program details on the other. Crucial for the success of MPSs is research on the methodologies and techniques required for integrated tool environments which scale to hundreds and thousands of processors.

The design and implementation of intelligent programming environments is another topic currently under intensive investigation. These environments will support the program design phase by providing user- and application-oriented, declarative problem specification formalisms. They will help to automate the difficult parts of programming MPSs with distributed address space, and address the problems of portability and software reuse on a very high level of abstraction. They will support interactive parallel programming and thus increase the programmer's productivity. Finally, these environments will also facilitate the teaching of MPS programming.

General purpose MPSs are still down the road. This goal is perhaps only of academic importance and may never be achieved. From our experiences gained over the last fifteen years with conventional high-performance computer systems, we know that even the goal of developing general purpose vector-computers with one or only a few processors was never achieved to full satisfaction. It appears that current expectations on the architectural characteristics of the next generation high-performance computing systems need to be generalized. Instead of arguing for either a multiprocessor vector-computer, or a massively parallel system, or a workstation cluster, etc., the tendency is towards transparently accessible heterogeneous meta-computer systems incorporating all these different hardware concepts. Such systems would optimally fulfill the requirements of application users to achieve good performance for a broad spectrum of distinct applications.

What are the long-term developments anticipated for the next three to four years ? With respect to hardware and architectures, we expect a heterogeneous mix of parallel vector processors and massively parallel processors (meta-computing environments). The size of the memory will drive performance and cost of these systems. Clusters of workstations will move upward in performance, connected by, for example, scalable ATM networks. Microprocessors for desk-top systems are generally considered to be not efficient for massively parallel systems. In the long run, optical computing, e.g., massively parallel processor systems with free-space optical interconnects, offers an interesting perspective to overcome some of the limitations of current day's technology.

With respect to software, the distributed memory, single address space programming model, which is uniformly addressable at not necessarily uniform speed, will probably become popular. This model will be supported by corresponding parallel languages which will also allow efficient programming of unstructured problems. Much more work will be devoted to the realization of intelligent programming environments. Particular emphasis will be on application-field specific user interfaces and interactive programming support. Methods and techniques for efficient reuse of software on different levels of abstractions by means of templates and algorithmic skeletons will be more intensively investigated. Finally, to manage and program meta-computing environments, new methods and techniques will be developed. First steps in this direction have already been taken: the user submits a job to a network of parallel vector processors, massively parallel processors, and clusters of workstations which then transparently executes the job in a way which optimizes the usage of resources.

It is research developments presented at conferences such as this one which will ensure that MPSs live up to their potential in the years to come: that MPSs gain the anticipated acceptance and fulfill the needs of academia and especially industry.

Programming Environments for Massively Parallel Distributed Systems, Monte Verità, Switzerland

The Cray Research MPP Fortran Programming Model

Tom MacDonald
Cray Research, Inc.
Eagan MN USA
tam@cray.com

Zdenek Sekera
Cray Research (Suisse) S.A.
Lausanne, Switzerland
zs@cray.com

Abstract

An integral part of any computer system is the programming model because most users program with high level languages. Programming model definition for massively parallel systems is an important research area. In their current Fortran product, Cray Research, Inc. has defined a Fortran based programming model that allows programmers to specify both explicit and implicit communication in a parallel program. The explicit communication is available through a message passing library that supports both a standard interface for sending and receiving data, and low level primitives that directly exploit addressing features available in the target machine, the Cray T3D® system. The implicit communication is available through language features called *data sharing* and *work sharing*. The data sharing and work sharing features are available through a set of directives that can be added to existing programs. There is also implied work sharing available through the use of array syntax statements involving shared data. There are other directives and intrinsic functions that provide access to explicit synchronization. One unique quality of this model is that both implicit and explicit communication styles can be combined within the same program.

1 Introduction

The Cray Research, Inc. (CRI) MPP Fortran Programming Model defines a feature rich implementation that caters to a diverse programming community still exploring the best way to exploit this relatively new technology called *massively parallel processing*. The guiding principles used to define the linguistic features found in this model are: it must be useful for constructing highly parallel programs, it must be general enough for future architectures, and it must permit an efficient implementation. The success of CRI's initial massively parallel system is dependent on the usability of the model and the ability to deliver high performance. Both the software implementation and architecture must cooperate to achieve these goals.

2 Architecture Assumptions

Some assumptions about the underlying hardware architecture are present in this programming model. The first assumption is that the architecture is a Multiple Instruction Multiple Data (MIMD) parallel architecture.

The CRI MPP Fortran Programming Model assumes that each PE has its own privately accessible memory module and other accessible memory modules that are *remote.* Remote references traverse an interconnection network to some uniquely identifiable PE on the network. This is called a *distributed memory* system. A high speed interconnection network is critical to providing high performance.

Although the memory system is physically distributed across the PEs, there is architectural support for viewing all of the memory systems as a *global address space* with nonuniform access time. The architecture also provides *memory latency tolerance* features that decreases the marginal cost of referencing a block of remote memory locations. This reduces the number of computational instructions required to hide the overhead of remote references. The *block transfer engine* is an asynchronous direct memory access controller that redistributes up to 65,536 64-bit words of data across the entire network (if desired) without interruption from the PE. There is also a low overhead asynchronous *prefetch queue* that stores up to sixteen 64-bit words of remote data.

Finally, there are assumptions that are not directly related to parallel execution, but necessary for efficiency and usability. These include fast PEs, sufficient range and precision in the underlying floating-point arithmetic, and 64-bit integers.

3 Message Passing Style

There are really two fundamentally different styles of programming available with the CRI MPP Fortran Programming Model. The first style uses explicit message passing defined by a set of library functions used for communication and synchronization. These functions are used to send data to, and to receive data from remote PEs.

Message passing allows existing message passing programs to execute on the Cray T3D system, and the development of new applications that can exploit high performance and portability through a standard interface. Both needs are accommodated. A pure message passing program does not need a global address space because communication does not use shared variables. All communication must be explicitly coordinated within the application with one PE sending data and another PE receiving. Since programming with explicit communication can be tedious, another programming style has been defined that permits communication through globally addressable shared variables. It is important to note that both message passing and global addressing can be combined within the same program.

4 Global Address Style

The global address style presents a *work sharing* model that distributes data objects and parallel work across tasks created at program startup time. The major linguistic features affect data declarations, parallel regions, distribution of loop iterations, array syntax, synchronization primitives, subroutine interfaces, and special intrinsic functions. These features allow a range of programming styles including explicit control over parallelism through multiple threads of independent execution, implicit parallelism through data parallel execution, and combinations of both styles.

5 Data Objects

Data objects are assigned to storage locations on the distributed memory modules associated with each PE. They include variables, common blocks and dynamically allocated stack and heap space. The global address style supports two additional attributes for data objects. Data objects are either *private* or *shared.* Data distributions allow programmers to distribute their data objects in a variety of ways. These data distribution features can help increase performance by decreasing the number of remote references, and by increasing *locality*, that is, increasing the number of references local to a PE.

A private data object can only be referenced by the task that owns it. (There is a one-to-one correspondence between tasks and PEs.) A reference to a private data object is never a remote reference. Private data is replicated on all tasks. The default attribute is the private attribute. All data objects are assumed to be private unless explicitly declared otherwise. In this paper, the term *private* is used to mean private to a task or PE (which is different than the use of the term private in the Fortran 90 standard).

A shared data object can be referenced by any task. Shared data is not replicated, in that there is only one data object shared by all tasks. Shared data objects must be declared as such, and can be distributed across all of the PEs executing the program. The individual entities within a common, local variables, and dummy arguments can be distributed. The one exception is entities declared within "blank common blocks," because the size of these data objects can expand.

5.1 Dimensional Distributions

The CRI MPP Fortran Programming Model allows different dimensions of a shared array to be distributed differently. The declaration of a *dimensionally distributed* array specifies the distribution for each dimension, and is intended to increase data reference locality by providing fine control over the placement of array elements. Each dimension can be distributed with one of the following distribution specifiers:

:BLOCK(N) a *block* distribution where N contiguous elements are in each block and each PE owns the same number of blocks

:BLOCK a *block* distribution where each PE owns exactly one block of contiguous elements

: a *degenerate* distribution specifies an entire dimension is resident on a PE (i.e., not distributed).

The following example shows a single dimensioned array that is distributed with a *block-size* of one, using the `:BLOCK(N)` distribution.

```
      REAL A(16)
CDIR$ SHARED A( :BLOCK(1) )
```

The following figure shows the distribution of the elements across four PEs.

Distribution Across 4 PEs															
PE0				PE1				PE2				PE3			
1	5	9	13	2	6	10	14	3	7	11	15	4	8	12	16

The first four elements of array A are all on different PEs. Similarly, for the next four elements. Notice that every block has the same number of elements and every PE has the same number of blocks. The next example shows the same array, only with a block-size of two.

```
      REAL A(16)
CDIR$ SHARED A( :BLOCK(2) )
```

The following figure shows the distribution of this array across four PEs when the block-size is two.

Distribution Across 4 PEs															
PE0				PE1				PE2				PE3			
1	2	9	10	3	4	11	12	5	6	13	14	7	8	15	16

This distribution places two contiguous elements in each block. The next example demonstrates the `:BLOCK` distribution for the same array.

```
      REAL A(16)
CDIR$ SHARED A( :BLOCK )
```

There is only one block assigned to each PE with the `:BLOCK` distribution.

In order to reduce the overhead associated with computing the address of arbitrary array elements, power of 2 restrictions are placed on dimension sizes, block-sizes, and the number of PEs assigned to a dimension. The formula for computing the block-size of a `:BLOCK` distribution is: `block_size = N / P` where `N` is the extent of the dimension, and `P` is the number of PEs assigned to that dimension. The following figure shows how the `:BLOCK` distribution for this array is spread across four PEs.

Distribution Across 4 PEs															
PE0				PE1				PE2				PE3			
1	2	3	4	5	6	7	8	9	10	11	12	13	14	15	16

In this example the block-size is 4 because `N=16` (the extent) and `P=4` (the number of PEs).

The degenerate distribution allows an entire dimension to be assigned to one PE. This is useful when, for example, it is beneficial to assign an entire row or column of an array to one PE. For example:

```
      REAL A(16,3)
CDIR$ SHARED A(:BLOCK,:)
```

declares the first dimension to always reside on a single PE. The following figure shows this distribution across four PEs.

Distribution Across 4 PEs											
PE0			PE1			PE2			PE3		
1,1	1,2	1,3	5,1	5,2	5,3	9,1	9,2	9,3	13,1	13,2	13,3
2,1	2,2	2,3	6,1	6,2	6,3	10,1	10,2	10,3	14,1	14,2	14,3
3,1	3,2	3,3	7,1	7,2	7,3	11,1	11,2	11,3	15,1	15,2	15,3
4,1	4,2	4,3	8,1	7,2	7,3	12,1	12,2	12,3	16,1	16,2	16,3

The above example declares a "block" of rows to be assigned to each PE. It is also possible to have just one row assigned to a PE with the following declaration:

```
      REAL A(N$PES,30)
CDIR$ SHARED A(:BLOCK,:)
```

Since this declares the first dimension's size to be the number of PEs, and the second dimension to be degenerate, each PE is assigned a row of array `A`. Note also that there is an exception to the rule that dimension sizes must be a power of 2. When the last (rightmost) dimension has a degenerate distribution, the size need not be a power of 2.

5.2 Geometry and Weights

The concept of *geometry* in this model is an abstraction of the dimensional distribution that simplifies the maintenance and declaration of several arrays with similar dimensional distributions. Change a single `GEOMETRY` declaration, and the distribution of all arrays distributed according to that geometry are changed automatically when the program is recompiled. The following example demonstrates how to declare a geometry.

```
CDIR$ GEOMETRY G(1:BLOCK, 2:BLOCK)
      REAL A(4,8), B(4,8)
CDIR$ SHARED (G) :: A, B
```

The declaration of the geometry `G` declares a named distribution (the meaning of the `1:` and `2:` is discussed later). In this example, the arrays `A` and `B` are declared to have the distribution specified by `G`. The following figure shows the distribution for these arrays across eight PEs.

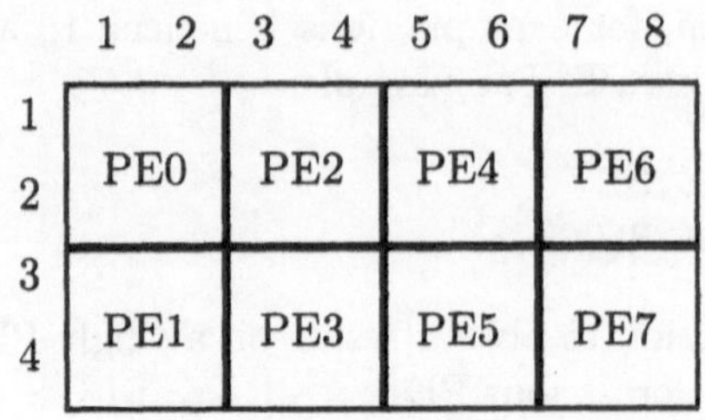

Note that two PEs are assigned to the first dimension and four PEs to the second. This factorization of the eight PEs was chosen because of the *weight* specifiers for each dimension. The weight specifiers are `1:` for the first dimension, and `2:` for the second dimension. This weighting indicates that the eight PEs should be divided up such that the second dimension is assigned twice as many PEs as the first. If no weight specifiers are present, the default is `1:`.

The variety of data distributions possible in this model can increase an application's performance by allowing programmers to increase data locality, while still using globally addressable data objects.

6 Subroutines

Two opposing goals arise in designing the behavior of subroutines in a distributed environment. High performance is crucial to user acceptance of the implementation, but maintaining the generality of the subroutine interface is necessary for ease of use, especially when defining general purpose libraries. The CRI MPP Fortran Programming Model adopts the principal that the efficiency of the generated code is dependent on the available information, and the programmer is allowed to specify different amounts of information. A subroutine's dummy arguments can be declared to be shared private, or unknown. When the declaration is shared or private, that declaration is used to generate more efficient code for references to those arguments. A dummy argument may have its distribution declared as being unknown with the following directive:

`CDIR$ UNKNOWN` $arg_1, arg_2, \ldots, arg_n$

The advantage of the `UNKNOWN` distribution is that a subroutine can be defined that accepts both shared and private arguments. A constraint placed on arguments declared `UNKNOWN` is that they cannot be used in constructs that require shared data objects (see Section **8.2**, **Shared Loops**). A dummy argument can be declared as both unknown and shared with the following directive:

`CDIR$ UNKNOWN_SHARED` $arg_1, arg_2, \ldots, arg_n$

Dummy arguments that are both unknown and shared can be used anywhere a shared data object is permitted, and the implementation assumes that a shared data object is passed as the actual argument. The disadvantage of unknown distributions is that references to these arguments are slower, because a general address calculation uses more instructions. If necessary, shared arguments are *redistributed* to the declared distribution upon entry, and redistributed back to their original distribution upon exit. The rules which apply to this redistribution are:

- If the dummy argument is declared private or shared, and the actual argument matches the distribution exactly, no redistribution is done and the addressing scheme used is tailored to the declared distribution.
- If the dummy argument is declared private but the actual argument is shared, then only local elements of the dummy argument can be referenced.
- If both the actual argument and dummy argument are declared `SHARED` but the two distributions do not match, the implementation redistributes the actual argument to the distribution specified for the dummy argument upon entrance to the subroutine, and redistributes it back upon exit.
- If the dummy argument is declared `UNKNOWN` or `UNKNOWN_SHARED` then a general addressing scheme is used and no redistribution is performed.

7 Parallel Execution

The MPP Fortran programming model is built primarily around the notion of work sharing. Constructs within this model provide access to mechanisms that distribute work among the available executing tasks. One task is assigned to each PE. The model supports both sequential regions (code segments executed by a single task) and parallel regions (code segments executed concurrently by one or more tasks). To simplify programming for some situations, each task is given a unique name (see Section **7.2**, **Task Identity** below). All tasks are created at program start-up time.

7.1 Parallel Regions

Programs initially begin executing in a parallel region on every PE. The program remains in a parallel region (with all tasks executing) until a special directive is encountered that delineates a sequential region. The syntax for this directive is:

`CDIR$ MASTER`

When this directive is encountered all of tasks, except the master task, wait at the end of the sequential region for the master task to finish executing the executable statements within the sequential region. The end of sequential region is delineated by the following directive:

```
      CDIR$ END MASTER
```

After exiting a sequential region a parallel region is reentered, and all tasks resume parallel execution of the program.

7.2 Task Identity

Each task executing within a program has a unique identification. The name given to each task is referenced by using the intrinsic function `MY_PE()`. It evaluates to an integer value between `0` and `N$PES-1`, inclusive. It can be used anywhere an intrinsic function is permitted.

8 Work Sharing

Work sharing is achieved by executing a *shared loop* or *array syntax* statement that reference shared data within a parallel region. The CRI MPP Fortran Programming Model defines both *shared* and *private loops*.

8.1 Private Loops

Private loops are executed in their entirety by any task that invokes them. No work is shared with other tasks. Private loops are defined, at the task level, as having exactly the same semantics as loops in standard Fortran. No special syntax is required to specify a private loop; it is the default.

8.2 Shared Loops

Shared loops specify the behavior of all tasks collectively, and define the behavior of individual tasks only implicitly. They permit work specified in the loop to be shared across all tasks. Shared loops do not guarantee the order in which iterations will be executed. The lack of a defined ordering allows the implementation to execute iterations concurrently.

Shared loops use a pre-scheduled mechanism to distribute loop iterations. A pre-scheduled mechanism is a low overhead loop distribution mechanism that assigns iterations to tasks prior to executing the first iteration. The general syntax for shared loops is as follows:

```
CDIR$ DOSHARED (I1,I2,...,In) ON  array-ref
      DO 10 I1 = L1, U1, S1
         DO 10 I2 = L2, U2, S2
            ...
               DO 10 In = Ln, Un, Sn
                  ...
   10 CONTINUE
```

where *array-ref* is a shared array that controls which loop iterations are assigned to which tasks. The iterations are assigned to tasks in a way that ensures references to *array-ref* are never remote.

The following example shows a doubly nested shared loop. Note that the loop control variables (I and J) must be specified on the DOSHARED directive in loop order.

```
CDIR$ DOSHARED (J,I) ON X(I,J)
      DO 10 J=1,N
        DO 10 I=1,M
          ... X(I,J) ...
   10 CONTINUE
```

All references to shared array elements X(I,J) are local because iterations are assigned in such a way as to ensure their locality. The proper choice of iteration alignment can often provide a high degree of locality when references in the iteration are close together. Shared loops are designed to place iterations within tasks on PEs where the references reside. For example, suppose that arrays X and Y have the same dimensionality, the same size, and the same distribution. The loop:

```
CDIR$ DOSHARED (I) ON X(I)
      DO 10 I = 1, N
   10    Y(I) = D * X(I) + Y(I)
```

is distributed such that each iteration I executes on the processor where X(I) resides. Since Y(I) resides on the same PE, all references are completely local.

9 Array Syntax

Array syntax is supported in the CRI MPP Fortran Programming Model. Array assignment statements are highly parallel operations. Unlike shared loops, their iteration distribution is controlled completely by the implementation. For example, given the declaration:

```
CDIR$ SHARED A, B, C
      REAL A(128), B(128), C(128)
```

The array syntax assignment

```
   A = B + C
```

is equivalent to:

```
CDIR$ DOSHARED (I)  mech
      DO I=1,128
10      A(I) = B(I) + C(I)
```

where *mech* is a mechanism chosen by the implementation.

10 Synchronization Primitives

The CRI MPP Fortran Programming model supports a standard set of shared memory synchronization primitives used in parallel programs including *barriers, locks, critical regions,* and *events.* Barriers are a fast way of synchronizing all tasks at once. They can be included anywhere in a program with the syntax:

```
CDIR$ BARRIER
```

Locks are a basic and primitive synchronization method that are generally used to serialize access to some piece of data. They are basic in the sense that they may be used to efficiently implement a wide variety of parallel constructs, including other synchronization constructs. They are primitive in the sense that serialization is enforced by convention only. Lock operations are supported by three intrinsics which use the syntax:

```
CALL SET_LOCK(lock)
CALL CLEAR_LOCK(lock)
L = TEST_LOCK(lock)
```

The SET_LOCK subroutine sets the lock. If the lock is set, it spin-waits until the lock is cleared, otherwise the lock is set immediately. The CLEAR_LOCK subroutine clears a lock whether it is set or not. The function TEST_LOCK atomically sets a lock and returns the state that the lock had (whether set or cleared) prior to the test.

Critical sections serialize access to a particular section of code rather than access to some data object. A critical section prevents more than one task from executing concurrently within the critical region. The syntax for a critical section is:

```
CDIR$ CRITICAL
      ...
CDIR$ END CRITICAL
```

Events provide a style of program synchronization that is different from locks. Whereas locks cause task suspension on setting the lock, events have an explicit blocking routine.

Events are supported by four intrinsic routines: SET_EVENT, WAIT_EVENT, TEST_EVENT, and CLEAR_EVENT. The subroutine SET_EVENT sets, or posts, an event.

The subroutine WAIT_EVENT suspends task execution until a specified event occurs. The function TEST_EVENT returns the state of an event, that is, whether it is posted or cleared. The subroutine CLEAR_EVENT clears the event. The syntax for each routine is:

```
CALL SET_EVENT(event)
CALL WAIT_EVENT(event)
CALL CLEAR_EVENT(event)
S = TEST_EVENT(event)
```

11 Conclusions

There are multiple forces that apply pressure to the definition of a programming model for a massively parallel system. Some programmers want very high level language features, others want very low level primitives that allow them to control every aspect of the program's execution. Some want a very MIMD model with extensive synchronizations, others want the implementation to "figure it all out" for them. The CRI MPP Fortran Programming Model is feature rich, because of this divergence of opinions in the user community over what is the best way to program massively parallel systems. It is an attempt to avoid burning any bridges until a clearer picture exists about which direction programming models are going. The hope is that this model allows programmers to experiment with a variety of styles, thereby aiding the process of focusing in on those features that prove to be the most beneficial.

This programming model is currently under development and scheduled for release in 1994. At the time of this writing, reliable performance numbers are not available. We tried to stress that attention has been paid to performance details, as well as to usability issues. Although there are constructs identified in this model that need to be used with care because of possible performance problems, there are other constructs that should yield excellent performance when used appropriately. When more performance testing results are available, performance concerns will be identified and either addressed through improvements, or documented appropriately. This model should be judged by how efficiently it is implemented and how useful it is found to be when implementing highly parallel solutions.

References

[1] D. Pase, T. MacDonald, A. Meltzer. *MPP Fortran Programming Model.* Cray Research, Inc., Eagan Minnesota, 1992.

[2] *American National Standard X3.9 1978, Programming Language FORTRAN.* ANSI X3J3 Committee. Global Engineering Documents, Inc., Santa Ana, California.

[3] *CF77 Compiling System, Volume 4: Parallel Processing Guide.* SR-3071 4.0, Cray Research, Inc., Eagan, Minnesota, 1991.

[4] *CM Fortran Reference Manual.* Thinking Machines Corporation, Cambridge, Massachusetts, 1991.

[5] *CRAY Y-MP, CRAY X-MP EA, and CRAY X-MP Multitasking Programmer's Manual.* SR-0222 F-01, Cray Research, Inc., Eagan, Minnesota, 1991.

[6] G. Fox, S. Hiranandani, K. Kennedy, C. Koelbel, U. Kremer, C. W. Tseng, and M. Y. Wu. *Fortran D Language Specification.* Rice University, Houston, Texas, 1991.

[7] F. Thomson Leighton. *Introduction to Parallel Algorithms and Architectures: Arrays, Trees, Hypercubes.* Morgan Kaufman Publishers, San Mateo, California, 1992.

[8] B. Chapman, P. Mehrotra, and H. Zima. *Vienna Fortran - A Fortran Language Extension for Distributed Memory Multiprocessors.* ICASE, NASA Langley Research Center, Hampton, Virginia, 1991.

[9] Constantine D. Polychronopoulos. *Parallel Programming and Compilers.* Kluwer Academic Publishers, Norwell, Massachusettes, 1988.

[10] Hans Zima and Barbara Chapman. *Supercompilers for Parallel and Vector Computers.* ACM Press Frontier Series, New York, New York, 1991.

[11] Karen Waren, Brent Gorda, Eugene D. Brooks III. *Programming in PFP.* Lawrence Livermore National Laboratory, UCRL-MA-107028, April 1991.

[12] Adam Beguelin, Jack Dongarra, Al Geist, Robert Manchek, and Vaidy Sunderam. *A User's Guide to PVM - Parallel Virtual Machine.* Oak Ridge National Laboratory, ORNL/TM-11826, July 1991.

Programming Environments for Massively Parallel Distributed Systems, Monte Verità, Switzerland

Resource Optimisation via Structured Parallel Programming

B. Bacci, M. Danelutto and S. Pelagatti
Department of Computer Science, University of Pisa, Italy
{bacci,marcod,susanna}@di.unipi.it

Abstract

When dealing with massively parallel architectures, many difficult problems have to be solved. In this paper we will show how, by adopting a structured style of programming and a set of template-based compiling tools, most of the burden required in writing massively parallel applications can be moved to the compiler design phase. In particular, we will discuss how the problem of implementing a parallel application onto a machine having a limited number of processing elements can be tackled. By exploiting information on the structure of the parallelism coming from the high level language and the templates in the compiling tools, we are able to devise a polynomial time procedure that achieves efficient implementation of structured parallel programs onto distributed memory, MIMD machines based on a regular interconnection topology and having a limited number of resources.

1 Introduction

P3L (the Pisa Parallel Programming Language) is a new, high level, parallel programming language explicitly designed to address massively parallel programming. It provides a set of statements, called the *parallel constructs*, that model the most common patterns used to exploit massive amounts of parallelism. These constructs can be used to build out parallel applications by composition, in much the same way as we can use `for` or `if-then-else` statements to build out sequential applications in the sequential imperative programming style.

The language is implemented by means of a set of *template based* compiling tools. Libraries of *implementation templates*, i.e. of (known) skeletons that can be used to implement the constructs present in the language, are included in the P3L compiling tools. The implementation templates stored in the libraries are *skeletons* (much in the sense of Cole's *skeletons* [Col89, DFH$^+$93, Kel89]), i.e. they are parametric in the number of resources (processing elements) that can be used to implement them on a target architecture and also provide some analytical models relating the performance they can achieve to the resources they use. The compilation process mainly consists in consulting libraries and in applying composition rules operating on the implementation templates. All of the details that one has to cope with in order to implement the parallelism exploitation patterns used by the programmer are dealt with in the compiling tools, and the programmer can concentrate his efforts on the qualitative aspects of parallelism exploitation, rather than on the implementation issues. It is worthwhile noticing that, by adopting the template based structure of the P3L compiling tools, most of the problems deriving from mapping, scheduling and load balancing can be solved directly at the compiler libraries design level. An exhaustive description of the P3L compiling tools can be found in [DMO+92, BDO+93a, BDO+93b].

Our group developed a first prototype version of a P3L compiler that cross compiles for a Meiko CS/1, an MIMD, Transputer based machine. The P3L cross compiler runs on a Unix workstation, takes a P3L source program and produces a set of C files, plus a number of `makefiles`. By "executing" the `makefiles` on the Meiko CS, the C files are compiled to generate the code that has to be placed on each one of the processing elements of the CS/1 that will be used to implement the program. The mapping, scheduling and load balancing code is also produced by the cross compiler under the form of commands and directives that can be understood by the Meiko C compiler and linker tools.

One of the features of the first (prototype) version of the P3L compiling tools, is that the compiling algorithm always performs compilation assuming that the number of resources available in the target parallel machine is unbounded, i.e. it compiles assigning resources to the implementation templates as long as the implementation templates behave below the 'saturation condition', (as long as the resources used are not used to their limit).

In this work, we will call *optimal implementation* of a P3L program P an implementation ω derived using the templates relative to the constructs and stored in the template library, in such a way that the tradeoff between the time spent in communications and the time gained by concurrent computations is achieved. It is obvious that this optimality *criterion* is relative to the templates stored in the compiler library and to the basic costs of elementary operations of the target architectures. The problem that we want to address in this paper is the following: given a P3L program P, its optimal implementation ω and a constraint S over the resources available for its implementation, we want to find a new implementation ω_S, using a number of resources which is less or equal to the number made available by the constraint, in such a way that this implementation could be considered optimal w.r.t. both that constraint and the templates included in the compiler, i.e. such that, using the same number of resources in a different way, it is not possible to use the templates in the compiler libraries to achieve a better service time. We call here this problem the *limited resource problem.* The purpose of this paper is to show how, taking advantage of the parallelism structuring in the source code *and* of the knowledge relative to the implementation templates, such an optimal implementation can be devised, using a polynomial time algorithm.

2 P3L

A P3L program is built out of a hierarchical composition of *modules*. Each module is a sequential module, a `main` module or a *parallel* module and it has an input and an output parameter list, denoting the parameters passed (by value) to the module, and those passed back (by result) by the module itself, and a name, allowing the module to be called from elsewhere in the program. Furthermore, each module has one or more *body* module calls. Each body module call can be a call to another module, i.e. the name of the module followed by the (actual) parameters, or an *in-line* module, i.e. a module declared in-line, with no name. Sequential modules are *functions* of the *host sequential* programming language, i.e. of the language we use to borrow a notation to write sequential code (in the current version of P3L such language is C++, but any other language could do the case). The `main` module represents the entry point of the program and simply calls another P3L module. Finally, a *parallel* module is the instance of one of the parallel constructs included in the language. Each parallel construct corresponds to a different paradigm of parallelism.

The parallel constructs included in P3L are the following (let us assume that $\mathcal{S}$ returns the function computed by a P3L module):

`pipe` modelling pipeline parallelism [KCN90]. `pipe` $mcall_1$ $mcall_2$ $mcall_3$ applied to an input stream $\ldots x_n, \ldots, x_1, x_0$ computes the 'function' $\mathcal{S}[mcall_3] \circ \mathcal{S}[mcall_2] \circ \mathcal{S}[mcall_1]$ over all the elements of the stream. Parallelism arises by the concurrent evaluation of the different body modules over different processing elements;

`farm` modelling stream parallelism [PJA+87]. `farm` *mcall* applied to an input stream performs the function $\mathcal{S}[mcall]$ over all the elements of the input stream $\ldots x_n, \ldots, x_1, x_0$. Parallelism arises because calls to the body module relative to different input data items are evaluated concurrently over a set of *worker* processing elements;

`reduce` modelling binary tree computations of an associative operator [Bir87]. `reduce` *mcall* applied to an input structure, say $\langle v_1, \ldots v_k \rangle$, computes $v_1 \oplus v_2 \oplus \ldots \oplus v_n$ (where $\oplus = \mathcal{S}[mcall]$). Parallelism is exploited according to the binary tree reduction model;

`map` modelling map parallelism [Bir87]. `map` *mcall* applied to an input data structure $\langle v_1, \ldots v_k \rangle$ computes a new structure $\langle f(x_1), \ldots, f(x_k) \rangle$ where $f = \mathcal{S}[mcall]$. Parallelism arises from the concurrent evaluation of f on different elements of the input structure;

`loop` modelling iterative computations. `loop` *mcall*, *termination* iteratively performs the module call $\mathcal{S}[mcall]$ over each item of the input data stream, until $\mathcal{S}[termination]$ becomes `true`. At that point, it emits the final value computed by $\mathcal{S}[mcall]$. Parallelism arises both from the pipeline evaluation of the *mcall* module and the *termination* module, *and* from the concurrent evaluation of different input data items.

The key points in the P3L language design can be summarised as follows. P3L is an *high level* language. The programmer has no way to express low level communications or to execute in parallel arbitrary (i.e. having no regular structure) process graphs. P3L is *structured*, as it only provides some basic parallel forms (the parallel constructs) and a way to compose them (hierarchical composition). Therefore, not all the possible process graphs can be expressed in P3L. Indeed, we claim that most of the computations that can benefit of massively parallel execution can be expressed in P3L. The study of a large number of existing applications suitable for massively parallel execution and the work of other authors [May90, PJA+87, Ski90, Kun88, Bir87] that recognised similar forms of parallelism exploitation as the 'useful' forms in the field of massively parallel programming, support our claim. Furthermore, it's easy to extend the language with new constructs, once a form is recognised to be 'typical' of massively parallel computation *and* some implementation templates are available for it. Moreover, P3L allows and encourage *reusability*. By using a well know and widely used sequential programming language as the 'host sequential language', re-usability of (dusty-deck) code is achieved, in that chunks of old code can be easily encapsulated in a sequential P3L module. Finally, P3L allows *modular* programming and incremental parallelism exploitation to be achieved; modules can be re-used in different programs as it happens with normal procedures. In addition, a programmer can start with a sequential application and refine its construct structure until a suitable parallel structure has been reached.

The P3L compiling tools can be considered the most innovative topic relative to the P3L design. They exploit the information relative to parallelism structuring and to the target architecture to achieve efficiency in program execution. The main parameter that the P3L compiling tools try to optimise is the application *service time*. The P3L compiling tools work out a P3L program in six phases.

Lexical analysis. In this phase the program file is scanned, syntax is checked and a *construct tree* is built. The construct tree has a node for each module in the program and each node is labelled with the name of the corresponding construct. The leaves are labelled with sequential module names. During this phase, the sequential code relative to the sequential modules is stored into "user" files, for further processing.

Construct tree optimisation. The constructor tree is scanned and some optimisations are applied, taken from an *optimisation library*, i.e. a library containing rewriting rules that transform construct trees into *more efficient* (w.r.t. the target architecture) construct trees. During this phase information is also gathered that will be used later on to pick up the right templates from the template library.

Template assigning. The *template library* is consulted and, starting from the leaves of the construct tree, one of the templates belonging to the library

```
init in() out(int x[10], float y[10])
   ${if (fscanf(stdin, "%d %f",
               &x[0], &y[0]) == EOF)
    p3l_exit();
for (int i=1; i<10; i++)
    fscanf(stdin, "%d %f",
                 &x[i], &y[i]);}$
end
fin in(int x[10], float y[10]) out()
    ${fprintf(stdout, "x:\t");
for (int i=0; i<10; i++)
    fprintf(stdout, "%-6d ", x[i]);
fprintf(stdout, "\ny:\t");
for (i=0; i<10; i++)
    fprintf(stdout, "%-4.1f ", y[i]);
fprintf(stdout, "\n\n");}$
end
```

```
work in(float y[10], int x[10])
     out(int x1[10], float y1[10])
    ${for (int i=0; i<10; i++)
{x1[i] = x[i] * 10;
    y1[i] = y[i] * 10.0;}}$
end
farm f in(int x[10], float y[10])
       out(int x1[10], float y1[10])
  work in(y, x) out(x1, y1)
end farm
pipe p in() out()
    init in() out(int x[10],float y[10])
    f in(x,y) out(int x1[10],float y1[10])
    fin in(x1,y1) out()
end pipe
main
  p in() out()
end
```

Figure 1: *A simple P3L program (Program A)*

relative to the current construct and to the current target architecture is assigned to the current node. The template is chosen in order to minimise the service time of the whole parallel application. In so doing, the relevant performance models of the templates are consulted, using the cost parameters relative to the target architecture, and the average execution times of the sequential portions of code, obtained by a profiling phase as described below. At the end of this phase, a process graph is obtained, which can be directly mapped onto the target architecture.

Code production. The process graph is scanned and for each process the appropriate *process template* is extracted from a *process template library.* These templates are then instantiated with the proper parameters, coming from the application code, such as the input and output parameter types and the proper calls to the user supplied code.

Template tuning. Some optimisations are performed onto the process graph, that do not change the behaviour of the parallel application but in the resource requirements. As an example, communication statements can be grouped in order to deliver bigger packets on the network, thus better exploiting the features of the interconnection network of the target architecture.

Object code generation. The instantiated process templates are compiled, along with the user code and code is produced to load and execute the application onto the target architecture, according to the computational model of that architecture.

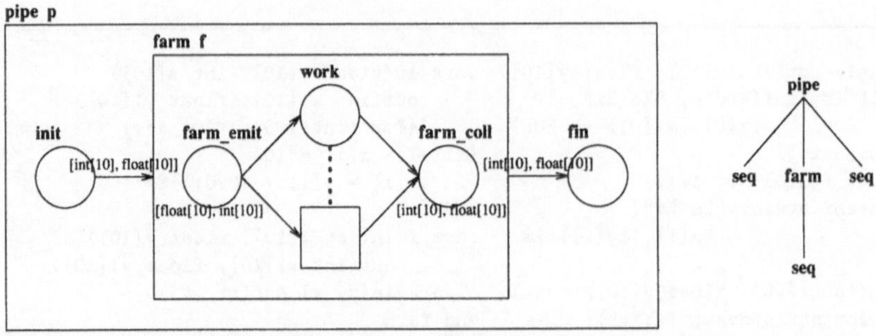

Figure 2: *Logical graph (left) and construct tree (right) relative to program A*

The P3L compiling tools present a number of innovative features.

- P3L applications turn out to be portable, as the machine dependent features are definitely hidden in the compiling tools. When a set of templates is available for a given architecture, all the existing P3L application can be ported to that target.
- Efficiency of P3L programs is achieved by adopting optimising compiling tools that have a deep knowledge of the target architecture features, such as the costs of (i.e. the time spent in) basic operations, or the topology used to interconnect the processing elements belonging to the architecture.
- In no way, the programmer of a P3L application can devise resource allocation or mapping information, nor it is charged of writing mapping and load balancing code. All this stuff is handled by the compiling tools, actually by exploiting the templates relative to the constructs.

Let us look at a simple example, to understand how all this process works. Suppose that the program we are going to compile is that of Fig. 1. This program corresponds to the 'logical' process graph of Fig. 2. It represents a small, typical P3L computation, structured as a pipeline, where the first stage reads a data stream from a file, the last one writes the data stream to a file and the inner one is built out of a farm, having a sequential module as the body module.

The output of the compiler, when run having as the target architecture a 2d-mesh MIMD architecture is graphically depicted in Fig. 3. The circles represent processors and the arcs represent communication channels implemented over inter-processor links. The (bold) names beside the processors are the names of the process templates running on that processor, the data types beside the arcs represent the type of messages flowing along the arcs. In this case, the inner `farm` construct has been compiled using one of the templates relative to the `farm` paradigm, namely the one having a distribution bus, built out of a string of processing elements that distribute tasks to the worker processing elements, a string of worker

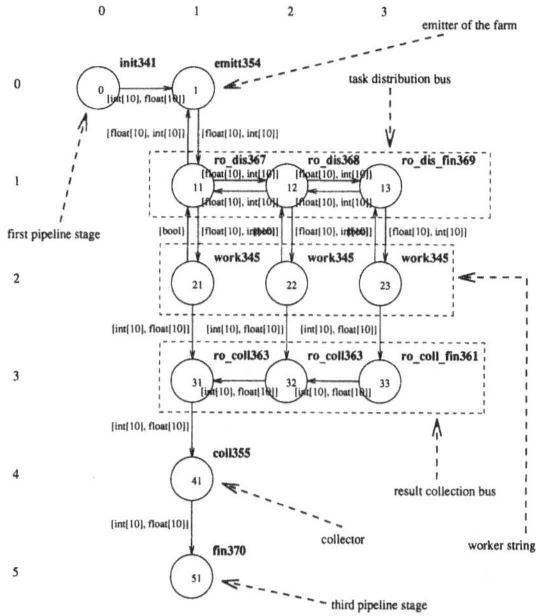

Figure 3: *Implementation of program A onto a 2d-mesh target architecture*

processing elements, and a collection bus, namely a string of processing elements collecting results from the worker processors and delivering them to the collector processing element, that is charged of the task of preserving the stream ordering.

In the P3L compiling tools, the main routine used to achieve the result presented here is a procedure `eval&map` that, given a P3L application P, its construct tree Γ, a service time T_ϵ and a set of costs (coming both from architecture abstraction and from sequential modules profiling) returns an implementation ω of the program P which is optimal with respect to the architecture and the templates included in the compiler, i.e.:

- has a service time $T_\omega \leq T_\epsilon$;
- for any other implementation ω_1 of P derived using the same template set, it holds that $T_\omega \leq T_\epsilon \leq T_{\omega_1}$;
- for any other implementation ω_1 of P derived using the same template set, it is not true that $A(\omega_1) < A(\omega) \wedge T_{\omega_1} \leq T_\epsilon$, where $A(\omega)$ is the number of resources (processing elements) used by the implementation ω.

A couple of things are worth mentioning, referring to the example.

- The number of worker processes is devised by the compiling tools, consulting the performance model relative to the farm template. This model allows to devise the optimal number of worker processes in such a way that: further workers added to the template do not affect the service time or slows it down; and less workers included in the template, lead to a greater service time.

- The template processes include load balancing strategies, that are effective also when the task execution time shows a great variance, provided that a rough estimate of the average computation time spent on each task by each processing element acting as workers is known. This estimate is obtained by first compiling the program with a fixed number of per-template resources (e.g. two workers for the farm template), then running the program on sample data and profiling the execution times, and finally using the data obtained to dimension the farm template in such a way that the optimality criterion already stated in section 1 is satisfied.

It's worthwhile noticing that the only code supplied by the programmer is that of Fig. 1, and, in particular, the programmer only specifies the 'qualitative' parallelism that he/she wants to exploit. All the quantitative aspects of parallelism exploitation are dealt with within the compiling tools, where exactly the knowledge necessary to target the features of the architecture is available. Finally, the implementation of the program A has been derived by using the 'unlimited resources' version of the compiler. This means that no constraint has been imposed over the number of resources used to implement the application of Fig. 1. In Section 3 we will outline the algorithm used to take into account such kind of constraints within the compiling tools. Here should suffice to say that, if a target architecture with less than 13 nodes was available, the object code of Fig. 3 cannot be run at all.

3 The 'limited resources' algorithm

In this section, we will outline the 'limited resources' algorithm, i.e. the algorithm that allows the P3L compiling tools to be used to devise an optimised implementation of a P3L application onto architectures with a limited number of processing elements.

The limited resources algorithm uses, as a coroutine, the procedure `eval&map` discussed in Sec. 2 as a coroutine. The algorithm starts looking at the unlimited resources optimal solution and iteratively 'takes away' resources from this implementation, in such a way that:

- at each step the exact number of resources is taken away, that produces the minimum increase in the service time of the program;

- at each step the implementation is kept optimal, i.e. it does not exist another combination of templates that implement the same program using the same number of resources and delivering a better service time.

The algorithm exploits the structuring information derived from the usage of constructs and templates in the source language and in the compiling tools. On the one hand, for each one of the templates used in the P3L compiler, some rules are stored in a *reduction library* that allow to 'reduce' the number of resources used for the template and to estimate the penalty paid in terms of the service time. These rules work both in the case that the body modules of a construct are sequential modules and in the case that they turn out to be an arbitrary nesting of other parallel constructs. On the other hand, by looking at the construct tree, the procedure taking away resources from the optimal implementation is able to understand which construct has to be affected at each step in order to retain the optimality of the implementation obtained by the reduction step. This means, for instance, that if we have to reduce the resources used to implement a construct tree built out of a `pipe` with two stages, we will take away resources from the implementation of the first stage *and* of the second stage, in such a way that the overall `pipe` turns out to be still balanced. In case the construct tree is built out of a `farm` having a worker process built out of a `pipe`, we will take away either resources from the `farm` (e.g. taking away the resources used for the implementation of a whole worker) or we will restructure (reduce) the resources used for the implementation of the inner `pipe`. In the latter case, this means that we first reduce the `pipe` implementation and then we use the reduced `pipe` for the implementation of all the workers of the outer `farm`.

The pseudo-code for the limited resources algorithm `lra` is the following:

$\texttt{lra}(\Gamma, T_\epsilon, S)$::
$\omega := \texttt{eval\&map}(\Gamma, T_\epsilon)$;
while $A(\omega) > S$ **do**
  $T_\alpha := \Delta(\omega)$;
  $\omega := \texttt{red}(\Gamma, T_\alpha)$;
end

Δ is the procedure that computes the minimum change in the service time of an implementation ω that decreases the resources used, `red` is the procedure that applies the reductions to the implementation templates according to the reduction rules stored in the reduction library (that is, `red` is a modified version of the `eval&map` procedure), and S is the constraint on the resource usage (i.e. the maximum number of resources to be used).

In particular, the procedure Δ looks at places in the construct tree where reductions can be applied, and, for each reduction, it looks up the reduction library. For every item in the reduction library matching the current template, the performance models of the current combination of templates used are consulted and the corresponding change in the service time is estimated. At the end, among all the possible reductions, the one delivering the minimum useful (i.e. leading to a decrease in resource requirements) change in the service time is chosen. At this point, the procedure `red` actually computes the new implementation ω according to that reduction.

This algorithm clearly terminates in polynomial time (in the number of resources of the optimal implementation ω_{opt} and in the number of constructs belonging to the construct tree) as:

- at each step it comes up with an implementation that uses less resources than the previous one, thus the number of resources is a decreasing function w.r.t. the iteration level;

- the library lookup and the construct tree lookup required by procedures `red` and Δ respectively, take a time proportional to the number of rules stored in the reduction library and to the depth of the construct tree.

The algorithm `lra` eventually comes up with an implementation ω_{last} that uses a number of resources that is less or equal to the input constraint S and that delivers a service time equal to T_{last}.

Some optimisations have been introduced in the algorithm currently implemented in the P3L compiler. As an example, let's consider the following. At step i, the `lra` algorithm computes a set of possible reductions along with the associated changes in the service time. Those that can be re-used at step $i+1$ are 'memoized' in such a way that at the next step they do not have to be re-computed, but simply looked up in the tables. This situation is quite common. Consider a pipeline program. If we reduce resources at stage k, it is likely that at the next iteration of the algorithm we will reduce resources of some other stage k' to keep the pipeline balanced. This means that the reductions computed for stage k' at iteration i (and not actually used at that iteration) can be used at iteration $i+1$, provided that they have been stored in suitable data structures.

The simplicity of the algorithm derives from two factors: on the one hand, the amount of information relative to the application structuring that is made available by the initial optimal implementation; on the other hand, by adopting a template-based approach, the procedures Δ and `red` can be kept reasonably simple. If the parallelism were not structured or the templates were not used at all, nothing comparable (in terms of simplicity) to the `lra` algorithm could have been written. In fact, in the general case, when dealing with implementation of a generic (unstructured, having any shape) process graph onto a generic architecture, problems such as mapping, scheduling and load balancing turn out to be $\mathcal{NP}$-hard. In our case, all what we do is to devise proper 'reduction' rules for the implementation templates (such as those depicted in Fig. 4), along with the relative models for the associated performance penalty.

4 An example

We will show the effectiveness of the limited resources algorithm with a simple example. Consider a P3L application, having as a construct tree the one depicted in Fig. 4.

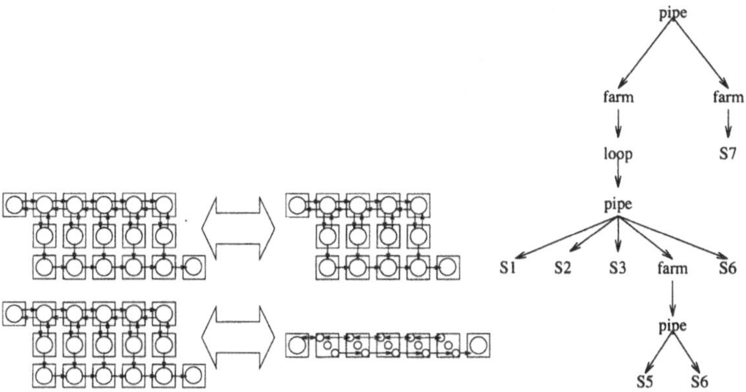

Figure 4: *Two reduction rules for the farm template (left). Constructor tree relative to program B (right)*

The implementation onto a 2D-mesh, MIMD, Transputer based architecture without resource constraints leads to a usage of 165 distinct processing elements. By imposing a constraint $S = 80$ and applying the limited resources algorithm , we get an implementation that actually uses only 73 nodes. In this implementation there is one worker less in both the inner and the outer farm of the first stage and 3 workers less in the second farm. This happens exactly to keep the outer pipeline balanced in such a way that no resources are wasted to implement a stage in a very efficient way, while the other stages of the pipeline have a much higher service time. By using the `lra` with the constrain $S = 20$, we get an implementation of the program that only uses 15 nodes. In this case the two farms have been completely collapsed in that emitter and collector processing elements have been discarded either, for they are not needed anymore. This is quite the smallest implementation possible for the original application. A further reduction step will simply merge some stages of the overall pipeline in such a way that they are executed by the same processing element. The complete pictures relative to the different implementations of this example program can be found in [BDP93]. Fig. 5 shows the completion time of the program w.r.t. the number of processing elements used.

It is clear that the less resources we assign to the program, the higher is the completion time. However, the intermediate points, indicating the completion time using an intermediate number of PEs, between 165 and 8, always are completion times relative to optimal implementations of the original parallel application.

The number 165, i.e. the maximum number of processing elements is the number that corresponds to the unlimited resources optimal implementation. This implementation corresponds to the implementation that the compiler is able to devise when no constraints are given on the amount of resources to use.

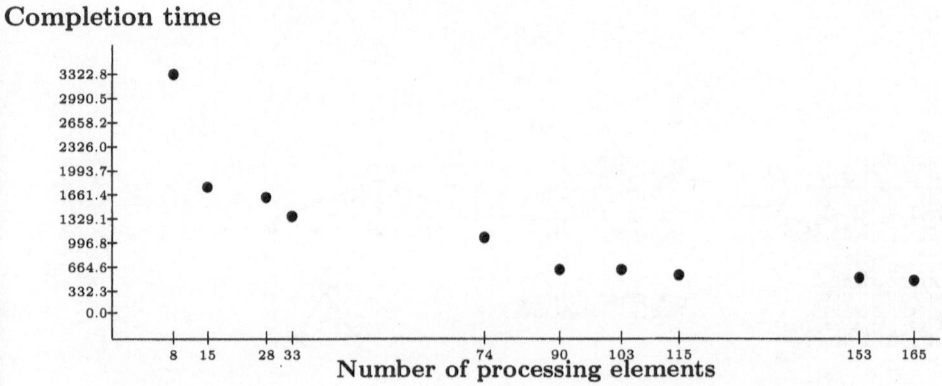

Figure 5: *Completion time vs. number of processors used (Program B)*

5 Conclusion

We showed here that by using a template-based compiler for a structured parallel programming language, we are able to devise an algorithm that compiles parallel applications for target architectures with a limited number of processing nodes. The problem of devising the exact number of resources that have to be assigned to different parts of the parallel application is solved by first compiling the application for unbounded resources, and then scaling down this implementation of the application in such a way that the "optimality" criterion used to devise the maximally parallel implementation is preserved. In so doing, we achieve automatic load balancing for the resources used to implement the parallel application. The main innovative points of this approach lie in the exploitation of the information relative to parallelism structuring and of the implementation templates. By separating the problems of devising an optimal implementation for an infinite number of processing elements and of 'reducing' this optimal implementation in order to satisfy a given constraint, we are able to devise an efficient, polynomial time algorithm for compiling P3L programs onto DM-MIMD machines with a limited number of processing elements. Another positive point of our approach is that, by structuring parallelism and by exploiting the implementation template concept, we are able to deal with problems that following other approaches turn out to be much more 'hard'.

Acknowledgments

This work has been founded by the Italian Netional Research Council (CNR) within the "Progetto Finalizzato Sistemi Informatici e Calcolo Parallelo", subproject *Architetture Parallele*.

References

[BDO+93a] B. Bacci, M. Danelutto, S. Orlando, S. Pelagatti, and M. Vanneschi. Efficient compilation of structured parallel programs for distributed memory MIMD machines. In *Proceedings of the PARCO'93 - Parallel Computing*, September 1993. Grenoble – France.

[BDO+93b] B. Bacci, M. Danelutto, S. Orlando, S. Pelagatti, and M. Vanneschi. P3L: a structured high level parallel language and its structured support. Technical Report TR-36/93, Dept. of Comp. Science – Univ. of Pisa, 1993. Available by fpt anonymous at `ftp.di.unipi.it`.

[BDP93] B. Bacci, M. Danelutto, and S. Pelagatti. Resource optimization via structured parallel programming. Technical Report TR-30/93, Department of Computer Science, University of Pisa (Italy), 1993. Available on ftp anonymous at the site `ftp.di.unipi.it`.

[Bir87] R. S. Bird. An introduction to the Theory of Lists. In Manfred Broy, editor, *Logic of programming and calculi of discrete design.* NATO ASI Series, 1987. International Summer School directed by F. L. Bauer, M. Broy, E. W. Dijkstra and C. A. R. Hoare.

[Col89] M. Cole. *Algorithmic Skeletons: Structured Management of Parallel Computations.* Research Monographs in Parallel and Distributed Computing. Pitman, 1989.

[DFH+93] J. Darlington, A. J. Field, P.G. Harrison, P. H. J. Kelly, D. W. N. Sharp, Q. Wu, and R. L. While. Parallel Programming Using Skeleton Functions. In M. Reeve A. Bode and G. Wolf, editors, *PARLE'93 Parallel Architectures and Langauges Europe.* Springer Verlag, June 1993. LNCS No. 694.

[DMO+92] M. Danelutto, R. Di Meglio, S. Orlando, S. Pelagatti, and M. Vanneschi. A methodology for the development and support of massively parallel programs. *Future Generation Computer Systems*, 8(1–3), July 1992.

[KCN90] C. T. King, W. H. Chou, and L. M. Ni. Pipelined data-parallel algorithms: Part I – Concept and Modeling. *IEEE Transactions on Parallel and Distributed Systems*, 1(4), October 1990.

[Kel89] P. Kelly. *Functional Programming for Loosely-coupled Multiprocessors.* Research Monographs in Parallel and Distributed Computing. Pitman, 1989.

[Kun88] H. T. Kung. Computational models for parallel computers. In *Scientific applications of multiprocessors*, pages 1–17. C.A.R. Hoare Series editor, 1988.

[May90] D. May. Towards general-purpose parallel computers. Draft, also presented at the CRAI Spring International Seminar on Higly Parallel Processing, Capri, May 1990.

[PJA+87] Pritchard, D. J., Askew, C. R., Carpenter, D. B., A. J. G. Hey, and D. A. Nicole. Pratical parallelism using transputer arrays. In *PARLE 1987*, volume 258 of *Lecture Notes in Computer Science*, pages 28–42. Springer-Verlag, 1987.

[Ski90] D. B. Skillicorn. Architecture-independent parallel computation. *IEEE Computer*, pages 38–50, December 1990.

Programming Environments for Massively Parallel Distributed Systems, Monte Verità, Switzerland

SYNAPS/3 - An Extension of C for Scientific Computations

V. A. Serebriakov A. N. Bezdushny
C. G. Belov
Computing Centre of the Russian Academy of Sciences
Moscow, 117967, Vavilova 40
e-mail:serebr@sms.ccas.msk.su

Abstract

Extensions for conventional programming languages are suggested that allow to write parallel algorithms for distributed memory machines. The main goal of these extensions is to supply a programmer with a strict, precise and transparent language for scientific applications. Main language constructs are discussed with appropriate examples. Performance results for some applications are given.

1 Introduction

It is well known that programming for distributed memory computers is a very hard problem, especially for a nonprofessional (applied) programmer. We suggest a language (SYNAPS/3) that can be viewed as an extension for conventional programming languages (the first of all to FORTRAN and C), and is very simple, transparent, and natural for scientific programming where loops are the main control structure and vectors and matrices are the main data structure.

2 Problem overview

There are two extreme points of view on programming style for MIMD machines: the first assumes that the user must describe parallelization in all details, and the second is based on the idea that user can know nothing about parallel processing and all the work has to be done by the compiler. The most popular approach is to suggest the user to define a data distribution between processors and to leave the task of program parallelization for the compiler. The most well known projects in this direction are High Performance FORTRAN (HPF) and Vienna FORTRAN.

But the problem of data distribution is not the only one that have to be overcome. Another important problem is the usage of replicated variables: either each processor must assign the same value to the variable on all iterations, so the program cannot be parallelized, or compiler can recognize, that the variable value is used only in the current loop iteration, and partition its assignments(privatize). The HPF does not give rules that manage these assignments, because there is no a distinction between private and replicated variables in HPF.

Partially the notion of reduction overcomes this problem. But due to the absence of the explicit division between private and replicated variables it is impossible to define and program **reduce**-statement. Language offers only a fixed set of reduce operations.

As an example, let us consider LU-decomposition with pivoting. Do programs for sequential computers fit for parallel ones? In the Vienna FORTRAN language specification one of the examples of LU-decomposition ([3]*pp.*72) is given (Figure 1 b). Sequential form of the program is shown in Figure 1 a. It is easily to see that this is not the pure sequential variant, but it is tuned for parallel computers in a way absolutely not evident from the sequential point of view. Instead of having scalar variable k array k is introduced to partition assignments of temporary value. This example shows that in most cases to get an appropriate result it is not sufficient simply to define data distribution, but it is necessary to do some more deep changes in the program.

All this leads to very diffused and vague language. The language is not now a strict tool to define a program, because it does not supply the programmer with understanding of the process of computations expressed in appropriate terms. To overcome this problem authors propose to introduce another, the second level of programming, the *environment* based upon text editor. This environment helps the user to understand what peculiarities of his program prevents parallelization. For example user can see data dependence graphs, sequence of calls etc. This is the typical case of double thinking: you formally consider the program as sequential, and the rules of the language does not supply you with some mechanisms to control the situation, but you cannot manage without this control, and you are forced to

```
Sequential program          Vienna FORTRAN program

real A(N,N)                 real A(N,N) dist(*)
real temp                   real temp (N) dist(=A.2)
real ipivot                 real ipivot (N) dist(=A.2)
do 30 k=1,N-1               do 30 k=1,N-1
...........                 ...........
temp=...                    temp(k)=...
 a)                          b)
```

Figure 1: *Comparison of a sequential and Vienna FORTRAN program specifications*

go out of these rules and attract another notions to understand the situation.

So, our purpose is to construct a language that must satisfy the following conditions:

- it must be a simple extension of conventional language (FORTRAN or C);
- it must not contain complex and unusual notions such as data communication, processes and so on;
- it must be strict in the sense that the language itself must be sufficient to express all notions that are needed; it should not be necessary to attract tools outside the language;
- it must supply the user with a possibility to manage the structure of the program and to control the quality of its program.

The only one principle difference that distinguish our language from HPF like languages is that the user must divide the program into two kinds of regions, the first can not contain assignments to replicated values that depend on its private and distributed variables, the second has no this restriction. Regions of the first kind we name *parallel*, regions of the second kind - *sequentional*. This requirement is sufficient to parallelize the program. Another result of this partitioning of the program body is that it makes possible to define **reduce**-statement precisely.

As a resume of the discussion we can say that we don't introduce any new concept in the language, but instead combine familiar concepts in a strict and precise mode.

SYNAPS/3 programs have following structure

```
  templ Tmpl[100:block];/* distribution scheme declaration */
  float A[Tmpl];        /* distributed array definition */
  float s;              /* replicated variable */
  par {float d; int i;/* private variables definition */
    for (;;;i in Tmpl)/* distribute iterations between processors*/
    { d=A[i];           /* Assignment to replicated variable s
                        (s=A[i]) the value that depends on private
                        or distributed variables is forbidden */
    }
    s=0;                /* assign the same value */
    reduce s+=d;        /* compute replicated variable value
                           on private data. */
}
```

2.1 Data distribution

Data that take part in parallel execution can be divided into two classes: *private* data that are declared in a parallel part and other ones that are declared in a sequential part, but are visible in a parallel part. The latter can be *distributed* and *non – distributed*. Distributed data are arrays for which some distribution rules are given. Other data are non-distributed. Private data are declared in a parallel block with usual rules.

From the **SPMD** point of view non-distributed variables are replicated variables and a parallel part differs from a sequential only in one restriction on use of replicated data: it is forbidden to assign them values that are dependent on private or distributed data.

Data distribution scheme is defined with *template* declaration **templ**. Data are distributed according with templates attached to them. For example,

```
templ t_a[100:block];
templ t_b[100:cyclic];
templ t_c[100:cyclic:10];
```

In this example data template *t_a* describes block distribution. Block size is determined by compiler. Distribution scheme may be defined as cyclic as for *t_b* template. Distribution scheme can be defined as block-cyclic as for *t_c* template. In this case blocks of data are distributed cyclically.

If templates are declared then distributed arrays can be defined in the following way:

```
float A[t_a];
float D[100][t_d];
float C[t_c][t_a];
```

Arrays are automatically dimensioned by being distributed. We name data that are declared as distributed *statically distributed* data.

3 Parallel control statements

3.1 Parallel block statement

par-statement allows to describe parallel execution of the same group of statements with distributed data. It is forbidden to assign to replicated variables values that depend on private or distributed variables. From the **SPMD** point of view **par**-statement serves to introduce private variables for processors and to limit assignments for replicated variables. To describe parallel execution it is necessary to point out the data and possible computations distribution. For this purpose the head of **par**-statement must contain templates according to which computations can be distributed in the par-statement and may define data that are dynamically distributed before the body of **par**-statement is executed and are collected after it. If **SPMD** model is used, data are not distributed before the statement, but it is necessary to "unify" data after the statement, i.e. to collect them on each processor.

If the head does not contain a list of dynamically distributed data then it has the form:

```
par (template_name,template_name...)
```

The list of templates in the head must contains all templates that define *dynamically* distributed data or schemes of a processors network for parallel **for**-statements of this **par**-statement. Statement sequence of the statement body is executed with replicated and distributed data and its own private data.

The head can contain a list of *dynamically* distributed data:

```
par (t1, t2, t3; A[][t1], B[t2][t3])
```

The dynamically distributed variable must not be statically distributed. Sizes of each dimension must be equal to corresponded sizes of the template.

3.2 Parallel form of the for-statement

The list of statements is executed in a **for**-loop. This statement is intended to distribute loop iterations between processors. To do this the head of the loop contains template that defines this distribution. Data that are used inside the statement as distributed can be as statically, as dynamically distributed. In the latter case the distribution is determined by the surrounding **par**-statement.

In general case the head of the **for**-statement has the following form:

```
for (I=L;I<=U;I+=S;I in template_name)
    { statement list}
```

The range defined by the template is distributed between processors. On each processor the loop variable gets values from intersection of the range assigned to the processor and the range $L..U$ from the head. The bounds $L..U$ must lie in the range determined by the template. Loop variable must be private with respect to parallel block.

If the loop variable range is equal to the range determined by the template, the definition of bounds can be skipped:

```
for (;;;I in template_name)
    {statement list}
```

Example 1. *jki*-form of LU-decomposition with pivoting is given below. In this example data are distributed by columns.

```
templ tmpl[N:cyclic];
int ipivot[N]; float A[N][N];
main ()
{
```

```
par (tmpl; A[][tmpl], ipivot[tmpl] )
{ int j:
  for (;;;j in tmpl)
  { int i,k, pivrow, tr[N];    float pivot;
    for (i=0; i<n; i++) tr[i]=i;  .
    if (j>0)
    { for ( k=0; k<j; k++ )
      {   pivrow=tr[k];
          tr[ k         ] = tr[ipivot[k]];
          tr[ipivot[k]] = pivrow;
          for ( i=k+1; i<N; i+=1 )
            A[ tr[i] ][j] = A[ tr[i] ][j] - A[ tr[k] ][j] *
                            A[ tr[i] ][k] / A[ tr[k] ][k];
    } }
    if (j<N-1)
    { pivot=0.0;             pivrow=-1;
      for (i=j; i<N; i++)
          if (abs(A[ tr[i] ][j]) > pivot)
          {   pivot=abs(A[ tr[i] ][j]);     pivrow=i;
          }
      if (pivrow>=0)        ipivot[j]=piv;
      else                  printf("Cannot solve the system\n");
}} } }
```

3.3 Reduce statement

reduce-statement ensures synchronous computation of replicated data on distributed and private data. **reduce**-statement has the form:

```
reduce statement
```

The statement sequence is executed sequentially in undefined order on every processor with its own private data. The statement body may contain assignments to replicated variables but not to private, distributed ones. We can compute the conjunction of private variable values in the following way:

```
int dis;
par (tmpl)
{ int flag;
  ....
  dis=0;
  reduce { dis |= flag; };
}
```

Example 2. Solving of linear system by Jakobi iterations:

```
templ  Tmpl   [N:block];
double A      [Tmpl][N];
double B[N], Y[N], X[N];
double Delta = 0.0001;  int j, dis;
do { for (j=0; j<N; j++) Y[j] = X[j];
     par (Tmpl; X[Tmpl] )
     { double s, Eps=0.0;  int i;
       for (;;; i in Tmpl)
       { s  = B[i];
         for (j=0; j<N; j+=1)  s -= A[i][j]*Y[j];
         s  /= A[i][i];
         Eps = fmax( Eps, fabs(X[i]-s) );
         X[i]= s;
       }
       dis=0;
       reduce dis |= (Eps > Delta);
     }
} while (dis);
```

Example 3. Fast Fourier Transform:

```
 enum     {       k = 13,    N = 8192 };
#define  M_PI    3.14159
 templ    Tmpl[N:block]; /* assumed that there exists */
 complex work_seq[Tmpl],/* the operations of complex type*/
         save[Tmpl];    /* to simplify program */
void main ()
{ int step, Power=1, Bit=1<<(k-1);
  par(Tmpl)
  { int i;
     for (;;; i in Tmpl) work_seq[i]= { (double)i/(double)N, 0. };
  }

  for (step=0; step < k; step++, Power *= 2, Bit >>= 1)
  {
     par (Tmpl)
     {  int e_vals[k];         /*The values of the e(k,j)*/
        complex omega_power; /*The value of omega^e(r,j)*/
        for (;;;i in Tmpl) save[i] = work_seq[i];

        for (;;; i in Tmpl)
        { int p=i, j;    complex shift_value;
          e_vals[k-1]=0;
          for (j=0;j<k;j++,p>>=1) e_vals[k-1  ]=(e_vals[k-1])+p%2;
          for (j=1;j<k;j++      ) e_vals[k-1-j]=(e_vals[k-j]<<1)%N;

          omega_power = { cos(2.0*M_PI*e_vals[k-1-step]/N),
                          sin(2.0*M_PI*e_vals[k-1-step]/N) };
```

```
        shift_value = (i % (N/Power) >= (N / (2*Power)))
                 ? save[i - N/(2*Power)] : save[i + N/(2*Power)];
        if (i & Bit)
          work_seq[i] = save[i] * omega_power + shift_value;
        else
          work_seq[i] = save[i] + shift_value * omega_power;
      }
    }
  }
  for (;;; i in Tmpl)
  {   printf("Value %d, real      part =%g\n",i,work_seq[i].re);
      printf("Value %d, imaginary part =%g\n",i,work_seq[i].im);
} }
```

4 Subroutines

We impose some restrictions on the use of parallel constructions in subroutines. The main is the following: if a function can be called from a parallel loop it must not have parallel loops inside. Distributed array in this case can be passed into the function on the place of the following formal parameter:

```
type A[i in tmpl], int i
```

where *i* is the formal parameter on the place of which loop control variable have to be passed, and *tmpl* is the template according to which actual parameter and parallel loop are distributed.

If the function is not called from parallel loops, it can have parallel loops inside. In this case distributed arrays can be passed into the function on the place of formal parameters that are described as usual distributed variables:

```
type A[tmpl]
```

and these arrays can be used in parallel loops inside the function.

5 Implementation and Performance Results

The first version of the compiler from the SYNAPS/3 language with some restrictions on the form of nonlocal index expressions is implemented. Each index of left-hand side distributed variable of an assignment must be a loop variable.

Some performance results for different forms of LU-decomposition and FFT are given in Table 1 and Table 2. The tables show the ratio speedup/number of processors. In the table 1 **p**, **b** and **c** mean pivoting, block distribution, and cyclic distribution, correspondingly. The first row of the table 2 corresponds to the use of not vectorized form of send/receive, the second - to the vectorized one. This

Size/Method	jkipb	ikjb	kjipb	kijb	kjipc	kijc	ikjc	jkipc
50	0.18	0.19	0.46	0.55	0.43	0.55	0.62	0.60
100	0.18	0.20	0.61	0.69	0.52	0.86	0.92	0.87
150	0.18	0.20	0.66	0.74	0.78	0.98	0.98	0.97
200	0.18	0.20	0.68	0.75	0.84	1.00	0.99	0.99
250	0.18	0.20	0.69	0.76	0.88	1.00	0.99	1.00
300	0.18	0.20	0.70	0.76	0.91	1.00	1.00	1.00

Table 1: *The results of parallelizing LU-decomposition*

measurements were done on the transputer board IMS B008 [7][8] connected with IBM PC. The transputer board has six IMS T805 transputer nodes, each equipped with 1 or 2 Mbytes of local memory.

6 Related works

There were proposed some extensions of C language for distributed memory multiprocessors. For example in Kali[5] the user must specify data distributions and after that he must associate this data distribution with loop iterations distribution.

The language DINO[6] requires the user to specify a distribution of data to an environment. The programmer does not specify communication explicitly, but must mark nonlocal references.

The most distinctive systems for distributed memory multiprocessors are based on FORTRAN: Fortran–D[1], HPF[2],Vienna Fortran[3]. The main idea of all of them is to save FORTRAN for its users. In principal, only one construction is added to pure FORTRAN, namely data distribution. From this data distribution description compiler extracts information about the distribution of computations. Of course, this approach simplifies programming (especially for FORTRAN programmers), but it violates one of the main principle of programming: program structure has to be in accordance with program data structures. As a result a user can't see the difference between different variants of an algorithm. For example, there are a lot of scheme for LU-decomposition, but only few of them are well suitable for distributed memory computers. In this case user have to draw some other tools to estimate his decision, for example a programming system that surrounds the compiler. In some cases such a system can suggest user a better decision. So, the construction of the program has at least two levels.

Another consequence of this disparity is the unnatural structure of an object

lg_2**Size**	6	7	8	9	10	11	12	13	14
w/o vectorization	0.18	0.28	0.33	0.35	0.40	0.40	0.44	0.41	0.41
with vectorization	0.54	0.90	0.93	0.96	0.98	1.0	1.0	1.0	1.0

Table 2: *The results of parallelizing FFT*

program. To support this difference between a data structure and a structure of computations, a lot of statements must be guarded by conditions [4].

Essentially our approach differs from that mentioned earlier in the following:

1) The user must to point out explicitly what loops are distributed; on one hand it simplifies a compiler and makes the object program more efficient, on the other hand - it stimulates the user to make the program structure more appropriate for parallel execution;

2) It is forbidden to assign replicated variables values that depend on private and distributed variables inside **par**-statement. Because this it is possible to avoid problems connected to parallelization of loop bodies and again force the user to care of the structure of its program;

3) **reduce**-statement coupled with **par**-statement allow to overcome easily the problem of computations of reductions;

4) Dynamic data distribution is performed in structural way but not so freely as in dialects of FORTRAN; this allows to avoid dynamic redistribution.

References

[1] G. Fox, S. Hiranandani, K. Kennedy, C. Koelbel, U. Kremer, C.-W. Tseng, and M.-Y. Wu. *FORTRAN D Language Specification.* Report COMP TR90-141, Rice University, Huston, Texas, April 1991.

[2] DRAFT, *High Performance FORTRAN Language Specification.* High Performance FORTRAN Forum, May 3, 1993, Version 1.0.

[3] H. Zima, P. Brezany, B. Chapman, P. Mehrotra, and A. Schwald. *Vienna FORTRAN - a Language Specification.* ICASE Interium Report 21, ICASE NASA Langley Research Center, Hampton, Virginia 23665, March 1992.

[4] S. Hiranandani, K. Kennedy, C.-W. Tseng.*Compiling FORTRAN D for MIMD Distributed Memory Machines.* Communications of the ACM, August 1992, V. 35, No. 8.

[5] P.Mehrotra and J.Van Rosendale, *Programming distributed memory architectutes using Kali.* Advances in Languages and Compilers for Parallel Processing, Cambridge, MA:Pitman/MIT Press, 1991, pp. 364-384.

[6] M.Rosing, R.W.Schnabel, and R.P.Weaver, *The DINO parallel programming language.* Journal of Parallel and Distributed Computing, v.13, 1991, pp. 30-42.

[7] Inmos Ltd. *Transputer Reference Manual.* Prentice-Hall, 1988.

[8] Inmos Ltd. *Transputer technical notes.* Prentice-Hall, 1989.

Programming Environments for Massively Parallel Distributed Systems, Monte Verità, Switzerland

The Pyramid Programming System

Zheng Lin* Songnian Zhou† Wenfeng Li‡

Abstract

A parallel programming system is presented in this paper. The system supports a parallel programming methodology that decouples parallel control from sequential codes by embedding computation into a special kind of directed-arc graphs, the fork-join graphs, in which many interesting applications are shown to be representable. We define a specification language called parScript that is able to conveniently encode a fork-join graph. We study the effectiveness of the proposal by building a prototyping system both in workstation clusters and on a NUMA multiprocessor. Experiments are performed with numerical as well as symbolic processing programs to evaluate the approach. Results show that programs in parScript are efficient and portable across different architectures. Many programs achieve speed-up comparable to that of their hand-tuned counterparts in the C language.
Keywords: Compilation, Fork-join Graphs, Parallelism, Performance.

1 Introduction

Parallelism can speed up the execution time of many computing applications. However, writing parallel programs is still a big challenge due to the fact that parallel computers are sophisticated and many problems do not naturally map well onto a parallel architecture. Abstract computing models are often necessary to help ease the task of programming. There are certain criteria we consider important for an abstract model:

- the abstraction shall be sufficiently easy to understand.
- the abstraction should not obscure parallelism, i.e. it ought to make control and data dependency readily obtainable.
- the abstraction should allow information pertinent to runtime performance to be expressed either implicitly or explicitly.

*NEC Research Institute, 4 Independence Way, NJ 08540, USA. E-mail correspondence to: zlin@research.nj.nec.com

†Department of Computer Science, University of Toronto, Toronto, Ontario M5S 1A1, Canada

‡Department of Computer Science,University of Maryland, College Park, Md 20742, USA

In this paper, we investigate a programming model which satisfies the above conditions. In this model, sequential computation is embedded into a special kind of directed-arc graph, fork-join graphs, and a runtime system will invoke the sequential tasks as it walks through the graph, possibly in parallel, at runtime. We show that fork-join graphs happen to reflect the control flow of a number of interesting parallel algorithms.

We propose a language, parScript, derived from Horn-clause-based logic programming language, that can encode a fork-join graph very conveniently. ParScript has a simple interface with the C language to allow performance critical sequential tasks to be programmed in C. A parallel program thus consists of a parallel control specification in parScript, and a number of sequential procedures in C. Figure 1 illustrates the structure of a program.

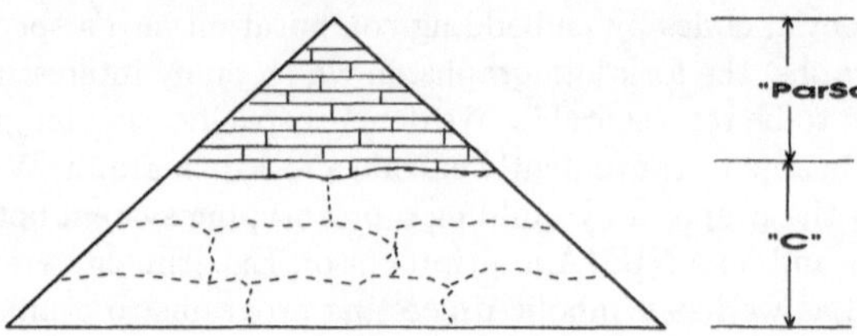

Figure 1: *A pyramid built of two different "materials".*

We have built a prototype system to experiment with the proposed method. The system consists of a parScript-to-C compiler, and a runtime kernel. The compiler translates parScript specification into C, and inserts parallel control codes into the object C program. We note that while a parScript specification normally need not be changed for different machines, parallel control codes generated by the compiler, as well as the runtime kernel are *architecture-specific.*

The system, to be referred to as Pyramid, is operational on a NUMA multiprocessor, Hector [7], and in a cluster of DEC5000 workstations connected by Ethernet. Hector is Non-uniform Memory Access (NUMA) shared memory multiprocessor with a hierarchical ring structure. It is considered a tightly-coupled architecture. The workstation cluster, on the other hand, is a highly loosely-coupled platform given its relatively fast CPU and slow interconnection network. These two machines are typical in the two classes of today's parallel architectures therefore they allow us to evaluate the proposed method with regard to its portability. We show that parScript programs can achieve performance result comparable to that of hand-tuned parallel C programs for the two architectures.

The paper is organized as following: section 2 describes the fork-join model and the parScript language; section 3 discusses some implementation issues; section 4 gives experimental results; section 5 discusses related works; and section 6 concludes the paper.

2 A Graph-based Computing Model

We begin with examining a number of program traces from some well-understood parallel algorithms. These traces show the control structures of the algorithms.

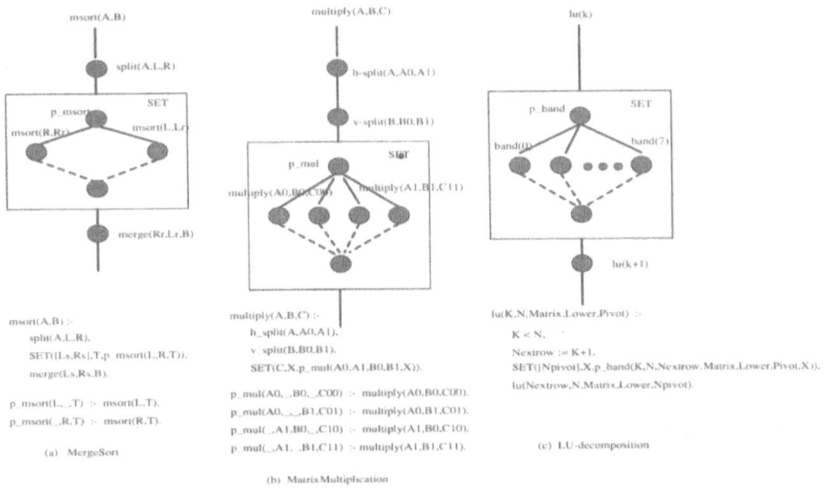

Figure 2: *Control flows of a mergesort, a matrix multiplication, and a LU-decomposition algorithms.*

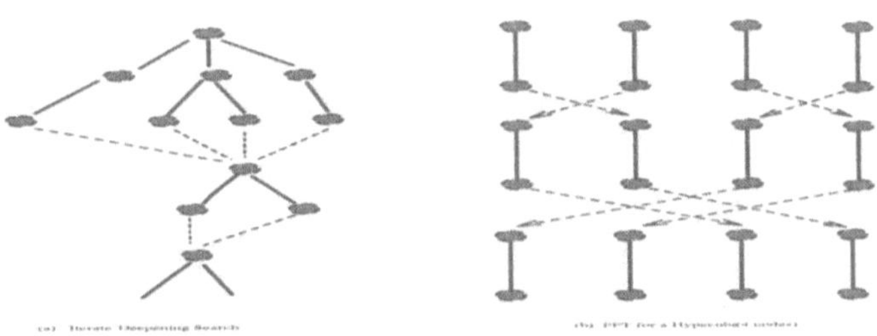

Figure 3: *Control flows of an iterate-deepening search and a FFT (on hypecube) algorithms.*

Figure 2 (a) is a trace from a merge sorting algorithm. The sorting process starts with splitting the input array, sort the sub-arrays (recursively), then merge the results. Figure 2 (b) is a (dense) matrix multiplication algorithm which computes the product by simultaneously computing the (four) sub-matrices of the product. Figure 2 (c) is a LU-decomposition algorithm which divides the input matrix into horizontal bands (eight bands shown in the graph), and processes the bands simultaneously.

Figure 3 (a) is a trace from an iterate-deepening search algorithm. Figure 3 (b) is a trace from a FFT algorithm designed for an (2-D) hypecube.

All traces exhibit a common graph structure , which we call a fork-join graph, to be formally defined it in the next subsection. The only exception in the examples here is the FFT algorithm whose control flow is not a perfect fork-join graph. But the misshape is minor and one can easily re-organize the graph to make it a fork-join graph. We believe that the fork-join structure is common for most divide-and-conquer algorithms, which constitute a large number of parallel algorithms.

2.1 Fork-Join Graph

Definition 2.1.1:

1. A tree is a fork-join graph.
2. Joining the leaves of a tree, i.e. creating a new node with every inciding arc coming from a leaf of the tree, results in a fork-join graph. We called the root of the tree a *fork* node, the new node a *joint* node.
3. Substituting a node in a fork-join graph with a fork-join graph results in a fork-join graph[1].

For our purpose, nodes in a graph are interpreted as *independent* tasks and the directed arcs as precedence relations between tasks. Note that computation and communication are *explicitly* represented in a fork-join graph.

2.2 ParScript Programs

In the following we define a simple language which can encode a fork-join graph conveniently. The language is derived from Horn clause-based logic programming language. Formally, ParScript program is a collection of clauses defined by the following syntax rules:

- **R1:** $f(X)$.
  This clause states that $f(X)$ is a solvable task. $f(X)$ is also called a fact in the program.
- **R2:** $h(X) : -b_1(X), b_2(X), ..., b_m(X)$.
  This clause states that $h(X)$ is solvable only if all b_i's are solvable. The clause is called a rule in the program. $h(X)$ is the head of the rule, and the conjunction of b_i's is the body of the rule.

In addition, a SET operator is defined as a special (built-in) task:

[1]By this definition, fork-join graphs are a subset of a mathematical object called *hygraph*. A hygraph is an extension of graph in that vertices are nestable, representing a (hy)graph underneath (referred to as a *blob*). In a fork-join graph, a pair of fork-join nodes defines a *fork-join component*, which can be *condensed* into one blob.

- **R3:** SET($finalset, template, goal(input, template)$)
  SET is used to computes all solutions to task *goal* with respect to the *template* and input variable *input*, and it puts solutions to $finalset$. Normally, the *template* are variables that are expected to be returned by the *goal*, and *input* are variables that are passed as parameters to the *goal*. SET also mandates that if there are more than one processes computing the SET every process will synchronize at the end of the computation.

Note that a task can be defined by multiple rules with the same head, representing alternative ways to solving the task. Also, facts in the program may be computed by external functions, possibly in other languages. In such cases, the fact shall be declared as $f(X) : -foreign(Argument\_Type)$.

Certain characteristics in parScript appear to have rendered it particularly suitable for describing a fork-join graph or expressing parallelism in general, comparing to languages relying on side-effects: 1). the program is *non-deterministic*, i.e., there are multiple choices of clauses for solving a task; 2) variables can be *bound only once*, i.e., the single-assignment property; 3) all variables in a clause are *local*; 4) there is *no global state* in a program. Examples of parScript codes can be found in figure 2. Notice that SET encapsulates an entire fork-join pair in a fork-join graph. Correspondence between a parScript program and a fork-join graph should be apparent. We do not further elaborate on this in the paper.

3 Implementation

The Pyramid system has been implemented on a NUMA multiprocessor, Hector [7], and in a network of DEC5000 workstations. Hector is a shared-memory multiprocessor with a hierarchical ring architecture [7]. It has 16 M88000 processors, each with 16 KB data, 16 KB code caches and 4MB memory. A key issue in the implementation is to achieve data locality so as to avoid contention on shared data, and to take advantage of the cache. The workstation cluster is a network of 8 identically configured DEC5000 workstations, each has 16 MB main memory. The PVM [4] software is used for communication support (message-passing) among workstations.

In both implementations, there is one operating system process (with its own address space) running on each processor. The fork-join graph underlying a program is mapped to processes using the self-organizing scheduling algorithm described in [5]. As mentioned in section 2, variables in a parScript program are mostly private variables, with the exception that variables inside the SET operator need to be shared. Private variables are always allocated in memory local to the process executing the task. Shared variables are treated differently in the two implementations. With the shared memory implementation, a mail box subsystem is implemented using shared memory to facilitate light weight synchronization and data exchanges among processes. When data is shipped through the mail box, the receiving process has to decide whether or not to make a local copy of the data.

At the meantime, the copying decision is made by the programmer by raising a special flag in the C modules. With the message-passing implementation, data is always transferred from one machine to another using the PVM send/receive calls as well as other synchronization primitives.

As one may observe, even in the shared memory implementation, we have used disjoint memory except when data sharing is absolutely necessary (e.g. variables in the SET operator). We believe this is an appropriate choice for NUMA machines similar to Hector as past experience with Hector [6] had shown that data sharing is not always beneficial because the existing cache control mechanism does not support hardware cache coherence. Even if cache coherence mechanism is available, using disjoint memory could still have advantages as it tends to render data being stored in memory pages private to the processor executing the task, avoiding the overhead of any remote memory reference.

4 Experiment

A set of numerical computing programs as well as symbolic processing programs were used in the experiment. Three numerical programs used are as follows[2]: 1) *msort*: sorting a set of records with the merge sort algorithm in Section 2. Note that a quicksort() procedure in C is called after the input array is split into 16 partitions; 2) *lu*: performing LU-decomposition on a dense matrix; and 3) *mm*: performing matrix multiplication on a dense matrix. In addition, three symbolic processing programs, the *queens*, *cube* and *zebra* programs, were used. These are all puzzle solving programs written entirely in parScript. The underlying fork-join graphs for these programs are large and can be highly irregular (e.g. the *cube* and *zebra* programs).

	ParScript	C
Sorting 100,000 records	23.5	22.0
LU-decomposition, 512x512	105	101
Matrix multiplication, 512x512	110	104

Table 1: *Uniprocessor execution time (in seconds).*

Uniprocessor runtime: Table 1 lists the execution time of parScript programs that rely on external C functions to perform the actual work. The timing was taken on a DEC5000 workstation. The overhead (compared to the C counterparts) of the parScript programs was measured at 6% or less. The reason the

[2]These programs are of different characteristics: the *mm* program requires little coordination among processes; the *lu* program frequently exchanges data among processes; and the *msort* program infrequently transmits data of large volume.

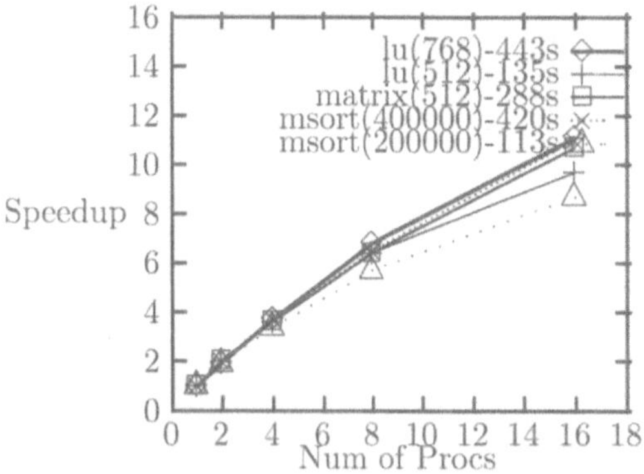

Figure 4: *Speed-up factors by parScript programs. Sequential runtime is listed next the labels.*

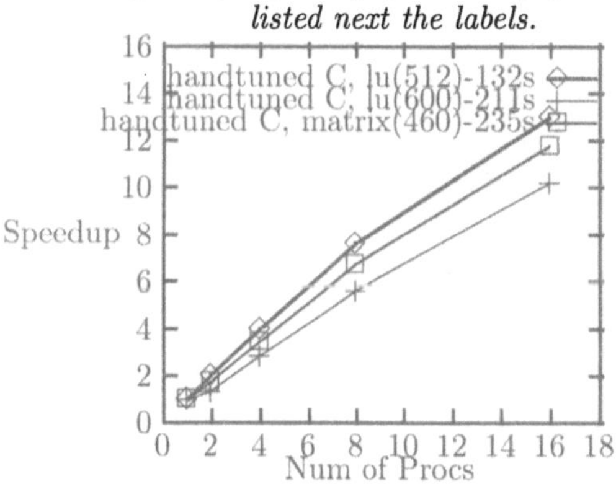

Figure 5: *Speed-up by handtuned C programs. Sequential runtime is listed next to the labels.*

overhead is so small is that the parScript code in a program is invoked only infrequently. For example, only the outer loop in the LU-decomposition program was coded in parScript. The overhead can be attributed mainly to the cost of manipulating choice points in the parScript part of the program.

Speed-up on Hector: Figure 4 gives the speed-up curves running the LU-decomposition, matrix multiplication and the sorting programs on Hector. To compare the performance with hand-written C programs, we give the speed-up curves for a LU-decomposition program and a matrix multiplication program in Figure 5 taken from [6]. The C programs were optimized to effectively utilize the cache memory on Hector. For matrix multiplication, the parScript program yields similar speed-up with up to 16 processors. For LU-decomposition, the hand-tuned C program yields better speed-up for the 512x512 matrix due to that 1) the C program schedules workload at the granule of *one row*, as opposed to *one band* (i.e., multiple rows) in the parScript program, achieving more balanced load distribution; 2) the hand-tuned C program exploits the advantage that a 512x512 matrix can have its rows aligned to page boundary [6] on Hector (with a page size of 4 KB), while the parScript program does not. Such advantage vanishes and the performance of the C program is not nearly as good for matrix of other sizes, such as 600x600. In fact, the speed-up by the parScript program on a 512x512 matrix is comparable to that of the C program on a 600x600 matrix.

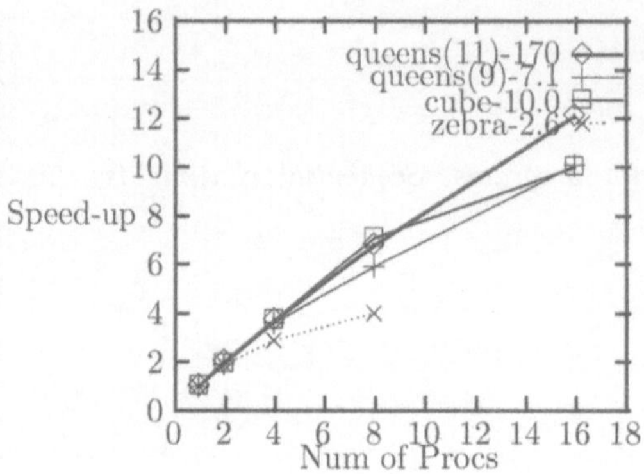

Figure 6: *Symbolic processing programs solving the* N-queens, cube *and* zebra *puzzles. Sequential runtime is listed next to the labels.*

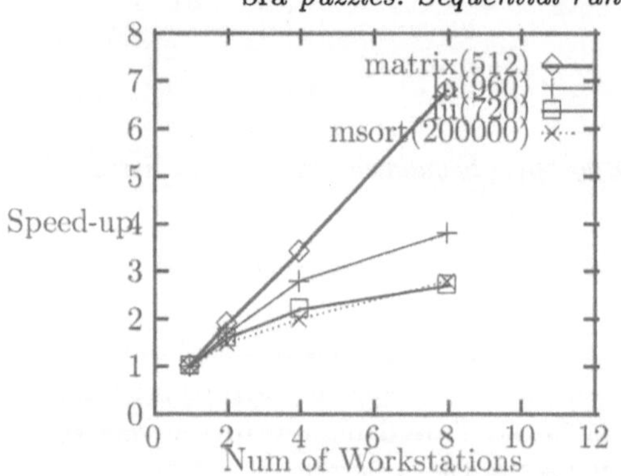

Figure 7: *Speed-up in the workstation cluster.*

Figure 6 depicts the speed-up for the three symbolic processing programs. We note that the *zebra* program is too small to measure its runtime on 16 processors, hence we used up to only 8 of them.

Speed-up in a network: Figure 7 depicts the speed-up curve for runtime some of the benchmarks in a network of workstations. The speed-up factors are not nearly as good as those from the NUMA multiprocessor. But the results are reasonable given the fact that communication cost is so high relative to the compute cost in a network. Programs requiring light communication, such as the matrix multiplication program, still do well. Others, such as the LU-decomposition and the sorting programs, show limited speed-up. The reasons are that the LU-decomposition program requires sending the pivot row to all processors frequently (i.e. every few tens of milliseconds); and the mergesort program transmits a large amount (i.e. a few megabytes) among processors to perform the merge, and in both cases the network was saturated. Limited bandwidth is clearly a performance bottleneck in a workstation cluster. This bottleneck cannot easily be alleviated even with hand-tuned C programs. In fact, a PVM program for LU-decomposition we tested gave speed-up results similar to that of the parScript program, indicating that the fact that speed-up is limited is not caused by the parScript implementation. Algorithms designed specially for alleviating the communication bottleneck may help improve speed-up. Whether those algorithms still conform to the fork-join model will be an interesting topic for future investigation.

5 Related Work

Presto [1] is a typical programming system using a runtime library for supporting parallelism. Compared to Presto, our system is built around a programming model based on fork-join graphs, and the system offers a language for encoding the graph. While our system is convenient and effective for applications conforming to to fork-join model, it is not be as flexible as Presto which permits imperative coding.

The difference between Pyramid and Linda [2] lies mainly in that the latter uses a shared tuple space to support parallel activities. It is not yet clear whether such a shared storage can be accommodated efficiently in a scalable architecture such as a network of computers or even NUMA machines. A fork-join graph, in contrast, appears to be less problematic with regard to mapping it to different architectures.

The cluster-M model [3] represents an interesting idea of exposing the *clustered* nature of many multi-computer systems to the programmer, in order to achieve a program that can be mapped effectively to the hardware. We believe that some of the mapping techniques in cluster-M can help handling the SET operator in Pyramid.

6 Summary

The Pyramid parallel programming system supports a methodology that decouples parallel control from sequential codes performing the actual computation. The system uses parScript as the parallel control specification language, taking advantage of its inherent parallelism and its correspondence the fork-join graph in which a great number of parallel applications are representable. Contributions of this research are:

- We have provided initial evidence showing that a number of interesting problems can be modeled in fork-join graphs.
- We have proposed adopting a Horn clause-based language, parScript, for the specification of parallel control.
- We have implemented a message-passing and a shared-memory prototype system to experiment with the proposed method. Results show that parScript programs are portable, and many of them can be as efficient as corresponding hand-tuned C programs.

We are in the process of writing large applications such as full text search and natural language processing applications with parScript. We plan to build a graphic environment for the Pyramid system.

References

[1] B.N. Bershad, E. D. Lazowska, and H. M. Levy. Presto: A system for object-oriented parallel programming. *Software - Practice and Experience*, 18(8), August 1988.

[2] N. Carriero and D. Gelernter. Linda in context. *Communications of the ACM*, 32(4), April 1989.

[3] M. M Eshaghian. Cluster-m parallel programming model. In *Proceedings of the 1992 international parallel processing symposium*, 1992.

[4] G. A. Geist. Network based concurrent computing on the pvm system. Technical report, Oak Ridge National Lab., 1991.

[5] Z. Lin. Self-organizing task scheduling for parallel execution of logic programs. In *Proceeding of the 1992 Conference on Fifth Generation Computer Systems*, Japan, 1992.

[6] H. S. Sandhu, B. Gamsa, and S. Zhou. The shared regions approach to software cache coherence on multiprocessors. In *Proceedings of the Fourth ACM SIGPLAN Symposium on Principles and Practices of Parallel Programming*, May 1993.

[7] Z. G. Vranesic, M. Stumm, D. M. Lewis, and R. White. Hector - a hierarchically structured shared-memory multiprocessor. *Computer*, January 1991.

Programming Environments for Massively Parallel Distributed Systems, Monte Verità, Switzerland

Intelligent Algorithm Decomposition for Parallelism with Alfer

S. N. McIntosh-Smith B. M Brown
S. Hurley
University of Wales at Cardiff
PO Box 916, Cardiff, U.K.
scmsns@cm.cf.ac.uk

Abstract

In this paper we present Alfer, a system that assists in the design of parallel programs that are to be run on distributed memory multicomputers. The user provides a high-level algorithm description, which may or may not contain any explicitly parallel constructs. Alfer then provides intelligent assistance to help in the parallelisation process. It does this by identifying certain features within the algorithm that can form parallel constructs either directly, or by applying some transformation. Minimum source change constraints are employed during transformation to improve readability, and ultimately maintainability of the generated parallel code. A prototype system exists, and initial results indicate that the system can provide useful assistance in the parallelising process, with significant improvements in the readability of the generated source in comparison to other restructuring parallelising compilers.

1 Introduction

Automatic transformation of sequential code into parallel programs has been the subject of intense research for some time, as shown by the plethora of tools available for performing such transformations [5]. The large sums of money invested in existing serial applications have resulted in industry encouraging and funding many projects in an attempt to parallelise "dusty-deck" programs automatically or semi-automatically. Many parallel machines in the early eighties were of the shared-memory type. However, shared-memory machines are restricted by technical problems which limit the number of processors a machine might contain [6]. Distributed-memory machines seemed to overcome the problems of restricted machine size, but new problems were introduced as program data then had to be efficiently partitioned. Gustafson showed that these efficiency problems could nearly always be overcome by increasing problem size, and in his paper showed that distributed memory machines had a future [2]. As traditional supercompilers were adapted for distributed memory environments, new difficulties were uncovered. Dependence analysis became increasingly complex in the attempt to refine old methods to cope with new partitioning problems, but code generated by such compilers often failed to make use of obvious parallelism. Instead, these restructuring compilers tended to parallelise certain classes of loops, a method that had proved ideal when dealing with shared-memory machines.

Another problem with current supercompilers is that automatically parallelised programs can be difficult to maintain [4]. The parallel code generated by them may not bear much resemblance to the original sequential code, so that even a program's original designers find it difficult to understandg what a compiler has done to their program. Such compilers reinforce the commonly felt "mysticism" about parallelism; that the subject is beyond most potential users and should be either avoided at all costs, or dealt with automatically. However, parallelism can prove to be a graceful and natural way of expressing algorithms, especially if software tools aid the process of software design [3].

In this paper we discuss some recent work designed to assist with the complicated problem of decomposing an algorithm in preparation for a parallel implementation. Alfer is a system that acts as an assistant to a programmer in the process of creating a parallel program. To keep the development process as familiar as possible, Alfer emulates a natural parallel algorithm design process. Alfer analyses an algorithm provided by the user and generates a near-optimal parallel version. The system simultaneously tries to maintain as much correspondence as possible between the original algorithm and the parallelised code, so that the resulting code is familiar to the user, hopefully improving its maintainability. An intention was to make Alfer easy to update with new methods by providing a mechanism for giving it additional or improved rules with which to work. An approach based on parallelisation rules kept in a knowledge base was developed to this end.

Alfer makes use of the Enterprise model of parallel computation in order to express parallel algorithms [7]. Enterprise programs consist of a set of sequential C subroutines together with a description of the parallelism between those routines. Parallel constructs in the model consist of pipelines, master-slaves and parallel recursion amongst others. Alfer only significantly changes the original algorithm under specific and limited circumstances; these will be described later in this paper.

2 A new approach: solutions based on alfs

When considering the parallel algorithm design problem, it was decided to adopt a method commonly used by human designers. In designing a parallel algorithm, one possible starting point is to outline a pseudo-code version that may or may not be explicitly parallel. The next step is to analyse the algorithm for any high-level parallelism that exists superficially in the pseudo-code, or that could be gained by small modifications to the pseudo-code. The designer would be looking for algorithmic features, which we term *alfs*, that are known to be parallelisable. An alf combines a set of the algorithm's subroutines to form a parallel construct. Hence a chain of subroutine calls might constitute a pipeline, multiple calls to a single subroutine could be suitable for master-slave type parallelism, and so on.

We shall now define the concept of an alf more formally. An *alf definition* is a categorisation for a set of sub-algorithms that together satisfy certain constraints. The set of sub-algorithms must be non-empty and constitute a sub-graph of an algorithms program graph. The definition is mainly the specification of the constraints.

An *alf instance* is an occurrence of a set of sub-algorithms from a real algorithm that actually satisfies some alf definition. We use alf definitions to search for alf instances in algorithms. Since we are primarily concerned with alf instances, these are more usually referred to as simply *alfs.*

Alfer allows the user to input a pseudo-code algorithm, and then to analyse that algorithm to find all possible alfs that can be constructed from its subroutines. Once the set of feasible alfs is known, the system attempts to generate a near-optimal parallel configuration of the algorithm. This consists of a subset of the alfs that could be generated from the algorithm, together with the set of sub-algorithms that make up the algorithm. The system finds this near-optimal configuration by evaluating candidate solutions against a fitness function. The fitness function is based on user specified criteria that can include maximising the solutions degree of parallelism, maximising the efficiency of resource utilisation, minimising execution time and minimising overheads. The sub-algorithms are then expanded to form proper C subroutines by the user before they, together with the near-optimal set of alfs, are passed to Enterprise for compilation into an executable parallel program. The following sections explain each of these stages in more detail.

2.1 Extracting alfs from a pseudo-code algorithm

Denote the set of all alf definitions by $\mathcal{F}$. $\mathcal{F}$ can be partitioned into three disjoint sets P, T and I. Any alf $f \in \mathcal{F}$ will belong to just one of these three subsets. The first subset P consists of alfs that exhibit parallelism as they stand. Examples of this kind of alf include pipelines, master-slaves, parallel recursion and so on. We will call this category the *parallelisable* alfs. The second subset T we shall term the *transformable* alfs. T contains alfs closely related to those in P, but restricted in some way, preventing them from exhibiting parallelism. An alf only qualifies for membership in T if there exists a transform (a simple rewriting rule) that removes the restriction on its parallelism, so changing the alf's classification to its related alf in P. This property means that the set of all transformations acts as a many-to-one function from T to P. Therefore each alf in T has a corresponding alf in P. The final subset I which we shall call the *irreducible* alfs, is for those alfs which do not exhibit any natural parallelism. Alfs in this category lack any parallelising transform that could be used to introduce parallelism, and as such are inherently sequential.

In practise many alfs will remain in I when no transform is currently known that would qualify it for membership of T. We predict that as more alfs are classified and new transforms discovered, so the size of P should increase slightly and the size of T grow significantly at I's expense.

Extracting alfs from an algorithm takes two steps. Firstly, Alfer's parser uses a modified version of traditional dependence analysis that generates Prolog facts representing the dependencies within the algorithm. Next Alfer's second stage uses Prolog rules on the dependence facts to recognise all possible alfs within the algorithm.

2.1.1 Alf recognition

Alfer's alf recognition works by analysing an algorithm first for any alfs that are parallelisable ($\in P$), then for any that are transformable ($\in T$). Any sub-algorithms (pseudo-code subroutines) that have not been included in an alf by the end of this process are classified as *atomic sub-algorithms* and hence members of I. In this way the system uses the sub-algorithms as building blocks with which alfs are created. For the purpose of the recognition, a special sub-algorithm is defined, called "start". This represents the environment from which the entire program will be called, and to which control will ultimately return. The purpose of start is to call "main"; in this way main can be treated as any other sub-algorithm, and can be included as a component of an alf. The system finds all alfs that can be built from the sub-algorithms; it is the task of the configurer stage of the system to choose which combination of alfs will result in the best parallel version of the algorithm.

A note on terminology: we need to distinguish between the programming constructs within an algorithm and those within the actual C source code that will eventually be created. We shall refer to the subroutines in the pseudo-code as *sub-algorithms* in order to make this distinction clear. To avoid confusion between the described abstract algorithmic features and their programmatic counterparts, we shall refer to alfs that represent pipelines as *cascades*, those that represent master-slaves as *multiple siblings*, and parallel recursion as *self-invocation*.

The prototype system concentrates on recognising three particular alfs in P: cascade, multiple siblings and self-invocation, and one alf from T: implicit cascade. These alfs represent important parallelism often found in algorithms but rarely exploited in current parallelising compilers. It is also possible to efficiently implement these constructs on medium/coarse grained parallel machines. The target machine for the prototype system is a local network of Sun workstations. This is essentially a distributed memory, message passing machine, and has been demonstrated to be well suited to executing such parallel constructs by Bemmerl et al in their work with the TOPSYS system [1].

Recognising alfs involves looking at a set of sub-algorithms and testing to see if the set constitutes an alf. The system tests for an alf by applying rules to the set and to any dependence information known about the sub-algorithms in that set. The rules state under what conditions a set constitutes a certain alf. If the rules are satisfied for the set then a fact is asserted into the database to record the recognition of an alf instance.

Rules to recognise cascade, multiple siblings, self-invocation and implicit cascade have been developed. The system uses the weakest rules that will correctly perform the recognition process. Stronger rules could be developed that would prevent weaker or less efficient alfs from being recognised. However, we believe that all potential alfs should be found and then selection of the optimal combination of alfs performed at a later, completely independent stage. Rules to recognise further alfs in P and common alfs from T are under development.

The recognition rules for one parallel alf, a cascade are described below. Each rule operates on a list L of n sub-algorithms $a_1, \ldots, a_n$. Dependence information is generated by Alfer's parser, and exists as Prolog facts. Facts about data dependence, call dependence and so on are all known for each sub-algorithm.

- $L = [a_1, \ldots, a_n]$
- $a_1, \ldots, a_n$ must be a path in the algorithm's call graph
- a_i only invokes a_{i+1} and is itself only invoked by a_{i-1}, $i = 2, \ldots, n-1$
- each a_{i+1} may only be data dependent on the a_i that invoked it, $i = 1, \ldots, n-1$
- a_i will always invoke a_{i+1} at least once
- n (the length of the cascade) ≥ 2
- a_1 must be guaranteed to be called more than once by a sub-algorithm $a \notin L$

A separate stage of the tool can analyse an individual sub-algorithm for any inner parallelism that could be exploited. Sub-algorithms in this category are alfs in themselves, and are called "complex atomic". These are transformable alfs, and so $\in T$. If such an alf is found, the system prompts the user for permission to "explode" the sub-algorithm into components that could be executed in parallel. Allowing the user the power of veto prevents the system from creating anything the user might not understand. Sub-algorithms exploded in this manner can be recombined by the user at any time. In a similar way, a set of sub-algorithms that contain little work can be combined into one for efficiency purposes. This is another alf, called a "simple set", and is a member of I since we force a sequential nature onto the sub-algorithms that make up the alf. Again the system will ask for the user's permission before any such grouping is performed. This transform is also reversible.

An advantage of this rule based approach is that more rules can be easily added to the rule base, and individual rules can be refined to reflect improved analysis techniques. It may be possible for a future version of the system to evaluate the effectiveness of its own rules, and so learn which perform well and which perform badly. In this way the system could improve its alf recognition process with experience.

2.2 Generating a near-optimal parallel configuration

Once the user has input the algorithm and Alfer has generated an alf for each possible parallel construct in the algorithm, the next step is to decide which configuration of parallel constructs would result in the best parallel program. The word "best" is taken to have several meanings, as detailed below. Alfer can currently think of best as a combination of factors, including fastest possible execution time, the most efficient use of resources, the smallest amount of overhead and the largest degree of parallelism. Most of these factors are interdependent; the fastest possible execution time depends on having the lowest overheads together with as much parallelism and the greatest efficiency possible. However, Alfer can be made to concentrate on one or more of these aspects. Making "best" the fastest possible execution time could conceivably result in the generation of a sequential program.

Earlier in the parallelisation process Alfer generated upper and lower bounds for the number of instructions each sub-algorithm would perform. This representation of the amount of "work" performed inside the sub-algorithm is now utilised to measure the quality of each alf we wish to assess. $\mathcal{P}$ is a measure of how many tasks are executing in parallel at any one time. In the normal course of a parallel program's execution $\mathcal{P}$ will vary with time. This suggests that there are several ways to interpret and measure $\mathcal{P}$. Alfer uses a method that takes into account the amount of work being performed in the tasks executing in parallel. For each $task_i$ we calculate a maximum and a minimum weight W_i^{max} and W_i^{min}, representing the upper and lower bounds for the number of instructions $task_i$ will execute. The sets $W^{max} = \{W_1^{max}, \ldots, W_n^{max}\}$ and $W^{min} = \{W_1^{min}, \ldots, W_n^{min}\}$ are the sets of all weights for a set of sub-algorithms $A = \{a_1, \ldots, a_n\}$. Multiplying $\mathcal{P}_i^{max}$ and $\mathcal{P}_i^{min}$ by W_i^{max} and W_i^{min} will reflect how worthwhile the parallelism in alf_i is relative to the other alfs found in the algorithm. This gives us the following:

$$\mathcal{P}^{min} = \frac{\sum_{i=1}^{n} \mathcal{P}_i^{min} \times W_i^{min}}{n}$$

$$\mathcal{P}^{max} = \frac{\sum_{i=1}^{n} \mathcal{P}_i^{max} \times W_i^{max}}{n}$$

The sets W^{min} and W^{max} are computed during the dependence analysis stage. This information is used to compute the sets $\{\mathcal{P}_i^{min}\}$ and $\{\mathcal{P}_i^{max}\}$, $i = 1 \ldots m$ where m is the number of alfs found in the algorithm, and $\mathcal{P}_i^{min}$ and $\mathcal{P}_i^{max}$ represent the minimum and maximum parallelism in alf_i respectively. When a configuration is generated from the set of alfs, $\mathcal{P}^{min}$, $\mathcal{P}^{max}$ and $\mathcal{T}$ can then be calculated, giving a measure of the quality of this configuration.

Alfer can use several different algorithms to generate a near-optimal configuration of alfs from an algorithm. It is hoped to make a comparison between these different methods, to determine if one will always perform better than the others. If this is not the case, the tool could have several different generation methods, applying the most suitable to a particular problem. An exhaustive search of all possible configurations would be computationally expensive. If we consider the case where we have n sub-algorithms, then the number of ways these can be combined into groups is described by the function $p(n)$ where

$$p(n) = \frac{1}{4n\sqrt{3}} \exp(\pi\sqrt{\frac{2n}{3}})$$

as shown by Ramanujan in [8]. Experimental results in Ramanujan's paper demonstrate that this factor would become prohibitive once algorithms with realistic numbers of sub-algorithms are to be considered. Calculating $p(30)$ we find that with only 30 sub-algorithms and if we place no restrictions on the way the sub-algorithms are to be grouped, then there already are over 6000 ways one could group the sub-algorithms together. An exhaustive search of all these groupings will therefore take exponential time to perform, and so alternatives to an exhaustive approach must be considered.

Alfer uses a configuration generation methods that involves generating several possible candidate configurations, and then measuring their suitability. The configuration that best fits the ideal solution criteria of maximum parallelism $\mathcal{P}$ and shortest execution time $\mathcal{T}$ is chosen. In order to generate a near-optimal configuration $C = (F', A)$ from a set of alfs $F = \{f_1, \ldots, f_m\}$ and a set of sub-algorithms $A = \{a_1, \ldots, a_n\}$, the system starts with $F' = \emptyset$. In generating a candidate configuration, the system starts with one of the parallelisable alfs $f \in F \cap P$. This is moved from F into F'. A greedy algorithm is then applied to F until every sub-algorithm in A has been involved in an alf in F'. Other candidate alfs are generated by starting with a different alf from $F \cap P$ each time. If there are p alfs in $F \cap P$, then p candidate configurations are generated. Each candidate configuration is compared to the best found so far, C^{best}. If the new candidate is better, C^{best} is updated. If there are m alfs in F, then the number of alfs in $F \cap P$ will be $< m$, as F will always contain at least n alfs $\notin P$. Each configuration takes time $O(m)$ to generate, and so the total time for this approach will be $O(m \times p)$. For large n it is likely that $\lim_{n \to \infty} m \times p = m$, making this an $O(m)$ technique.

Once the configuration has been generated, the user can examine how well the algorithm parallelised, and if satisfied can expand the pseudo-code until the sub-algorithms are correct C code. Only source in legitimate C can be passed to Enterprise, so before a working parallel program can be created the user must confirm the parallel algorithm design, altering the original pseudo-code first if so desired. When a satisfactory parallel algorithm is obtained, the sub-algorithms can then be used to generate C subroutines. The configuration and the set of subroutines are then passed through the Enterprise precompiler. Enterprise creates a parallel program from these components that can then be executed on a network of Sun workstations. Enterprise also provides facilities to animate the execution of the program, and also to monitor its performance and record timing information which can be used by Alfer for further program refinement if the user so wishes. To facilitate such an iterative development process both the pseudo-code templates and full C versions of the sub-algorithms are retained by Alfer.

3 Results

To measure how effectively Alfer can recognise coarse-grained, algorithmic parallelism, we used Alfer to parallelise some example code presented in [7] for which the optimal parallel solution had been derived experimentally. The code was "reverse-engineered" into an algorithm and given to Alfer. A much simplified version of the code, which is for a real application in image processing, is given below.

```
algorithm model() {
    for ( i=0; i<frame_count; i++) {
        /* compute location and motion of objects */
        polyconv(frame);
    }
}

polyconv(frame) {
    /* perform transformations and projections */
    split(frame, polygons);
}

split(frame, polygons) {
    /* hidden surface removal and anti-aliasing */
}
```

We must emphasise that we have left in the most important parts of the algorithm, the parts that determine the call structure. The rest of the code is only considered for its effect in inter-procedural dependencies. Alfer generated 5 candidate parallel configurations of this algorithm. The one Alfer chose as the best was the optimal version that had been obtained by hand in the Enterprise paper [7].

Alfer spent relatively little time in dependency analysis, an advantage over most other source-to-source parallelising compilers. Instead it spent most of it's time reasoning with the information it had about the algorithm, deciding which would be the best way to parallelise it. A breakdown of Alfer's execution time example is given. The example was run on a loaded Sun SPARCserver 10.

Initialisation of the Prolog environment accounted for 0.72 seconds of the recognising time. This startup time remained almost constant for all test runs, and so has not proved to be a limiting factor. Alfer found a total of 8 alfs in the example, of which 5 were parallel alfs ($\in P$) and 3 were irreducible alfs ($\in I$).

Timings for the "model" example	
	Time in seconds
parsing	0.05
recognising	2.6
optimising	0.09
conversion to Enterprise format	0.01
Total	2.75

Developing a measure of the "readability" of a parallel program is difficult, as the concept is inherently subjective. Alfer utilises a readability metric that measures a generated parallel program in terms of its similarity to the sequential program from which it was derived. The assumption behind this metric is that a user will be familiar with their own code, i.e. the sequential original. If the parallel version is identical to the sequential, we determine it to be 100% readable. If there is a 50% correspondence between the two versions then the parallel source is 25% readable, and so on.

$$readibility = \left(\frac{number\ of\ lines\ preserved}{total\ lines}\right)^2 \times 100$$

In the example, Alfer used only parallel and irreducible alfs, and so the resulting parallel version had a readibility of 100%.

The example shows that Alfer's approach can give high-quality parallelisation strategies in a reasonable time period in comparison to other techniques. This is due to Alfer's high-level analysis and reasoning process and its reluctance to indulge in exhaustive dependence analysis. Alfer is thus able to tackle large codes in reasonable time while still yielding results comparable with those of other currently available parallelising compilers.

4 Conclusions

The system described in the above sections attempts to provide an intelligent tool to assist in the development of parallel programs. Our design philosophy has been to develop a tool that will assist in the parallelisation of new algorithms; as such we would expect that our tool will be of more use to a developer writing new parallel code than to a programmer parallelising "dusty deck" programs. Further, we believe that our tool will reduce the development time for new applications with a significant reduction in the development costs.

Alfer exists in prototype form, and tests are being developed to measure its performance and compare it to that of other restructuring parallelising compilers. Early results indicate that the parallelisation technique based on pattern matching utilised by the system produces code with performance comparable with code produced by other restructurers, whilst the readability of the parallel code has been greatly increased. Indeed, if the parallel program is generated from only parallelisable and/or irreducible alfs, no lines of source are altered to produce the parallel version. The system also trivially recognises what would appear to be "obvious" parallelism to a user, but often missed by source directed restructuring compilers.

Acknowledgments

We would like to thank Jonathan Schaeffer and the Enterprise team at the University of Alberta, Canada for allowing us to use their system for our work, and for the example code used to generate our results. One of us, SNMS, wishes to acknowledge the support of the British SERC through the award of a research studentship.

References

[1] Thomas Bemmerl and Bernhard Ries. Programming Tools for Distributed Multiprocessor Computing Environments. In *Proceedings of the EIT Workshop on Parallel and Distributed Systems.* IAM, University of Berne, Switzerland, September 1991.

[2] Robert E. Benner, John L. Gustafson, and Gary R. Montry. Development of Parallel Methods for 1024-Processor Hypercube. *SIAM Journal on Scientific and Statistical Computing*, 9(4), July 1988.

[3] K. Chandy and Carl Kesselman. Parallel Programming in 2001. *IEEE Software*, 8(6):11–20, November 1991.

[4] Michael H. Coffin. *Parallel Programming: A New Approach.* Prentice Hall, 1992.

[5] Warren Harrison. Tools for Multiple-CPU Environments. *IEEE Software*, 7(3):45–51, May 1990.

[6] Thomas J. LeBlanc and Evangelos P. Markatos. Shared-Memory Multiprocessor Trends and the Implications for Parallel Program Performance. Technical Report 420, University of Rochester, Computer Science Department, Rochester, New York 14627, May 1992.

[7] Greg Lobe, Ian Parsons, Jonathan Schaeffer, and Duane Szafron. The Enterprise Model for Developing Distributed Applications. *IEEE Parallel and Distributed Technology*, 1(3):85–96, August 1993.

[8] Srinivasa Ramanujan. Asymptotic Formulae in Combinatory Analysis. In G.H. Hardy, P.V. Seshu Aiyar, and B.M. Wilson, editors, *Collected Papers of Srinivasa Ramanujan*, chapter 36, pages 276–310. Cambridge University Press, 1927.

Programming Environments for Massively Parallel Distributed Systems, Monte Verità, Switzerland

Symbolic Array Data Flow Analysis and Pattern Recognition in Numerical Codes

Christoph W. Keßler
Graduiertenkolleg Informatik
Universität des Saarlandes
D-66041 Saarbrücken, Germany
kessler@cs.uni-sb.de

Abstract

The PARAMAT approach to fully automatic distributed–memory parallelization consists of three basic ideas: First, we observe that we can cover large parts of many numerical codes by a small set of typical programming patterns. Second, we give a fast and powerful pattern recognition algorithm which tries to locally recover the semantics of the program while being robust against many common code modifications like loop distribution, loop interchange, loop blocking or loop unrolling. Third, we use the restored program semantics information to guide data partitioning, run time prediction and sophisticated optimizing code transformations including algorithm replacement.

In this paper we focus on the symbolic array dataflow analysis techniques of PARAMAT's pattern recognition tool. We introduce a compact symbolic access descriptor and use it to compute array data flow that guides the recognition process. As an example, we show the application of this method to recognize and reroll unrolled loops.

1 Introduction

Distributed memory systems (DMS) are well–known to be difficult to program. The most important reasons are: (1) Parallel code must contain explicit message passing statements, and programming explicit message passing is complex, tedious and error-prone. (2) The efficiency of the target program heavily depends on choosing a suitable data distribution (and sometimes, also redistribution) — for larger applications, this is a very hard problem. (3) SPMD programs must in general be transformed to be efficient — just applying the owner-computes-rule will usually not suffice. There is, however, no guidance in which optimizing transformations to choose, and in which order to apply them. (4) Run time prediction for non-trivial codes on real machines is a very problematic matter for reasons of network contention, message protocols, buffering, undocumented hardware features, and others.

Message passing statements can be generated automatically today by *semi-automatic* parallelization. The user has to provide data distribution and optimizing transformations, either in the form of interactive commands in tools like SUPERB [Ger89] or in the form of language constructs or compiler directives in an explicitly parallel language such as Fortran-D [HKT91], Vienna Fortran [CMZ92], HPF [HPF93] and others.

Nevertheless, there are hard problems involved in automatic data distribution and redistribution, in automatic guidance in optimizing transformations, and in suitably accurate performance prediction. These problems arise from the fact that there is often not sufficient knowledge available on the source program and on the target machine characteristics. So what we should do to make fully automatic DMS parallelization feasible at all is to gain as much of this knowledge as possible. This works, of course, not for all programs.

Many numerical programs are, however, in particular good-natured for this purpose. We have examined a lot of typical application codes that are to be run on distributed memory systems. As a result, we have observed that there is only a rather limited number of typical programming idioms, called *patterns*, that often occur in these programs, in particular in the time–consuming inner loops, and we have collected around 150 typical patterns and also typical modifications (transformations) of them, called *templates*, in a *basic pattern library* [Keß93b]. We claim that these few patterns cover large parts — especially the time–critical ones — of numerical application codes that are actually run on distributed–memory multiprocessors. We exemplified this by examining the source codes of standard numerical benchmark programs [KP93, Keß93b].

From this observation, we construct a sophisticated automatic DMS parallelizer called PARAMAT [KP93, Keß93a, Keß93b] with the following key ideas: A pattern recognition tool working fast and reliably locally recognizes pattern incarnations and replaces them by a pattern *instance*, looking similar to a Fortran90 intrinsic function call. By this information, we can infer a lot of additional knowledge on mathematical properties, efficient implementations, favorable data distributions and run time behaviour, to guide a sophisticated parallelization process including high–level program transformations up to local algorithm replacement.

In this paper we focus on the symbolic array dataflow analysis techniques of PARAMAT's pattern recognition tool that are responsible for a significant part of its performance. We introduce a compact symbolic access descriptor. We use it for two purposes: to analyze data dependence and to compute array data flow that guides the recognition process. We give an example for the application of this method by showing how to recognize unrolled loops and how to reroll them to obtain a target-machine-independent program representation.

2 Pattern Recognition

In order to be able to do a proper job, the source program must be preprocessed first to make the program as *explicit* as possible, for instance to propagate constant expressions forward to the place where they are needed, to get rid of induction temporaries, to inline procedures, to make the program well-structured by getting rid of GOTO's, to simplify arrays with dimensions of low extent, etc.

Pattern Hierarchy Graph The pattern library is hierarchically organized. We represent it as a directed acyclic graph, the pattern hierarchy graph (PHG). A PHG edge connects a pattern p_1 to a pattern p_2 iff p_1 may occur as a direct subpattern in a template of p_2. The PHG edges are used to trigger pattern matching. Usually, a pattern has only a few predecessors and a few successors in the PHG. The pattern matching algorithm only needs to inspect the PHG successor's templates of an already matched pattern p when looking for a possible pattern containing p as a subpattern. That results in faster pattern recognition compared with simple testing of all predefined templates.

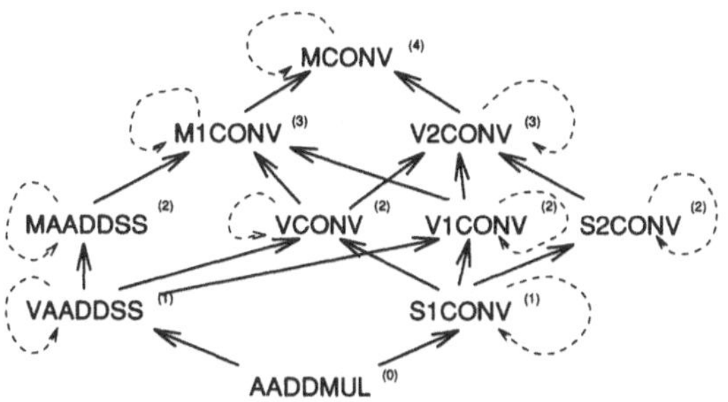

Fig. 1: The PHG of 1D (VCONV$^{(2)}$) and 2D (MCONV$^{(4)}$) convolution. Each solid edge into a pattern stands for a particular 'vertical' template of this pattern; the dashed edges represent templates for matching along cross edges. For the reason of improved performance, self-cycles from a pattern to itself are admitted.

Pattern Recognition Strategy The source program's syntax tree is traversed bottom-up and from the left to the right. A recognized node is replaced by a pattern instance. Each node is visited only once, and for each node, there are only a few possible patterns due to the PHG structure. Thus, matching time is guaranteed to be linear in the size of the source program.

We have designed the templates in such a way that pattern recognition is robust against typical code transformations like expression reordering, statement reordering, loop interchange, loop distribution, loop unrolling, loop peeling, loop blocking or introduction of temporary variables.

Example The PHG of 2D convolution is given in Fig. 1. Suppose the programmer has coded a 2D convolution as follows:

```
  for (i = 1; i <= u1-1; i++) {
    for (j = 1; j <= u2-1; j++)
S1:   y[i][j] = 0.0;
    for (j = 1; j <= u2-1; j++)
      for (k = 1; k <= u3-1; k++)
        for (l = 1; l <= u4-1; l++)
S2:         y[i][j]=y[i][j]-a[k][l]*x[i-k][j-l];}
```

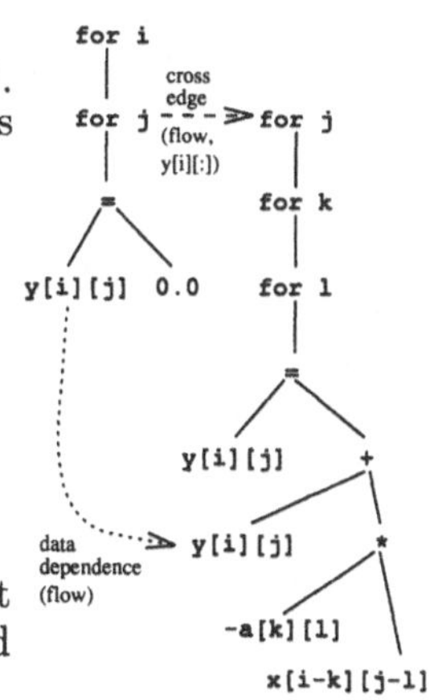

The pattern matcher traverses the syntax tree in leftmost postorder. First the assignment node at S1 will be replaced by the pattern instance SINIT(y[i][j],0.0).

Thereafter, the `for j` loop around S1 will be matched as a new pattern instance `VINIT(j, c(i,:), 0.0)` (vector init.). The *range* slot for the loop variable `j` also contains information on loop bounds and step size.

Then the algorithm descends towards S2, replaces the assignment statement at S2 by `AADDMUL(y[i][j], -a[k][l], x[i-k][j-l])` and, following the suitable edge in the PHG, merges it with the `do l` loop giving the instance `S1CONV(l, y[i][j], y[i][j], -a[k][:], x[i-k][j-:])`. Note that `a[k][:]` denotes a vector, as well as `x[i-k][j-:]`. ':' stands for a ranging loop variable. From its range, the spanned vector elements can easily be computed. The `S1CONV` instance matches then with the `for k` loop into `S2CONV(l,k, y[i][j], y[i][j], -a[:][:], x[i-:][j-:])`, with `a` and `x` now being matrices. This instance, in turn, can be matched with the `for j` loop, as shown in the following picture:

```
for (i=1; i<=u1-1; i++) {
S1': VINIT(j, y[i][:], 0.0);
S2': V2CONV(j, k, l, y[i][:], y[i][:],
             -a[:][:], x[i-:][:-:]); }
```

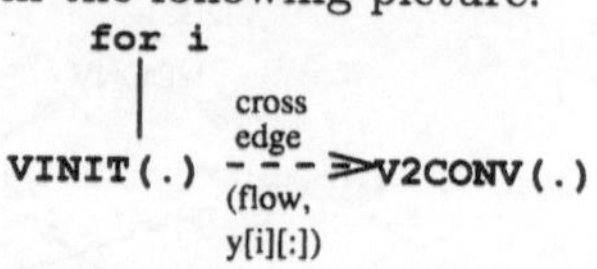

There is a cross edge from S1' to S2' of type FLOW, caused by the vector `y[i][:]` (`i` is a constant at this point; the second dimension of `y` is bound by `j` ranging from `1` to `u2-1`). For V2CONV$^{(3)}$, VINIT$^{(1)}$ is a mergeable cross predecessor, according to the matching rules supplied with the PHG. Merging these two instances along the cross edge yields a new pattern instance `V2CONV(j, k, l, y[i][:], 0.0, -a[:][:], x[i-:][:-:])`. Matching this with the `do i` loop gives `MCONV(i, j, k, l, y[:][:], 0.0, -a[:][:], x[:-:][:-:])` representing the entire piece of code. In the PHG (Fig. 1), the pattern matching algorithm has taken the path AADDMUL$^{(0)}$, S1CONV$^{(1)}$, S2CONV$^{(2)}$, V2CONV$^{(3)}$, MCONV$^{(4)}$ which corresponds to this particular coding of 2D convolution.

There are many ways to code 2D convolution: The four loops may be permuted in any order. Each coding then results in a different path being taken by the pattern matcher in the PHG towards MCONV$^{(4)}$. Moreover, in each of these cases, the initialization may be more or less distributed over the `for i` and the `for j` loop. Furthermore, each loop may be unrolled or blocked, and additional conditions may be inserted to avoid redundant computations. All these coding possibilities (exponentially many in terms of PHG size) are covered by the PHG of Fig. 1: Only 9 patterns with 25 templates (16 vertical, 9 cross) altogether suffice to represent all codings.

3 A compact descriptor for trapezoidal matrices

For each slot of a pattern instance that contains an array reference, we compute a compact *descriptor* that exactly summarizes which part of the array's index domain is accessed, e.g., trapezoidal or triangular parts of a matrix, diagonal vectors, or a rectangular region, perhaps with excluded row, column or diagonal vectors. Although the descriptor is, in principle, not limited to matrices, this two–dimensional case is most interesting for our application domain.

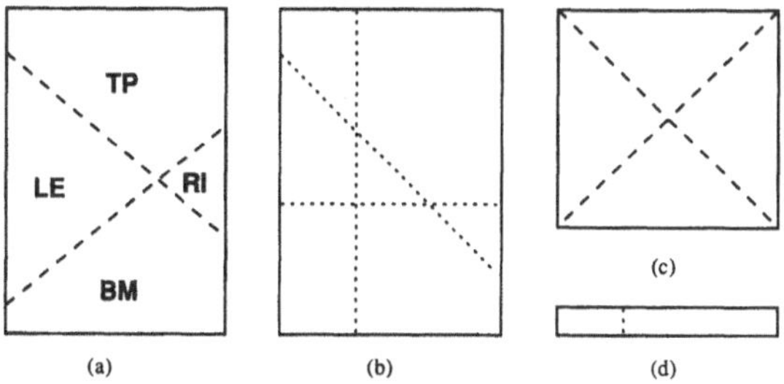

Fig. 2: Possible descriptor variations: (a) the four areas for tridiagonal matrices, (b) excluded row, column or diagonal for rectangular matrices, (c) diagonal or counterdiagonal vector in a matrix, and (d) excluded position in a vector.

```
for i from 1 to 4
  for j from i+1 downto 1
    ... A[2*i][k-j] ...
```

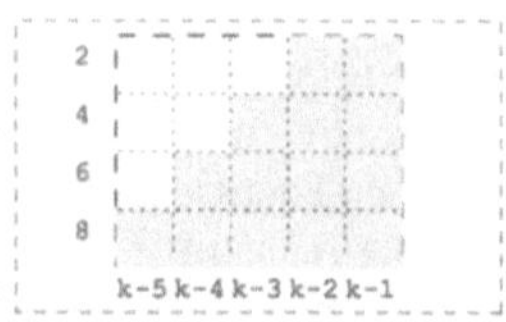

Fig. 3: Descriptor for an example array occurrence. The vertical axis represents the possible values of the first index expression (`i`), the horizontal axis (ascending values towards the right) these of the second (`k-j`). The shaded array elements are accessed.

Descriptor definition Let us consider a subtree of the syntax tree representation of the sequential source program. An integer variable is called *ranging* if it is the loop variable[1] of a loop occuring in this subtree. For an occurrence of a (possibly higher–dimensional) array A, call a dimension d of A ranging if there occurs at least one ranging variable in A's dth index expression. A *scalar* is either a common scalar variable or an array occurrence with no ranging dimension. A *vector* is an array occurrence with exactly one, a *matrix* with exactly two ranging dimensions. Thus, a diagonal vector is treated as a special matrix.

Let a be an array occurrence. We show now which parameters of its descriptor d_a can be controlled: The *accessed index domain* of a scalar, vector or matrix is defined as the smallest enclosing rectangular polytope of all index positions of ranging dimensions that are accessed in a loop nest. The rectangle is represented by the boundaries in each ranging dimension. Lower and upper bound are set such that the stride is always positive or symbolic. The axes are addressed in ascending order: the descriptor should describe *which* array elements are accessed, but not in which order or how often.

In the most interesting case of two ranging dimensions, the accessed index domain is (a subset of) a rectangle. Fig. 3 shows a triangular resp. trapezoidal access shape.

For a trapezoidal access shape, either the *diagonal* (directed from top left to bottom right) or the *counterdiagonal* (vice versa) of the rectangle are defined in a natural way such that (1) there is at least one row and at least one column that are completely accessed, and (2) there is exactly one column or exactly one row or both accessed completely. The diagonal resp. the counterdiagonal divide the rectangle into two trapezoidal sections (Fig. 2(a)) that can be described as combinations of any two neighbouring of the four areas TP (top), LE (left), RI (right) and BM (bottom). To describe the accessed trapezoidal part of a matrix,

[1]Other induction variables have been transformed away.

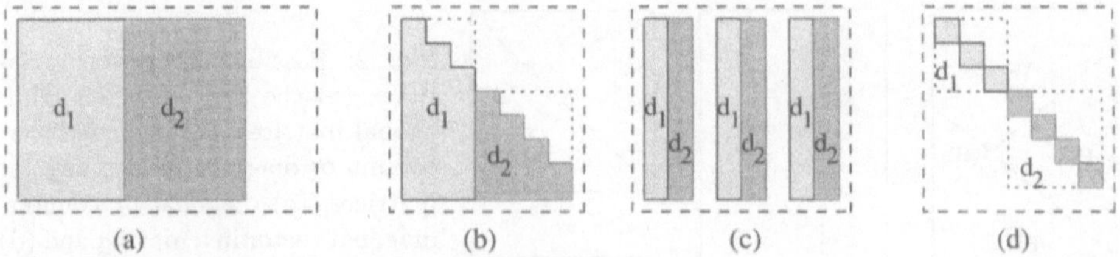

Fig. 4: Some examples for neighboured descriptors.

there are just the corresponding two of the *area bits* TP, LE, RI and BM to be turned on. In the example from Fig. 3, the area bits RI and BM are 1 and the other two are 0. — If all four bits are set, then the matrix is accessed in a rectangular way (*full* access). However, there may be exceptions specified: If an exceptional row index *excidx*[1] is defined, then this row vector is not accessed (Fig. 2(b)). Similarly, *excidx*[2] excludes a column vector, *excdiag*[1] denotes the offset[2] for an excluded diagonal, and similarly *excdiag*[2] for an excluded counterdiagonal. — Finally, if all four bits are zeroed, the *diag* bit indicates whether the diagonal or the counterdiagonal are accessed.

All descriptor parameters (except for the area bits, of course) can be *symbolic* expressions. The descriptor is unique, i.e. if two descriptors are different, then the accessed regions that they describe are also different.

Operations on descriptors The PARAMAT pattern recognition tool requires three important operations on descriptors:

disjdescr(d_1, d_2) returns TRUE if d_1 and d_2 can be proved to access disjoint sections of the same array, and FALSE otherwise. We use this as the main data independence test in PARAMAT. The operation is conservative since descriptors always describe a superset of the array elements that are actually accessed. Note that we are only interested in whether $d_1 \cap d_2 = \emptyset$ but not in $d_1 \cap d_2$ itself. Thus, we can avoid computing the intersection explicitly.

eqdescr(d_1, d_2) returns TRUE if d_1 and d_2 can be proved to be equal, and FALSE otherwise. *geqdescr*(d_1, d_2) returns TRUE if all array elements described by d_2 can be proved to be also described by d_1, and FALSE otherwise. These operations are required for computing data flow edges as described in the next section.

neighbdescr(d_1, d_2) returns TRUE if d_1 and d_2 can be proved to be neighboured array sections, and FALSE otherwise. Two disjoint descriptors d_1 and d_2 of the same d-dimensional array are *neighboured* if (1) their non-ranging index expressions equal, (2) the ranges of d_1 and d_2 are neighboured for exactly one ranging dimension (for a diagonal matrix: two ranging dimensions), and (3) for all other ranging dimensions, the ranges fit together as shown in Fig. 4, i.e. have the same strides, share at least one bound, and the other bounds match according to the situation. Neighbourhood of descriptors is also of great importance for computing special data flow edges, e.g. to recognize unrolled loops.

[2]The offset is absolute in terms of the vertical axis entries.

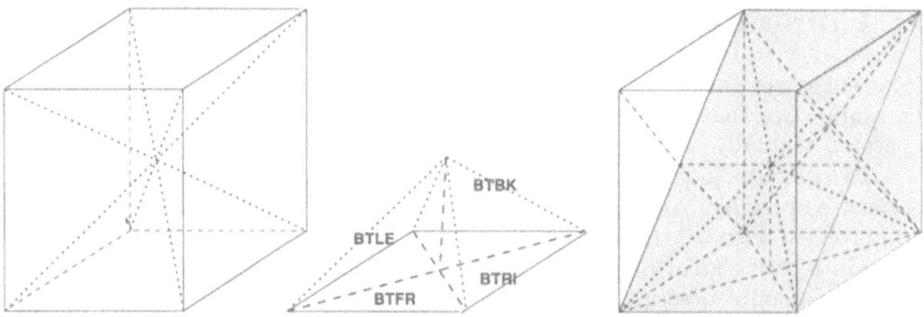

Fig. 5: For three ranging dimensions, the areas move into a fourth of one of the six pyramids separated by the inner diagonals. there are now 24 bits required, like e.g. BTFR for "bottom pyramid, front part". For the prism on the right hand side, all bits of the bottom and the back pyramid are turned on and also the bits LEBM, LEBK, RIBM, RIBK.

Extending the area bit concept to higher dimensions Non-rectangular array accesses with more than two ranging dimensions require an extension of the area bit concept to higher dimensions. This is, at least in principle, straightforward. For the three–dimensional case, we can still visualize graphically (Fig. 5) how the four inner diagonals (defined similar to the 2D case) divide the rectangular cube into six pyramids, each of which consists of four parts that are separated by the face diagonals (as already known from the 2D case), thus 24 bits will suffice to code these parts. We can assemble them to describe prisms, pyramids, diagonal faces, or inner diagonal vectors. Since there occur no patterns so far in our library that would handle objects with more than two ranging dimensions, we did not implement this extension up to now.

Discussion Our descriptor is in some aspects similar to that described in [BK89]. It is is simpler in that it only allows trapezoidal access structures. We however claim that "parallelogram" or "octogonal" access structures very rarely occur in real programs[3]. In fact, they do not occur in our pattern library at all. On the other hand, our descriptor allows to specify exceptional row, column or diagonal vectors in matrices which is not supported by [BK89]. It further allows non-unit, even symbolic, loop strides and symbolic linear access functions in each dimension. The expensive union and intersection operations from [BK89] are not required for our system: union is handled explicitly by the pattern recognition tool, and regarding intersection, we are only interested in the fact whether the intersection of two descriptors is (provably) empty or not, but not how it does look like. Furthermore, we do not need any information about how often or in which order the data is accessed. The area bit concept provides great compactness of access representation. Due to the area bits, descriptors can be compared very fast.

[3]Since we do not need the intersection and union operations for descriptors, this source of non-trapezoidal access shapes is also eliminated.

4 Computing Cross Edges

Cross edges are caused by data dependence. They connect parts of the code in the syntax tree that belong to the same thread of computation, even if they are separated textually. They are of crucial importance for pattern recognition.

To compute cross edges properly, we need array data flow analysis to be as exact as possible. Although exact array data flow analysis is generally a very hard problem [Fea91, MAL93], it is highly simplified here since our patterns access arrays in a very regular manner.

We compute descriptors and array data flow immediately before they are needed for the computation of the cross edges, since then maximal data access information is supplied by the pattern instances, and only one loop level has to be considered at a time. For non-matched statements, worst case assumptions must be made (the whole array may be accessed); for matched statements, the access information supplied by the descriptor is tight if some conditions (see above) are met.

Each slot of a pattern instance has one of four access modes: I (ignore), R (read), W (write), RW (read and write). R-slots are upwards–exposed, W-slots are downwards–exposed, and RW-slots are both. Let I_1, I_2 belong to the same block, I_1 preceding I_2. There are five different types of *cross edges*:

FLOW: If I_1 writes d_1 and I_2 reads d_2 and $geqdescr(d_1, d_2)$ holds and all descriptors d_3 of the same array written by instances between I_1 and I_2 fulfill $disjdescr(d_3, d_2)$, then a cross edge of type FLOW is drawn from I_1 to I_2. It corresponds to a loop-independent data flow dependence from I_1 to I_2.

ANTI: If I_1 reads d_1 and I_2 writes d_2 and $geqdescr(d_1, d_2)$ holds and all descriptors $d_3$of the same array written by instances between I_1 and I_2 fulfill $disjdescr(d_3, d_2)$, then a cross edge of type ANTI is drawn from I_1 to I_2. This corresponds to a loop-independent anti-dependence from I_1 to I_2.

INPUT: If I_1 reads d_1 and I_2 reads d_2 and $eqdescr(d_1, d_2)$ holds and all descriptors d_3 of the same array written by instances between I_1 and I_2 fulfill $disjdescr(d_3, d_1)$ (and thus also $disjdescr(d_3, d_2)$), then a cross edge of type INPUT is drawn from I_1 to I_2.

DISJOUT: If I_1 writes d_1 and I_2 writes d_2 and $neighbdescr(d_1, d_2)$ holds and all descriptors d_3 of the same array written by instances between I_1 and I_2 fulfill $disjdescr(d_3, d_1)$ and $disjdescr(d_3, d_2)$, then a cross edge of type DISJOUT is drawn from I_1 to I_2.

DISJIN: If I_1 reads d_1 and I_2 reads d_2 and $neighbdescr(d_1, d_2)$ holds and all descriptors d_3 of the same array written by instances between I_1 and I_2 fulfill $disjdescr(d_3, d_1)$ and $disjdescr(d_3, d_2)$, then a cross edge of type DISJIN is drawn from I_1 to I_2.

In general, the cross edges of a block of statements form a directed acyclic graph. Pattern recognition along a cross edge is guided by the type of the cross edge and the pattern names of the instances involved. If there are several cross edges coming into a pattern instance I_2, all candidates I_1 are tested successively. As in the vertical case, cross matching is deterministic such that there is always at most one matching template.

If a template for cross matching matches, then I_1 and I_2 are contracted and

I_2 is replaced by the new pattern's instance. If d_1 and d_2 are not completely equal then a residual instance of I_1 must remain, as in the following example:

```
I1: VINIT(j=[1:u2], y[i][1:u2], 0.0);
I2: V2CONV(j=[1:u2-1],1,k,y[i][1:u2-1],y[i][1:u2-1],-a[:][:],x[i-:][:-:]);
```

can be matched along the FLOW cross edge caused by `y[i][1:u2-1]`. It remains

```
I1': SINIT(y[i][u2], 0.0);
I2': V2CONV(j=[1:u2-1], 1,k, y[i][:], 0.0, -a[:][:], x[i-:][:-:]);
```

5 Example: Loop Rerolling

Former machine-specific optimizations, such as redundant IF conditions, loop unrolling, statement reordering and expression reordering, 'encrypt' the meaning of the code. Many of these transformations can be undone on-the-fly at low expense in the pattern recognition phase.

Loop Rerolling undoes loop unrolling that may appear (1) as replication at the expression level, (2) as replication at the statement level, or (3) as blocking at the loop level, also known as strip mining (one-dimensional) or tiling (more-dimensional). Loop rerolling and unblocking is, for instance, of crucial importance when matching the Level 1 BLAS routines that are almost all unrolled in some way. As an example, consider the following daxpy routine (after the preprocessing transformations)[4] that is 4-way-unrolled at the statement level:

```
for (j=1; j<=mod(n,4); j++)  dy(j) = dy(j) + da*dx(j)
for (i=mod(n,4)+1; i<=n; i+=4) { dy(i)   = dy(i)   + da*dx(i);
                                 dy(i+1) = dy(i+1) + da*dx(i+1);
                                 dy(i+2) = dy(i+2) + da*dx(i+2);
                                 dy(i+3) = dy(i+3) + da*dx(i+3); }
```

To recognize this as an occurrence of the VAADDSV$^{(1)}$ pattern, we must reroll the loop. Loop distribution and "vertical" pattern matching generate

```
I1:   VAADDSV(j=[1:mod(n,4)], dy,da,dx)
I2:   VAADDSV(i=[mod(n,4)+1:n:4], dy,da,dx)
I3:   VAADDSV(i=[mod(n,4)+2:n:4], dy,da,dx)
I4:   VAADDSV(i=[mod(n,4)+3:n:4], dy,da,dx)
I5:   VAADDSV(i=[mod(n,4)+4:n:4], dy,da,dx)
```

For each slot of each pattern instance, a descriptor is computed and the cross edges are computed as outlined in the previous section. There are now four cross edges of type DISJOUT: from I2 to I3 and I5, from I3 to I4, and from I4 to I5. These cross edges show the neighbourhood relations and guide the pattern recognition process to use the appropriate template that collects all instances in this connected component (I2,I3,I4,I5), merges[5] them and produces

```
I1:   VAADDSV(j=[1:mod(n,4)], dy,da,dx)
I2':  VAADDSV(i'=[mod(n,4)+1:n], dy,da,dx)
```

[4]As n is symbolic, mod(n,4) is treated as a symbolic expression.

[5]Merging would not be prohibited by other statements that were textually located between these instances and would not write to dy[mod(n,4)+1:n].

For the new instance I2', we again compute descriptors and now obtain a new cross edge of type DISJOUT from I1 to I2'. Merging finally yields `VAADDSV(j'=[1:n], dy,da,dx)`.

6 Status of Implementation

A prototype of the pattern recognition tool has been implemented and tested. The current implementation consists of around 12000 lines of C code and reliably recognizes 91 nontrivial patterns with around 150 nontrivial templates[6], including loop rerolling and identification of difference stars. More patterns can easily be added. The high degree of robustness against loop interchange, loop distribution, loop unrolling and statement reordering has been exemplified in practice.

A block diagram of the Pattern Recognition Tool is given in Fig. 6(a).

7 Knowledge–Based Code Generation

The matched intermediate representation is machine independent and opens access to very sophisticated program transformations.

Instances of recognized patterns can now be replaced by their best known parallel implementation. There exists at least one for each pattern. These implementations are machine dependent and are parameterized in problem size and data distributions.

As the recognized pattern's names are available, we can now access mathematical background information, e.g., on convergency properties to replace, for instance, a Gauss-Seidel Wavefront relaxation by its Red-Black variant or by two steps of Jacobi relaxation which is much better suited for parallel execution (depending on the target machine). The basic motivation for this "aggressive" local replacement of implementations is that the average user just wants to get the actually fastest parallel implementation on *this* target machine — independent of, for instance, a particular relaxation coding.

This is a first important step away from the classical SPMD semiautomatic code generation method [Ger89] that only inserts masks and communication statements but leaves the original computation structure unchanged. It is now also no problem to locally get rid of the owner-computes rule.

Local algorithm replacement also enables re-introducing machine-specific code transformations such as loop blocking that may have been removed by the loop rerolling technique described above. Now the compiler itself is free to choose a suitable blocking scheme for optimizing vector register allocation [KPR92] or cache utilization [WL91].

If, for a given pattern instance, the problem size is known at compile time and if it is small, PARAMAT may also decide to prohibit parallelization if sequential

[6]Each template is implemented as a C routine of around 20 to 50 lines that tests syntactic and semantic conditions and, if successful, generates the pattern instance and fills in the slot entries. Since many useful syntactic and semantic predicates have been predefined, writing code for templates is handy and straightforward.

execution will be faster, thus avoiding speed-down of the target program. If the problem size is not known at compile time, a suitable run time test should be inserted into the generated code. All these optimizations are hidden for the user.

Each pattern implementation accesses data in an individual manner. Thus, for each pattern implementation, PARAMAT knows (at least) one favorite alignment (to minimize communication) and one favorite distribution (to maximize parallelism) of all the arrays which this pattern is operating on.

The alignment and distribution recommendations for different pattern instances in a given program will usually conflict with each other. The problem of resolving this conflict by determining globally optimal data alignment and distribution is well-known to be NP-complete [LC90], thus automatic partitioning may take exponential time in the worst case. To help with the combinatorial complexity, we make use of our favorite-partitioning knowledge as starting configurations when performing a global search for the optimal data distribution, e.g. by branch and bound, as in [DHR93]. [DHR93] also enables *static array redistribution* which is also a NP-complete problem [Kre93].

For each pattern implementation, PARAMAT can inspect a table of run times — again parameterized in problem size and data distribution — that have been measured at an earlier time on the target machine. As a consequence, run time prediction considerably gains accuracy since now actual run times of high-level implementations on the target architecture are available which reflect hardware properties (traffic on the network, message buffer sizes, message protocols, overlapping of computation and communication etc.) better than theoretical, idealized estimation functions.

Fig. 6(b) summarizes the PARAMAT system design.

References

[BK89] V. Balasundaram and K. Kennedy. A technique for summarizing data access and its use in parallelism enhancing transformations. In *ACM SIGPLAN Programming Language Design and Implementation*, pages 41–53, 1989.

[CMZ92] Barbara Chapman, Piyush Mehrotra, and Hans Zima. Programming in Vienna Fortran. *Scientific Programming*, 1(1):31–50, 1992.

[DHR93] Anne Dierstein, Roman Hayer, and Thomas Rauber. Automatic parallelization for distributed memory multiprocessors. In *C.W. Keßler (Ed.): Automatic Parallelization — New Approaches to Code Generation, Data Distribution and Performance Prediction*, pages 192–217. Verlag Vieweg, 1993.

[Fea91] Paul Feautrier. Dataflow Analysis of Array and Scalar References. *Int. Journal of Parallel Programming*, 20(1):23–53, Feb. 1991.

[Ger89] Hans Michael Gerndt. *Automatic Parallelization for Distributed-Memory Multiprocessing Systems*. PhD thesis, Universität Bonn, 1989.

[HKT91] Seema Hiranandani, Ken Kennedy, and Chau-Wen Tseng. Compiler–Support for Machine–Independent Parallel Programming in Fortran-D. Technical Report Rice COMP TR91-149, Rice University, March 1991.

[HPF93] High Performance Fortran Forum HPFF. High Performance Fortran Language Specification, Final Version 1.0, May 1993.

[Keß93a] Christoph W. Keßler. Knowledge–Based Automatic Parallelization by Pattern Recognition. In *C.W. Keßler (Ed.): Automatic Parallelization — New Approaches to Code Generation, Data Distribution and Performance Prediction*, pages 110–135. Verlag Vieweg, 1993.

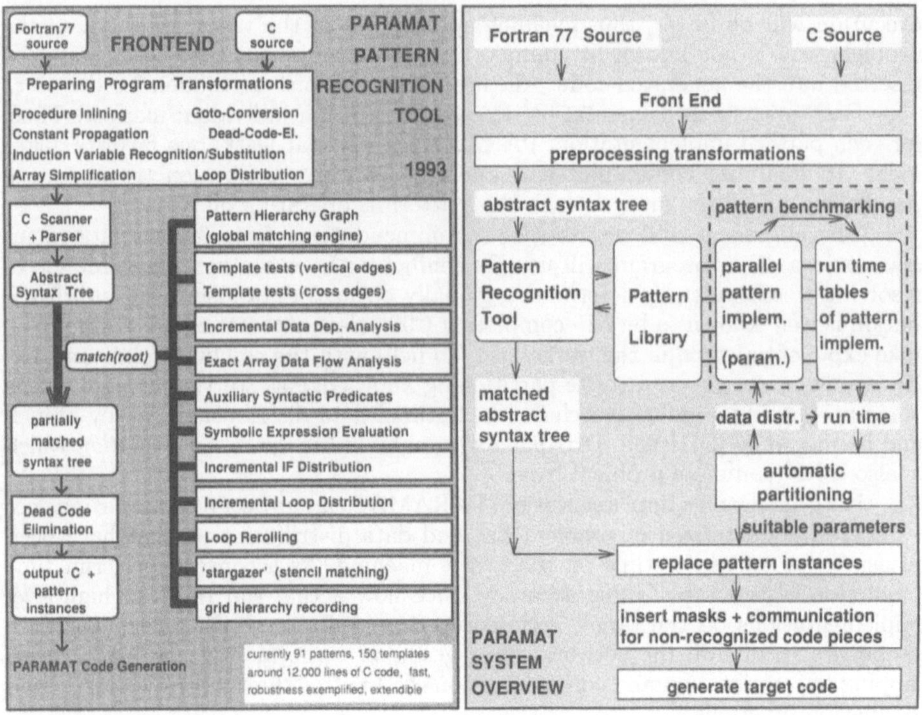

Fig. 6: (a) PARAMAT Pattern Recognition Tool; (b) PARAMAT system design

[Keß93b] Christoph W. Keßler. Pattern Recognition Enables Automatic Parallelization of Numerical Codes. In *Proc. of the Fourth Int. Workshop on Compilers for Parallel Computers, Delft, NL*, Dec. 1993.

[KP93] Christoph W. Keßler and Wolfgang J. Paul. Automatic Parallelization by Pattern Matching. In *Proc. of Second Int. Conference of the Austrian Center for Parallel Computation*, pages 166–181, Oct. 1993.

[KPR92] C.W. Keßler, W.J. Paul, and T. Rauber. Scheduling Vector Straight Line Code on Vector Processors. In R. Giegerich and S.L. Graham, editors, *Code Generation – Concepts, Tools, Techniques*, pages 77–91. Springer Workshops in Computing Series, 1992.

[Kre93] Ulrich Kremer. NP-Completeness of Dynamic Remapping. Technical Report CRPC-TR93330-S, Center for Research on Parallel Computation, Rice University, Houston, TX, Aug. 1993. see also: Proc. Fourth Workshop on Compilers for Parallel Computers, Delft, Dec. 1993.

[LC90] Jingke Li and Marina Chen. Index Domain Alignment: Minimizing Cost of Cross–referencing between Distributed Arrays. In *Third Symposium on the Frontiers of Massively Parallel Computation*, pages 424–433, 1990.

[MAL93] Dror E. Maydan, Saman P. Amarasinghe, and Monica S. Lam. Array data-flow analysis and its use in array privatization. In *ACM SIGPLAN Principles of Programming Languages*, Jan. 1993.

[WL91] Michael E. Wolf and Monica S. Lam. A Data Locality Optimizing Algorithm. In *ACM SIGPLAN Programming Language Design and Implementation*, pages 30–44, 1991.

Programming Environments for Massively Parallel Distributed Systems, Monte Verità, Switzerland

A GUI for Parallel Code Generation

Mark R. Gilder*
gilderm@cs.rpi.edu

Mukkai S. Krishnamoorthy*
moorthy@cs.rpi.edu

John R. Punin*
puninj@cs.rpi.edu

Abstract

Developing applications for parallel architectures is a very complicated and arduous task even for expert programmers. There are several issues that must be considered, i.e., the number of CPU's available, vector processing capabilities, shared memory issues, process communications, and process synchronization, to name a few. Software developers have been trained to view the solution to a selected problem as a sequence of dependent steps or transitions which are applied to some input in an effort to produce the desired results. This approach to problem solving has been enforced by the traditional languages of C, Pascal, and Fortran. In this paper we describe the *Interactive Visualization Tool* (IVT) developed for the HICOR interactive parallelizing compiler. In particular, the IVT allows users to interactively manipulate a graphical representation of the program to be parallelized. Parameters describing the target architecture may be manipulated interactively to create *what-if* scenarios for architectural simulation.

1 Introduction

Current analysis tools for parallelization are typically constructed as an internal part of the compiler [5, 6]. Tools constructed in this manner rely on the underlying intermediate representation chosen; however, since no standardized intermediate representations yet exist, the tool is limited in scope to the existing framework of the compiler and, therefore, becomes extremely difficult to port to multiple platforms. Also, the fine line which separates the tool from the compiler is not clearly defined making extraction of the tool almost impossible. This design methodology has greatly hindered the ability to rapidly prototype current research ideas [3] for lack of a common interface into the existing compilation systems [4]. To solve this problem, we provide a high-level *Tool Interface Layer* into an object-oriented intermediate code representation called HICOR. The HICOR representation provides

*Rensselaer Polytechnic Institute, Department of Computer Science, Troy, NY 12180

the ability to extract and/or manipulate information available in the underlying intermediate representation. This design greatly simplifies the design of parallelization tools for the following reasons:

1. The tool no longer needs knowledge of the underlying intermediate representation and hence may manipulate information at a much higher level of abstraction,
2. the tool remains immune to any low-level changes made to the underlying representation,
3. the tool remains consistent across different platforms, and
4. the tool need not be altered as new HICOR objects are added due to polymorphism.

The *Interactive Visualization Tool* has been constructed using X11R5 and the Athena widget set. The tool uses the *Tool Interface Layer* in order to manipulate the HICOR representation. Currently, the tool processes three types of displays. These include the HICOR representation itself, the data dependency graph, and the compile-time schedule. We note that only information necessary for understanding the *Interactive Visualization Tool* are presented herein. A detailed description of the HICOR parallelization system may be found in [1, 2]. The remainder of this paper is organized as follows: Section 2 describes the specification of the *Interactive Visualization Tool* developed, Section 3 describes the graphical displays; and Section 4 concludes with an evaluation of the IVT.

2 IVT - Interactive Visualization Tool

The *Interactive Visualization Tool* (IVT) allows users to graphically interact with the HICOR parallelization system developed. The IVT displays source programs in the same hierarchical format that is provided by the underlying HICOR representation. Users are given a top-down view of all program constructs extracted from the source program, i.e., objects, functions, statement blocks, and statements. This technique provides the ability to convey information in the best possible manner. First, high-level information about the source program may be extracted. Then, by analyzing portions of the representation at lower levels of the representation hierarchy, more detailed information may be extracted. The IVT allows users to familiarize themselves with the intricate dependencies that exist between all components of the source program. A graphical representation of the parallel solution may be generated at any time. The user may then interact with the graphical solution to see how components of the original source program were mapped into the parallel solution. In Figure 1 a C-function called MINMAX, which locates the minimum and maximum values of the array a, is provided. Lines labeled by $Obj_{<num>}$ indicate that the associated source code is contained in the HICOR object numbered by *num*. Figure 2 illustrates the graphic display produced by the IVT tool for this function. The hierarchical information in the source program is clearly illustrated. HICOR object 94, which represents the entire MinMax function, can be viewed as the ordered collection of its immediate children, i.e., objects 11, 12, 51, 53, 54, 69, 71, 72, 87, 90, and 93. Similarly, each of these children can be viewed as the ordered collections of their respective immediate children.

The HICOR representation is an object oriented intermediate representation which provides a hierarchical view of all program constructs. Each object in the representation encapsulates the internal intermediate code corresponding to the source construct it represents. Internal object information is provided through a set of common access routines or *methods.* It is these methods that provide the *Tool Interface Layer* on which parallelization tools may be constructed. In most instances a single HICOR object may be decomposed into an ordered collection of smaller, more detailed, objects. For example, a HICOR object which represents a *Function* in some source language may be viewed as a collection of objects, each representing the immediate basic blocks it consists of. In this respect, the grain size represented by a particular HICOR object is related directly to its position in the hierarchy. Objects occurring at higher levels are more computationally complex than those occurring at lower levels. Therefore, as we descend through the hierarchy, the grain-size represented decreases. The IVT provides the user with the ability to navigate throughout the HICOR instance, allowing operations to be applied to selected objects.

The design issues are focused in three main areas: the display and manipulation of the HICOR objects for a particular program instance; the display and manipulation of graphs representing data dependencies and the compile-time execution schedule; and the manipulation of parameters which describe the current target architecture.

2.1 HICOR Object Display

To display the HICOR representation for a particular program instance, the tool need only access the starting HICOR object. This object may be viewed as the root of the HICOR representation which is generated by the front-end of the compilation system. To access this object a special static method called `GetStartObj` may be invoked. Once performed, selected information about the object may be displayed using the methods described below. The `ParentOf` method may then be applied to retrieve the immediate children of the object. By recursively applying the `ParentOf` method to the children of each object, the entire HICOR instance may be rendered. The DisplayRep algorithm provided in Figure 3 illustrates how this is accomplished.

```
Obj94       void MinMax() { /* N is even */
                int i, j, a[N], b[N/2], c[N/2], min, max;

Obj11           for(i = 0; i < N; i++)
Obj6                a[i] = random()%10000;

Obj12           j = 0;
Obj51           for(i = 0; i < N; i = i + 2)
Obj47               if(a[i] > a[i + 1]) {
Obj33                   b[j] = a[i];
                        c[j++] = a[i + 1];
                    }
                    else {
Obj46                   b[j] = a[i + 1];
                        c[j++] = a[i];
                    }

Obj53,54        max= b[0];
Obj69           for(i = 1; i < N/2; i++)
Obj64               if(b[i] > max)
Obj63                   max = b[i];

Obj71,72        min= c[0];
Obj87           for(i = 1; i < N/2; i++)
Obj82               if(c[i] < min)
Obj81                   min = c[i];

Obj90           printf("Minimum value is: %d\n",min);
Obj93           printf("Maximum value is: %d\n",max);
            }
```

Figure 1: MinMax*: function to find the minimum and maximum values of array a*

Figure 2: *Descendants of HICOR object 94*

Algorithm:	DISPLAYREP
Input:	*Obj* HICOR object to be displayed
Output:	None
Description:	Graphically displays the HICOR object, *Obj*, along with selected internal information. It is called recursively on each child of *Obj*.

1. Display *Obj* along with selected internal information.
2. Let C represent the ordered collection of immediate children for this object found by invoking the `ParentOf` method, i.e.,

$$C = Obj.\texttt{ParentOf}()$$

3. **foreach** child $c_i \in C$

$$\textsc{DisplayRep}(c_i)$$

Figure 3: *Algorithm to display HICOR representation*

The following methods are used to retrieve internal HICOR object information in step 1 of the DISPLAYREP algorithm:

- `GetObjectType`: returns the type of the HICOR object.
- `GetCost`: returns the estimated cost of executing the object.
- `GetIndexNumber`: returns the implicit executing order of the HICOR object in the original source code.

The following methods may be applied to any selected HICOR object. These methods generate information to be displayed in a popup window.

- `GetModUseVarSet`: returns all variables either modified and/or used by the HICOR object.
- `GetSourceCode`: retrieves the source code represented by the HICOR object.
- `GenCCode`: generates the C-code for the underlying intermediate code represented by the object.
- `GenerateDependencies`: generates a *Dag* object containing the dependencies between the immediate children of the selected object.
- `BuildExecutionDag`: generates a *LayerRep* object containing the compile-time schedule for the code to be generated.

A HICOR object may be selected by using the left mouse button. The object becomes highlighted to indicate its selection. By default, subsequent selections of other objects will deactivate the previously selected object; hence, only one object can be selected at any one time in this manner. To select multiple objects, the "meta" key must be depressed during object selection. This blocks deactivation of any previously selected objects. Once a HICOR object has been selected, the operations available in the *popup menus* may be applied. The middle mouse button may be used to move a HICOR object in the main window. This is done by pressing and holding the middle mouse button on the HICOR object to be moved. The object may then be dragged to its new position on the window. All arcs are maintained to any connected objects.

2.2 Conveying Parallel Information

The *Interactive Visualization Tool* allows for the display and manipulation of two types of graphs. The first graph represents data dependencies that exist in the original source program. The second graph represents the near-optimal compile-time schedule which is generated using architectural specific parameters. The vertices of each graph are labeled with the corresponding number of the HICOR object it represents.

The data dependency graph provides valuable insight into the dependencies that inhibit parallelization. Figure 4 illustrates the dependency graph for the immediate children of HICOR object 94. These children represent the first level of basic blocks for the MINMAX program. The number over each vertex provides the estimated execution time for the represented code on the selected target architecture. This figure also illustrates the popup window generated by selecting the "*Display Source Code*" operation for object 51. In this way, the user can view the source code represented by each vertex in the graph.

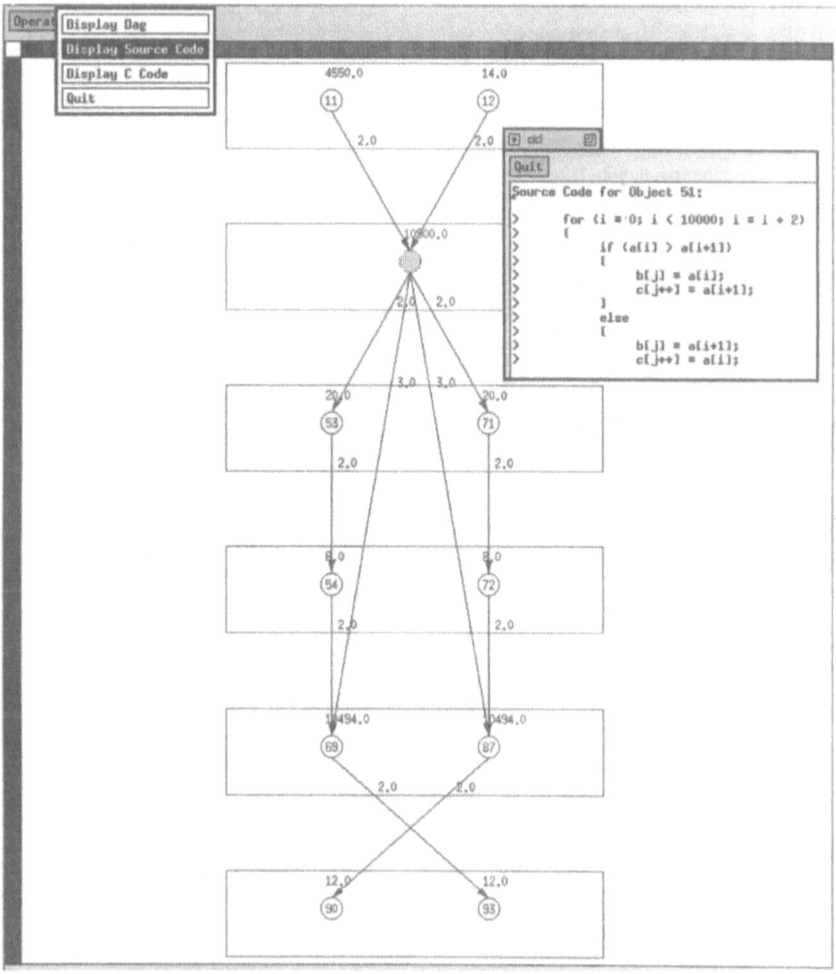

Figure 4: *Dependency graph for the immediate children of HICOR object 94. The* "Display Source Code" *operation is illustrated for object 51*

The graph representing data dependencies consists of tasks which may vary greatly with respect to computational grain size each task comprises. It is therefore imperative that the graph be manipulated to guarantee that the generated parallel code, along with the incurred overhead, produces a better result then the sequential version. This problem differs from traditional scheduling in that we allow tasks to

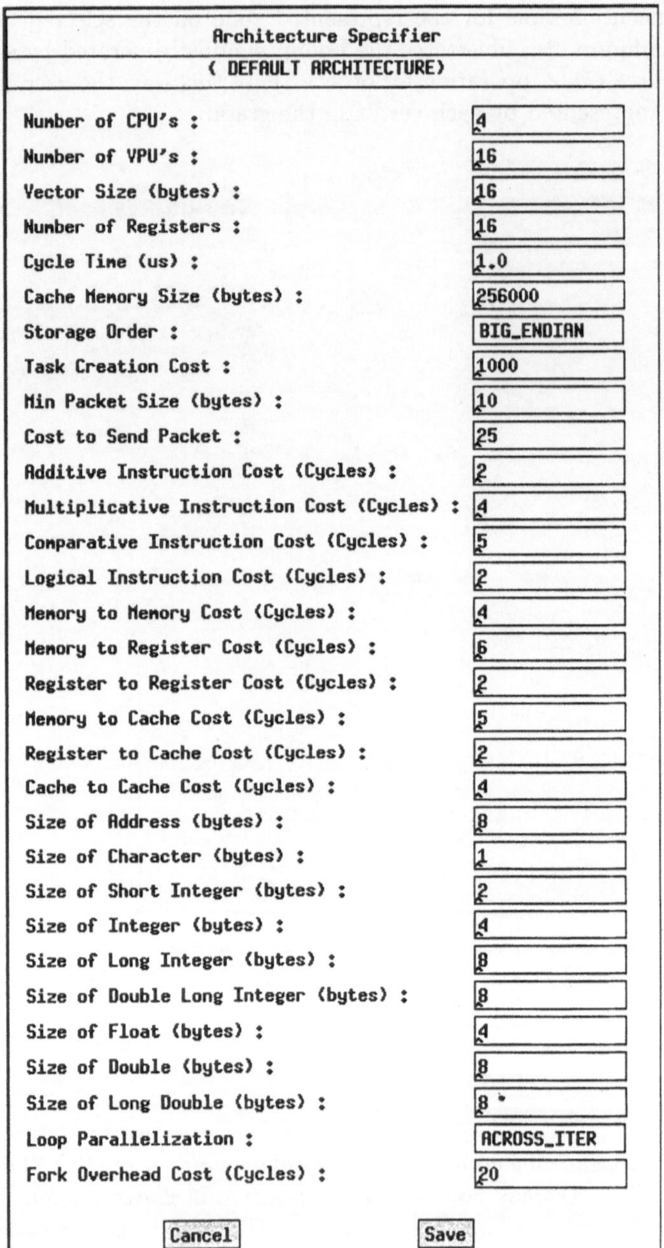

Architecture Specifier
(DEFAULT ARCHITECTURE)
Number of CPU's : 4
Number of VPU's : 16
Vector Size (bytes) : 16
Number of Registers : 16
Cycle Time (us) : 1.0
Cache Memory Size (bytes) : 256000
Storage Order : BIG_ENDIAN
Task Creation Cost : 1000
Min Packet Size (bytes) : 10
Cost to Send Packet : 25
Additive Instruction Cost (Cycles) : 2
Multiplicative Instruction Cost (Cycles) : 4
Comparative Instruction Cost (Cycles) : 5
Logical Instruction Cost (Cycles) : 2
Memory to Memory Cost (Cycles) : 4
Memory to Register Cost (Cycles) : 6
Register to Register Cost (Cycles) : 2
Memory to Cache Cost (Cycles) : 5
Register to Cache Cost (Cycles) : 2
Cache to Cache Cost (Cycles) : 4
Size of Address (bytes) : 8
Size of Character (bytes) : 1
Size of Short Integer (bytes) : 2
Size of Integer (bytes) : 4
Size of Long Integer (bytes) : 8
Size of Double Long Integer (bytes) : 8
Size of Float (bytes) : 4
Size of Double (bytes) : 8
Size of Long Double (bytes) : 8
Loop Parallelization : ACROSS_ITER
Fork Overhead Cost (Cycles) : 20
Cancel
Save

Figure 5: *Target architecture parameters*

be merged in an effort to reduce both task creation and task communications overhead. Hence, the compile-time schedule represents the near-optimal schedule, which minimizes these costs, for a particular target architecture. The scheduler uses parameters which provide a description of the target machine. Figure 5 illustrates the popup window that is used to enter these parameters.

The graph in Figure 6 illustrates the compile-time schedule produced for the immediate children of HICOR object 94. Note that this graph consists of the same number of vertices as in the dependency graph; however, the scheduler has merged selected tasks to reduce task creation and communications overhead. In particular, tasks representing HICOR objects 53,54,69,93 and objects 71,72,87,90 were merged into single tasks, respectively. The graphical representation clearly conveys the result of the scheduler, i.e., the loops to find the minimum and maximum values of the array *a* may proceed in parallel once the loop which partitions the array *a* has completed. The same operations are available for the compile-time schedule as for the dependency graph, as illustrated by the display of source code for object 11.

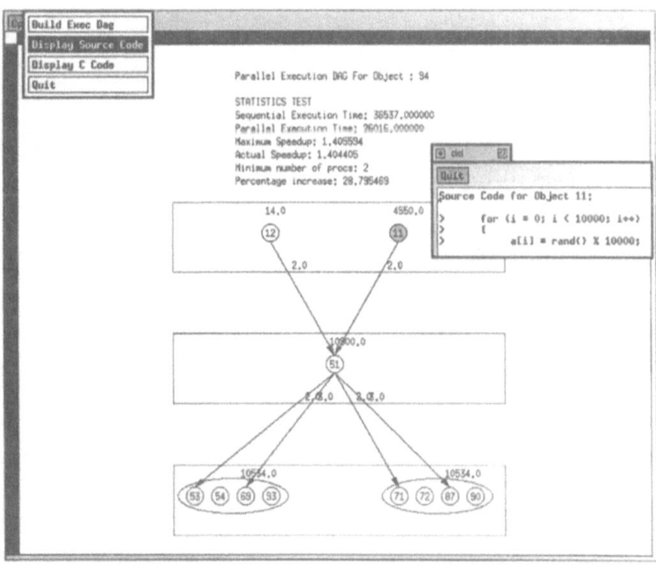

Figure 6: *Compile-time schedule for immediate children of HICOR object 94*

The schedule illustrated in Figure 7 was generated by increasing the task creation and communications costs by approximately 50%. The schedule depicted in Figure 8 was generated by setting the number of available processors to one. The result clearly indicates that all tasks are to be merged into a single task for execution.

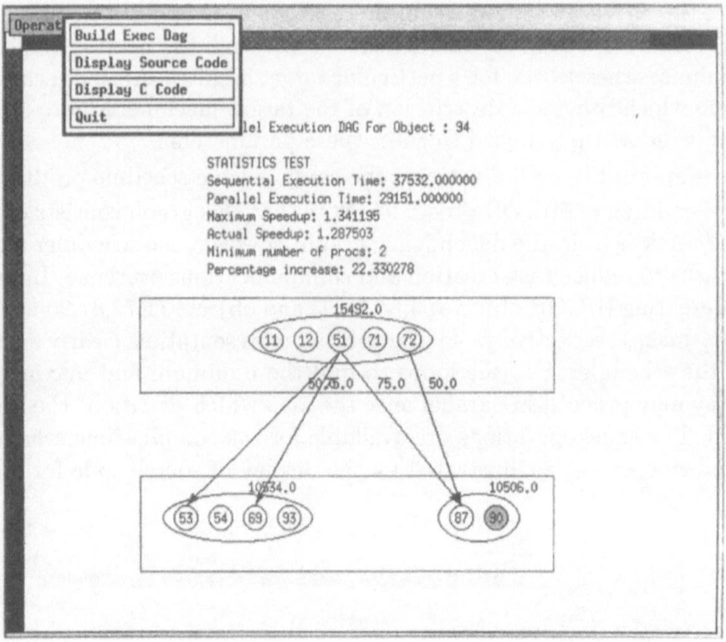

Figure 7: *Compile-time schedule after modification of task creation and communication overhead parameters*

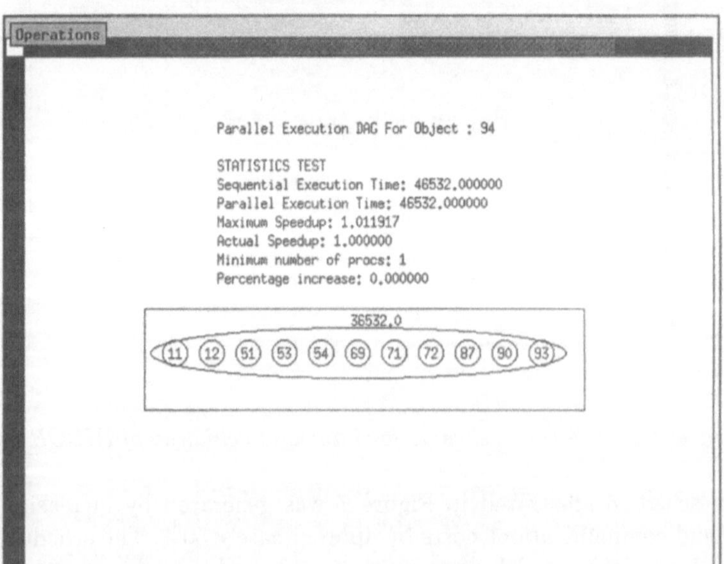

Figure 8: *Compile-time schedule with one available CPU*

3 Conclusion

We have shown that by providing a GUI which presents source program constructs as graphical objects, as well as providing user interaction capabilities, conveying information regarding parallelization can be easily accomplished. The HICOR representation and associated *Tool Interface Layer* described provide a data encapsulation model which allows the *Interactive Visualization Tool* to both manipulate and extract program information; hence, the tool is completely independent of the underlying representation and therefore can not be affected by any internal changes. The *data dependency* and *compile-time schedule* graphs provide alternate views of the source program. These views illustrate how program constructs are mapped into the parallel solution for a particular architecture. We feel that the IVT will play an important role in providing users with an in depth understanding of the issues involved in developing applications for parallel architectures.

References

[1] M. R. Gilder. *An Object Oriented Intermediate Code Representation For An Architecturally Independent Parallelizing Compiler.* PhD thesis, Rensselaer Polytechnic Institute, Troy, NY, October, 1993.

[2] M. R. Gilder and M. S. Krishnamoorthy. An Object-Oriented Intermediate Code Representation for the Development of Parallelization Tools. *Journal of Object-Oriented Programming*, 1994 (To appear).

[3] M. Girkar and C. Polychronopoulos. Compiling Issues for Supercomputers. *IEEE Computer*, pages 164–173, September 1988.

[4] A. F. Halford. Parallel Compilers: the key to 90s software performance. *Electronic Design*, 38:63–64, August 1990.

[5] K. Kennedy, K. S. Mckinley, and C. W. Tseng. Interactive Parallel Programming Using the ParaScope Editor. *IEEE Transactions on Parallel and Distributed Systems*, 2(3):329–341, July 1991.

[6] B. Shei and D. Gannon. SIGMACS: A programmable programming environment. In *Proc. Third Workshop Languages and Compilers for Parallel Computing*, Irvine, CA, August 1990.

Programming Environments for Massively Parallel Distributed Systems, Monte Verità, Switzerland

Formal Techniques Based on Nets, Object Orientation and Reusability for Rapid Prototyping of Complex Systems

Fabrice Kordon
Laboratoire MASI, Institut Blaise Pascal,
Université P. & M. Curie, 75252 Paris Cedex 05
kordon@masi.ibp.fr

Abstract

This paper presents a technique based on both nets and object orientation for rapid prototyping of parallel systems. The technique described here is currently implemented under a software environment.

1 Introduction

Once a satisfactory system specification is established, it has to be implemented. This operation is quite critical [Murphy 89]. The specification may be misunderstood or implementation choices may change the system's behavior.

Most of the time, the implementation operation is so expensive that its result overwrites the application specification. Modification, extensions and maintenance are performed at the prototype level. A solution to these problems is to automate the prototyping process [Luqi 89], a quick and low cost procedure that allows the system designer to work at the specification level. Rapid prototyping is already experimented in an exploitation context [Burns 93], even for real time applications [Luqi 92].

Prototyping however should not be confused with compiling while this operation deals with the system semantics. There are many types of prototyping. Each one corresponds to a given objective and integrates different constraint. [Hallmann 91, Asur 93] propose the following classification :

Incremental approach: New parts of a system are added to a kernel and the software architecture remains all over the development phases.

Throw-away approach: This kind of prototype generally implements a subset of the requirements and is not reused.

Evolutionary approach: The main idea is to preserve the flexibility of both the system architecture and functions.

Most of the studies outline the following points:

- It is rather difficult to determine when a model becomes a prototype [Hallmann 91];
- The quality of results relies on the formalism used to design the specification of the system [Luqi 92];
- While there is no universal formalism which fit any problem; the choice of an input formalism is not easy [Murphy 89].

This paper presents a methodology based on refinement and enrichment of a system specification. This methodology takes in input a structured high level specification [Kordon 93, Bachatène 94] and aims to produce a prototype. The prototyping process involves Petri nets [Jensen 92] as an internal representation. Petri nets are useful for a formal verification of the specification. In section 2, we summarize studies about Petri Net prototyping and section 3 exposes our method.

2 Parallel systems prototyping from Petri Nets

Many studies summarized in [Colom 86] have been performed on the prototyping of parallel systems specified by means of Petri Nets. There are three successive approaches of Petri-Net prototyping.
The first one aimed at implementing a centralized "Petri net player". An executor investigates all possible transitions and checks its firability. Very efficient evaluation filters are studied to avoid the bottleneck induced by the size of the net [Colom 86, Murata 86]. However, the executor is a sequential task.
Then some work studied a totally distributed execution [Hauschildt 87, Taubner 87]. Each transition and place are implemented by means of a task. This approach becomes inefficient when the net grows or has large sets of colors.
Finally, a hybrid approach proposes to decompose the Petri Net into a set of sequential and concurrent processes. Several decomposition techniques of model into state machines are studied. This approach provides an efficient implementation but some Petri nets cannot be processed.
It appears that prototyping from formal specification is very valuable [Colom 86, Tu 90, Kordon 93]. The specification level can be used as a high level programming language that fit both design and validation requirements.

3 Principle of a hybrid prototyping technique

The strategy we consider belongs to the hybrid family. We do not aim at the prototyping of any Petri net specification.

Our prototyping technique relies on two main concepts : integration with the environment and generation objects. We present both (sections 3.2 and 3.3) and explain in section 3.4 the generic architecture we have defined. This procedure is applicable if the input model verifies some characteristics [Kordon 93]. This is the case when we consider the Petri net construction exposed in section 3.1.

3.1 Petri net structuration and Higher level formalism

The Petri net specification we aim to prototype is semi-automatically produced during a translation step (Figure 1). In this phase, the Petri net is built and structured by mean of *Modeling Units* [Bachatène 94].

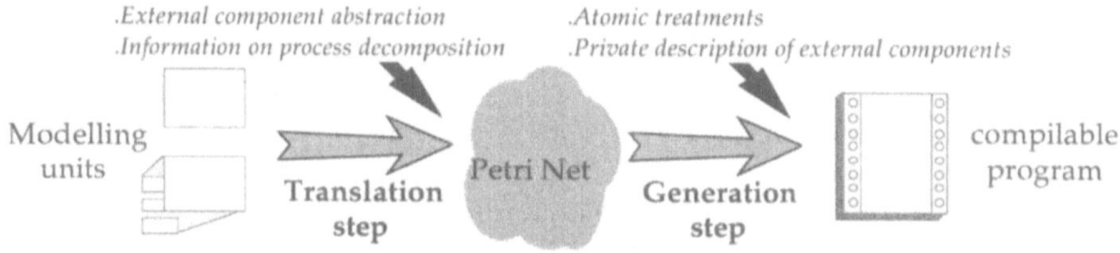

Figure 1: *Pieces of information involved in the prototyping process*

A Modeling Unit is a black box containing either a set of sub-units or a Petri net model that describe its behavior (the unit is then *elementary*). Each modeling unit is connected to other by mean of services either provided by the unit or required to other units [Kordon 93, Bachatène 94]. Each required service must be provided somewhere in the system. This constraint is an easy way to check the completeness of a model. When a Petri net is generated from a Modeling Unit description, characteristics of each service are used to connect Petri net of all elementary units according to the relations defined by the system designer (Figure 2).

In model (a), two modeling units are connected by means of an asynchronous service. In the unit providing it, it is modeled by only one transition (*accept*). Place DT is generated to connect private descriptions. It represents the buffer that stores information from the caller unit to the invoked unit.

In model (b), two modeling units are connected by means of a synchronous service. In the unit providing it, it is modeled by a path connecting two transitions (*BeginA* and *EndA*). *BeginA* represent the beginning of the service and *EndA* its end. The invocation does not have to consider this aspect : only transition *invoke* exists in the original model. During the translation phase, places DT and RR are generated. On the invocation side, the place *Wait* and the transition *Invoke* are automatically created to model the synchronization.

Services of a unit constitute its public description. A private description also exists. When the designer reaches the most detailed level, he must provide the Petri net description of all elementary units.

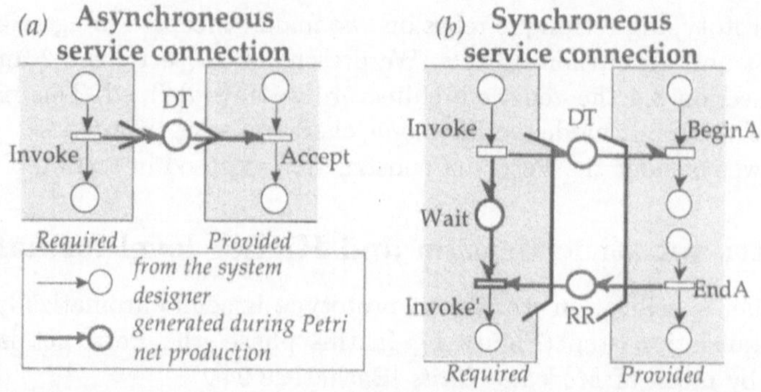

***Figure 2**: Generated places and transitions during the translation step*

The structured model computed by the translation step insures all required properties of the input model.

3.2 Integration with the environment

A specification consists in two different parts:

- Model of the system behavior : this part of the specification has to be prototyped.
- Description of the environment behavior : this part of the specification is only needed to validate the system in its environment. Only primitive calls must be generated since the environment already exists.

3.2.1 External treatment associated to transitions

The environment behavior is expressed by means of procedures associated to transitions and linked during the code generation step (Figure 1). Such procedures must have no side effect. Otherwise, their execution can raise erroneous states while the specification seems to be correct.

3.2.2 External components

An *external component* is the abstraction of an outside subset of the environment the prototype has to deal with. External components may be reused for other specifications if they are defined properly. It is valuable to manage external component libraries. The designer has to outline their location in the net.

The description of an external component consists in two aspects:

- the abstraction, defined by means of a Petri net model, which expresses relations between services; it does not deal with any implementation aspect;

- the private description, defined by means of a programming language; it *is* the implementation of the piece of environment. If a system has to be prototyped into several target languages, the private description must exist for every one.

3.3 Generation Objects

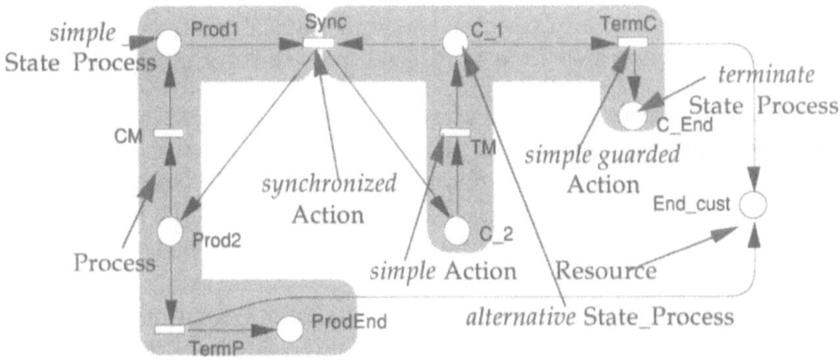

***Figure 3**: Example of Generation objects*

There are four Generation Objects (Figure 3):

- The **Processes** are subsets of the net in which no parallelism is possible. A Process defines a generic state machine instanciated upon the initial marking of the subnet.

- The **Actions** are deduced from Petri net transitions and represent atomic treatments. They may be *simple* (one Process involved) or *synchronized* (rendez-vous between several Processes). An Action may also be *guarded*; its firability is then submitted to some marking constraints.

- The **State_Processes** are deduced from discrete places of the net and represent possible states of a Process. They may be *simple* (sequence of transitions), *alternative* (choice between several actions) or *terminate* (no possible action).

- The **Resources** are deduced from places that are not State_Processes. They represent data storage zones that can be used for communication between processes.

Each Generation Object corresponds to an element of a model that can be interpreted in both Petri net theory and software component. They are computed on the specification of the system. External component abstraction must be removed first.

3.4 Generic architecture of a prototype

Generation Objects are a software interpretation of a Petri net specification:

- The Resource manager deals with resources of the Petri net.
- The Synchronization manager deal with Synchronized Actions (transitions shared by several processes).
- Each process can be implemented by a unit which describes its behavior. The automaton is generated from State_Processes and Actions of the process.

These modules belong to two different types. There is only one resource manager and one synchronization manager in the prototype, if at least one corresponding generation object is located in the model. On the contrary, there is one process module per process in the Petri net specification.

The final architecture of the prototype looks like to the one proposed for software environments in [ECMA 91] (Figure 4). Communication is performed by a unit : all modules of the prototype must use its functions to exchange data and invoke services.

Functions, like initialization, termination or communication between units are performed by the Prototype manager. Finally, external treatments (atomic procedures) and external components must also have to be linked to the prototype. External treatments are directly connected to synchronization and process

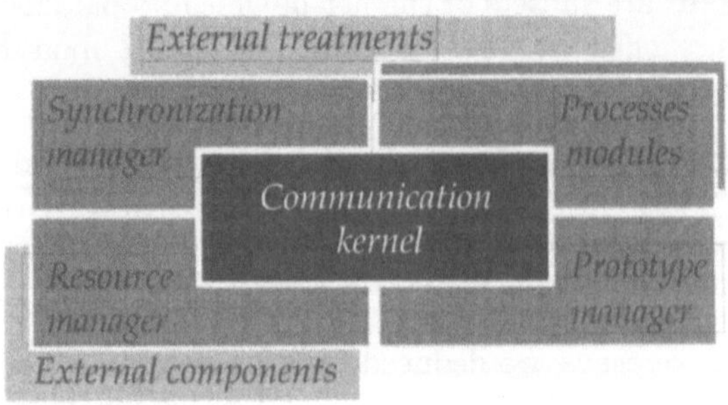

Figure 4: *Generic architecture of the prototype*

modules. External components are connected to the resource manager. Interface places are then considered as specialized resources.

The prototype architecture is generic: it can be implemented several ways using different languages.

A valuable feature, for a prototyping tool, is to perform task distribution over a given architecture. [Burns 91, Bréant 93] propose to separate the description of the architecture and the description of the system. In that case, it may be possible to manage libraries of architecture. This is the approach we have considered.

Generation Objects may be associated to Location-objets that describe strongly connected components of the system. A procedure to map the software architecture of the prototype to a hardware description is also investigated [El Kaim 94].

4 Conclusion

The method we have described in this paper is based on enrichment and refinement of a specification:

- The enrichment is achieved by adding more and more information (details) about the system. The global system architecture is first described using the object paradigm. The behavior of elementary components is then specified by means of small Colored Petri Nets.

- The refinement is performed using information from analysis and/or execution of the prototypes. Results must be available for all representations involved in the process.

Such an approach is allowed by the combination of two different paradigms: the object oriented approach bringing its power of structuration and the use of a formal model, bringing results extracted from the theory. The technique takes advantages of both waterfall [Vonk 92] and incremental [Hallmann 91] approaches.

Our rapid prototyping technique relies on a generic architecture [Kordon 93]. So, several programming languages may be considered. An Ada code generator is already available [MARS 93] and C language prototyping is planned.

The prototype may include self-evaluation mechanisms. It allows the system designer to study his system at both model (formal verification) and prototype (performance evaluation) level.

References

[Asur 93] S. Asur, S. Hufnagel. *Taxonomy of Rapid-Prototyping Methods and Tools.* Proceedings of the 4th International Workshop on Rapid System Prototyping. Research Triangle Park Institute, North Carolina, USA, June 1993.

[Bachatène 94] H. Bachatène and P. Estraillier. *Composing Objects: state of the art and definition of a general support for specification composition.* To appear in the proceedings of IFIP WG 10.3 Concurrent systems, International Conf on Applications in Parallel and distributed computing, Caracas, Venezuela, April 1994.

[Bréant 93] F. Bréant, J. F. Peyre. *OCCAM Prototyping of Massively Parallel Applications using colored Petri Nets.* 7th IEEE Int. Parallel Processing Symposium, pp. 842-848 , Newport Beach, California, April 1993.

[Burns 91] C. Burns. *Parallel PROTO — A prototyping tool for analyzing and validating sequential and parallel processing software requirements.* 2nd International Workshop on Rapid System Prototyping, Research Triangle Park, June 1991.

[Burns 93] C. Burns. *REE — A Requirements Engineering Environment for Analyzing & Validating Software and System Requirements.* Proceedings of the 4nd International Workshop on Rapid System Prototyping, Research Triangle Park, June 1993.

[Colom 86] J. M. Colom, M. Silva, J. L. Villarroel. *On software implementation of Petri Nets and colored Petri Nets using high-level concurrent languages.* 7th Workshop on Application and Theory of Petri Nets, pp207, 1986.

[ECMA 91] ECMA. *A Reference Model for Frameworks of Software Engineerings Environments.* ECMA report number TR/55 (version 2), NIST Report Number SP 500-201, December 1991.

[El Kaim 94] W. El Kaim, F. Kordon. *An Integrated Framework for Rapid System Prototyping And Automatic Code Distribution.* To appear in proceedings of the 5th International Workshop on Rapid System Prototyping, Grenoble, June 1994.

[Hallmann 91] M. Hallmann. *A process model for prototyping, Software engineering & its applications.* Toulouse, 9-13 December 1991.

[Hauschildt 87] D. Hauschildt. *A Petri Net Implementation.* Fachbereich Informatik, Universität Hamburg, Hamburg, February 1987.

[Jensen 92] K. Jensen. *Coloured Petri Nets. Basic concepts, analysis method and practical use (vol 1).* EATC monographs on Theoretical Computer Science, Springer Verlag 1992.

[Kordon 93] F. Kordon. *A generic prototype model for distributed systems based on high level object oriented specification.* Proceedings of the 4th International Workshop on Rapid System Prototyping, Triangle Park Institute, June 1993.

[Luqi 89] Luqi. *Software Evolution through Rapid Prototyping.* IEEE Computer 22(5), May 1989.

[Luqi 92] Luqi. *Computer Aided System Prototyping.* 3rd International Workshop on Rapid System Prototyping, Triangle Park Institute, June 1992.

[MARS 93] MARS-Team. *The CPN-AMI environment.* MASI lab, Institut Blaise Pascal, Université P. & M. Curie, 4 place Jussieu, 75252 Paris Cedex 05, October 1993.

[Murata 86] T. Murata, N. Komoda, K. Matsumoto. *A Petri Nets based Factory Automation controller for flexible and maintainable control specification* IEEE Trans on Industrial Electronics, vol IE-33(1), February 1986.

[Murphy 89] S. C. Murphy, P. Gunningberg, J. P. J. Kelly. *Implementing protocols with Multiple Specifications: Experiences with Estelle, LOTOS and SDL.* 9th IFIP WG 6.1 International Symposium on Protocol Specifications, Testing and Verification, Enschede, The Netherlands, June 1989.

[Taubner 87] D. Taubner. *On the implementation of Petri Nets.* 8th European Workshop on Application and Theory of Petri Nets, Saragosa, Spain, June 1987.

[Tu 90] S. Tu, S. M. Shatz, T. Murata. *Applying Petri Net reductions to support Ada-tasking deadlock detection.* Proceedings of the IEEE 10th International Conference on Distributed Computing Systems, Paris, May 1990.

[Vonk 92] R. Vonk. *Prototypage : l'utilisation efficace de la technologie CASE.* MASSON & Prentice Hall, Paris, 1992.

Programming Environments for Massively Parallel Distributed Systems, Monte Verità, Switzerland

Adaptor — A Transformation Tool for HPF Programs

Thomas Brandes Falk Zimmermann
German National Center for Math. and Computer Science (GMD)
P.O. Box 1316, 53731 St. Augustin, Germany
zimmermann@gmd.de

Abstract

Due to the existence of a global name space, the data parallel programming model is very comfortable to use. All communication requirements are implicit and therefore left to the compiler. To support this model even to general classes of parallel architectures, i.e. MIMD machines with distributed memory, High Performance Fortran (HPF) was developed. Beside a data parallel point of view the programmer has the ability to specify data distributions explicitly via directives.

ADAPTOR (Automatic Data Parallism Translator) is a compilation tool for transformating programs written in data parallel Fortran style to programs with explicit message-passing constructs.

This tool has been used to make experiences with HPF and to develop efficient and reliable compilation technology for future HPF compilers.

1 Introduction

Usually, MIMD architectures with distributed memory are programmed by explicit message passing. The data parallel programming model offers a more comfortable environment to program a wide range of scientific applications. This model stands for single threaded, global name space, and loosely synchronous parallel computation.

Language extensions and modifications for Fortran 90 have been defined by the High Performance Fortran Forum [Hig93] to take advantage of data parallelism. This High Performance Fortran language (HPF) allows code tuning for various architectures and should guarantee top performance on MIMD and SIMD computers with non-uniform memory access costs. The Adaptor system makes it possible to translate these programs to message passing programs already now. It transforms data parallel programs written in Fortran 77 with array extensions, parallel loops, and layout directives to parallel programs with explicit message passing. Therefore code containing global data references together with a user specified or implicitly defined data distribution is translated into a program with local and non-local references, where the latter are satisfied by automatically inserting message-passing statements.

2 The Adaptor Compilation System

Adaptor [1] transforms Fortran 77 or Fortran 90 programs with explicit data parallelism into parallel programs for MIMD architectures with explicit message passing. Utilizing a run time system these programs are able to run on most available parallel architectures. Though the user will need to understand some issues of parallelism and has to know for efficiency reasons where message passing will be generated, the effectiveness of Adaptor is based on the fact that the user neither has not to know any message passing command nor to manage the control of the data partitioning. He can change types of variables (e.g. single to double precision) and data distributions without rewriting any other statement in his program. He is not forced to write two versions of code (host and node program) and many global array operations are translated to the most efficient code for the underlying architecture. The parallel program can be written in such a way that it can be developed on a serial machine and is also suitable for vector machines or parallel machines with shared memory. Furthermore many features supported by Adaptor result in good execution times for these architectures, too. Similiary, it helps to design programs that run efficiently on nearly all architectures. Adaptor takes only advantage of the parallelism in the array operations and of the parallel loops. It has no features for automatic parallelization! Adaptor supports the development of parallel codes that scale with the number of processors.

2.1 Overview of Adaptor

The essential parts are the interactive source-to-source transformation (fadapt) and the run-time system DALIB (distributed array library). For compiling and linking of the generated programs, the available Fortran compilers of the parallel machines are utilized.

The input language of Adaptor can be regarded as Fortran 77 with some restrictions, but with many extensions like dynamic arrays, array operations, parallel loops and layout directives taken from HPF and Fortran 90.

In Adaptor the specification of data layouts is handled with directives like it is done in HPF. Also the parallel `FORALL` statement supported by Adaptor has the same syntax and semantic as proposed in the data parallel language.

---

[1]The Adaptor compilation system ia available via anonymous ftp ftp.gmd.de:gmd/adaptor

2.2 Realization of the Translation

The following steps are done during the source to source transformation of Adaptor:

1. The source program is parsed and an abstract syntax tree generated.

2. Symbol tables are created for usage in semantic analysis.

3. The program (abstract syntax tree) is normalized to reduce the translations complexity.

4. The real translation on the internal abstract syntax tree and symbol tables has four phases:

   (a) In the *analysis phase* the code is checked to verify that there are no violations of the current restrictions.

   (b) Normalizations reduce the number of rules for all following phases. They are also important for generating correct code, e.g. the definition of an aligned object has to follow the definition of the object to which it is aligned.

   (c) In many cases array assignments need communication. In this case Adaptor tries to split up the assignment in primitive array assignments with communication and local array assignments. Sometimes new temporary arrays have to be created.

   (d) In the *initial transformation phase* local array operations will be translated to parallel loops, the forall statement will be translated to equivalent do loops. After this phase only parallel loops without communication will exist.

   (e) During the *classification* communication is detected and classified (shifts, broadcasts, reductions)

   (f) In the *optimization phase* transformations are executed that reduce communication and loop fusion to take advantage of cache effects on the node processors

   (g) During *code generation* loops will be restricted to the array parts that are owned by one processor and communication statements or movements are translated to corresponding subroutine calls of the underlying run time system.

5. The new internal abstract syntax tree is unparsed back to source text.

Except the graphical interface, the whole source-to-source transformation of Adaptor is generated with a toolbox for compiler construction [GE90]. These tools have a great flexibility and can generate very efficient code. For the intermediate language, abstract syntax trees will be used where the program module that defines the structure of the abstract syntax trees and provides general tree manipulating procedures is also generated by a tool.

For the analysis and transformation components the compiler tool *Puma* is utilized. This tool cooperates with the generator for abstract syntax trees and supports the transformation and attribution of attributed trees. It is based on pattern-matching, unification and recursion. The flexibility of this tool allows not only a modular design but also to extend it in a way as one would expect from a knowledge-based system.

2.3 Support of Data Mapping

The latest version of Adaptor can handle block and cyclic distributions up to three dimensions with full support of alignment, whereas the previous versions could only deal with block distributions along one dimension. The improvement requires additional data structures and index transformations for packing of elements.

2.4 Support for block-structured Applications

One big class of scientific and engineering applications involves irregularly coupled meshes. These problems have the following characteristics:

- The data is divided into several interacting regions.
- There is a computational phase during which computation in each block can be carried out independently.
- The data access patterns within each block are regular.
- Communications between the subdomains are restricted to regular array sections.

These kind of applications are on the way to be supported by Adaptor. One necessary extension is that either blocks or arrays can be distributed onto a portion of the processor space. This is possible with the new version. Some more extensions might be required for more efficient codes. Currently there are two levels of parallelism available: Coarse-grain parallelism can be used for processing the blocks concurrently. Fine-grain parallelism is given by the data parallelism for each block. This allows some kind of MIMD execution of different blocks.

2.5 Communication Schedules

If an array operation requires communication, the transformation tool generates corresponding calls to the runtime system DALIB. These calls are always structured in such a way that at first a communication schedule is computed and afterwards the communication schedule is used for the data exchange.
Thus communication schedules are explicit data structures of the runtime system.

With the help of this feature, optimizations can be realized by reusing communication patterns or combining communications.

```
      integer A(N), B(N), P(N)
!hpf$ distribute (*) :: HA
!hpf$ distribute (CYCLIC) :: A
!hpf$ align with A :: B, P
      ...
      call global_get (B, A, P)
!     same as
      B = A(P)
```

2.6 Overlap Areas

The translation of parallel loops and array operations is always done by splitting operations into chunks of data movements with (global operations) and without (local operations) communication. This approach needs temporary arrays and many data movements.

```
      REAL A(N,N), B(N,N)
!ADP$ OVERLAP B(1:1,1:1)
!HPF$ DISTRIBUTE (BLOCK,BLOCK) :: A, B
      ...
      FORALL (I=2:N-1, J=2:N-1)
         A(I,J) = (B(I,J-1) + B(I,J+1) + B(I-1,J) + B(I+1,J)) * .25
      END FORALL
```

If arrays A and B are distributed by block, many redundant local data has to be moved. By using an overlap area for array B, these movements and the usage of temporary arrays are no longer required. Instead, the overlap area has to be updated. Currently, overlap areas are defined by the user choosing a special syntax which is only used by Adaptor. In a future version features will implemented that determine the overlap area automatically.

3 Conclusion

The Adaptor tool provides mechanisms to translate even large data parallel programs into message passing programs, that are nearly as efficient as their hand written counterparts. Due to this possibility MIMD architectures can be utilized by a wide range of scientists, who have not the *programming know how* and the time to develop message passing programs for their applications.

4 Related Work

The ADAPT system of Merlin [Mer91] compiles Distributed Fortran programs for execution on MIMD distributed memory architectures. Hatcher, Quinn et al. have realized a similar system for data parallel C* programs [HLJ+91]. The Fortran 90D/HPF compiler at Syracuse [BCF+93] deals also with data and computation partitioning, communication detection and generation. This compiler is the Fortran 90 counterpart of the Fortran 77D compiler [FHK+91] that is being developed at Rice. The used compilation methods are based on previous work by Koelbel and Mehrotra [KM91] and by Gerndt [Ger89]. Due to the introduction of High Performance Fortran, some other compilers are in development [BBZ93]. The commercial parallelization tool FORGE90 can deal with HPF extensions [9093].

References

[9093] FORGE 90. xHPF 1.0 Automatic Parallelizer for High Performance Fortran on Distributed Memory Systems - User's Guide. Technical report, Applied Parallel Research, Inc., April 1993.

[BBZ93] S. Benkner, P. Brezany, and H. Zima. Compiling High Performance Fortran in the PREPARE Environment. In *Fourth International Workshop on Compilers for Parallel Computers*, pages 105–116, Delft, Netherlands, December 1993.

[BCF+93] Z. Bozkus, A. Choudhary, G. Fox, T. Haupt, and S. Ranka. Fortran 90D/HPF Compiler for Distributed Memory MIMD Computers: Design, Implementation, and Performance Results. Technical Report, Syracuse Center for Computational Science, April 1993.

[FHK+91] G. Fox, S. Hiranandani, K. Kennedy, C. Koelbel, U. Kremer, C. Tseng, and M. Wu. Fortran D language specification. Technical Report TR90079, Department of Computer Science, Rice University, April 1991.

[GE90] J. Grosch and H. Emmelmann. A Tool Box for Compiler Construction. *Lecture Notes of Computer Science*, 477:106–116, October 1990.

[Ger89] H.M. Gerndt. *Automatic Parallelization for Distributed-Memory Multiprocessing Systems.* PhD thesis, University of Bonn, 1989.

[Hig93] High Perforamnce Fortran Forum. High Performance Fortran Language Specification, May 1993.

[HLJ+91] P. Hatcher, A. Lapadula, R. Jones, M. Quinn, and R. Anderson. A production quality C* compiler for hypercube machines. In *3rd ACM SIGPLAN Symposium on Principles Practice of Parallel Programming*, pages 73–82, April 1991.

[KM91] C. Koelbel and P. Mehrotra. Compiling global name-space parallel loops for distributed execution. *IEEE Transactions on Parallel and Distributed Systems*, October 1991.

[Mer91] J. Merlin. ADAPTing Fortran 90 Array Programs for Distributed Memory Architectures. In *Proc. 1st International Conference of the Austrian Center for Parallel Computation*, Salzburg, October 1991.

Programming Environments for Massively Parallel Distributed Systems, Monte Verità, Switzerland

A Parallel Framework for Unstructured Grid Solvers

D. A. Burgess P. I. Crumpton
M. B. Giles
Oxford University Computing Laboratory,
Wolfson Building, Parks Road, Oxford, OX1 3QD

Abstract

The aim of this work is to solve large two and three dimensional CFD problems using unstructured meshes. These problems are too large and too slow to put on sequential machines so parallel machines are required. Writing one off, machine specific parallel programs is time consuming, expensive and difficult to maintain. Consequently a general *framework* has been formulated to enable parallel and sequential execution of a single source FORTRAN 77 code. This is achieved via the straightforward insertion of OPlus library routine calls (Oxford Parallel Library for Unstructured Solvers). Hence, the user's code can be developed, debugged and maintained on a sequential machine and executed in parallel when required.

The OPlus interface provides a software platform for efficient execution of an application on a wide variety of parallel architectures. This generality and flexibility is derived from abstracting these application programs into sets, pointers between sets and functions defined over sets. This facilitates detailed runtime data dependency analysis.

1 Introduction

Algorithms for unstructured grids are becoming more popular, especially within the CFD community, where the geometrical flexibility of unstructured grids enables whole aircraft to be modelled. The resulting calculations are huge, hence the need to fully exploit modern parallel hardware. A *framework* has been formulated to enable parallelisation of unstructured grid solvers which execute efficiently on a wide variety of machines. To utilise the library the application program needs to be written in a certain style which accommodates OPlus library calls. Thus a single source FORTRAN 77 code can be developed, debugged and maintained on a sequential machine and executed in parallel when required. This is of great benefit since parallelising unstructured grid codes is a time consuming process.

There have been several authors who have pursued the idea of constructing a library for parallelising programs for MIMD machines. These are mainly aimed at structured grids. De Keyser developed a software tool called LOCO [Key93] for structured grids with refined regions. Dellagiacoma *et al* constructed PARAGRID [DPPV] which uses overlapping domain decomposition techniques on block–structured grids. Williams created DIME (Distributed Irregular Mesh Environment) [Wil90] and Das *et al* developed PARTI (Parallel Automated Runtime Toolkit at ICASE) [DSB93] for unstructured mesh algorithms on distributed machines. However, DIME restricts the user to two dimensional triangular grid calculations. PARTI parallelises problems in any dimensions, but is not believed to be as communication efficient and easy to use as the current work.

The OPlus framework uses a data parallel approach. Consequently certain algorithmic restrictions must be enforced to ensure the solutions from parallel and sequential executions are identical, to within machine accuracy. For example, algorithms involving matrix–vector multiplications can be handled, such as conjugate gradient methods with simple preconditioning, explicit time stepping methods and Jacobi relaxation. Excluded algorithms are globally implicit methods, such as ADI and sweeping relaxation schemes like Gauss–Seidel.

This paper will first describe the concepts behind the OPlus framework, then implementation issues for the distributed memory library and finally some results for a code predicting the inviscid flow over an aircraft.

2 Top Level Concepts

The concept behind the OPlus framework is that unstructured grids can be described by a number of *sets*. Depending on the application, these sets might be of nodes, edges, triangular faces, quadrilateral faces, cells of a variety of types, far-field boundary nodes, wall boundary faces, etc. Associated with these sets are both *data* (e.g. coordinate data at nodes, volumes at cells, normals on faces) and *pointers* to other sets (e.g. edge pointers to the two nodes at each end of the edge). All of the numerically-intensive operations can then be described as a *function* operating on all members of a set (eg. looping over cells, calculating volumes from the nodal coordinate values). The function can operate on data associated directly with the set or with another set through a pointer.

The OPlus framework makes the important restriction that a function will operate on all members of a set and the order it operates on the members will not affect the final result. If a function needs to be applied on a subset of members then another set should be formed containing only these members. Consequently, the OPlus routines can choose an ordering to achieve maximum parallel efficiency. It is this restriction that negates the framework being applied to Gauss–Seidel relaxation or globally implicit methods.

Before parallel execution can proceed, three main initialisation phases take place:

partitioning All sets are partitioned and each partition is assigned an *owner* processor. Processors must compute and store the values of the members they own.

halo construction If the application of a function to an element of a set (and other data pointed to by that element) requires data which is not locally owned that element is referred to as a "halo" member. The data at the halo member itself may, or may not, be owned. Copies of the required data must be communicated before halo execution.

local renumbering All sets are locally renumbered to minimise the memory requirements of each process. The pointers have to be similarly renumbered to ensure consistency.

The following example is given to illustrate how a loop is parallelised. Suppose that a triangular cell area, **AREAC**, is distributed to the cell's nodes using a pointer, NCELL, which points from the cell to its three nodes. This can be carried out for all the cells in the triangular mesh by the following DO–loop:

FORTRAN 77 code for distributing cell areas to the nodes

```
DO IC = 1, NCELLS
  I1 = NCELL(1,IC)
  I2 = NCELL(2,IC)
  I3 = NCELL(3,IC)
  AREAN(I1) = AREAN(I1) + AREAC(IC)/3.0
  AREAN(I2) = AREAN(I2) + AREAC(IC)/3.0
  AREAN(I3) = AREAN(I3) + AREAC(IC)/3.0
ENDDO
```

Suppose that a triangular mesh is partitioned which results in processor 1 owning five nodes 1 to 5 and four cells 1 to 4, as depicted in Figure 1. In order to have node values AREAN(1:5) consistent with the sequential code, after the loop has finished, local cell numbers 1 to 6 need to be executed within the loop. Thus, unowned halo cell data AREAN(5:6) needs to be transferred from the processor that owns them. The parallel execution of this loop on processor 1 would be:

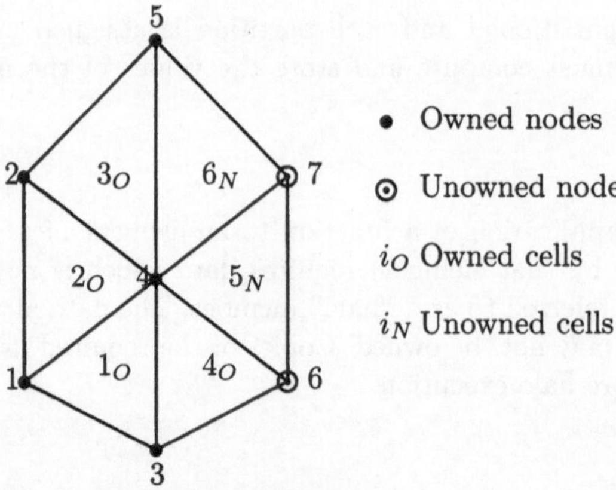

***Figure 1**: An example partition.*

Cells	Cell to Node(Owned/Not owned) Pointer	Cell Section
1_O	3 (O), 4 (O), 1 (O)	interior region
2_O	4 (O), 5 (O), 2 (O)	interior region
3_O	1 (O), 4 (O), 2 (O)	interior region
4_O	3 (O), 6 (N), 4 (O)	owned halo
5_N	6 (N), 7 (N), 4 (O)	unowned halo
6_N	4 (O), 7 (N), 5 (O)	unowned halo

***Table 1**: The cell–to–node pointer stored by processor 1 determines the sections of the local cell array for the example in Figure 1*

Parallel execution of DO–loop

Step 1. send `AREAC(4)` to neighbouring processor,

Step 2. execute DO–loop for `IC = 1, 2` and 3,

Step 3. receive `AREAC(5)` and `AREAC(6)` from neighbouring processors,

Step 4. execute DO–loop for `IC = 4, 5` and 6.

At the end of this loop `AREAN(i), i=1,2,3,4` and 5 will be up to date on processor 1. Redundant calculations which distribute cell areas to nodes `AREAN(6)` and `AREAN(7)` will be performed in this loop on processor 1, as these values will also be determined by the processor that owns them. These unowned members will have incorrect data on processor 1 after the loop is completed, and will need

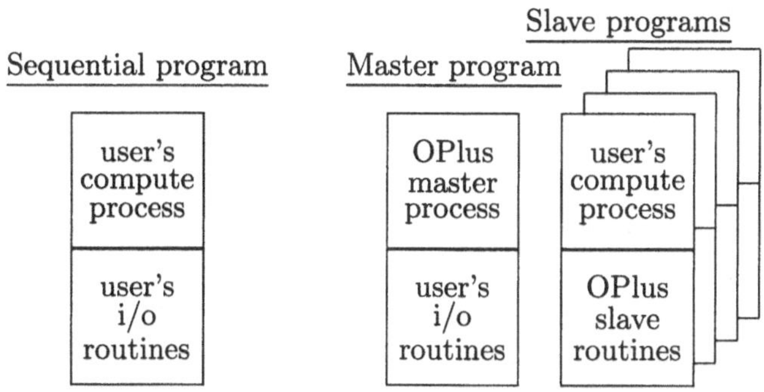

Figure 2: *Sequential and parallel versions of user's program*

to be replaced by values from their owners if they are required in a subsequent DO–loop.

This strategy of performing redundant calculations on unowned data only requires one communication phase per loop. The alternative is to communicate partial sums which requires two communication phases per loop, but no redundant calculation, see [FS94]. Clearly there is a tradeoff between computation and communication, the redundant calculation approach has been pursued here because:

1. The trend in hardware is toward very powerful processors ($\sim$ 100 Mflops); each will perform computations for a large number of cells/nodes, so the fraction of redundant computation is small.

2. This enables a simple loop syntax which facilitates:

   (a) efficient parallel execution of a loop,

   (b) hiding the parallelism from the application programmer.

   This is very important when developing large codes.

3 Implementation Issues

3.1 Input/Output

An aim of the framework is to allow users to write a *single source code* which will execute either sequentially or in parallel depending on how the executable is linked. To achieve this it is necessary for the program to handle all disk and terminal i/o via appropriate subroutines.

1. For sequential execution the user's main program is linked to user–written subroutines which handle all i/o. This will enable the user to develop, debug

and maintain their sequential code without any parallel message passing libraries.

2. For parallel execution the OPlus framework creates master and slave programs from the user's single source, Figure 2. The master program is formed by linking the OPlus master process to the user's i/o routines, while the slave program is created by linking the user's compute process to OPlus slave routines.

3.2 Parallelising DO–loops

The sequential loop given earlier, becomes, using the OPlus framework:

FORTRAN 77 DO–loop with framework calls

```
DO WHILE(OP_PAR_LOOP(NCELLS, ISTART, IFINISH))
  CALL OP_ACCESS_R8('read'  ,AREAC,1,NCELLS,NULL ,0,0,1,1)
  CALL OP_ACCESS_R8('update',AREAN,1,NNODES,NCELL,1,1,1,3)
  DO IC = ISTART, IFINISH
    I1 = NCELL(1,IC)
    I2 = NCELL(2,IC)
    I3 = NCELL(3,IC)
    AREAN(I1) = AREAN(I1) + AREAC(IC)/3.0
    AREAN(I2) = AREAN(I2) + AREAC(IC)/3.0
    AREAN(I3) = AREAN(I3) + AREAC(IC)/3.0
  ENDDO
END WHILE
```

Essentially the `DO WHILE` loop is similar to a colouring loop that would be necessary for vectorisation. `OP_PAR_LOOP` is a logical function which returns as arguments the start and finish indices of the inner loop. For sequential execution, `ISTART` and `IFINISH` are set to `1` and `NCELLS` respectively. `OP_ACCESS` tells the library how the arrays in the main loop are to be accessed and enables the library to perform runtime data dependency analysis. The contents of the inner loop have not changed during parallelisation. Full details of the arguments and other routines can be found in [BCGS93]. With this syntax the OPlus library can concatenate slave to slave messages to reduce latency, minimise the size of message sent and overlap communication with computation.

3.3 OPlus framework operations

The OPlus master process is responsible for the following operations:

1. initiates and terminates slaves,
2. reads in set and pointer information using user's i/o routines,
3. partitions, halo construction and local renumbering,
4. transfer of sets and pointers to the slaves,
5. handle all i/o from the slaves,

while the OPlus slave process is responsible for:

1. transfer of halo information to ensure consistent parallel execution,
2. overlap of communication and computation,
3. minimisation of latency and message length.

Other than the special treatment of i/o, there are just a few additional subroutines needed to achieve parallelism. The sequential versions of these subroutines do almost nothing. The initial implementation of the OPlus library uses PVM3.2.6 message passing for portability onto a wide variety of parallel machines.

3.4 Partitioning

An optimal partitioning for a distributed memory machine should evenly distribute the workload and minimise the communication cost between processors. As illustrated by Mavriplis *et al* in [MDSV92] the partitioning of the mesh can take as much time as solving the CFD problem itself. This shows that it is important to implement efficient partitioning algorithms that will give an approximate though satisfactory answer to the partitioning problem in a reasonable time frame. Hence, heuristics are used to obtain a near–optimal solution. In most CFD applications an unknown is updated in the grid by combining contributions from neighbouring cells. Thus, the grid should be partitioned into contiguous sections. There is a plethora of partitioning methods which attempt to do this. It is beyond the scope of this paper to describe these methods. The present implementation uses a straightforward recursive coordinate bisection, and has the facility to read a partition from elsewhere.

4 Results

To demonstrate the library a realistic industrial application has been chosen. This models the steady inviscid flow past an aircraft, which is discretised using an unstructured tetrahedral grid, see Figure 3. A Lax–Wendroff pseudo timestepping algorithm is used as the solver. The sets required for this are

set	size of set
nodes	137094
cells	746286
boundary nodes	16123
boundary faces	31536

and the pointers are

from	to	geometrical object	length
cell	nodes	tetrahedra	4
boundary faces	nodes	boundary faces	3
boundary nodes	nodes	list of boundary points	1

Timings are presented for the following machines:

- an 8 node distributed memory IBM SP1,
- 4 processor shared memory SGI Challenge.

E is the amount of redundant calculation, defined as

$$E = \frac{\sum \text{halo cells}}{\text{ncells}} \times 100$$

since the main computational loop is over cells. Elapsed times for a single iteration on an empty machine are quoted; many thousands of iterations are required for numerical convergence.

		IBM(Enet)		IBM(switch)		SGI	
p	E	time	S U	time	S U	time	S U
1	0.0	23.4	1.0	23.4	1.0	45.3	1.00
2	2.0	12.3	1.9	12.3	1.9	23.0	1.97
3	3.8	9.3	2.5	9.0	2.5	15.9	2.85
4	5.4	7.6	3.1	7.1	3.3	12.4	3.65
5	6.6	7.1	3.3	6.4	3.6	—	—
6	7.9	7.5	3.1	5.5	4.2	—	—
7	8.0	7.7	3.0	5.0	4.7	—	—
8	9.7	8.0	2.9	4.5	5.2	—	—

Two timings are quoted for the SP1, one using ethernet for communication (Enet) the other using the switch. The ethernet timings are equivalent to using a cluster of workstations. All timings use the PVM3.2.6 software. Improvements in the switch and SGI timings are possible by using the native message passing routines.

It is worth noting how E increases with the number of processors, giving about 10% more work for eight processors. At first sight this might indicate a lack of scalability to a large number of processors. However, scalability for a fixed problem size is not the objective. The aim of this project is to utilise parallel hardware for large and complex industrial applications. The problem size for this example is only 0.75 Million cells; it is envisaged future viscous calculations will have 10 Million cells. In this case the proportion of redundant calculations will remain small for more processors.

5 Conclusions

A flexible and general approach has been demonstrated to parallelise unstructured grid applications. This involves the programmer adopting the OPlus loop style of programming and all i/o being sent through specific subroutine calls. The resulting code will execute on a sequential machine (without the need for *any* parallel libraries) or in parallel (on a MIMD architecture). This single source is of major benefit for development and maintenance of the code.

The OPlus parallel execution is fully optimised to concatenate messages, minimise number of messages sent and overlap communication with computation. This library is intended for large applications, which warrant the use of parallel machines, and has been demonstrated by a 3D Euler solver for a complete aircraft configuration. For this realistic industrial application a worthwhile speed up has been achieved, with little effort from the application programmer.

Acknowledgements

This work was performed within Oxford Parallel, with financial support from Rolls–Royce plc, DTI and SERC.

References

[BCGS93] D. Burgess, P.I. Crumpton, M.B. Giles, and G.N. Shrinivas. OPlus programmer's manual. Oxford University computing laboratory, 1993.

[DPPV] F. Dellagiacoma, S. Paoletti, F. Poggi, and M. Vitaletti. PARAGRID: a parallel multi–block environment for Computational Fluid Dynamics. IBM ECSEC,Viale Oceano Pacifico 173, 00144 Rome, Italy.

[DSB93] R. Das, J. Saltz, and H. Berryman. *A Manual for PARTI Runtime Primitives, Revision 1.* ICASE, NASA Lagley Research Centre, Hampton, USA, May 1993.

[FS94] C. Farhat and Lanteri S. Simulation of compessible viscous flows on a variety of MPPs: computational algorithms for unstructured dynamic meshes and performance results. INRIA Report No. 2154, 1994.

[Key93] J.De Keyser. *LOCO1.0: a library supporting data parallelism on MIMD computers.* Department of Computer Science, Katholieke Universiteit Leuven, Leuven, Belgium, March 1993.

[MDSV92] D. J. Mavriplis, R. Das, J. Saltz, and R. E. Vermeland. Implementation of a parallel unstructured Euler Solver on shared and distributed memory architectures. *ICASE Report 92–68*, 1992. appearing in Supercomputing '92 proceedings and J. of Supercomp.

[Wil90] R. D. Williams. *DIME Distributed Irregular Mesh Environment.* California Institute of Technology, 1990.

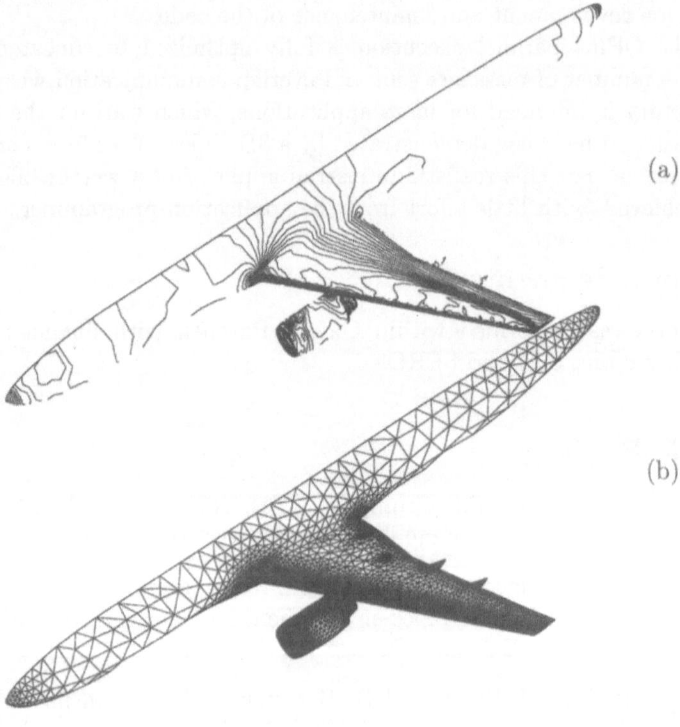

Figure 3: *(a) contours of pressure, (b) surface grid*

Programming Environments for Massively Parallel Distributed Systems, Monte Verità, Switzerland

A Study of Software Development for High Performance Computing

Manish Parashar, Salim Hariri, Tomasz Haupt and Geoffrey Fox
Northeast Parallel Architectures Center
Syracuse University
parashar@npac.syr.edu, hariri@cat.syr.edu

Abstract

Software development in a High Performance Computing (HPC) environment is non-trivial and requires a thorough understanding of the application and the architecture. The objective of this paper is to study the software development process in a high performance computing environment and to outline the stages typically encountered in this process. Support required at each stage is also highlighted. The modeling of stock option pricing is used as a running example in the study.

1 Introduction

Software development in any High Performance (Parallel/Distributed) Computing (HPC) environment is a non-trivial process and requires a thorough understanding of the application and the architecture. This is apparent from the fact that applications currently achieve only a fraction of peak available performance [Zor92]. HPC software development requires the developer to resolve and tune a large number of available design options. For example, during the course of software development, the developer is required to select the optimal hardware configuration for a particular application, the best decomposition and mapping of the problem onto the selected hardware configuration, the best communication and synchronization strategy to be used, etc. Using conventional techniques, this would require extensive experimentation, data collection and post-processing. The set of reasonable alternatives that have to be evaluated is very large and selecting the best among these is a formidable task. As a result the exploitation of the vast potential of HPC systems will largely be governed by the availability of suitable tools and application development environments to support application developers.

The objective of this paper is to study the software development process in a high performance computing environment and to outline the stages encountered. Further, the nature of supporting tools that can assist the developer at each stage are identified. Parallel modeling of stock option pricing is used as an illustrative example in the study. The rest of the document is as organized follows: Section 2 presents the study of HPC software development process and outlines the stages (subsections 2.3 - 2.7). Section 3 presents some conclusions.

2 HPC Software Development

The HPC software development process is described as a set of stages which correspond to the phases typically encountered by a developer. At each stage, a set of support tools which can assist the developer are identified. The stages can be viewed as a set of filters in cascade (see Figure 1) forming a development pipeline. The input to this system of filters is the application description and specification which is generated from the application itself (if it is a new problem) or from existing sequential code (porting of dusty decks). The final output of the pipeline is a running application. Feedback loops present at some stages signify step-wise refinement and tuning. Related discussions pertaining to parallel computing environments and spanning parts of the software development process can be found in [BM91, BBDK91, RL88]. A survey of existing tools and techniques corresponding to the developemnt stages is presented in [PHHF93a]. The stages in the HPC software development process are described in the following sections. Parallel modeling of Stock Option Pricing [MCV+92] is used as an illustrative, running example in the discussion.

2.1 Parallel Modeling of Stock Option Pricing

Stock options are contracts that give the holder of the contract the right to buy or sell the underlying stock at some time in the future for an agreed upon striking or exercise price. Option contracts are traded just as stocks and models that quickly and accurately predict their prices are valuable to the traders. Stock option pricing models estimate the price for an option contract based on historical market trends and current market information. The model requires three classes of inputs: **Market Variables** which include the current stock price, call price, exercise price and time to maturity. **Model Parameters** which include the volatility of the asset (variance of the asset price over time), variance of the volatility and the correlation between asset price and volatility. These parameters cannot be be directly observed and must be estimated from historical data. **User Inputs** which specify the nature of the required estimation; e.g. American/European call, constant/stochastic volatility, time of dividend payoff, and other constraints regarding acceptable accuracy and running times. A number of option pricing models have been developed using varied approaches, e.g. non-stochastic analytic models, Monte Carlo simulation models, binomial models, binomial models with forced recombination, etc. Each of these models involve a set of tradeoff's in the nature and accuracy of the estimation and suit different user requirements. In addition, these models make

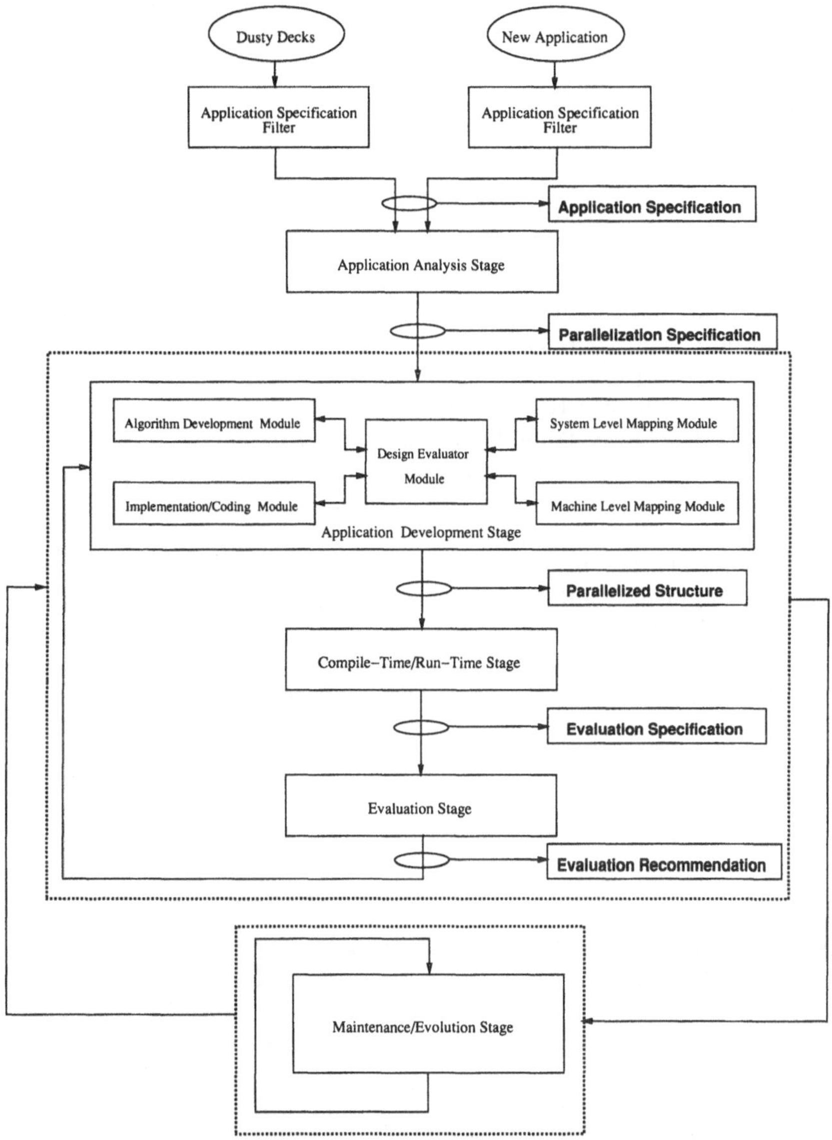

Figure 1: *The HPC Software Development Process*

varied demands in terms of programming models and computing resources.

2.2 Inputs

The HPC software development process presented in this section addresses "new" application development as well as the porting of exiting applications (Dusty-

Decks) to HPC environments. The input to the development pipeline is the application specification in the form of a functional flow description, which is a very high-level flow diagram of the application outlining the sequence of functions to be performed. Each node (termed as functional module) in the functional flow diagram is a black-box and contains information about (1) its input(s), (2) the function to be performed, (3) the desired output(s) and (4) the resource requirements at each node. The application specification can be thought of as corresponding to the "user requirement document" in a traditional life-cycle models.

In the case of new applications, the inputs are generated from the textual description of the problem and its requirements. In the case of dusty decks code porting, the developer is required to analyze the existing source code. In either case, expert system based tools and intelligent editors, both equipped with a knowledge base to assist in analyzing the application, are required. In Figure 1, these tools are included in the "Application Specification Filter" module.

The stock price modeling application comes under the first class of applications (i.e. new applications). The application specifications based on the textual description presented in Section 2.1, is shown in Figure 2. It consists of three functional modules: (1) The input module which accepts user specification, market information and historical data and generates the three classes of inputs required by the model. (2) The estimation module consists of the actual model and generates the stock option pricing estimates. (3) The output module provides a graphical display of the estimation to the user. The feedback from the output module to the input module represents tuning of the user specification based on the output displayed.

2.3 Application Analysis Stage

The first stage of the HPC software development pipeline is the application analysis stage. The input to this stage is the application specification as described in Section 2.2. The function of this stage is to thoroughly analyze the application with the sole objective of achieving the most efficient implementation. The problems dealt with in this stage are: (1) module creation problem, i.e. identification of tasks which can be executed in parallel; (2) module classification problem i.e. identification of standard modules; and (3) module synchronization problem, i.e. analysis of mutual interdependencies. The output of this stage is a detailed process flow graph called the "Parallelization Specification" where the nodes represent functional components and the edges represent interdependencies. This stage corresponds to the "design phase" in standard software life-cycle models and its output corresponds to the "design document". Tools which can assist the user at this stage of software development are: (1) smart editors which can interactively generate directed graph models from the application specifications; (2) intelligent tools with learning capabilities which can use the directed graphs to analyze dependencies, identify potentially parallelizable modules and attempt to classify the functional modules into standard modules; and (3) problem specific tools equipped with a

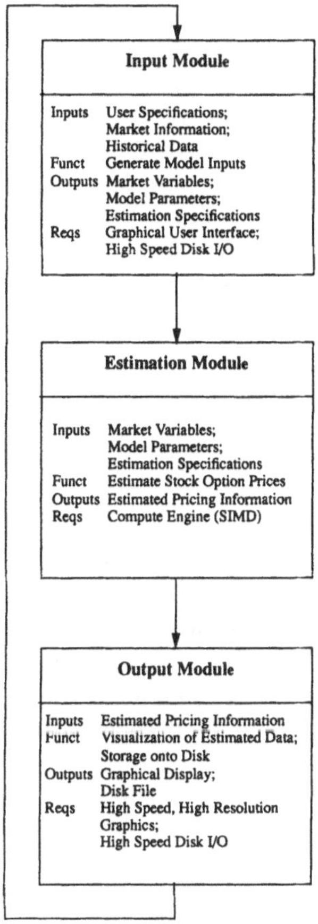

Figure 2: Stock Option Pricing Model: Application Specifications

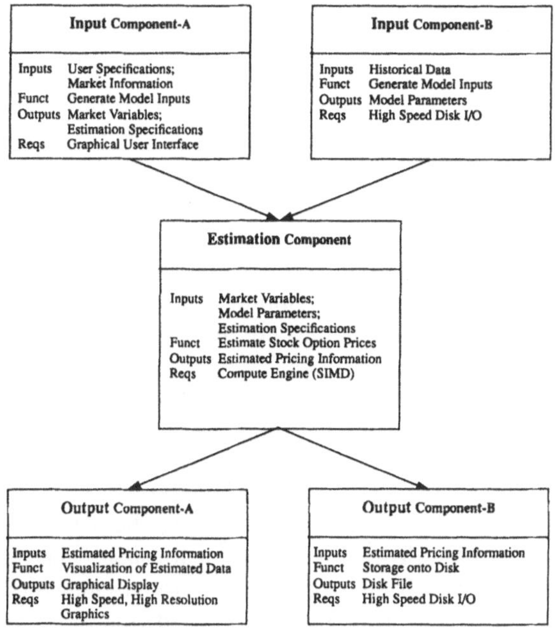

Figure 3: Stock Option Pricing Model: Parallelization Specifications

database of transformations and strategies applicable to the specific problem.

The parallelization specification for the running example is shown in Figure 3. The Input functional module is subdivided into two functional components: (1) analyzing historical data and generating model parameters; and (2) accepting market information and user inputs to generate market variables and estimation specifications. The two components can be executed concurrently. The Estimation module is identified as a standard computational module and is retained as a single functional component. The Output functional module consists of two independent functional components: (1) rendering the estimated information onto a graphical display; and (2) writing it onto disk for subsequent analysis.

2.4 Application Development Stage

The application development stage receives as its input the Parallelization Specifications and produces the Parallelized Structure which can then be compiled and executed. This stage is made up of 5 modules: (1) Algorithm Development Module; (2) System Level Mapping Module; (3) Machine Level Mapping Module; (4) Implementation/Coding Module; and (5) Design Evaluator Module. It should be noted, however, that these modules are not executed in any fixed sequence or a fixed number of times. There exists instead, a feedback system from each module to the other modules through the design evaluator module. This allows the development as well as the tuning to proceed in an iterative manner using step-wise refinement. The modules are described below:

2.4.1 Algorithm Development Module

The function of the algorithm development module is to assist the developer in identifying functional components in the parallelization specification and selecting appropriate algorithmic implementations. The input information to this module includes: (1) the classification and requirements of the components specified in the parallelization specification; (2) hardware configuration information; and (3) mapping information generated by the system level mapping module. It then uses this information to select the best algorithmic implementation and the corresponding implementation template from its database. The algorithm development module uses the services of the design evaluator module to select between possible algorithmic implementations. Tools needed during this phase include an intelligent algorithm development environment (ADE) equipped with a database of optimized templates for different algorithmic implementations, an evaluation of the requirements of these templates and an estimation of their performance on different platforms.

The algorithm chosen to implement the Estimation Component of the stock option pricing model (shown in Figure 3), depends on the nature of the estimation (constant/stochastic volatility, American/European calls/puts, dividend payoff time, etc) to be performed and the accuracy/time constraints. For example, models based on Monte Carlo simulation provide high accuracy. However, these models are computationally intensive and slow and thereby cannot be used in real-time systems. Further they are not suitable for American calls/puts when early dividend payoff is possible. Binomial models are less accurate than Monte Carlo models but are more tractable and can handle early exercise. Models using constant volatility (as opposed to treating volatility as a stochastic process) lack accuracy but are simplistic and easy to compute. The algorithmic implementations of the input and output functional components must be capable of handling terminal and disk I/O at rates specified by the time constraint parameters. Further, the output display must provide all information required by the user.

2.4.2 System Level Mapping Module

The function of the system level mapping module is to use the information provided by the algorithm development module to appropriately map the functional components of the application to the appropriate computing elements of a distributed (possibly heterogeneous) HPC environment. The objective is to map each functional component to the computing element that maximizes the performance of the application. Some data and load distribution issues may have to be resolved in this module. In addition, this module may also cluster functional component nodes specified in the parallelization specifications to obtain a better mapping. The system level mapping module uses feedback from the evaluation module to select between different mapping candidates. System level mapping can be accomplished in an interactive mapping environment equipped with intelligent tools for analyzing the requirements of the functional components, and a knowledge base consisting of analytic benchmarks for the different computing elements and interconnection media in the HPC environment.

The algorithms for stock option pricing have been efficiently implemented on architectures like the CM2 and the DECmpp-12000 [MCV+92]. Thus, an appropriate mapping for the estimation functional component in the parallelization specification in Figure 3 is an SIMD architecture. The input and output interfaces (Input/Output Component-A) require graphics capability with support for high speed rendering (output display) and must be mapped to an appropriate graphics stations. Finally, Input/Output Component-B requires high speed disk I/O and must be mapped to an I/O server with such capabilities.

2.4.3 Machine Level Mapping Module

The machine level mapping module performs the mapping of the functional component(s) onto the processor(s) of the computing elements. This stage resolves issues like data partitioning, load distribution, control distribution, etc. and makes transformations specific to that computing element. It uses the feedback from the design evaluator module to select between possible alternatives. Machine level mapping can be accomplished in an interactive mapping environment similar to that described for the system level mapping module, but equipped with information pertaining individual computing elements of a specific computer architecture.

The performance of the stock option pricing models are very sensitive to the layout of data onto the processing elements. The optimal layout is dictated by the input parameters (e.g. time of dividend payoff, terminal time, etc.) and by the specification of the architecture onto which the component is mapped. For example, in the binomial model, the continuous time processes for stock price and volatility are represented as discrete up/down movements forming a binary lattice. Such a lattice is generally implemented as asymmetric arrays which are distributed onto the processing elements. It has been found that the default mapping of these arrays (i.e. in two dimensions) on architectures like the DECmpp-12000, lead to poor load balancing and performance, specially for extreme values of the dividend payoff time. Further the performance in case of such a mapping, is very sensitive to this value and has to be modified for each set of inputs. Hence, in this case it is favorable to explicitly map them as one dimensional arrays. This is done by the machine level mapping module.

2.4.4 Implementation/Coding Module

The function of the implementation/coding module is to handle all code generation and perform the code filling of selected templates, so as to produce parallel code which can then be compiled and executed on the target computer architecture. This module incorporates all machine specific transformations, optimized libraries and codes; handles the introduction of calls to communication and synchronization routines; and takes care of the distribution of data among the processing elements. It also handles any input/output redirection that may be required.

With regard to the pricing model application, the implementation/coding module is responsible for introducing the machine specific communication routines. For example, the binary estimation model makes use of the "end-of-shift" function for its nearest-neighbor communication. The corresponding function call in C^* (CM2) or MPL (DECmpp-12000) are introduced by this module. A possible machine specific optimization that can be introduced by this module is to reduce communication by making use of in-processor arrays. This optimization can improve performance by about two orders of magnitude [MCV+92].

2.4.5 Design Evaluator Module

The design evaluator module is a critical component of the application development stage. Its function is to assist the developer in evaluating different options available to each of the other modules, and identifying the option that provides the best performance. It receives information about the hardware configuration, the application structure, the requirements of the selected algorithms and the mappings. This input information is then used to estimate the performance of the application on the target configuration. Further, it provides insight into the computation and communication costs, the existing idle times and the overheads. This information can be used by the other modules to identify regions where further refinement or tuning is required. The keys features of this module are: (1) the ability to provide evaluations with the desired accuracy, with minimum resource requirements and within a reasonable amount of time; (2) the ability to automate the evaluation process; and (3) the ability to perform the evaluation within an integrated workstation environment without running the application on the target computers. Support applicable to this module consists primarily of performance prediction and estimation tools. Simulation approaches can also be used to achieve some of the required functionality. A novel approach which uses interpretive techniques to realize a performance prediction framework that can meet these requirements, is presented in [PHHF93b].

2.5 Compile-Time & Run-Time Stage

The compile-time/run-time stage handles the task of executing the parallelized application generated by the development stage to produce the required output. The input to this stage is the parallelized source code (parallelized structure). The compile-time portion of this stage consists of set of cross compilers for the computing elements and tools for scheduling and allocation. The run-time portion of this stage handles run-time functions like debugging, scheduling, dynamic load balancing, migration, irregular communications, etc. It also enables the user to (non-intrusively) instrument the code for profiling and debugging and allows checkpointing for fault-tolerance. During the execution of the application, it accepts outputs from the different computing elements and directs them for proper visualization. It intercepts error messages generated and provides proper interpretation.

2.6 Evaluation Stage

In the evaluation stage, the developer, retrospectively evaluates the design choices made during the design process and looks for ways to improve the performance. The evaluation stage performs a thorough evaluation of the execution of the entire application, detailing communication and computation times, synchronization overheads and existing idle times at every execution level (application level, node level, procedure level, etc.). It uses this evaluation to identify regions in the implementation where performance improvement is possible. Further, it allows a cost-effective evaluation (in terms of time and resources) of the application for a representative inputs set as well as the effect of various run-time parameters like system load, network contention, on performance. The scalability of the application with machine and problem size is also evaluated. The key requirement of this stage is the ability to provide desired accuracy and granularity of evaluation while maintaining tractability and non-intrusiveness. Support applicable to the evaluation stage include different analytic tools, monitoring tools, simulation tools and prediction/estimation tools.

2.7 Maintenance/Evolution Stage

In addition to the above described stages encountered during the development and execution of HPC applications, there is an additional stage in the life-cycle of this software which involves its maintenance and evolution. Maintenance includes monitoring the operation of the software and ensuring that it continues to meet its specifications. It involves detecting and correcting bugs as they surface. The maintenance stage also handles modifications needed to incorporate changes in the system configuration. Software evolution deals with improving the software, adding additional functionality, incorporating new optimizations, etc. Another aspect of evolution is the development of more efficient algorithms and corresponding algorithmic templates and the incorporation of new hardware architectures. To support such a development, the maintenance/evolution stage provides tools for the rapid prototyping of hardware and software and for evaluating the new configuration and designs without having to implement them. Other support required during this stage includes tools for monitoring the performance and execution of the software, fault detection and recovery tools, and system configuration and configuration evaluation tools.

3 Conclusions

Software development in any Parallel/Distributed environment is a non-trivial process and requires a thorough understanding of the application and the architecture. This apparent from the fact that currently, applications are able to achieve only a fraction of peak available performance. This paper studies the software development process for in a High Performance Computing environment. It describes the stages typically involved in this process and outlines the support required at each stage. The development of a parallel model for stock option pricing is used as a running example.

References

[BBDK91] J. E. Boillat, H. Burkhart, K. M. Decker, and P. G. Kropf. Parallel Computing in the 1990's: Attacking the Software Problem. *Physics Report (Review Section of Physics Letters)*, 207(3-5):141 – 165, 1991.

[BM91] Victor R. Basili and John D. Musa. The Future Engineering of Software: A Management Perspective. *IEEE Computer*, 24(9):90–96, September 1991.

[MCV+92] Kim Mills, Gang Cheng, Michael Vinson, Sanjay Ranka, and Geoffrey C. Fox. Software Issues and Performance of a Parallel Model for Stock Option Pricing. *Proceedings of the* 5th *Australian Supercomputing Conference, Melbourne, Australia*, December 1992.

[PHHF93a] Manish Parashar, Salim Hariri, Tomasz Haupt, and Geoffrey C. Fox. An Integrated Software Development Model for Heterogeneous High Performance Computing. Technical Report SCCS-453, Northeast Parallel Architectures Center, Syracuse University, Syracuse NY 13244-4100, April 1993.

[PHHF93b] Manish Parashar, Salim Hariri, Tomasz Haupt, and Geoffrey C. Fox. An Interpretive Framework for Application Prediction. *Procs of the 1993 Int'l Conference On Parallel and Distributed Systems*, 668–672, Dec. 1993.

[RL88] Lucian Russell and R. N. C. Lightfoot. Software Development Issues for Parallel Processing. *Proceedings of the* 12th *Annual International Computer Software and Applications Conference*, 306–307, 1988.

[Zor92] Glenn Zorpette. Teraflops Galore. *IEEE Spectrum*, 29(9):26–76, sep 1992.

Programming Environments for Massively Parallel Distributed Systems, Monte Verità, Switzerland

Parallel Computational Frames: An Approach to Parallel Application Development based on Message Passing Systems*

M.Fruscione, P.Flocchini, E.Giudici, S.Punzi, P.Stofella
ACS (Advanced Computing Systems)
Via Rombon 11
20134 Milano, Italy

Abstract

The main goal of this work is to provide a set of tools able to give direct support for the most known parallel processing techniques when developing parallel application. While a lot of work is being done by researchers in this field, trying to delineate those applications and those software engineering practices which can allow automatic parallelization of code based on the Communicating Sequential Processes (CSP) programming tools (e.g. Express, CSTools, PVM), the idea underlying to this work is that, as a first step, higher level development tools have to be produced to help the programmers of parallel applications and to cover the broader range of applications. Our approach departs from the classification of parallel computing paradigms and the associated parallelization techniques and from the definition of a set of structures and procedural interfaces able to partially solve the problems associated with these paradigms, such as load balancing, domain decomposition, communication, synchronization and mapping. When developing a parallel application these different aspects are tackled togheter and embedded in a parallelization technique able to solve most of the involved details. We define the concept of Parallel Computational Frames (PCF) for the combination of those parallelization techniques and related solutions.

1 Introduction

Since the definition of the CSP computational model [Hoa78], a number of hardware systems and software tools for parallel applications development [Flo90]

*Partially supported by CNR "Progetto Finalizzato Calcolo Paralleli e Sistemi Informatici Sottoprogetto 3" and from the esprit Project "Palace"

[Mei93] [Oak93] have been developed that conform in some way with the basic ideas explored by Hoare. The main functionalities these software environments provide are extensions to commonly used languages with communication primitives or functions resembling the main features of CSP model. Added values are deadlock free routing mechanism and distribuited system services over the network of processors; in some cases, direct support is provided for specific parallelization techniques, as for domain decomposition data parallel model. Tools for static code analysis oriented to parallelization or post mortem profilers for performances evaluation and optimization are also generally provided. Even if the support provided by such environment is clearly useful in the context of parallel application development, there is a lack of direct support for the solution of the major problems involved in parallel programming, such as high level logical communications, load balancing, synchronization. Using these specific environments users and their applications also tend to be strictly tied to the kind of used parallel architecture giving to the code no chance of portability on different hardware platforms. The main goal of this work is to build a set of software tools able to provide direct support for the most common parallel processing techniques with a methodology and a specific language to better exploit the tools: while most part of the development environments provide a tool kit for solving particular parallel problems [Dec93], the aim of this project is to provide a more general solution kit for parallelization problems in building real world applications. Our approach is based on the definition of the Parallel Computational Frame (PCF) concept as a building block for the development of parallel applications. Final objective of this work is the definition of a computational model able to represent parallel solutions as basic structures to be combined togheter to form a parallel application. The PCF approach introduces a new methodology for solving problems on parallel computers or networked workstations, allowing the user to work on high level structural aspects of their applications, rather than concentrating on low level details both of parallel hardware and of parallel programming. A set of ready to use solutions for parallelization problems will dramatically increase the programmer's productivity, reducing one of the most frustrating limits to the diffusion of parallel architectures. After a brief description about parallel computing paradigms the approach based on PCF is presented, with its formal definitions in Chapter 3. In Chapter 4 there is a discussion about the PCF implementation and in Chapter 5 follows an example of parallelization using the PCF approach. Conclusions and further developments end this paper.

2 Parallel computing paradigms and PCF

There exist in literature a rich set of works treating and defining different parallelization models [Hey89], [Kun89] and [Fox88] suggesting their related parallelization technique. Each computational model captures and encapsulates parallel algorithms proper to a specific range of programming applications [Van91], [Dar93].

Our approach starts from the definition of specific parallel frames togheter with the implementation of the associated parallelization techniques. Data Parallel model encapsulates parallel algorithms where different processes execute the same set of instructions on different data. Domain decomposition techniques are usually employed to fully exploit the data parallelism. In Master Slave (Task farm) model parallelism is embedded by splitting a large task to several subtasks (slave or worker processes). Load balancing techniques strongly influences runtime performances. In the Client Server model parallelism arises from the interaction between server and client processes while the Pipeline model implements a sort of linear parallelism. In addition to this computational models we thougth that a Shared Memory Emulation model to share common variable without explicit message passing could improve the programmer productivity and the source code readability. All these computational models (except the Pipeline model) are the building blocks in a set of developed libraries called Arnia [Fru90]. Further developments plan the implementation of the Pipeline model and of a Producer Consumer like model with implicit worker processes. The programming techniques of each PCF are implemented by a different library of functions. Each library is well suited to solve a specific simple application, which can be parallelized following one decomposition technique. When the problem to solve is inherently complex, Arnia libraries can be used in combination at the cost of a stronger programming effort. This is the evidence for a higher level tool, which permits to combine easily the Arnia libraries. The approach proposed is founded on a precise programming methodology: the programmer have to make a decompostion of its problem recognizing the different patterns in which parallelism can arise. Each one of these patterns stands for a subproblem of the original one. This methodology should be iterated until each one of the obtained frames is simply parallelizable using one of the Arnia libraries. We name Parallel Computational Frame (PCF) the different parallelization techniques and PCF instances the patterns obtained through the problem decomposition just described. A PCF instance is composed by the processes which work in the same context of the problem, using one of the Arnia libraries (so we speak about PCF Master Slave instance, PCF Client Server instance etc.). Each process is identified by the role played inside the PCF instance, so, to each process is associated a process type (for example master or slave in the PCF Master Slave) describing its behaviour inside the instance. A PCF application is made up by a set of instances eventually intersecting. An intersection is made up by process belonging to more than one PCF instance. The programmer must define the structure of its application in terms of PCF instances. No high level tool has been implemented to help the user in this decision making. The Parallel Computational Frame library (PCFlib) implements the concept of PCF and provides the user the possibility to easily combine the Arnia libraries.

3 PCF: formal definition

The concept of Parallel Computational Frame is build upon the Communicating Sequential Processes model; a program built in terms of PCF will always result in a set of communicating sequential processes. In the following a process can be seen as a CSP process or a process in any CSP like language, extension or environment.

- Def.1: we define a Parallel Computational Frame as a pair (T,F), where $T = T_1.., T_n$ is a set of proces types and F is a set of PCF specific functions.
- Def.2: a Process is a list $P = d_1, d_2, ..., d_m$ of pairs. Each d_i=(pcf_i, t_i), called Process Descriptor, is a pair where pcf_i =(T,F) is a PCF and $t_i \in$ T is a process type.
- Def.3: let I be a set of processes $I = P_1, P_2, ..., P_k$ where P_i=(pcf_{i1}, t_{i1}) ,.., (pcf_{im}, t_{im}). Then I is a Parallel Computational Frame Instance of the PCF H if, for each i=1,2,...,k there is a j for which pcf_{ij}=H.
- Def.4: A PCF application is a set of (possibly intersecting) PCF instances.

An intersection occours whenever a process belongs to more than one PCF instance. The last formal definition is the key point in order to structure a parallel application. If the single PCF represents a solution to a certain parallel computational model, combining different PCFs means to combine different solutions inside the same complex application.

4 PCF implementation

Our approach is built on the definition and implementation of a set of parallel computational models togheter with high level tools which permit to develop a parallel application as a combination of these models. The resulting programming environment is structured in five different layers, see Figure 1, and is available both with C and Fortran interfaces.
The Communication Network layer provides the functionalities of message passing systems implementing the CSP computational model with basic routines for inter process communications. In order to enhance portability, a message passing interface, named Stratos, has been implemented on different message passing systems (CSTools, PVM, Express).

4.1 Stratos

Stratos consists of a set of functions supporting a message passing system. All the communication functions provided by Stratos are based on the mailbox concept, the main structure which allow the exchange of messages between processes. The functions of Stratos can be grouped in mailbox functions, for the management of

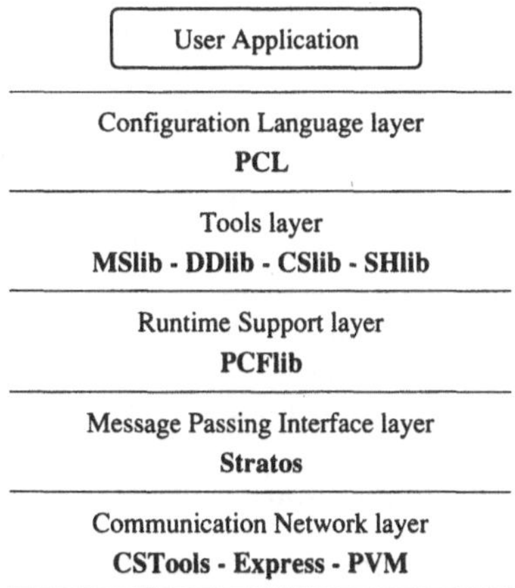

Figure 1: *The programming environment structure*

mailboxes and communicating functions for the operation of sending and receiving messages in mailboxes. Blocking, non blocking, one to one and multi to one communications are supported.

4.2 Runtime support layer

Runtime support layer provides mechanisms and data structures needed for the management of multiple PCF instances. The PCFlib library implements the concept of PCF through the definition and management of particular data structure describing the application and its building processes. Such data structures contain information concerning every PCF instance, such as the referenced PCF model, the number of cuncurrent processes and their types, the descriptors of the processes belonging to a particular instance. Process descriptors contain the list of mailbox used in communicating with other processes belonging to the same instance and the logical process identifiers. The PCFlib functions can be grouped in declaration functions, registration functions and data retriving functions. Declaration functions are used in the declarative part of a PCF application, where each process states the instances to which it belongs. After that, a registration phase collects declaration data and organizes information in data structures describing instances. Due to the fact the employed algorithm is fully centralised there is the evidence to redistribute the data structures among every process. During the normal execution phase of the application a process usually needs to retrive information concerning its instances such as particular mailboxes connected to a process or the number of processes of a specified type (for example the number of slave processes in a Master Slave instance). Retrival data functions give the possibility to get these encapsulated data easily and in a secure way.

4.3 Tools layer

At the tools layer a set of parallelizing tools (corresponding to the Arnia libraries) is defined and implemented according to the different PCF models proposed. These classes of tools perform the most of the work usually in charge to the programmer. Solutions to a certain kind of parallel problems (domain decomposition, load balancing etc.) are well known, so they can be available to the programmer. The MSlib library implements the PCF Master Slave, providing direct support to the parallelization of application that can be developed following this model. MSlib insulates all of the low level communication and parallelization structures providing a set of higher level procedures with the following main functionalities:

- High level communication primitives between master and slaves
- Automatic decomposition and distributions of n dimensional data structures
- Automating management of overlapping areas
- Automatic collecting of subgrids from slave processes
- Data broadcasting and collecting from/to slaves
- Global binary operation between slaves processes
- Automatic self scheduling based load balancing

In particular, automatic load balancing ensures best performance togheter with the simplicicty of use given by high level primitives. Automatic domain decomposition happens in two phase: first, given the dimension of the data domain to decompose (which can be monodimensional, bidimensional or threedimensional), a dimensional decomposition is found, i.e., it is calculated the number of processes associated to each dimension of the domain. This decomposition can be twofold. From one hand, homogeneus domain can be calculated (the subgrid dimensions will be the same in each slave node, if it is possible). From the other hand subdomains dimensions are possibly not homogeneus. This computation maximizes the fraction area/perimeter for each subdomain, in order to achieve less communication overhead. The second phase in the automatic domain decomposition calculates the local dimensions of a subgrid assigned by the master to each slave process. The Data parallel library (DDlib) implements the Data Parallel PCF providing high level communication functions and domain decomposition primitives among the running processes. In a DDlib instance a collection of node processes organized in a regular n-dimensional grid topology executes the same code on different parts of a domain. Complex systems simulation are usually based on some data structure representing physically distributed variables: a geometrical decomposition of these data structures on a set of processes is the most frequent approach to parallelization. The purpose of the domain decompostion functions is to take a user specified problem domain and perform a mapping to the underlying processor topology so that the user has not to understand the location of processes in the application or which nodes have to communicate. The user has only to specify the dimensions of the problem, the dimensions of domain and the number of processors to use, then the system automatically decides the number of processors to assign to each dimension, operates a decomposition of the original data structure and assign to each processor a portion of data, automatically managing overlap area, if specified. The data structure could be both decomposed and recomposed reading and writing both from I/O and memory. Once the specification of the problem domain has been set, the user is provided by DDlib with a set of communication primitives on the n-dimensional grids. Shortly, the main functionalities DDlib provides are:

- Logical communication primitives on n-dimensional grids
- Domain decomposition and data structures automatic distribution
- Overlapping areas managing support with automatically swap operations
- Global binary operations between node processes

Global binary operations between node processes perform distributed operations on data replicated globally. The algorithm implemented ensures a number of communication needed that varies with the logarithm of N (where N is the number of running processes). The Client Server library (CSlib), provides direct support in applications where a collection of processes, called clients, possibly executing different codes on local data structures, interact with a distinct collection of processes, called servers, providing services needed and explicitly requested by the clients themselves. Services can be replicated and partitioned in the server' set: server processes must declare which services they offer and notify them to the clients, while client processes must explicitly ask for services to the appropriate server or servers. The interaction between servers and clients may cause data exchange and behaves following a fixed protocol. The main functionalities CSlib provides are:

- Services declaration and notification
- Automatic load balancing strategies for services requests
- High level communication primitives between servers and clients

Whenever a client requires a service makes a random selection of the server which will offer the service (obviously among the servers offering that particular service). Actually, for sake of simplicity, the involved communications are blocked. The Shared Memory library (SHlib) creates a global memory abstraction accessible from all the nodes using a set of read/write primitives. Shared memory emulation is implemented using the following techniques:

- Data distribution among the nodes

- Direct memory access
- Page based memory management
- Both strict and weak consistency supported
- Read replication/invalidation technique

The fundamental primitives that can be used from the programmer are shread and shwrite; a special data type (shared) is supported to represent global data structures.

4.4 The configuration language layer

The PCFlib is based on the declaration of the structure of the parallel application in terms of PCF instances: the way the programmer can specify it is twofold. First, the user can declare explicitly the fact that a process belongs to a certain instance using the PCFlib primitives PCFInstanceIs() and InitializeInstances(). Second, the user can declare the full structure of its application using PCL (Parallel Configuration Language) a simple ad hoc configuration language to specify the PCF instances building a PCF application. The correct calls to the parallel PCFlib primitives will be automatically generated in a source C module (future developments will permit to generate also Fortran modules). This approach seems to be a good choice: algorithmic part, contained in the user source files, would be split from descriptive application structure concerns, contained in a separate description file. Also, this separation influences user's programming methodology to follow the programming discipline proposed in the PCF approach.

5 An example

In this chapter we illustrate an example of application developed and parallelized with PCF, taken from the ESPRIT Project Palace (PArallelization of a LArge CodE) [Eur94]. Geant [Cer93] code is a MonteCarlo program used to simulate the effects of radiation in matter. When nuclear radiation traverses matter, the initial energy is converted into new lower order energy radiations. One incoming particle can generate a large number of secondary particles. Each of the particles produced is indipendent from all the others. Each particle is followed along its path in the physical object under study. In the sequential code the initialization steps are followed by a production phase in which the primary interaction (event) is generated. Then a dedicated set of routines performs the simulation of the secondary interactions and finally the result of the simulation can be collected. One possible parallelization of the algorithm, decompose it into a mixture of Master Slave and Client Server instances, depicted in Figure 2.

A master process (Monitor) performs task scheduling and monitoring reading configuration files. In the second Master Slave instance, a producer process, after

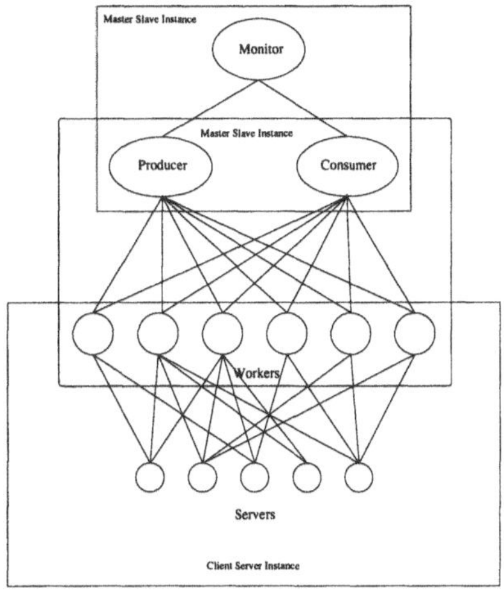

***Figure 2**: Application structure in terms of PCF instances*

the generation of the primary tracks, builds secondary track packets and begin a workload decomposition session using a set of workers. The workers receive the tracks from the producer and simulate their behaviour, calculating their paths and the relative involved physic charcteristics. A second Master Slave instance is made up by a consumer process and by the same workers and is useful to execute concurrently the simulation of secondary interactions with the collection phase of the computed tracks. The consumer process collects partial data and organizes them building the complete event. Worker processes are also client processes in a third instance (a Client Server one) asking for services furnished by a set of server processes during their simulation of the secondary interactions.

6 Conclusions and further developments

Actually Arnia library is available both with C and Fortran interfaces, excepted for the PCFlib, currently available only for C language. The Parallel Computational Frame approach to the development of parallel application is based on a detailed knowledge about the application structure. An automatic makefile generator, able to build a makefile schema from the information contained in the configuration file, enriches the environment. Moreover, the same information can be kept to develop a module which performs the mapping of the user processes on the underlined parallel architecture in order to minimize overhead communication time and optimize the communication bandwidth. Further developments will be the development of new parallel computational models (such as pipeline,and recursive models) and the development of a graphical interface for the configuration language (running on X Window environment) providing the user a more suitable way in the task of defining the application structure.

References

[Cer93] Cern Geneva. *Geant Users Guide*, 1993.

[Dar93] J. Darlington. Parallel programming using skeleton functions. In *Parallel Languages And Architectures, Europe: PARLE 1993*, 1993.

[Dec93] K. M. Decker. A knowledge-based scientific parallel programming environment. Technical report, Swiss Scientific Computing Center, 1993.

[Eur94] Eurosim 1994 International Conference. *Status Report on Esprit Project P7519 Palace*, 1994.

[Flo90] Jon Flower. *A packet History of Message Passing Systems.* Parasoft Corporation, 1990.

[Fox88] G. Fox. *Solving problems on concurrent processors.* Prentice Hall, 1988.

[Fru90] M. Fruscione. Arnia reference and user manuals. Advanced Computing Systems Milan, 1990.

[Hey89] A.J.G. Hey. Experiments in mimd parallelism. In Springer Verlag, editor, *PARLE 1989*, 1989.

[Hoa78] C.A.R. Hoare. Communicating sequential processes. *Communications of ACM*, 21(8), 1978.

[Kun89] H.T. Kung. *Scientific applications on multiprocessor*, chapter Computational models for parallel computers, page 1. Prentice Hall, 1989.

[Mei93] Meiko Ltd. *CSTools Reference Manual*, 1993.

[Oak93] OakRidge University. *PVM on line Referenece Manual*, 1993.

[Van91] M. Vanneschi. Language constructs for easy massively parallel computing. Technical report, Hewlett Packard Laboratories, 1991.

Programming Environments for Massively Parallel Distributed Systems, Monte Verità, Switzerland

A Knowledge-Based Scientific Parallel Programming Environment

Karsten M. Decker Jiri J. Dvorak
René M. Rehmann
CSCS–ETH Zurich
CH–6928 Manno, Switzerland
{decker,dvorak,rehmann}@cscs.ch

Abstract

Distributed memory parallel systems are still lacking simple and economic programmability, since, from the scientific programmer's point of view, first generation tools and environments for distributed memory parallel processor systems are largely insufficient. In this paper, we present an overview of our approach to parallel distributed programming environments overcoming these limitations: a knowledge-based problem-solving environment for programming parallel distributed systems. The environment features a problem-oriented specification formalism and is based on a skeleton-oriented programming methodology. The large set of fine-grain algorithmic skeletons used in the system is managed with a knowledge-based component. Skeletons are completed with computational components by means of automatic program synthesis techniques. We describe in detail a working prototype that, for the class of stencil-based problems, supports transparent programming of parallel distributed systems, while successfully addressing and solving some of the problems of performance, portability and software reuse.

1 Introduction

Parallel systems with distributed memory are difficult to program, since the programmer is requested to take full responsibility for the management of the distributed address space. This duty is not known from conventional systems, e.g. single-processor systems or multi-processor systems with shared memory.

First generation tools and tool environments developed over the last years (for a review see [Tur93]) did not yet succeed in overcoming this problem and make programming of distributed memory parallel processor systems as simple as programming of conventional systems. Existing tools can be criticized in several ways [DDR93]. Most notably, they were not developed in a user- and application-driven way. As a result, the tools were too complicated to use for non-computer scientists or non-specialists in parallel computing. Other problems with existing tools include lack of portability and scalability.

It is the purpose of this paper to propose, from the scientific programmer's point of view, a viable approach to solve the problem of programming parallel systems with distributed memory. The paper is based on a critical analysis of existing tools and tool environments and a detailed discussion of the profile and the requirements of the scientific programming community presented in [DDR93]. The design objectives underlying the system to be presented in this paper have also been deduced in [DDR93].

Section 2 presents an overview of our approach to parallel distributed programming environments: a knowledge-based problem-solving environment for the problem of programming parallel distributed systems based on a large set of fine-grain algorithmic skeletons organized and maintained in the central knowledge base. Besides the knowledge base, the system features a problem-oriented specification formalism to formulate the problems to be solved, and automatic program synthesis techniques to support generation of programs in a way transparent to the users. Section 3 describes a working prototype in detail that, for the class of stencil-based problems, supports transparent programming of parallel distributed systems while successfully addressing and solving the problems of performance, portability and software reuse. By means of a simple example, section 2.4 illustrates the different steps handled by the system, from the initial problem specification up to the generated code. Finally, section 4 summarizes the paper and discusses future developments.

2 A Knowledge-Based Parallel Programming Environment

2.1 Programming Methodology

To realize the objectives derived in [DDR93], a programming environment with user support starting much earlier in the program development path seems most appropriate [Kuc92]. The *Program Development Environment* (PDE) to be discussed subsequently covers important parts of the complete program development path from problem specification and design through to code generation. Emphasis is put on user interactions at a high level of abstraction, well above the level of standard high-level programming languages.

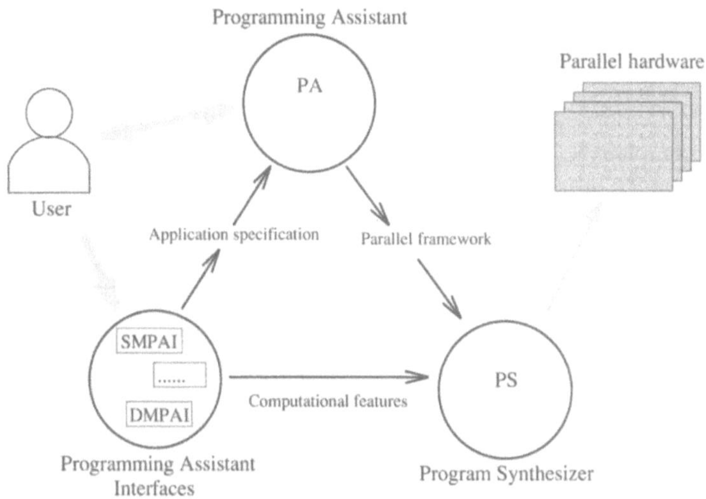

Figure 1: *The conceptual structure of the program development environment with programming assistant interfaces, programming assistant, and program synthesizer.*

The programming methodology supported by PDE consists of the following three steps:

1. Problem-oriented specification using a formal language
2. Interactive refinement and completion of the specification
3. User-transparent generation of compilable program code

From the scientific programmer's point of view, the problem-oriented specification language formalism is probably the most important ingredient of the methodology. It supports specification of the problem in a problem-oriented way, using a terminology which is derived from the terms used in the scientist's problem domain, and avoiding the jargon of computer science to a large extent. This strategy ensures that the programming methodology is readily managed by scientific users.

2.2 System Overview and Operation

The realization of the above programming methodology by means of three functional components is depicted in Figure 1.

In a typical session, the programmer gives an initial specification of the problem under consideration using one of the *Programming Assistant Interfaces* (PAIs). This specification is then decomposed into the purely computational features and the features relevant to the parallel structure. The first are passed directly to the *Program Synthesizer* (PS), and the latter go to the *Programming Assistant* (PA). The PA extracts the information needed to select an appropriate parallel framework. If the PA detects that the information available is incomplete, it queries the user to complete it. Functions and procedures that may be needed within the selected framework are also requested from the user. The PA is the central, largely AI-based component of the PDE, relying on expert knowledge about parallel programming, parallel hardware, software engineering, and the problem area. The parallel framework of the application, declarations, and references to functions to be generated or fetched from libraries are passed to the PS. The PS combines the computational features with the data received from the programming assistant into compilable, hardware specific, parallel C++ or C programs.

2.3 Restrictions on Problem Domain

To implement and test our parallel programming concept, we have chosen the domain of stencil-based computations for the first programming interface. A *stencil* is a local computation prescription that is usually iteratively executed for all members (*cells*) of multidimensional *grids*. On the one hand, this class of applications is of particular importance in high-performance computing, covering applications from many scientific disciplines. Examples are computational fluid dynamics, a large class of simulations, and image restoration and analysis. On the other hand, the domain is sufficiently restricted and regular to serve as an ideal initial testbed for the development of the programming environment. It can also be expected that by relaxing the restrictions and extending the specification formalism used in the programming interface for stencil-based problems, a development path to an interface covering increasingly more general data-parallel applications exists.

2.4 Description of the Functional Components

The following sections describe the functional components of the program development environment PDE. The capabilities of each component are illustrated with a particular example.

2.4.1 The Stencil Modeling Programming Assistant Interface

The *Stencil Modeling Programming Assistant Interface* (SMPAI) interfaces the PA and provides special support for the particular case of programming stencil-based problems. The graphical tool and the language allow specification of the problem type to be solved, the geometry of the problem domain, the size and dimensionality of the grids, the structure of a grid cell, the geometry of the relaxation stencil, a function for the boundary condition for each physical boundary of the grid, the data structure decomposition scheme, and the coloring scheme used for the grid.

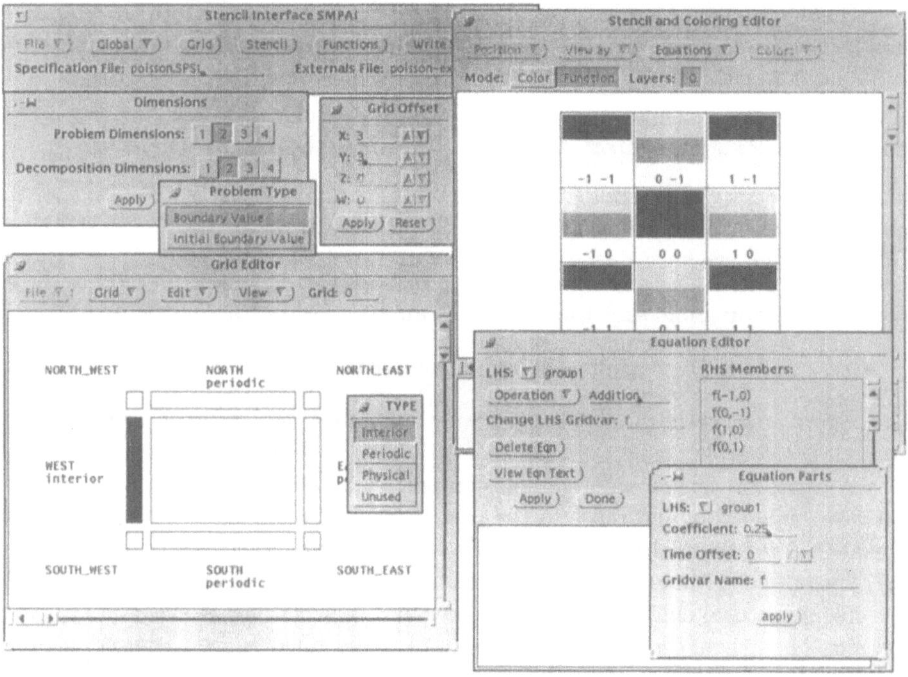

Figure 2: *Programming interface for stencil-based applications (SMPAI) that can be used for all applications relying on local, iterative computations on multidimensional grids.*

Figure 2 shows the users' view of the SMPAI. All relevant parts of the definition of a complete program for the solution of the Poisson equation using a 5-point stencil in two dimensions are at least partially visible. The important characteristic of such an abstract, domain-oriented problem specification is that the user gives only a declarative description of the problem. It is the tool that has complete control over the generation of the parallel algorithmic structure. The declarative problem specification provides a much more efficient and reliable basis for this task of parallelism extraction and exploitation than applications formulated in common programming languages. The generation of the parallel structure for the application is completely transparent to the programmer: there is no explicit mention of parallelism in any specification part.

Where the graphical means of specification reach their limits, e.g., when the problem domain has more than three dimensions, or when stencil functions go beyond the basic operations offered in the stencil editor, the user can add parts of the specification in textual form. The textual form is equivalent in concept to the graphical form and uses the same declarative, domain-oriented terms. Its full definition is given in [Rot93].

Finally, the SMPAI invokes a parser to verify the syntax of both the graphical and textual user input and produce a problem representation suitable for the subsequent steps.

2.4.2 The Programming Assistant: Finding the Right Skeleton

Our programming methodology relies fundamentally on a large collection of *algorithmic skeletons* forming the central knowledge base. A parallel distributed program in the program development environment is thus modeled:

- as an algorithmic skeleton serving as an integrating framework, and
- as a number of sequential computational components.

The algorithmic skeleton separates purely computational aspects of a program from all the complex aspects of parallelism.

Algorithmic skeletons or similar components have already been proposed for software engineering and reuse in the past [Wat82]. Cole [Col89] proposes the use of skeletons for parallel computation. He describes four skeletons that cover various types of algorithms. The basic idea underlying these approaches is to encode reusable structural characteristics of algorithms in skeletons. A skeleton typically contains open, i.e., *generic*, parts that have to be filled in by the user in order to adapt the skeleton to the given situation and to get a complete algorithm or algorithm part.

The initial task of the PA is to find a skeleton suitable as a parallel framework using information received from the SMPAI or other programming interfaces to be developed in the future. According to the requirements of this search task, the skeleton collection is organized as a tree-like hierarchy with unspecific skeletons at the top and most-specific skeletons at the leaf-level. Descending down the skeleton hierarchy, successively more aspects of the skeleton are elaborated and the applicability of the skeleton gets smaller. The process of selecting the skeleton most suitable for the problem under consideration is a rule-driven descent in this skeleton hierarchy, based on the initial problem specification given by the user. Expertise from the application domain as well as expertise in parallel processing and knowledge on the various hardware platforms is encoded in the rules that control this skeleton selection.

To illustrate the reasoning process with an example, the coloring specification given by the user is exploited to take one of the first decisions in the skeleton tree descent. The coloring scheme determines the basic control structure of the processes. The skeletons for problems using two-colored grids contain roughly the following algorithmic framework:

```
communicate data color 0
iterate till some termination criterion fulfilled
    communicate data color 1
    compute stencil at color 0
    communicate data color 0
    compute stencil at color 1
```

In this sense, the declarative description of the coloring scheme given by the user is exploited to generate such a parallel framework first and later need to generate the parallel code. The entities shown above, such as *communicate data*, are still very general, and other required parts are still missing. Descending further down the skeleton tree, other parts of the problem specification are subsequently employed to refine and complete the above framework. The stencil geometry and the types of boundary conditions for the grids, for example, are analyzed to expand the entity *communicate data* in a sequence of more specific data gather, exchange, and scatter steps. The following simple rule illustrates the process of stencil analysis:

```
(defrule STENCIL::stencil-extent-north
  ?inst <- (object (is-a stencil_prop_class)
                   (rhs_gridvars $? ?x $?)
                   (north_extent ?ext))
  (test (> (send ?x get-dim1) ?ext))
  =>
  (send ?inst put-north_extent (send ?x get-dim1)))
```

Matching all members of the attribute `rhs_gridvars`, which holds all previously extracted grid references of the stencil function, the maximum extent of the stencil in the north direction is determined. Based on this maximum extent, subsequent rules decide whether communication in the north direction is needed, what depth the northern boundary has, and what kind of communication is appropriate in this direction. Of course, the same scheme does not only work for the north direction, but it applies to all uni- and multidimensional communications.

Still later in the reasoning process, knowledge about hardware characteristics is used to determine the specific communication functions, e.g., selecting among blocking and non-blocking communication variants.

Using the SMPAI to define an application, the whole reasoning process and code generation is most likely to happen without further user interaction, provided suitable skeletons are present. This is due to the fact that the declarative problem description given by the user contains enough information to take all necessary decisions and steps within the reasoning process. However, such a high level of automation is not anticipated with programming interfaces handling less structured problem areas. To cope with unexpected situations or with situations where there is not enough information available to perform a complete descent, there are two ways of improving the general usability. First, the user is included in the reasoning process. If there is insufficient information for a particular decision, the expert system seeks to get the information through a user query formulated in an easily understandable way. Second, it is not necessary to descend down to the leaf level. The skeleton frame hierarchy is organized in such a way that information is stored as high as possible and inherited down the tree. In this respect, a frame at an intermediate level in the hierarchy represents a more coarse-grain skeleton than its descendants. It thus will either contain more open parts that have to be filled with user-provided code, or less efficiency can be expected from the resulting code. In the previous example, if the reasoning process would stop at the coloring level, which is very early in the whole process, the user would have to provide expansions for the abstract entities, such as *communicate data*, into statements, substituting for the otherwise automated generation. This code would probably run less efficiently, unless the user has good parallel programming and hardware expertise.

Currently, the PA generates a pseudo-code output for a general *master-slave model of computation* [DR92] and passes it to the program synthesizer. Parts of the output generated for the simple Poisson equation example are shown below. Some statements are slightly simplified for demonstration purposes.

```
FOR number_of_iterations DO
  FOR all_colors DO
    INTERACTION
      IF (not physical_boundary(grid, NORTH)) THEN
        fill_buf(grid, n_obuf, NORTH, color)
        exchange(s_ibuf, SOUTH, n_obuf, NORTH)
        scatter_buf(grid, s_ibuf, SOUTH, color)
      ENDIF

      (* ditto for any other communication directions ...  *)

    PHYSICAL_BC
      IF (physical_boundary(grid, NORTH)) THEN
        scatter_bc(grid, boundary_condition(NORTH), NORTH, color)
      ENDIF

      (* ditto for any other physical boundaries ...       *)

    CALCULATION
        update(grid, color)
```

This pseudo-code formalism used in the interface to the program synthesizer consists of four parts: declarations/definitions (not shown above), processor communications (`INTERACTION`), handling of physical grid boundaries (`PHYSICAL_BC`), and the computation of the stencil functions (`CALCULATION`). The above example is for a communication model with synchronous, blocking communications. Output can also be generated for other models, such as a non-blocking model where for efficiency reasons communications overlap with computations. In the non-blocking case, care has to be taken to start computations on subsets of the grid where no dependencies to communicated data exist.

As an important part of the complete code is generated automatically from the skeleton knowledge base, the PA presents a solution not only to parallel distributed programming, but also to portable software reuse at an abstract level.

2.4.3 The Program Synthesizer: Generation of Compilable Code

The pseudo-code mentioned above is then passed to one of the two components of the program synthesizer, called TINA [Gut93], which is developed at the University of Basle. TINA generates the process topology, the data distribution, the communication calls for various message-passing interfaces, and calls the computational components defined by the PA. TINA does not generate any code which is dependent on the grid structure of the problem domain, the coloring scheme or the boundary conditions defined by the user. These missing parts are generated by the second component of the program synthesizer developed at CSCS [Reh94]. This component gets an abstract definition of the computational units of the application and the definition of the grid structure, and from there generates the code of the function which calculates the user-defined stencil, the functions for filling and scattering the communication buffers from and to the grid, and the function calls for the various types of boundary conditions.

The result of the invocation of the two components of the program synthesizer is a complete compilable C-program including calls to a message passing interface library which solves the problem specified by the user.

3 Status

Three prototypes of the program development environment PDE have been realized [Dvo93]. All prototypes are running and present different aspects, such as top-down or bottom-up views, of the programming environment.

The first prototype serves primarily as a working specification of the PDE and contains a first attempt at a skeleton hierarchy, a skeleton tree browser, and a few rules reasoning about the current state of skeleton selection and completion. It is implemented using Common Lisp, the Common Lisp Object System CLOS, a self-developed hybrid AI tool and a comfortable GUI builder producing CLOS-based LispView code.

Whereas the first prototype presents a top-down, overall view of the PDE, the objective of the second prototype was to elaborate on the central part of the PDE, the programming assistant PA. Here, the PA is realized using mainly a bottom-up strategy. It is completely reimplemented using the CLIPS expert system shell [GR94] and C++ together with a GUI builder. Knowledge representation and inference techniques from artificial intelligence play major roles for the task of the PA. The PA of this prototype is complete in the sense of performing all important steps needed to select and complete an appropriate skeleton.

The organization of the skeleton hierarchy follows a systematic classification of the information received from the SMPAI. The decisions for subclassing correspond to concepts relevant to the generation of the parallel structure, with a decreasing importance from root to leaves. The most important criteria, i.e., the most discriminating information, are used for subclassification near the root of the skeleton hierarchy. Less important decisions are moved to the lower levels of the tree. The hierarchy contains skeletons mainly for stencil-based example applications and has an average depth of eight levels on average with an estimated final depth of around eleven levels. Figure 3 shows a view of the PA in use. The CLIPS interaction window and the skeleton tree browser window displaying the path from root node to the currently selected skeleton are shown.

The third prototype extends the second, bottom-up PA prototype towards a complete programming environment by integrating it with SMPAI, parser, PS, and a coherent graphical user interface. Demonstrator applications from a restricted subset of the domain (e.g., currently only one grid and at most two-dimensions) are supported from high-level graphical problem specification to completely automated generation of C code with communication calls for the PVM [GS91] library.

4 Summary and Future Developments

In this paper we have presented the design and implementation of a program development environment which is deduced from analysis of the requirements of scientific programmers, or in more general terms, computational scientists. This analysis has led to a programming methodology comprising a problem-oriented specification formalism, interactive refinement and completion of the specification, and a user-transparent generation of compilable program code. Tool support for this methodology centers around a knowledge-based system with a skeleton-based approach to the reuse of important software parts and to portability across different platforms.

The current PA and PS prototypes do not provide detailed target architecture dependent optimization of the communication steps. To achieve this, the next PA prototype will be supplemented by a hardware knowledge base. Other limitations of the existing PDE, such as the restriction to a single grid with at most two dimensions will be removed.

Besides that, we are investigating the definition of other programming assistant interfaces which either will cover more general problem specification paradigms, such as an interface for data-parallel applications, or will support other scientific problem domains relevant to high-performance computing.

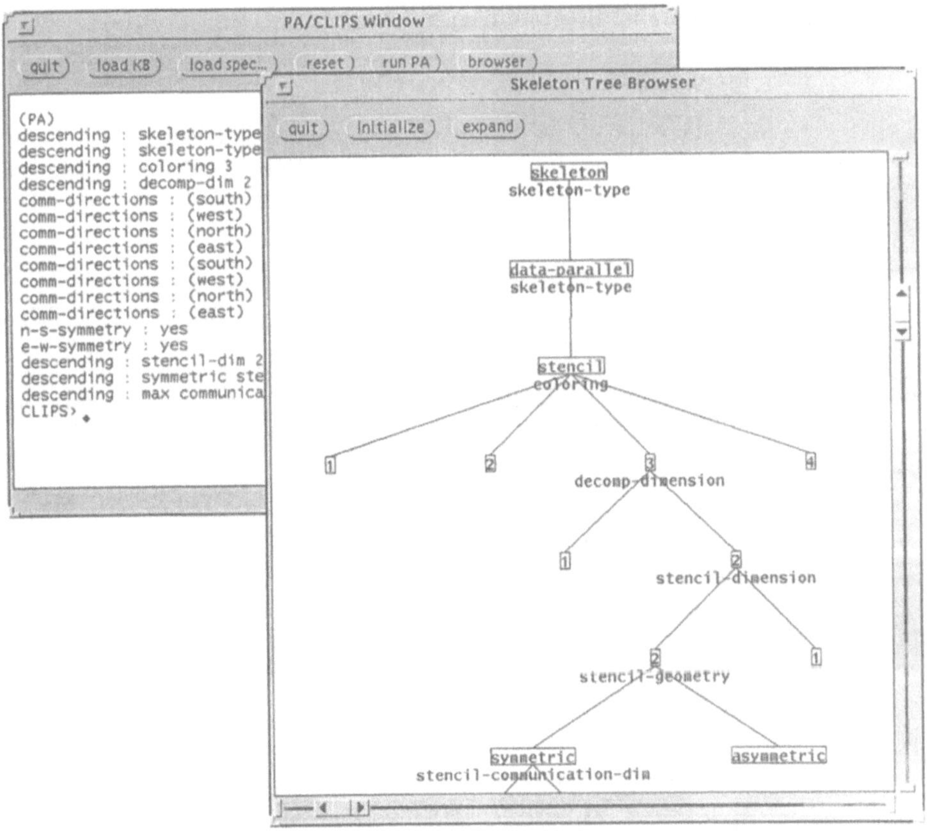

Figure 3: *CLIPS and browser windows. In the skeleton tree, the framed labels contain the specialization value, the labels below the nodes hold the criterion for the next specialization.*

Acknowledgment. The project is funded by the Swiss National Science Foundation in the framework of the Swiss Priority Program Informatics, Grant-No. SPPIF-5009-034402. Additional funding has been received from SNF Grant-No. 20-33949.92.

References

[Col89] M. Cole. *Algorithmic Skeletons: Structured Management of Parallel Computation.* Research Monographs in Parallel and Distributed Computation. The MIT Press, Cambridge, MA, USA, 1989.

[DDR93] K. M. Decker, J. J. Dvorak, and R. M. Rehmann. A Knowledge-Based

Scientific Parallel Programming Environment. Technical Report CSCS-TR-93-07, Centro Svizzero di Calcolo Scientifico, Via Cantonale, CH-6928 Manno, Switzerland, December 1993.

[DR92] K. M. Decker and R. M. Rehmann. Simple and Efficient Programming of Parallel Distributed Systems for Computational Scientists. Technical Report IAM-92-019, IAM, University of Berne, Switzerland, October 1992.

[Dvo93] J. J. Dvorak. An AI-based Approach to Massively Parallel Programming. Technical Report CSCS-TR-93-04, Centro Svizzero di Calcolo Scientifico, Manno, Switzerland, August 1993.

[GR94] J. Giarratano and G. Riley. *Expert Systems: Principles and Programming.* PWS Publishing, Boston, MA, USA, 2nd. edition, 1994.

[GS91] G. A. Geist and V. S. Sunderam. The PVM system: Supercomputing level concurrent computations on a heterogeneous network of workstations. *Sixth Distributed Memory Computing Conference Proceedings*, pages 258–261, April/May 1991.

[Gut93] S. E. Gutzwiller. *Werkzeuge und Methoden des skelettorientierten Programmierens von Parallelrechnern.* PhD thesis, University of Basle, Switzerland, November 1993. In German.

[Kuc92] D. J. Kuck. A User's View of High-Performance Scientific and Engineering Software Systems in the Mid-21st Century. In J. R. Rice E. N. Houstis and R. Vichnevetsky, editors, *Expert Systems for Scientific Computing*, pages 69–87. Elsevier Science Publishers, 1992.

[Reh94] R. M. Rehmann. Automatic Generation of Programs for a Scientific Parallel Programming Environment. Technical Report CSCS-TR-94-02, Centro Svizzero di Calcolo Scientifico, Manno, Switzerland, May 1994. To be published.

[Rot93] M. Roth. Generation of Algorithmic Skeletons from Stencil Specifications. Master's thesis, IAM, University of Berne, Switzerland, May 1993. In German.

[Tur93] L. H. Turcotte. A Survey of Software Environments for Exploiting Networked Computing Resources. Technical report, Engineering Research Center for Computational Field Simulation, USAE Waterways Experiment Station, Vicksburg, MS, June 1993.

[Wat82] R. C. Waters. The Programmer's Apprentice: Knowledge Based Program Editing. *IEEE Transaction on Software Engineering*, SE-8(1):1–12, January 1982.

Programming Environments for Massively Parallel Distributed Systems, Monte Verità, Switzerland

Parallel Distributed Algorithm Design Through Specification Transformation: The Asynchronous Vision System

Didier Buchs* Daniel Monteiro† Fabrice Mourlin‡
Denis Brunet†

1 Introduction

The main purpose of this paper is to introduce, through the case study of a new class of general approach of vision processing, the use of formal techniques to model complex concurrent systems using abstract specification. Moreover, we want to show that it is possible to derive implementations on parallel machines by specification transformation. The implementation is derived from the abstract specification by introducing concrete aspects of the realization, for instance the algorithms used to distribute the global knowledge of time, producing a concrete specification. The CO-OPN (Concurrent Object Oriented Petri Nets) language [4,5] is used to model both specifications, the abstract one and the concrete one. This example proves the wide spectrum of application that can be modelled using CO-OPN. CO-OPN is supported by a complete environement called SANDS (Structured Algebraic Net Development System) including a graphical editor, a compiler, a temporal logic prover and a simulator [5]. The concrete specification is used for producing the code for the parallel machine, in our case a transputer machine. The idea of developing a vision system in a modular fashion has already been raised by many authors [1]. Anatomical, physiological and psychological studies show that despite separation and specialization of visual processing, common underlying principles and mechanisms seem to apply. Moreover if modules are casted from the same mold, reusability can significantly save development time. The goal of this work is not to propose a universal vision system, but rather to investigate promising concepts. One of these is the active use of time [3] in desynchronizing data in a specific way in order to improve the various processings. A second concept is

*LGL-DI, Swiss Federal Institute of Technology, 1015 Lausanne, Suisse, Didier.Buchs@di.epfl.ch
†CUI, Université de Genêve, 24 rue du général Dufour, 1211 Genêve, Suisse
‡LRI, Bat. 490, Université de Paris Sud, 91405 Orsay, France

to group pieces of information in more and more elaborated ones [1]. Continous components of the abstract vision model are discretized into an user defined small amount of interaction zones. The implementation must incorporates more concrete features than the abstract specification, for instance in order to eliminate the explicit reference of time. A distributed algorithm has been defined that distribute the time reference, preserving the logical causallity between the forward and the backward flow of information.

2 The specification language: CO-OPN

As the goal of this paper is not to introduce a specification language, the description of the specification language we will use, CO-OPN, will be brief and presented in an intuitive way. Interested readers can find complete and detailed description of this language in [4,5]. The project CO-OPN has been developed in order to propose a formal specification language for the design of large parallel systems. This aim is reached by using a modular specification language combined with Petri Nets. More precisely, the CO-OPN objects are interconnected modular entities described by algebraic nets. In fact, CO-OPN is based on two simple and elegant concepts, algebraic data types [7] and Petri nets, gathered into a more general model, algebraic nets [9]. Although algebraic nets are an important improvement of Petri nets, they are quite useless when facing to large problems. Therefore, some facilities has been included in the CO-OPN model, including: standard constructors on data types,iterators on algebraically specified arrays, structuring capabilities. Both abstract data type and the theory of algebraic specification find their origin in the impossibility to manage and to develop large software system without methods and tools. Before going deeper in details we need to introduce some terminology. An abstract data type is the representation of a data structure coupled with a set of operations that manipulate this data structure independently (data type) of any particular implementation (abstract). The algebraic approach to specification considers a system in terms of abstract data types represented, in the mathematical discourse, by many-sorted algebra together with axioms or equations. An algebra is simply a domain provided with a set of operations.

Petri nets and algebraic nets

Petri nets are used to modelize and analyse discrete systems in which notions such as interacting components, concurrency and synchronization play a key role. Petri net modelization embeds both the structural aspect of the system and its evolution. Systems are modelled through the use of places and transitions. Their behavior is described using rules including pre and post conditions on the states. We use the following textual convention: $transition : condition \Rightarrow pre \rightarrow post$ The use of tokens with an internal structure greatly increase the modelling power of Petri nets. Structured tokens give an insight into the way data structures evolve during the system running and many aspects of the modelization are described in a more accurate and concise manner. The evolution of the structured tokens are specified by rules of the underlying formalism used to represent these tokens. By its abstractness and soundness, algebraic specifications turn out to be well-suited for this purpose. The high-level nets obtained by describing structured tokens in the algebraic framework are called algebraic nets [9].

The CO-OPN formalism

A CO-OPN specification is composed of objects described by algebraic Petri nets, in which transitions are classified into two classes: the methods representing the external accesses and the internal transitions representing the reactions of the object, and a synchronization mechanism linking these nets together. These synchronisation mechanism are defined in order to keep object state encapsulation, allowing us to specify independently each object. The language CO-OPN has a textual and a graphical equivalent notation, both notations are used in the rest of the paper. Some examples for the use of CO-OPN can be found in [5]. Some properties are formalized within the CO-OPN framework [4], such as the equivalence allowing to refine an abstract CO-OPN specification by progressively replacing abstract object and specification by more concrete ones.

3 The abstract specification of the vision system

This section shortly describes the main components of the vision system using CO-OPN objects and algebraic specifications. The figure 1 shows the generic objects used in the vision system and their relation to the instance object such as the Timer. One concrete specification is composed with instances derived from these generic objects. Moreover, algebraic specification describing for instance the tokens of the vision system are based on primitive types such as Bool, Nat not described here. The evolution of the system is based on a time model, each token evolves in the system according to the time evolutions which is modelled by discrete values. The reference of time is given by the object Timer. This object provides two services, the time is incremented after activating the method tick and the current time value is given when activating the method gettime. Concurrent access to gettime and tick is allowed although the method gettime is not auto-concurrent and the its access is sequentialized.

```
object Timer;
use Time,Bool;
places tickcount:[bool]; currenttime:[time];
methods tick; gettime:time;
internal incr;
axioms
axtick: tick :: => -> tickcount([b]);
```

```
axgettime: gettime(t):: => currenttime([t]) -> currenttime([t]);
axincr: incr::  => tickcount([b]) , currenttime([t])
                  -> currenttime([succ(t)]);
marking currenttime([zero]);
where b:bool; t:time;
end
```

The channel description

A channel looks like a bidirectionnal communication buffer into a producer consumer system. In fact its internal protocol is much more complex. In order to be able to model a channel with a sequence of interactions between the tokens, the continous interactions are modelled by discrete ones. A channel is decomposed into slices connected by channel processors, each slice representing one point of interaction. The interaction, in a slice, is made between the outgoing forward token and the other tokens staying into the slice. The result of an interaction is a token staying into the slice. A channel must only know the first and the last slice of this sequence which are given by the parameter object sliceleft and sliceright.

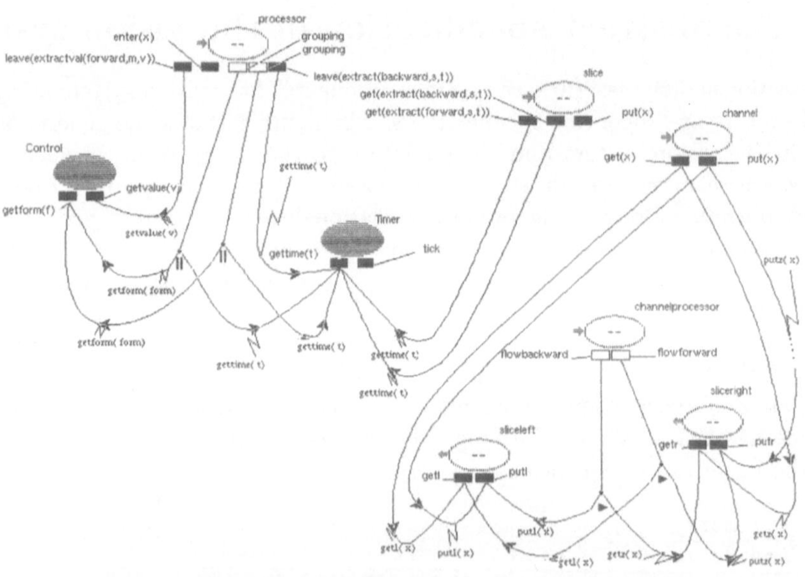

Figure 1: *The interconnection of the generic objects (white ovals) slice, processor and channel to the instance object (grey ovals) Timer and the parameter objects sliceleft or sliceright. The arcs between methods (black rectangles) represent the synchronization expressions.*

```
generic object channel(sliceleft, sliceright);
use Messages, sliceleft, sliceright;
methods put:message; get:message;
axioms
  ax1put: put(x) with putl(x)::whichdirection(x) = forward => -> ;
  ax2put: put(x) with putr(x)::whichdirection(x) = backward =>->;
  ax1get: get(x) with getr(x)::whichdirection(x) = forward => -> ;
  ax2get: get(x) with getl(x)::whichdirection(x) = backward =>->;
where x:message;
end
```

3.1 Simulation on the SANDS environment

The development of such a large application needs the assistance of a tool including simulation, analysis and debugging facilicilities. The CO-OPN language is supported by the SANDS environement allowing to perform such kind of activities. Furthermore, due to the modular nature of the CO-OPN formalism it is possible to partially explore and analyze, module by module, the behavior of an application. The simulation in SANDS is performed by interpreting the generated Prolog code.

4 The distributed algorithm

4.1 Construction of the distributed coherent time algorithm

We are interrested to elaborate a stable global property, the causal time consistency, of a set of distributed processes through the definition of a distributed algorithm. This property must be maintained during the whole life of the application which end when no communication can occur. The application is made of processes that can be either grouping processors or slices. The slices collect tokens and form a chain. The grouping processors can have several slices as left or right neighbours, they includes also tokens. The processes communicate through message passing along communication channels. Any process of the system knows its left and right neighbors.

Structure of the solution

We use the wave principle [10] to find a unique global time to the nodes of the system, it is the minimum of next moving time of the tokens of the slices and the grouping processors. Two waves are necessary to compute this minimum. The first one, the analysis wave, collecting the information of the processes from the left to the right and the second one, the distributing wave, giving the result to all processes in the opposite direction. Starting with the unstructured topology of the vision system we build a system with two new processes: the Feeder on the left and the Consumer on the right of the oriented topology. All processes without left neighbor are connected to the Feeder and all processes without right neighbors are connected to the Consumer. The analysis wave is initiated by the Feeder and arrives to the Consumer after visiting all the nodes. The message transmitted to the right neighbor contains the minimum token time collected during all previous visits. The distributing wave is initiated by the Consumer after receiving all the message comming from the analysis wave. It gives to all processes the minimum time collected by the analysis wave. It must be noted that launching the analysis and distributing waves is a repetitive process which ends when the minimum does not increase.

5 Implementation of the Distributed Algorithm

The abstract algorithm must be introduced into the initial formal specification. The global structure of the specification and the signatures of all components will not be changed, nevertheless the internal behavior of the slices and processors will include the new algorithms. In order to deal with synchronization different kinds of modifications will be made: the inclusion of local behavior modelling the phases of the algorithm and an encapsulation of messages into new sorts modelling the two waves (analysis and distribution wave);the inclusion of the analysis wave initiating the algorithm into the 'Feeder' object and terminating the algorithm into the 'Consumer' object; the inclusion of the distribution wave initiating the algorithm into the 'Consumer' object terminating the algorithm into the 'Feeder' object. Due to the lack of space it is not possible to explain the transformation techniques introducing the algorithms, in [2] the treatment of the vision problem is fully described while in [6] CO-OPN transformation language and tools are also explain. The implementation on parallel machine was a direct translation of the concrete specification into the parrallel C language availlable on our network of transputer (VOLVOX machine) [2].

References

[1] D. Marr. Vision. W.H. Freeman and Co., 1982.

[2] D. Monteiro. *Etude, spécification et implantation sur machine ripartie d'un système modulaire de vision.* Diplôme en Informatique, Université de Genêve, Novembre 1993.

[3] D. Brunet and T. Pun. *A modular architecture for asynchronous visual processing.* Swiss Vision, Sept. 1993.

[4] D. Buchs, N. Guelfi. *CO-OPN: A Concurrent Object Oriented Petri Net Approach.* 12th International Conference on theory and application of Petri Nets, Aahrus, pp. 432-454, 1991.

[5] D. Buchs, J. Flumet, P. Racloz. *SANDS/CO-OPN Structured Algebraic Net Development System* Petri Nets Tool Presentation, 1993 Chicago.

[6] Buffo M. Transformations: théorie et outils. 1993, Cahier du CUI No 78, Université de Genêve.

[7] H. Ehrig and B. Mahr. *Fundamentals of algebraic specification 1: equations and initial semantics.* 1985, EATCS Monographs, Springler Verlag.

[8] B. Krieg-Brückner. PROgram development by SPECification and TRAnsformation. Article in TSI 9(2).

[9] Reisig W. *Petri nets and algebraic specifications.* 1991, in Theoretical computer science 80.

[10] Raynal M. *Networks and distributed computation: concepts tools and algorithms.* London, North Oxford academic, 1987.

Programming Environments for Massively Parallel Distributed Systems, Monte Verità, Switzerland

Steps Towards Reusability and Portability in Parallel Programming*

Helmar Burkhart Stephan Gutzwiller
Informatics Department
University of Basel, Switzerland
{burkhart,gutzi}@ifi.unibas.ch

Abstract

Skeleton-oriented programming is a new technique that aims towards reusability of software components in massively parallel systems. Carefully tested and efficiently implemented coordination schemes and data distributions are collected in a library of algorithmic skeletons. Programmers inspect the library, access the appropriate element and fill in the application-dependent parts. Our approach has several benefits, such as improved portability, reusability, and correctness of software.

After a short introduction, we summarize BACS (Basel Algorithm Classification Scheme) and present a sample algorithm. Next, we introduce TINA, the skeleton generator, and describe the basics of its script input language. We sketch our implementation testbed and report on measurements done in a transputer environment. Finally, we conclude with some remarks on the project state and related work.

1 Introduction

One challenge in software development is the software factory, i.e. the availability of building blocks that may be reused. We cannot expect that complete application programs are reusable, because – even in the same problem domain – there are always slight differences, e.g., different input/output formats. We can, though, expect to get reusable components for the coordination part of a parallel program, because real-world applications are quite regular regarding the process structure. Our current research has shown that only a small number of coordination schemes are used in algorithms and applications. On massively parallel systems this trend is emphasized because hundreds or thousands of different processes cannot possibly be managed individually. The percentage of code for the coordination part is

*This research is funded by the Swiss National Science Foundation, research grant SPP IF 5003-34357: "Skeleton-Oriented Programming".

definitely much smaller compared to the computation part; but it is the crucial part. It is this portion of code that we will make reusable by providing a library of algorithmic skeletons. We call this approach *skeleton-oriented programming (SOP).*

Our research work combines aspects of portability and algorithmic reusability and aims towards a machine-independent classification and description of parallel algorithms. By supporting the most common parallel computation schemes on the most widely distributed virtual machine models and computation languages, we intend to improve the programmer's situation.

Many research projects emphasize the need for more "programming tools". There is no doubt that tools are needed to develop parallel processor software; however, first a methodology and a framework have to defined before tool developments can start.

2 BACS and a Sample Algorithm

While several classifications for computer architectures have been proposed and some of those are really used (for example Flynn's taxonomy), widely accepted classifications for parallel algorithms do not exist. The few approaches that can be found in literature are either too simple, too close to the hardware, or too theoretical.

During the last year, BACS [1] has been defined at the Basel Parallel Processing Laboratory. BACS should provide a basic classification and description methodology allowing to build a programming environment.

2.1 BACS Summary

Parallel algorithms can be regarded as a collection of processes consisting of different building blocks:

Process and Data Management (daemon call): Services that belong to this category are process administration (creation and deletion), as well as data binding. All these operations are managed by an entity we call daemon; daemon functions can be implemented at the programming level, operating system level, and hardware level, respectively.

Interaction: Interactions define the coordination of the processes at runtime. Coordination operations are used for data exchange, signalling of events, and for consistency purposes.

Calculation: These consist of all statements that do computations; for example arithmetic operations, bookkeeping operations, and local data access.

Control structures: Finally the three previous items are controlled by sequence, loop, and conditional statements, respectively.

In BACS we refine this list and end up with a generic description tuple which fully characterizes a parallel algorithm (Figure 1). The tuple itself is structured into process attributes, data attributes, and interactions. Most of the tuple elements are described and structured by hierarchical representations that are extensible. As we will later see, concrete algorithms are represented by tuples for which all fields are filled with corresponding items.

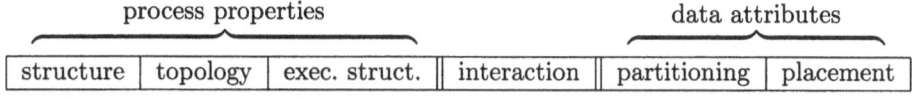

process properties				data attributes	
structure	topology	exec. struct.	interaction	partitioning	placement

Figure 1: *Tuple for the classification of parallel algorithms*

Process structure: We distinguish between static and dynamic process structures. An algorithm is called static if the daemon is only called at the beginning (to create all processes) and at the end (to delete them), but not during the execution of the actual algorithm. Today, static algorithms are dominating the field.

Process topology: This component defines the geometric structure of the process set. We concentrate on regular topologies, which split into homogeneous topologies (all processes have identical instructions) and inhomogeneous ones (at least two processes have different operations; e.g., master-worker relationship).

Execution structure: While the two previous elements define static process attributes, this component describes the dynamic behaviour. We are only interested in regular execution patterns (multiphase structures).

Interactions: The purpose of interactions has already been mentioned. BACS identifies direct interactions which exactly link two process nodes, and global interactions involving several processes which coordinate their activities by means of anonymous synchronization elements (e.g., mailbox) or signals to process groups (e.g., broadcast).

Data partitioning: For distributed data it is important to know how they are partitioned. Arrays for example can be partitioned into elements, rows, columns, and blocks, respectively.

Data placement: This component defines the binding of processes and data. Local data are private to a process, while non-local data can either be global (all processes can have access), be interaction data (data explicitly used for interactions), be static or dynamically placed data.

The next subsection presents an example that should clarify these concepts.

2.2 LU-Decomposition

The LU-decomposition algorithm transforms a nonsingular matrix A into a lower triangular matrix L and a upper triangular matrix U, such that

$$A = L \times U$$

If L und U are known, systems of linear equations can be computed more efficiently.

The matrix A is rowwise distributed in a cyclic scheme (because of workload balancing). The parallel algorithm eliminates for each column all elements below the main diagonal element and replaces the generated zero values by the elements of matrix L. Thus, both L and U are stored within matrix variable A. The BACS tuple description is shown in Figure 2.

Process attributes

Structure	Topology	Execution structure
static	Worker	$Fix_w(I_{bcst}, C^p)$

Interactions
{Broadcast}

Data attributes

Partitioning	Distribution
A[n,n](1,p),(1,p),(None,Cyclic)	

***Figure 2**: Classification tuple of LU-decomposition*

As the process structure does not change during execution, it is static. The topology used is a set of workers, interacting with each other by means of a broadcast facility.

With the basic operations *Calculation, Interaction* and *Daemon Calls*, as well as the basic structures *Sequence, Loop* and *Selection* for composition, the execution structure of the LU algorithm may be written as

$$FIX_w(I_{bcst}, C^p)$$

i.e. a vector will be sent by one of a set of processes to all the others (broadcast interaction I_{bcst}) be performed by a process group (C^p)[1]. This happens a fixed number of times and the processes form a uniform set of workers for this action (FIX_w – the subscript w refers to the set of workers).

The data used is the matrix, which is partitioned into rows. These are placed at the beginning by the daemon (static placement) on the worker processes. The rows may be placed in blocks as well as cyclic.

[1]A superscript p indicates that only a partial set of processes is active; if all processes participate, an index t is used instead.

Partitioning and placement are specified using several parameters:

A[n,n] represents the n×n matrix. *"(1, p) , (1, p)"* is the partitioning specification, *"(None, Cyclic)"* the distribution specification. As a result, the rows of the matrix A are distributed among p processes in a cyclic order.

3 Skeleton Generator TINA

We have designed and implemented a skeleton generator, called TINA, that supports both reusability and portability of parallel program components.

As a programmer you have to provide TINA the following information:

- The algorithmic core of the program in mind: The BACS tuple information provides a first, coarse grain view of the algorithm. However it is too informal in order to be useable as input for a program generator tool. Therefore, we refine these concepts towards a formal description language.
- The parallel virtual machine and the programming language for which code shall be generated.

3.1 Input script

The input script is structured into three parts:

General informations: The first part reports on

- Name of the algorithm
- Virtual machine
- Programming language
- Process topology
- Interaction mechanisms

For the LU-decomposition example, the script information is shown in Figure 3:

```
NAME:             "lu-decomposition-kij";
MACHINE:          EXPRESS;
LANGUAGE:         C;
PROCESS_TOPOLOGY: STATIC Worker(p);
INTERACTIONS:     Broadcast;
%%
```

***Figure 3**: Part 1 of LU script*

Declarations: Part 2 of the script consists of several algorithm-dependent declarations:

- Data types
- Variables
- Function prototypes

It is important to notice that for each topology, several variables are implicitly introduced. For instance, for a mesh topology the variables p (total number of processes), px/py (number of processes per row/column), me (private process number), north/east/south/west (identifications of processes in the relevant direction) are defined.

Part 2 of the LU script (Figure 4) introduces the matrix variable A, the line buffer *line* for a matrix row to be broadcasted, and some local variables. For the matrix variable, partitioning and distribution information is given according the BACS classification tuple. Two functions are declared that are later filled in by the programmer: PrepareElimination and Eliminate.

```
TYPES:                     double matrix(n,n);
                           double buffer(n);
GLOBAL_VARIABLES:          ;
DISTRIBUTED_VARIABLES:     matrix A STATIC(NONE,CYCLIC,1,p,1,p)\INOUT;
                           buffer line STATIC (NONE, 1, 1)\TEMP;
INTERACTION_VARIABLES:     buffer bcst_buffer;
LOCAL_VARIABLES:           long sender, global_k, global_i;
FUNCTION_PROTOTYPES:       PrepareElimination(POINTER, POINTER);
                           Eliminate();
%%
```

Figure 4: *Part 2 of LU script*

Execution structure: Finally, the third part, called frame, defines the overall execution structure (Figure 5). For LU there is a For-loop in which each row is broadcasted to all other processes such that they can execute their local elimination computations in parallel. As the frame reveals, parallel elimination is precisely controlled. All processes execute the global_i loop, but elimination only takes place when the OwnIMatrix-function returns true, ie. processes only operate on their distribution chunks.

3.2 TINA Basics

The basic design decision has been to build up a support library in which parametrized text pieces (called templates) are collected.

```
FRAME:
  FOR (global_k = 0; global_k < n-1; global_k++) DO
    INTERACTION
      PrepareElimination (bcst_buffer, sender);
      Broadcast (bcst_buffer, sender)
    END;
    CALCULATION
      FOR (global_i = global_k+1; global_i < n; global_i++) DO
        IF (OwnIMatrix(A, global_i, *)) THEN
          Eliminate()
        ENDIF
      ENDFOR
    END
  ENDFOR.
```

***Figure 5**: Part 3 of LU script*

TINA concatenates these templates according to the input script specification and substitutes all parameter information.

Figure 6 gives a pictorial view of the processing. In the first step, all parameter information is generated by analyzing the script. In the second step, the relevant templates are imported, filled with the parameter data, and the program skeleton is generated. It is important to notice that TINA has been designed to support several virtual machines (and programming languages). This is achieved by supporting a template library for the different choices. The current prototype generates C source code for Express, PVM, and a subset of MPI.

TINA generates a skeleton program which is split into several files. The prototype implementation is based on a host-node model; so separate files for the host and the nodes, as well as common data files are generated.

As the programmer has to provide the algorithm-specific part (eg., calculations) it is essential to guide him/her during this process. Therefore, a detailled report is generated that tells the programmer where to fill in missing information.

3.3 Implementation Testbed

TINA itself runs on a NeXT workstation.

It has been implemented by using the Lex and Yacc translator tools of Unix. The workstation is interfaced to a 486 PC via NFS, such that the transfer of skeleton source files can easily be managed. The PC serves as a host system for the 16-node transputer network. Both the PC and the transputers modules (T805 with 8 MB RAM each) have the system software Express installed. Express is a virtual parallel machine consisting of about 75 basic functions (process creation, deletion, message transfer functions, global combine operations etc.) and a few tools for

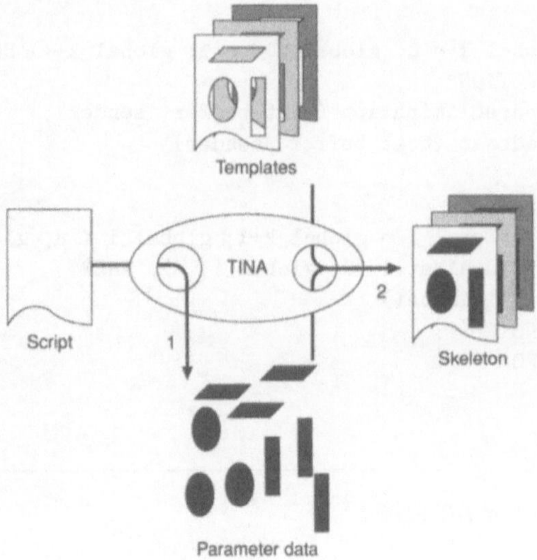

Figure 6: *TINA execution flow*

debugging and tuning of programs. Express offers two operation modes: Cubix-Mode allows parallel input/output while Host-Node mode restricts input/output to the host system. Our experiments have been made using the host-node mode.

3.4 Results for LU-decomposition

Because of space restrictions we cannot refer to the generated skeleton code. TINA generates a skeleton file consisting of 430 lines C code. The programmer has to write just another 24 lines of application-dependent source code in order to get an executable version for the LU-decomposition. If the programmer wants to switch to a PVM environment, for instance, it is sufficient to replace "EXPRESS" by "PVM" in part 1 of script. All other modifications are automatically done by TINA, and C skeleton source files for PVM are generated.

TINA favours algorithmic experiments with parallel programs. For instance, in the LU example we are interested in performance values for increasing matrix dimensions. Figure 7 shows the speedup values measured on the transputer system.

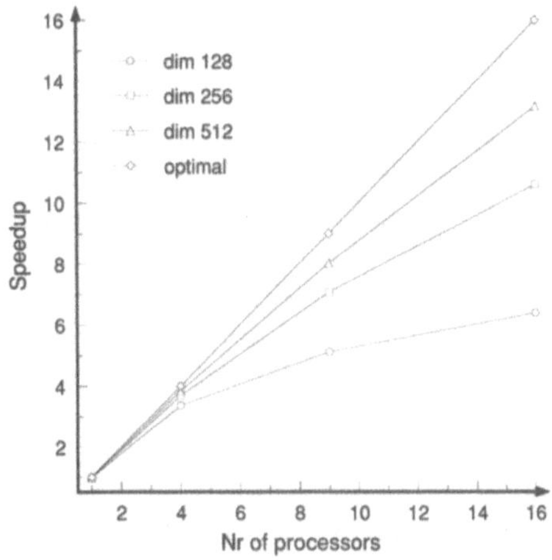

Figure 7: *Speedup LU-decomposition*

4 Project State

We have reported on a project that is still under development. The TINA prototype has been successful for delivering early experience regarding the practicability of the approach (for further details see [2]). The script language as well as some implementation aspects are under major revision.

The algorithm base needs to be broadened. Within the Swiss Priority Programme for Informatics we have a collaboration to link our system to an environment where application-specific descriptions are used [3].

Further research projects at our laboratory are related to the work presented in this paper. YAPPE (Yet Another Parallel Programming Environment) is a LINDA-based parallel programming environment for master-worker algorithms using the BACS data mapping primitives [4]. ParStone is a synthetic benchmark for parallel processor systems using algorithmic skeletons [5].

All major High Performance Computing initiatives currently emphasize the importance of cost-effective software production for parallel systems. In fact we think that this is the real Grand Challenge, because today's techniques and tools are at a rather poor level. We have presented concepts and a research direction towards software reusability. As our work is based on widely distributed virtual machine models and programming languages, external users will benefit from our results.

5 Related Work

Reusability is a "hot topic" in software engineering. The number of papers is immense; we refer to [6] for a survey of the state-of-the-art.

For parallel programming, the idea of skeletons has been reported in the thesis of Cole [7]. He, Rabhi, Skillicorn, and the authors of [8] have concentrated on the functional paradigm, however. These and other references can be found in the proceedings of the Leeds [9] and Berlin [10] conferences, respectively.

The P4 methodology (P3L language and P3M machine model) developed at the University of Pisa addresses portability and abstract machine issues.

P.B. Hansen has published a set of examples that serve as model programs for parallel programming [11].

While most of the virtual machines ignore the data aspect, the VMMP environment [12] as well as the High Performance Fortran Forum discuss data partitioning and distribution primitives.

[13] presents concepts and an environment based on object-oriented technology.

Acknowledgements

The list of past and present laboratory members includes Helmar Burkhart, Carlos Falcó Korn, Niandong Fang, Robert Frank, Stephan Gutzwiller, Guido Hächler, Walter Kuhn, Peter Ohnacker, Jean-Daniel Pouget, Gerald Pretot, and Stephan Waser.

References

[1] Helmar Burkhart, Carlos Falco Korn, Stephan Gutzwiller, Peter Ohnacker, and Stephan Waser. BACS: Basel Algorithm Classification Scheme. Technical Report 93-3, Institut für Informatik, University of Basel, Switzerland, March 1993.

[2] Stephan Gutzwiller. Methoden und Werkzeuge des skelettorientierten Programmierens. PhD thesis, University of Basel, to appear 1994 (in german).

[3] K. M. Decker, J. J. Dvorak, and R. M. Rehmann. A Knowledge-Based Scientific Parallel Programming Environment. IFIP Working Conference WG10.3 on Programming Environments for Massively Parallel Distributed Systems, 1994.

[4] Jean-Daniel Pouget. YAPPE – Eine tupelorientierte Programmierumgebung für Parallelrechner. PhD thesis, University of Basel, June 1993 (in german).

[5] Stephan Waser. Benchmarking Parallel Computers. PhD thesis, University of Basel, July 1993.

[6] C. Krueger. Software Reuse. *ACM Computing Surveys*, 24(2):131-183, 1992.

[7] M. Cole. *Algorithmic Skeletons: Structured Management of Parallel Computation.* MIT Press, Cambridge, Massachusetts, 1989.

[8] J. Darlington, A. Field, P. Harrison, P. Kelly, D. Sharp, and Q. Wu. Parallel Programming Using Skeleton Functions. Proc. 5th Int Conf PARLE, 146-160, Springer, 1993.

[9] Workshop on *Abstract Machine Models for Highly Parallel Computers.* Leeds, April 1993, Oxford Univ. Press.

[10] Conference on *Massively Parallel Programming Models.* Berlin, September 1993.

[11] P. B. Hansen. Model Programs for Computational Science: A Programming Methodology for Multicomputers. *Concurrency – Practice and Experience.* Jan 1993.

[12] E. Gabber. VMMP: A Practical Tool for the Development of Portable and Efficient Programs for Multiprocessors. IEEE Trans. on Parallel and Distributed Systems, 1(3), July 1990.

[13] G. Alverson and D. Notkin. Program Structuring for Effective Parallel Portability. *IEEE Trans. on Parallel and Distributed Systems*, Vol 4, No 9, 1041-1059, Sep 1993.

Programming Environments for Massively Parallel Distributed Systems, Monte Verità, Switzerland

An Environment for Portable Distributed Memory Parallel Programming

C. Clémençon, A. Endo*, J. Fritscher,
A. Müller, R. Rühl, B. J. N. Wylie

CSCS–ETH, Section of Research and Development (SeRD),
Swiss Scientific Computing Center, CH-6928 Manno

* NEC, SX-Center, Switzerland

Abstract

As part of the *Joint CSCS–ETH/NEC Collaboration in Parallel Processing*, we are currently developing an integrated tool environment consisting of an extended High Performance Fortran (HPF) compiler, a parallel performance monitor and analyzer, and a parallel debugger for distributed memory parallel processors (DMPPs). The environment is implemented on top of a subset of the emerging Message Passing Interface standard (MPI), running on several platforms, among others a NEC Cenju-2 DMPP. We develop a sequence of prototypes, which are continuously evaluated by a team of application developers. This document describes the first prototype currently installed on our systems.

1 Introduction

Advances in VLSI technology continue to ease replication and interconnection of many identical processing elements, and as the price/performance ratio of parallel processors decreases, they become increasingly attractive to numerical scientists. In MIMD distributed memory parallel processors (DMPPs) most investment is put into local computation and communication power at the expense of global communication performance. This potentially provides high performance, at least for problems with physically-local interactions which easily map to such architectures.

On many DMPPs the basic programming model supported by the vendor is the Single Program Multiple Data (SPMD) paradigm. SPMD programs are based on low-level *message passing*, i.e., all processors execute the same program and communicate by explicitly exchanging messages. Explicit message passing programs are difficult to implement and maintain, because multiple threads and separate address domains have to be managed. Therefore several higher-level languages providing portability and additional programming comfort were proposed. High Performance Fortran (HPF) [HPF93] for instance, provides a data parallel single-threaded execution model. Similar message passing interfaces, the above higher-level languages and the potential scalability promise to the scientific programmer both portability between DMPPs from different vendors, and portability *in time*, i.e., portability to future more powerful upgrades of a given DMPP.

In practice, DMPP programs are hardly portable because vendors continue to support their own different message passing libraries. Different basic architectural parameters (such as, for instance, the communication/computation speed ratio [APR89]) also strongly influence the efficiency of DMPP programs. Although the development of message passing programs is much more complex than the development of sequential or vector supercomputer programs, on most commercial DMPPs the programmer is supported—if at all—only with primitive profiling, monitoring, and post-mortem debugging facilities [Che93]. This lack of programming comfort and the current non-portable programming practice discourage many scientific application developers from moving from their familiar comfortable vector supercomputers to new massively parallel architectures.

To demonstrate that comfortable DMPP programming using standardized programming languages is possible, we are currently developing a complete integrated tool environment as part of the *Joint CSCS–ETH/NEC Collaboration in Parallel Processing* [Dec93, CDE+94]. This environment supports *both* high-level parallel programming based on HPF, as well as low-level programming based on the emerging Message Passing Interface (MPI) standard [MPI94]; interactive debugging, and performance monitoring on DMPPs will be possible on both levels. A team of tool developers is designing and implementing a sequence of tool prototypes, which are used and evaluated by a team of application developers. This prototype evaluation allows rapid feedback and requests of the application developers for functionality enhancements can be immediately considered for inclusion in future tool prototypes.

This paper describes the first results of our tool development effort. It is organized as follows: after a detailed description of the DMPP platforms and the message passing interface used, we first present our design objectives and a short overview of our tool environment, and then describe the functionality of its components. We show an example of the use of the tools on a large application.

2 Platforms

We work with four different hardware platforms: a NEC Cenju-2, a Meiko CS-1, single Sun (multi-processor) workstations, and networks of Sun workstations, running SunOS 5.2. The Cenju-2 [MYNK93] is provided by NEC Corporation as part of the CSCS/NEC collaboration and is expected to be upgraded in June 1994 to a larger Cenju-3 system.

The current Cenju-2 configuration consists of 16 computational nodes, featuring a MIPS R3000 chip-set (25 MHz), 64 Mbytes of main memory and two 64 Kbyte caches for data and instructions. The nodes are connected with a multi-stage shuffle-exchange network.

We decided to use the same communication platform for the low-level program development and as a common base for all our tools. MPI was chosen as such platform because it is an emerging standard and a variety of DMPPs will support it in the near future. Therefore we believe that using MPI guarantees portability. We do not support the full standard, but only an efficient subset which is complete enough to provide an efficient message passing interface (using standard MPI syntax) to the tool developer and to the low-level message passing programmer.

Our MPI subset is implemented in three layers. The lowest layer consists of three hardware-dependent basic functions, i.e., non-tagged send, receive and poll operations. The second layer consists of tagged point-to-point communication of contiguous data streams. On top of these, the third layer consists of collective communication routines.

Basic communication tracing facilities have been included to support performance monitoring. The strategy was to incorporate the trace functionality of PICL [GHPW90] into our communication platform. With trace files generated by the communication library in this format, the ParaGraph [HF93] trace visualization tool can be used, which can be particularly useful for analyzing low-level interprocessor communication.

In future versions of the communication platform we will extend the MPI subset: for instance, we will also support process groups and Cartesian process maps.

3 Tool Environment

3.1 Design Objectives

Before outlining the design objectives and the basic structure of our tool environment, we summarize the functionality of environments provided by some DMPP vendors and other research groups. Note that this list is not complete. We believe, however, that it contains the most advanced and commonly used DMPP programming environments for commercial DMPPs currently available. For a more complete overview of existing tools and for a lists of references describing the tools mentioned below, the reader is referred for instance to [Che93].

Meiko and Intel provide instrumented versions of the proprietary message passing libraries, CSN and NX respectively. Instrumented programs drive modified versions of the ParaGraph trace visualization tool. Both vendors also provide parallel debuggers with their machines — Intel `ipd`, and Meiko the `pdb` debugger. Thinking Machines offer an integrated environment called Prism for program debugging and visualization on their CM series of DMPPs in their proprietary

Fortran and C language variants. Distributed data can be visualized during program execution, or performance data analyzed after execution completes. On their CM-5 series, individual nodes can open separate debugger windows. Applied Parallel Research market an interactive Fortran program browser and analyzer, called Forge, which can also assist parallelizing programs for a number of distributed- and shared-memory platforms. This tool has been recently enhanced to support HPF, and can assist conversion of Fortran programs to (and from) HPF.

Bearing in mind the work done for the development of the tools described above, we formulate our major design objectives as:

- Designing and implementing an integrated tool environment which *both* allows parallel program development in a *high-level* data-parallel MIMD language and *low-level* message passing.
- Support of standardized programming languages and machine interfaces. At the high level, HPF and possible future HPF extensions are supported. At the low level, the MPI standard is used as the machine interface.
- Proposing and implementing HPF language extensions to also provide parallelization, debugging, performance monitoring, and analysis support for scientific applications considered today difficult to parallelize on DMPPs (e.g., unstructured sparse matrix computations).
- Application-oriented tool design. That is, the tools are developed in a sequence of prototypes, and a team of application developers is continuously providing feedback when using and testing the prototypes.

3.2 Overview

Three component tools are envisaged within our tool environment, sharing a common *User Interface* (**UI**):

PST *Parallelization Support Tool*
PMA *Performance Monitor and Analyzer*
PDT *Parallel Debugging Tool*

The integrated environment accepts high-level extended HPF programs and low-level message passing code. PST acts mainly as a compiler for both paradigms. PMA and PDT are designed with the same philosophy, i.e., it will be possible for the user to obtain information at different levels of abstraction. The lowest level of abstraction, providing the most detailed information, is as close as possible to the DMPP's hardware. Since we are also interested in porting the environment to several DMPPs, this lowest level of abstraction is the common communication platform (MPI) installed on all machines considered. For instance, a detailed breakdown of parallelization overhead in communication, computation, and idle times on all processors will be provided at any time of program execution. A higher

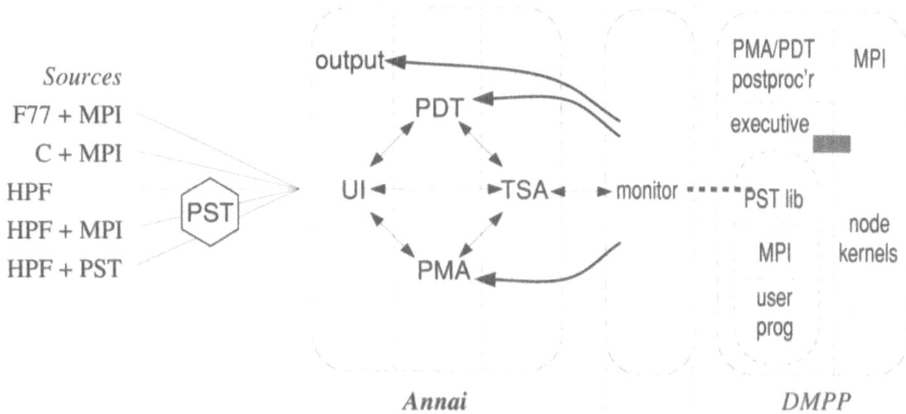

Figure 1: *CSCS 'Annai' tool environment overview*

level of abstraction is provided by considering features of the high-level language, such as global name space and data distribution, or data parallel execution mode which appears to the user as a single program thread. The inter-relationship of the components within the tool environment is shown in Figure 1.

PST aims to provide extensive run-time support for scientific applications today considered difficult to parallelize on massively parallel distributed systems. Working as a preprocessor on source programs, the application sources will be instrumented to generate both performance information for PMA and debugging information for PDT.

PMA utilizes trace information generated during the execution of a parallel program, and assists the performance tuning and interpretation of program execution through visualization and analysis of this information. Different levels of abstraction are supported, from the analysis of communications and memory utilization of individual processes through to global views of the data-parallel execution.

PDT similarly supports debugging at different levels of abstraction, often with support from PST and PMA. Debugging of single node programs at the source level through to high-level support of the parallel distributed program (mostly) presented as a single-thread is planned.

The user interface provides a single interface between the component tools and the user. It primarily consists of a source code browser, which can also be directed (and possibly annotated) by PMA and PDT to show features or source regions of interest. Output from a running program, sent to both standard output and error streams by processor nodes, is also displayed under the control of the UI in a separate window.

The UI also directs the operation of the other tools and controls parallel program construction and execution. This latter role is performed in conjunction with the TSA, *Tool Services Agent*, which provides the interface between the tools and the monitor which directs the parallel machine. Because we support the SPMD paradigm, breakpoints can be specified globally, i.e., TSA sets a breakpoint on all processors executing the parallel program. Instrumentation levels and regions specified by PMA are handled similarly.

Communication between PDT, PMA, TSA, the UI and the monitor is done via pipes with simple ASCII protocols. The monitor controls the executive running on the parallel machine, with a different packet-based protocol. Within the parallel machine, the user program executes utilizing the MPI and PST libraries, and directing the kernels running on the processor nodes. Bulk output from the executing program—user program output, trace information introduced by PMA, and debugging information required by PDT—may be processed within the parallel machine prior to transfer via streams or files to the desired destination.

3.3 The Tool Services Agent (TSA)

The tool services agent is currently based on Free Software Foundation's GNU `gdb` debugger with extended functionality for the control of parallel programs. (In due course, this may be replaced by other software components which provide the required functionality.)

TSA will be the interface to the parallel platform for both PMA and PDT. The interaction with PDT is obvious, whereas the interaction with PMA becomes clear when considering its requirements. PMA needs to have appropriate instrumentation (levels and regions) set within the parallel program, perhaps additionally instrumenting subroutine boundaries, and TSA can do this. Statistics generated by PMA can also be stored in global data structures which are part of the run-time library of the system, and these global data structures can be read via TSA.

3.4 The Parallelization Support Tool (PST)

PST currently consists of the Oxygen compiler [Rüh92]. Oxygen is a parallelizing Fortran compiler providing a global name space on distributed memory parallel processors. It accepts Fortran 77 annotated with compiler directives for data distribution and loop parallelization and generates parallel C code with communication primitives for execution on DMPPs.

Several research groups have defined languages and implemented compilers that increase DMPP programming comfort and allow portable coding at least of applications requiring highly structured computations, like dense matrix linear algebra, or finite difference and finite element methods applied to regular grids. The definition of the HPF standard is an attempt to standardize various efforts based on Fortran language extensions (and for a more complete list of references to such systems the reader is referred to [HPF93]). However, this first specification of HPF only provides minimal support for the parallelization of more irregular computations like linear algebra on general sparse matrices. As we have shown in [PR94], for the efficient parallelization of such applications, a high-level language DMPP compiler must support extensive run-time analysis, and the language—in contrast to HPF—must include constructs to dynamically distribute data and control flow.

To a limited extent, this run-time analysis is included in some data-parallel compilers, such as for instance Fortran D, Kali and Vienna Fortran. For critical code sections, compilers generate *inspectors* and *executors*, where the inspector pre-processes the executor to compute non-local data accesses at run-time; the executor performs the actual computation and executes communication statements based on information prepared by the inspector. Another approach is to implement such run-time analysis in libraries such as PARTI, which provide essentially the same inspector/executor mechanism, but require a little more user interaction.

The current PST prototype features run-time analysis more completely than the other above systems. Data and loop annotations allow data and control-flow distribution using either the well known static block or cyclic distributions or dynamic user-defined distributions. Critical code segments are also compiled into pre-processing phases (known as the "symbol handler") and executor. However, the symbol handler can consist of additional iterations as required by how non-local data are accessed in the critical code segment. If nested dependencies on non-local information exist, the compiler generates code slices, which only operate on local data to generate data fetches and updates for the next symbol handler iteration or for the executor.

As for the other above mentioned systems, PST generates more efficient parallel code if communication patterns, once they are generated by inspector or symbol handler, can be re-used. In fact, with PST, several different communication patterns may be computed and re-used as specified by the user for the same code segment.

NEC Corporation provides as part of the Joint CSCS-ETH/NEC Collaboration an HPF system which is the base for future PST prototypes. That is, we are currently integrating the above Oxygen features into existing HPF system components already available to us.

3.5 The Performance Monitor and Analyzer (PMA)

PMA provides facilities to assist with the instrumentation and analysis of program execution. Initially, PMA is used to configure parallel program instrumentation. Subsequently it interprets trace information generated during execution, assisting with performance tuning and interpreting program execution through visualization and analysis of this information. Different levels of abstraction are supported, from the analysis of communications and memory utilization of individual processes through to global views of the "data-parallel" execution.

In the first prototype, PMA drives a collection of ParaGraph displays after the execution of a parallel program has completed and execution trace information from the instrumented communications library has been collated. Meiko's CSNgraph also provides this functionality. This role will be retained in later PMA prototypes, providing extensive visualization of low-level program execution, which will be particularly relevant for localized regions of code which use message passing, such as those which would be automatically generated by PST.

Future prototypes will include additional performance statistics generated (as a first step) by post-processing the trace files. Additional statistics generated by PST, concerning memory consumption and dynamic data distributions, will also be included. Customized displays will also be designed, to provide increased insight into the program execution. These displays can also be interactively rescaled, to allow the resolution of finer details, or to provide a more general impression of program behavior. One such display will show each thread of the parallel program represented by its own utilization time-line, with communication highlighted between threads. Other metrics can also be selectively combined in the display, sharing the same annotated time-axis to facilitate relating associated properties.

In PMA displays, direct association between program statements (and blocks) and the performance metrics is an important part of the process of understanding program execution behavior. The tool environment user interface can be directed to display the section of code relevant to a selected metric, and the source code shown there can have detailed metric figures annotated in a margin. Thinking Machines' Prism environment provides similar performance annotations.

In conjunction with the source browser of the UI, PMA will set instrumentation "checkpoints," i.e., source lines defining regions where communication tracing is switched on or off. These instrumentation regions, with an appropriate instrumentation level (from a simple execution path to a detailed performance profile), are configured by PMA in liaison with the TSA. It is the TSA which modifies the program instrumentation state and maintains the instrumentation of the parallel program during execution.

It should be noted that our final target is *interactive* (rather than post-mortem) profiling of parallel programs. To minimize PMA's impact on program execution, and reduce the amount of trace information which might otherwise burden the system I/O and disk capacity, efforts will be made to process the communication traces in parallel on the distributed memory platform. This will also remove some sequential bottlenecks in trace data transfer and processing, providing scalable support for larger systems.

3.6 The Parallel Debugging Tool (PDT)

PDT is a source-level, interactive parallel debugger. The first PDT prototype makes use of TSA offering the functionality and commands of a conventional sequential source-level debugger, plus some features for debugging parallel programs on DMPPs. Commands are provided to attach to and detach from the target platform, to load and run a parallel program, to deal with global breakpoints and exceptions, and to switch from one processor to another when the program is stopped for stack, registers and data examination. This functionality is similar to that supported by Meiko's pdb and Thinking Machines' Prism debuggers.

In future prototypes we plan to fully support source-level debugging of PST programs presented as single-threaded programs, and we will facilitate interpretation of large distributed arrays by providing graphical views of the data layout (such as views supported by Prism and Forge) and how it is redistributed as the program executes. At the message-passing level, we are adding facilities for run-time deadlock detection, conditional breakpointing, and race condition detection.

For the first prototype we concentrated our efforts on a straightforward strategy to handle breakpoints and exceptions. In a parallel environment two particular problems have to be considered: (1) identifying which processors a breakpoint has to be set on, and (2) how to stop the machine and give control back to the user when a breakpoint or any other exception occurs. Problem (1) is easy to solve when considering programs of multiple processes with identical source code blocks (the SPMD model of computation), where each process is running on its own processor (one-to-one mapping). In this context, it is natural to set breakpoints globally on all processors executing the program. Problem (2) is more difficult to handle, because multiple breakpoints may be hit during the stopping phase, or even worse, these hits may come from different breakpoints. When an exception occurs, PDT freezes all of the participating processes. Such an exception can be one of the following events: a user stop, a breakpoint hit, a division by zero, a segmentation fault, etc. If different breakpoints are hit simultaneously, these are serialized, i.e., the breakpoint reached first is considered the breakpoint at which the program has stopped, and is presented as such to the user. PDT then prints the identifiers of processors hitting this breakpoint during the stopping phase. Possible exceptions coming from other breakpoints are delayed. When the user resumes execution, a pending exception immediately causes a new breakpoint stop.

3.7 The User Interface (UI)

The UI currently supports browsing through program source files, selecting breakpoints and checkpoints, possibly invoking different compilers (i.e., C, Fortran 77, and PST, with automatic selection of appropriate compilation flags and libraries). It allows PDT and PMA to be invoked and managed from the one unifying interface.

Future enhancements to UI will provide feedback between PMA and UI to allow, for instance, direct display of the most important global performance statistics in the source browser beside related lines of source code, or annotations of an interactive program call-graph structure display.

4 First Application Experience

PILS [Pom92] is a software Package of Iterative Linear Solvers for very large, irregularly sparse, unsymmetric, ill-conditioned systems of linear equations. PILS was developed at the Integrated Systems Laboratory at ETH Zurich, and was parallelized with Oxygen on DMPPs prior to the beginning of the CSCS/NEC collaboration. It was shown [PR94] that Oxygen's run-time parallelization support eased migration of PILS from vector supercomputers—platforms PILS was originally optimized for—to distributed memory parallel machines.

To meet the requirements for data structuring and flexibility, PILS is mainly implemented in C++. However, the most time-critical, vectorizable parts of PILS are written in Fortran. These Fortran parts consist of 50 subroutines which account for more than 99% of the run-time in a typical application and handle all linear algebra operations on the main data structures, i.e., the sparse matrix and the vectors. In the parallelized version, the C++ part is executed sequentially on the Cenju-2 on processor 0. The Fortran subroutines are compiled by Oxygen and run in parallel on all processors of the machine.

An example of the use of the instrumented MPI communication library, and the resulting visualization from ParaGraph is shown in Figure 2, which was produced from a trace of PILS running on 8 Cenju-2 processors. Time is on the horizontal axis, and processors are arranged along the vertical axes. The display depicts in different shades of gray the different phases (also called "tasks") of program execution on each processor. The different phases are marked by insertion of appropriate trace annotations into the user program prior to execution—this process is assisted by PMA in future prototypes.

For the trace, PILS was applied to a system of equations, stemming from the three-dimensional finite-element simulation of a sub-micron DRAM cell with trench capacitors, and has 46,692 unknowns and 986,042 nonzeros. As iterative solution method Bi-CGSTAB was used, preconditioned by a D-ILU preconditioner in split position.

Figure 2 shows one iteration of the program. Task 0 denotes sequential C++ overhead on processor 0. Task 1 denotes a subroutine performing vector-scatter operations and task 2 denotes a subroutine performing vector-gather operations. Task 3 denotes simple linear algebra operations on distributed vectors. White space denotes idle time.

5 Conclusions

We observe that recent DMPP architectures from different vendors resemble each other more than older generation machines do, in particular regarding architectural parameters which strongly influence parallel program efficiency. It is now for instance widely recognized that the communication speed has to match the computation speed for a well-balanced, versatile DMPP.

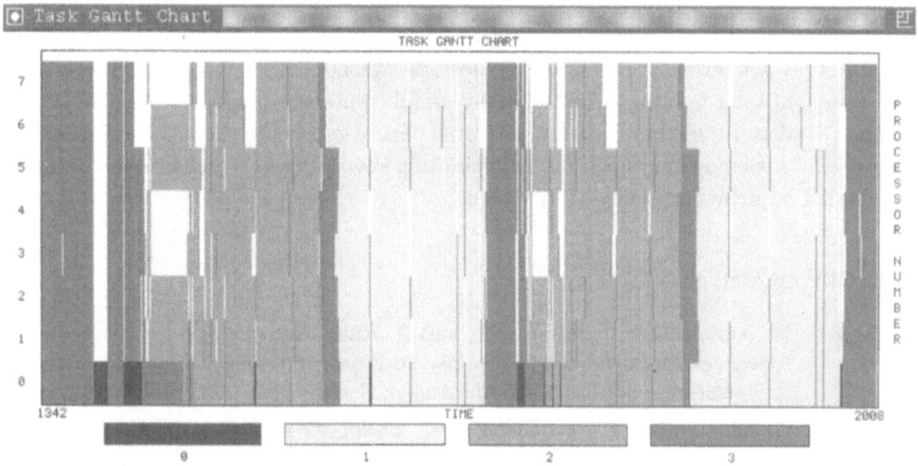

Figure 2: *ParaGraph display of one PILS iteration on Cenju-2*

The definition of MPI is now almost complete, whereas the definition HPF was completed at the beginning of 1993, and already the first production compilers are available. More importantly, many DMPP vendors have participated in the definition of both MPI and HPF and agreed to support these on current and future products.

Taking MPI and HPF as starting point, we have designed an integrated tool environment for programming DMPPs. This paper describes the implementation of a first prototype. The environment's key features include: support of both high-level data parallel and low-level message passing programming for flexibility; standardized programming languages and machine interfaces for portability; and run-time parallelization support beyond HPF with comprehensive parallel program profiling and debugging tools for user comfort.

We believe that the current state of our programming environment already shows that comfortable programming environments, which allow interactive debugging and tracing of parallel message passing programs, can be provided to developers of scientific applications. A key feature here is the support of a standardized communication interface. In addition, we propose an HPF extension to address irregular problems and envisage supporting this extended HPF language with a compiler, debugger and performance analyzer. We hope that such an environment, implemented on a DMPP with reasonably efficient communication characteristics, will make the computational power of a such machines accessible to the majority of developers of numerically intensive applications.

Acknowledgements

We gratefully acknowledge K. Decker, G. Jost, N. Masuda, W. Sawyer and E. de Sturler for testing our tools and for providing many useful comments. As part of the 1993 CSCS Summer Student Internship Program, an initial port of **gdb** to the Cenju-2 EWS front-end was done by J. Blandy and functions for generating PICL-format traces were incorporated in our MPI implementation by M. T. Nyeu.

References

[APR89] M. Annaratone, C. Pommerell, and R. Rühl. Interprocessor communication speed and performance in dmpps. In *Proc. 16th Symposium on Computer Architecture*, pages 315–324, Jerusalem, Israel, June 1989. IEEE-ACM.

[CDE+94] C. Clémençon, K. M. Decker, A. Endo, J. Fritscher, G. Jost, N. Masuda, A. Müller, R. Rühl, W. Sawyer, E. de Sturler, and B. J. N. Wylie. Application-Driven Development of an Integrated Tool Environment for DMPPs. Technical Report CSCS-TR-94-01, April 1994.

[Che93] D. Y. Cheng. A Survey of Parallel Programming Languages and Tools. Technical Report RND-93-005, NASA Ames Research Center, Moffet Field, CA, March 1993.

[Dec93] K. M. Decker. Methods and Tools for Programming Massively Parallel Distributed Systems. *SPEEDUP Journal*, 7(2), November 1993.

[GHPW90] G. A. Geist, M. T. Heath, B. T. Peyton, and P. H. Worley. A User's Guide to PICL: A Portable Instrumented Communication Library. Technical Report ORNL/TM-11616, Oak Ridge National Laboratory, TN, October 1990.

[HF93] M. T. Heath and J. A. E. Finger. ParaGraph: A Tool for Visualizing Performance of Parallel Programs. User Guide, UIUC/ORNL, August 1993.

[HPF93] HPFF (High Performance Fortran Forum). High Performance Fortran Language Specification: Version 1.0. *Scientific Programming*, 2(1&2), 1993.

[MPI94] MPIF (Message Passing Interface Forum). Document for a Standard Message-Passing Interface. Technical Report, Oak Ridge National Laboratory, TN, February 1994. Draft.

[MYNK93] S. Matsushita, T. Yamauchi, T. Nakata, and N. Koike. The Architecture of the NEC Cenju-2 Parallel System. HPC Select News, article 352, June 1993. Reprinted from the Winter and Spring'93 issues of *NEC SX World*.

[Pom92] C. Pommerell. *Solution of Large Unsymmetric Systems of Linear Equations*. PhD thesis, ETH-Zürich, 1992. Published by Hartung-Gorre Verlag, Konstanz, Germany.

[PR94] C. Pommerell and R. Rühl. Migration of Vectorized Iterative Solvers to Distributed Memory Architectures. In *Colorado Conference on Iterative Methods*, Breckenridge, Colorado, April 1994. Preliminary proceedings.

[Rüh92] R. Rühl. *A Parallelizing Compiler for Distributed-Memory Parallel Processors*. PhD thesis, ETH-Zürich, 1992. Published by Hartung-Gorre Verlag, Konstanz, Germany.

Programming Environments for Massively Parallel Distributed Systems, Monte Verità, Switzerland

Reuse, Portability and Parallel Libraries

Lyndon J. Clarke   Robert A. Fletcher*   Shari M. Trewin
R. Alasdair A. Bruce   A. Gordon Smith
Simon R. Chapple
Edinburgh Parallel Computing Centre, University of Edinburgh,
James Clerk Maxwell Building, Edinburgh EH9 3JZ, UK

Abstract

Parallel programs are typically written in an explicitly parallel fashion using either message passing or shared memory primitives. Message passing is attractive for performance and portability since shared memory machines can efficiently execute message passing programs, however message passing machines cannot in general effectively execute shared memory programs. In order to write a parallel program using message passing, the programmer is often obliged to develop a significant amount of code which manages distributed data and events and parallel input/output, and such code may have little or nothing to do with the application. However many parallel applications have common structural elements and much of this additional code can be encapsulated within a parallel library and reused in several programs. We discuss the requirements the library writer and user makes of the basic message passing interface and describe how we have addressed these requirements in our Common High-Level Interface for Message Passing (CHIMP) project. We also describe how these requirements are supported in the new standard Message Passing Interface (MPI). We then describe a selection of the parallel libraries which we have written in our Parallel Utility Library (PUL) project. These libraries encapsulate common approaches to parallel data and event management and parallel input/output.

1 Introduction

Parallel programs are typically written in an explicitly parallel fashion using either message passing or shared memory primitives for process coordination. Message passing is attractive for portability and performance since shared memory architectures can efficiently execute message passing programs whereas the reverse is not generally the case. In order to write parallel programs using message passing

*Contact Email: bobf@epcc.edinburgh.ac.uk

primitives the programmer is often obliged to develop a significant amount of software which manages distributed data and events and input/output of distributed data structures. Many parallel applications have similar structural components and much of the additional support software is potentially reusable. Such common software can be encapsulated in parallel utility libraries for reuse in many applications. The utilisation of parallel libraries reduces the additional effort required to exploit parallel systems to an understanding of the parallel concepts and relieves the programmer from the implementation of detailed message passing. Furthermore, encapsulation and reuse affords the opportunity to increase the time and effort involved in optimisations, since that cost can be spread over many applications. We describe a suite of libraries which we have written in the Parallel Utilities Library (PUL) project which support parallel input/output and parallel data and event management.

In order to realise the benefits of software reuse through utility libraries, such libraries must be portable across parallel computing platforms. Thus we require a uniform set of message passing primitives which support safe and efficient library implementation and utilisation. The message passing interfaces provided by vendors of parallel computing platforms differ, which has undermined the potential portability of message passing software. There have been a number of efforts to provide portable message passing libraries which have gone some way to solving this problem but have not addressed the requirements of library writers and users. We discuss these requirements and describe how we have provided support in our Common High-Level Interface for Message Passing (CHIMP) project. We also describe how these requirements are supported in the new standard Message Passing Interface (MPI).

2 Parallel Libraries and Message Passing

This section discusses facilities that parallel libraries require from the base message passing interface. The support for these requirements in two message passing interfaces is described: our Common High-level Interface to Message Passing (CHIMP) [14, 3]; and the new standard Message Passing Interface (MPI) [11].

2.1 Parallel Library Requirements

In order to provide generality, it is important to allow use of parallel libraries in conjunction with other communicating parallel libraries and with application message passing. The communications required by a library must be isolated from other communications in order to prevent interference. This can be achieved by assigning one or more different message *contexts* to each independently communicating agent within the same process. The defining property of a context is that a message cannot be received in a context other than that within which it was sent. Most existing message passing interfaces provide only a single global context. The message tag mechanism [17, 10, 2] alone is not sufficient as the user is entirely responsible for the interpretation of tag values [18].

Many useful parallel procedures involve collective communication within a group of processes. In general, users will apply these operations to arbitrary groups of processes, requiring an ability to form process groups in a general way. Most existing message passing interfaces provide collective operations that are applicable only to all processes in the system. This is unsatisfactory as it prevents uninterested processes from opting out of collective operations to perform other work. Process grouping can also be used to distinguish processes that have different functions. Some library implementations involve interaction with processes dedicated to providing certain services. An example is a client-server model where it is useful to group server processes separately from clients.

Portability of parallel libraries is enhanced by a logical process addressing scheme. For clarity, a library should be able to expose the structure of the algorithm or paradigm encoded within it in terms of the logical process names it uses (for example, a grid based algorithm addressing its constituent processes in a grid like fashion). Specification of the *virtual topology* of processes is also necessary if an implementation intends to map an algorithm onto hardware in an efficient manner.

2.2 CHIMP Parallel Library Support

In the CHIMP interface all communications are addressed through Service Access Points (SAPs). The CHIMP "send" primitives send a message through a SAP at the sender process to a SAP at the receiver process. The CHIMP receive primitives receive a message through a SAP at the receiver process from a SAP at a sender process. Messages may only be received through the SAP to which they were sent, which provides the required message context.

CHIMP service access points are configured into SAP groups such that each SAP is a member of exactly one group and each process may have SAPs in any number of such groups, although no process may have more than one SAP in the same group. A SAP group thus defines a group of processes, comprising the processes that own each constituent SAP.

Groups are identified by a textual name and manipulated by a group handle. Individual members of a group are identified by a membership identifier which is usually a number between zero and the number of members of the group. This provides a primitive virtual topology which is a simple one dimensional array.

Parallel libraries can create private communication contexts by creating private SAP groups. In the short example shown in Figure 1 a library initialisation call accepts a group handle which it duplicates, creating a new SAP group with a new context, and stores it in the library object for private use in further library calls. The initialisation is called by all processes in the identified process group. This call would also initialise any additional library state retained in the library object. The private message context and associated process group can be used in subsequent library calls without interference from other communications

```
typedef struct {
int group;
...             /* library data */
} LIB_OBJECT;

LIB_OBJECT *lib_init(int group)
{
  LIB_OBJECT *lib = lib_objInit();

  lib->group = chp_join_duplication(group, NULL);
  return (lib)
}

void lib_shift(LIB_OBJECT *lib, void *in, void *out, int count)
{
  int nb;
  int size = chp_group_size(lib->group);
  int rank = chp_group_member(lib->group);

  nb = chp_recv_nb(lib->group, lib->group, (rank+size-1)%size, in, count);
  chp_send(lib->group, lib->group, (rank+1)%size, out, count);
  chp_test(&nb, 1, CHP_ALL, NULL);
}
```

Figure 1: *Simple collective library example with CHIMP*

in progress. The example also shows how a group wide operation (in this case a cyclic shift of data across the group members) might be implemented.

EM [23] is a parallel utility library implemented using CHIMP message passing. It provides collective communication routines, applicable across processes in a CHIMP SAP group, to complement the facilities provided by CHIMP. The functionality of EM includes: a barrier operation; one-to-one, one-to-all and all-to-all message exchange such as concatenation and permutation; and global summation, minimum, maximum and logical operations. Although EM provides separate functions for the base data types, generic combination and selection services are also provided, permitting the user to define binary operations on arbitrary data types. EM demonstrates a trade-off between code reuse and performance in attempting to optimise communication patterns for particular target architectures. There are two alternative implementations, based on binary trees or parallel prefixes, which can be selected by the user, depending on the platform used. A more attractive solution would involve EM querying the platform in order to decide which implementation to adopt. This might involve lower level system software making machine parameters available to modules, or having modules execute test codes in order to determine these parameters at first hand. However, it is not clear how this querying could be achieved in a platform-independent manner or, indeed, what would constitute an adequate machine-independent set of parameters.

2.3 MPI Parallel Library Support

The support for parallel libraries in MPI is broadly similar to that in CHIMP. In MPI messages are addressed through a *communicator* object which can be viewed as a bundle of a message context and a process group, providing a safe communication space for library writer and user alike. The communicator may be implemented for example in terms of the port model of CHIMP or the extended tag model of Zipcode [20, 19].

The support for virtual topologies in MPI is more extensive than that in CHIMP and is broadly comparable to the process topologies support provided by PARMACS[2]. Cartesian and graph topologies are supported. These facilities enhance the basic process group and rank addressing methodology with structural information about the spatial relationship between component processes, and provide assistance with effective mapping of process group topologies onto hardware resources.

The communicator object also contains a user data cache which stores arbitrary data using a simple key mechanism. The communicator cache can be used to implement the virtual topology and collective communication layers of MPI which can be thought of as internal libraries. The communicator cache also makes MPI extensible since the library programmer can write MPI libraries with the same "look and feel" as the MPI internal libraries.

The code fragment in Figure 2 shows how the MPI interface can be used to implement the simple library example from the previous section, making use of the communicator cache mechanism. No explicit initialisation procedure is required and the communicator supplied by the caller is used to store the library state which is the reverse of the equivalent CHIMP example. In the first ever call, the library gets an attribute key value and specifies functions that the MPI caching mechanism should use to copy and to delete attributes. The attribute key is used to search the cache associated with the given communicator for an object holding library state. If there is no library object, the communication context defined by the communicator is duplicated to isolate library communications and the library object is allocated, initialised and inserted into the cache under the allocated key value. The secure communications context is used to perform the data shift in later calls with the same user level communicator.

3 Parallel I/O

There are two principal issues concerning I/O for MIMD machines. The first is the arbitration of access by a group of processes to a common, shared file. This is addressed by the GF (Global File) utility [4]. The second is the provision of scalable I/O performance through the distribution of a file over multiple discs. The PF (Parallel File) utility [6] adds this capability to a variation of the functionality of GF.

```
static int LIB_key = MPI_NULL_KEY;

typedef struct {
MPI_Comm comm;
...             /* library data */
} LIB_OBJECT;

void lib_shift(MPI_Comm comm, void *in, void *out, int count)
{
  LIB_OBJECT *lib;
  MPI_request req;
  int found, size, rank;

  if (LIB_key == MPI_NULL_KEY)
    MPI_Attr_get_key(&LIB_key, lib_cpObj, lib_rmObj);

  MPI_Attr_get_value(user, LIB_key, &lib, &found);
  if (! found) {
    lib = lib_initObj();
    MPI_Comm_dup(user, &(lib->comm));
    MPI_Attr_put_value(user, LIB_key, lib);
  }

  MPI_Comm_size(lib->comm, &size);
  MPI_Comm_rank(lib->comm, &rank);

  MPI_Irecv(in, count, type, (rank+size-1)%size, 0, lib->comm, &req);
  MPI_Send(out, count, type, (rank+1)%size, 0, lib->comm);
  MPI_Wait(&req, NULL);
}
```

Figure 2: *Simple collective library example with MPI*

3.1 Multiple Processes and Global Files

GF provides structured and unstructured access by a group of processes to shared files. The I/O functionality is based on the `C stdio` library, providing formatted and unformatted I/O, and adding operations to read and write arbitrary sub-blocks of arrays.

The utility supports four Parallel File Access Modes (PFAMs) which determine the behaviour of I/O operations. The first two are *single*, where all processes in a group synchronously access the same data and *multi* where they synchronously access contiguous data. These modes are similar to their namesakes in the CUBIX operating system [16], although GF does not enforce an SPMD model. The other modes are *random* and *independent*, where processes may independently access arbitrary data using either a shared or local file pointer. Figure 3 summarises how the modes modify the semantics of the I/O operations.

Applications often require the ability to alter the PFAM whilst accessing an open file. A typical example is an application which reads common header information for each process at the beginning of the file (in *single* mode), and then reads specific data for each process from the remainder of the file (in *multi* or *random* mode).

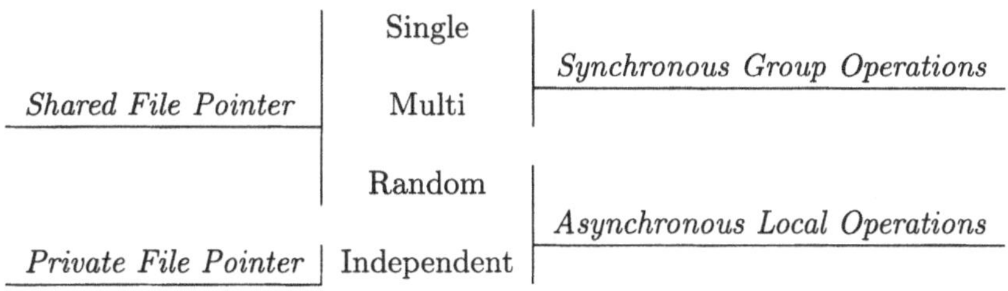

Figure 3: *Comparison of GF parallel file access modes.*

The current implementation uses a client-server architecture, thus allowing GF to provide non-blocking reads and writes, enabling the application to control the overlap of computation with I/O.

3.2 Multiple Discs and Distributed Files

I/O is one of the major bottlenecks that affects parallel codes. Parallel file systems represent a solution by multiplying the number of streams over which I/O is performed and thereby increasing the bandwidth. Such facilities are provided by the newest parallel computing systems (including Thinking Machines Corporation's CM-5, Meiko's Computing Surface 2 and Fujitsu's AP1000), but as is frequently the case, software support lags hardware capability.

It is the objective of the PF utility to provide a transparent, efficient and portable interface to parallel discs. The goal of transparency implies that the file should be presented as a single, logical unit to the processes accessing it. Thus, the I/O operations are unaware of the actual distribution of the parallel file. This ensures a simpler programming model, and a clean separation of the issues of functionality (access to the file) and performance-tuning (distribution of the file).

However, while PF provides the PFAMs supported by GF, we believe that for efficient parallel I/O, it is necessary to abandon the "Unix" byte stream model of GF. Instead, we allow the structure of application data to be embodied in the file access operations, so that the distribution pattern of the file may be matched to the access patterns of the application. To this end, PF uses an *I/O atom*, defined to be an addressable, user-defined record type, possibly of variable length. The name "atom" has been chosen because this is the finest unit of file distribution.

Files may be distributed by PF over discs in a variety of strategies, which are partly based on a taxonomy by Crockett [8]. A *Multi-Instance* distribution replicates the file on a set of discs as in RAID [13] Level 1. The *Partitioned-Interleaved* distribution stripes contiguous blocks of atoms across the discs, and the *Partitioned* and *Interleaved* distributions are special cases of this. *User Defined* distributions are also permitted by PF.

A single parallel file may have a number of concurrently-existing, equivalent instances with different distributions, from which the utility chooses the most appropriate on opening the file, or it may determine that the generation of a new distribution is required. In order to allow PF to determine what is an appropriate distribution, the user may provide the utility with "hints" about access patterns, such as the predominant PFAM. The "hints" mechanism also allows an appropriate caching strategy to be determined. The existence of a distributed, replicated cache is likely to be the source of a significant proportion of the performance gained [9].

4 Parallel Data Management

Many important classes of application, such as computational fluid dynamics (CFD) or seismic data processing, are expressed as regular local operations over a very large spatial data set. Parallelism offers a significant performance improvement to such applications, by splitting the data set between different processors and assigning processing according to the *owner computes* rule. Processes responsible for neighbouring portions of the data set must communicate to ensure that data elements on the boundaries of these portions are kept consistent. Applications amenable to this kind of parallelisation are commonly based on data structures such as rectilinear *grids*, or irregular *meshes.*

These paradigm specific requirements may be encapsulated within a library, such as the RD utility within PUL [5], which supports regular domain decomposition. This technique is appropriate for balanced grid-based problems, and involves dividing up the (multi-dimensional) array-based data set into a set of similarly sized blocks which are allocated to a logical grid of processes.

RD introduces the concept of an *operator stencil* to define the pattern of data access for updating the data elements. The operator stencil is used by RD to calculate the inter-process communications for internal boundary updates and may be changed over the lifetime of the grid.

Two interoperable levels of interface are provided. Under the *skeletal* level both the control and data-flow of the paradigm are managed automatically by RD, and the application need only provide a function to update an arbitrary region of the data set. This strategy owes much to Cole's "algorithmic skeletons" [7], and can allow very rapid parallelisation. With the *procedural* interface, boundary updates are still performed by the utility, but under the control of the application. Boundary updates may be non-blocking, allowing computation to be overlapped with the communication.

The class of applications which is probably the largest current consumer of supercomputing cycles is that of irregular mesh-based problems, such as finite element or volume codes, often used in CFD. These typically suffer from load imbalance [15], which becomes more severe when adaptive meshes (those which change shape as the computation proceeds) are implemented. Even meshes with a static structure may still be dynamically unbalanced.

The SM utility in PUL [24] supports two or three dimensional meshes. The utility includes procedures to ensure the consistency of data lying at process boundaries and also supports the migration of data elements between processes, in order to obtain optimal load balancing. Any dynamic load balancing technique must be cost effective, that is, the cost of making changes in processor responsibility and migrating data between processes must be greatly outweighed by the efficiency gained from the better load balance. Accordingly, the load balancing algorithms employed by SM use local decision-making and element migration. This approach is scalable, and although decisions are based on partial knowledge it has been shown to yield good results at low costs [1].

SM provides two load balancing functions in order to achieve cost-effectiveness under different conditions. The first migrates all mesh elements on a boundary, which is very inexpensive to execute, as it can use existing boundary update communications. The second migrates only a certain number of the "highest energy" elements, which is more costly to execute, but provides more accurate load balancing.

One alternative to the PUL approach of providing libraries explicitly supporting message-passing parallel programming paradigms is the approach taken in the High Performance Fortran (HPF) initiative [12]. In this case the user annotates almost serial source code with directives specifying how the data is to be distributed. The compiler generates a parallel executable using the owner computes rule, inserting parallel data management code as appropriate. This approach is excellent for the class of regular, static balanced problems tackled by RD. For unbalanced mesh problems, however, HPF is not powerful enough to provide the dynamic load balancing required to achieve efficient utilisation of a parallel machine. Run-time utility libraries such as PUL are flexible enough to tackle these difficult problems, while hiding the details of the parallel implementation from the application programmer.

5 Parallel Event Management

This approach is suitable for applications whose task can be split into two or more smaller, independent sub-tasks, the results of which are combined to solve the original problem. The sub-tasks may themselves be further subdivided, or solved directly. An advantage of over the data parallel approach is that unbalanced problems (which divide into tasks of varying degrees of difficulty) are easily load balanced.

This kind of *event parallelism* is typically found in ray tracing and tree search problems. Event parallel problems are often tackled by some form of *task farm*. In the classical task farm there is one source process, which generates tasks, a set of worker processes which transform tasks into results, and one sink process which collates results to form the final solution.

Within the PUL library, the TF utility [25] embodies a classical task farm. As with RD, two interoperable levels of interface as are provided. The higher, *skeletal* level encapsulates both the data and control flow of the application, where the user need only specify the source, worker and sink functions, and the *procedural* level provides facilities to distribute and collect tasks and results.

The basic task farming approach is inherently non-scalable, as task creation and result collation become bottlenecks with large numbers of workers. More powerful is the "divide-and-conquer" strategy, where the task is recursively broken down into a tree of sub-tasks, whose branches may be solved independently. Since the depth and breadth of the tree is unknown, the allocation of branches should be dynamic in order to balance the computational load, each process taking on work from a heavy branch when it has finished all local branches. A PUL utility to support this strategy would manage the computation tree, and be responsible for work migration.

6 Conclusion

In order to promote portable parallel software, there is a need for a common message passing interface. Portability need not be achieved at the expense of performance, if there is some form of communication of attributes between platform and messaging system. Building libraries on top of a messaging system requires it to have secure communication contexts (as in CHIMP, MPI and Zipcode), and is aided by allowing user data to be associated with communication contexts (as in MPI).

Effective use of I/O on MIMD architectures requires the co-ordination of multi-process access to a common file. The provision of scalable, but usable I/O performance necessitates providing a global view of a file distributed in an application-specific form over multiple discs. The PUL GF and PF utilities support these goals.

Many important parallel applications comprise regular, local operations on large spatial data sets, typically rectilinear grids or unstructured meshes. Effective parallelisation strategies for these may be encapsulated in libraries, which can accommodate irregular datasets and dynamic load-balancing more effectively than a compiler-based approach. The PUL RD and SM utilities encapsulate decompositions of rectilinear grids and unstructured meshes.

For applications whose task can be partitioned into independent sub-tasks, then an event-parallel paradigm can be suitable. This can take the form of a classical task farm (realised in the TF utility), or for amenable problems, a divide and conquer approach can be used.

The feasibility of employing a portable, library-based approach in large-scale applications is demonstrated by the use of CHIMP and PUL in industrial and academic applications such as global weather modelling, seismic image processing [22], network-management and a parallel genetic algorithm framework [21].

Acknowledgements

Lyndon J. Clarke acknowledges support for this work from the Science and Engineering Research Council. Shari M. Trewin acknowledges support from Software Engineering for Parallel Computers programme of the Information Systems Committee.

References

[1] A. Barah and A. Shiloh. A distributed load balancing policy for a multicomputer. *Software: Practice and Experience*, 15(9):901–913, 1985.

[2] Luc Bomans and Rolf Hempel. The Argonne/GMD macros in FORTRAN for portable parallel programming and their implementation on the Intel iPSC/2. *Parallel Computing*, 15:119–132, 1990.

[3] R. Alasdair A. Bruce, James G. Mills, and A. Gordon Smith. Chimp version 2.0 interface. Technical Report EPCC-KTP-CHIMP-V2-IFACE 1.7, Edinburgh Parallel Computing Centre, University of Edinburgh, February 1994.

[4] Simon R Chapple. PUL-GF Prototype User Guide. Technical Report EPCC-KTP-PUL-GF-PROT-UG, Edinburgh Parallel Computing Centre, University of Edinburgh, 1992.

[5] Simon R Chapple. PUL-RD prototype user guide. Technical Report EPCC-KTP-PUL-RD-PROT-UG, Edinburgh Parallel Computing Centre, University of Edinburgh, 1992.

[6] Simon R. Chapple and Robert A. Fletcher. PUL-PF prototype functional specification. Technical Report EPCC-KTP-PUL-PF-PROT-FS, Edinburgh Parallel Computing Centre, University of Edinburgh, 1993.

[7] Murray Cole. *Algorithmic Skeletons: Structured Management of Parallel Computations.* Research Monographs in Parallel and Distributed Computing. Pitman, 1989.

[8] Thomas W. Crockett. File Concepts for Parallel I/O. ICASE Interim Report 7, Institute for Computer Applications in Science and Engineering, 1989.

[9] David Kotz and Carla Schlatter Ellis. Caching and Writeback Policies in Parallel File Systems. *Journal of Parallel and Distributed Computing*, 17, 1993.

[10] J. Dongarra, A. Geist, R. Manchek, and V. Sunderam. Integrated PVM framework supports heterogeneous network computing. *Computers in Physics*, 7(2):166–175, April 1993.

[11] Message Passing Interface Forum. Document for a standard message-passing interface. Technical Report CS-93-214, University of Tennessee, November 1993. Available on **netlib**.

[12] High Performance Fortran Forum. Draft High Performance Fortran Language Specification. Technical report, Center for Research on Parallel Computation, Rice University, Houston, TX, U.S.A., November 1992.

[13] Randy Katz and Garth Gibson. Case for redundant arrays of inexpensive disks. University of California at Berkely, 1987.

[14] James G. Mills, Lyndon J. Clarke, and Arthur S. Trew. Chimp concepts. Technical Report EPCC-KTP-CHIMP-CONC, Edinburgh Parallel Computing Centre, University of Edinburgh, April 1991.

[15] D. M. Nicol and J. H. Saltz. Dynamic remapping of parallel computations with varying resource demands. *IEEE Transactions on Computers*, 37(9):1073–1087, 1988.

[16] ParaSoft Corporation, 27415 Trabuco Circle, Mission Viejo, CA 92692. *Cubix*, 1988. Release 1.0.

[17] Paul Pierce. The NX/2 operating system. In *Third Conference on Hypercube Concurrent Computers and Applications*, 1988.

[18] A. Skjellum, N. Doss, and P. Bangalore. Writing libraries in MPI. Computer Science Department and NSF Engineering Research Center for Computational Field Simulation, Mississipi State University. Available on **netlib**, 1993.

[19] A. Skjellum and A. Leung. Zipcode: a portable multicomputer communications library atop the reactive kernel. In D. W. Walker and Q. F. Stout, editors, *Fifth Distributed Memory Concurrent Computing Conference*, pages 767–777. IEEE Press, 1990.

[20] A. Skjellum, S. Smith, C. Still, A. Leung, and M. Morari. The Zipcode message passing system. Technical report, Lawrence Livermore National Laboratory, September 1992.

[21] Patrick D. Surry and Nicholas J. Radcliffe. RPL2: A language and parallel framework for evolutionary computing. Technical Report EPCC-TR94-10, Edinburgh Parallel Computing Centre, 1994.

[22] C. Thornborrow, A. Wilson, and C. Faigle. Developing modular application builders to exploit MIMD parallel resources. In G. Neilson and D. Bergeron, editors, *Proceedings Visualization '93*, pages 134–141. IEEE Press, 1993.

[23] Shari Trewin. PUL-EM prototype user guide. Technical Report EPCC-KTP-PUL-EM-PROT-UG, Edinburgh Parallel Computing Centre, University of Edinburgh, 1992.

[24] Shari Trewin. PUL-SM prototype user guide. Technical Report EPCC-KTP-PUL-SM-PROT-FS, Edinburgh Parallel Computing Centre, University of Edinburgh, 1992.

[25] Shari Trewin. PUL-TF prototype user guide. Technical Report EPCC-KTP-PUL-TF-PROT-UG, Edinburgh Parallel Computing Centre, University of Edinburgh, 1992.

Programming Environments for Massively Parallel Distributed Systems, Monte Verità, Switzerland

Assessing the Usability of Parallel Programming Systems: The Cowichan Problems

Gregory V. Wilson
Edinburgh Parallel Computing Centre
gvw@epcc.ed.ac.uk

Abstract

The only control-parallel programming model to win wide acceptance to date has been procedural message passing. One reason that higher-level systems have not been widely accepted is that there is no consensus on what they should offer; one reason for this is that there has been no systematic comparison of the usability of alternatives models and systems. This paper describes a problem suite with which the usability, rather than performance, of parallel programming systems may be assessed.

1 Introduction

While data parallelism is now widely accepted, most control-parallel programming systems are used only by their authors, or not used at all. The only general exceptions are low-level procedural message-passing (PMP) systems such as `PVM` and `PARMACS` [GS92, BRH90]. While these are appropriate for systems-level programming, they make applications programming tedious and error-prone. Like the VT100, the PMP model does not offer much, but is the only reliable common denominator between different platforms.

One reason higher-level systems have not displaced PMP is that their benefits have not been clearly demonstrated. In particular, there has been no systematic comparison of the usability of alternative models and systems. A paper describing a new parallel programming system (PPS) usually contains speedup curves or MFLOPS figures, but not a discussion of how easy the system is to learn, or how well it supports large-scale software engineering. This is partly because most developers of PPSs put far more effort into writing their systems than into using them. Often, the only applications implemented toy problems such as matrix multiplication, the Game of Life, Mandelbrot set generation, the N-queens problem, and all-pairs shortest-paths.

The aim of this work is therefore to compare several representative parallel programming systems in two related ways. The first, which will assess how well systems can support large-scale software engineering, will compare implementations of a standard set of problems using software engineering metrics such as lines of code, Halstead's "program volume" measure [Hal75], McCabe's cyclomatic complexity [McC76], and more modern measures based on the decomposition of flowgraphs [Fen91]. In the second, which will measure how easily systems can be learned, and how quickly code can then be developed, we will measure the time taken by both novice and expert users of each system to achieve reasonable performance using each system.[1] [SS94] presents the surprising results of such an experimental comparison of the high-level parallel applications construction tool Enterprise with low-level message-passing, and will be a model for our work.

This paper presents the problem suite which will form the basis of this work. This suite is called the Cowichan Problems, after a place and tribal name from the Canadian Northwest, and has been chosen to acknowledge the debt this work owes to the Salishan Problems of Feo *et al.* [Feo92]. The author is grateful to Allen Malony (University of Oregon), Jonathan Schaeffer (University of Alberta), Richard Brent and Robin Stanton (Australian National University), and Henri Bal (Vrije Universiteit, Amsterdam) for their support during this work, and to the many students who have implemented these problems over the years.

2 Dynamic Programming

The first problem has been chosen to assess how easily shared structures can be created and accessed, and how easily regular, predictable data movement can be exploited. The author and Felicity George of the Edinburgh Parallel Computing Centre have produced prototype message-passing and Linda implementations; a complex, but efficient, shared-memory implementation is discussed in [ECG93].

Suppose a program is to multiply N matrices M_i, $0 \leq i < N$, each matrix with r_i rows and c_i columns. The number of scalar multiplications which must be performed to obtain the product of two matrices is $r_i c_i c_{i+1}$. If the matrices' dimensions vary, different multiplication orders may have very different costs. For example, if matrices A, B, C, and D have dimensions 6×3, 3×5, 5×12, and 12×2, the total costs can range from 186 for $A(B(CD))$ to 594 for $((AB)C)D$.

Dynamic programming can find an optimal ordering by filling in each element $C_{i,j}$ of an upper-triangular cost matrix C with the cost of the least expensive way to multiply the matrices from M_i to M_j. For each k, $i < k < j$, the algorithm determines the least cost of multiplying $M_i \ldots M_k$ and the least cost of multiplying $M_{k+1} \ldots M_j$, then uses these to find the cost of multiplying the results $M_{i \to k}$ and $M_{k+1 \to j}$.

If the values of C are determined diagonal by diagonal, then $C_{i,k}$ and $C_{k+1,j}$ will be known when $C_{i,j}$ is to be calculated. Since they are independent, the values of all elements on a diagonal may be calculated concurrently. The calculations to

[1] By analogy with Hockney's $n_{1/2}$ measure (the vector length on which a pipeline achieves 1/2 its theoretical peak performance) this metric is sometimes referred to as $p_{1/2}$.

determine possible values for each element may also be done concurrently, so long as the conditional replacement of an old minimum with a newly-found one is atomic.

A data-parallel implementation can work by shifting copies of the cost matrix so that the values needed on a diagonal arrive at the appropriate time. A control-parallel PPS which supports fine-grained access to, and synchronization on, shared data structures can use the dovetailing discussed in [ECG93] to amortize synchronization costs.

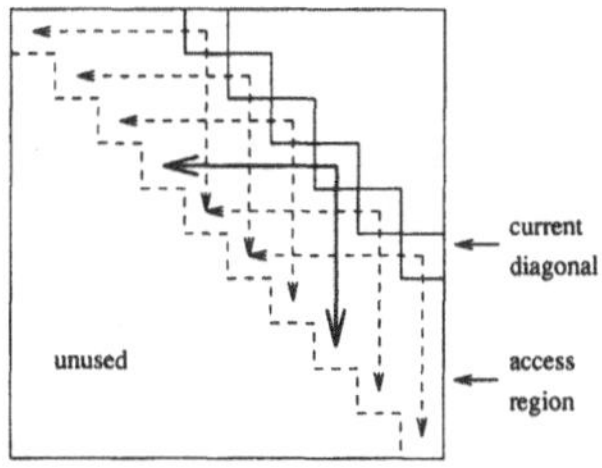

Figure 1

Programmers using a coarse-grained disjoint-memory system have a more difficult task. As can be seen from Figure 1, cost matrix values are accessed both along rows and down columns. If the cost matrix is decomposed by rows, each processor can read half of the values it needs locally, but must read the others remotely. Decomposing the cost matrix by columns or into blocks has analogous problems.

One technique is to duplicate the matrix, and store one copy by row and the other by column [WG92]. This results in two types of processes: calculators, which calculate costs, and line managers, which are responsible for storing and updating rows and columns of C. Implementations using this technique reflect the usability cost of not providing shared memory: while the dataflow and shared-memory versions of this code are only slightly larger than the serial code, the message-passing version is more than ten times as large, and was correspondingly more difficult to debug.

3 The Turing Ring

The problem has been chosen to assess how easily dynamically-changing workloads can be managed. Mark Smith, of the Edinburgh Parallel Computing Centre, has implemented it using Meiko's CS Tools and Thinking Machines Corporation's CM-FORTRAN.

In [Tur52], Alan Turing analyzed the interaction of two chemicals in a ring of cells using a pair of coupled differential equations, similar to those developed by Lotka and Volterra to describe predatory/prey systems. These have the form:

$$\frac{dX_i}{dt} = X_i(r_X + c_{XX}X_i + c_{XY}Y_i) + \mu_X(X_{i+1} + X_{i-1} - 2X_i)$$
$$\frac{dY_i}{dt} = Y_i(r_Y + c_{YX}X_i + c_{YY}Y_i) + \mu_Y(Y_{i+1} + Y_{i-1} - 2Y_i)$$

where $r_{X,Y}$ are birth rates, $c_{a,b}$ represent local interactions, and $\mu_{X,Y}$ are migration rates between neighboring cells. [Smi93] describes how the choice of parameters governs the degree of instability in the system, the ratio of desired wave number to world size, and the sizes of the equilibrium populations.

To simulate the system's evolution, these equations are discretized, and cell populations updated probabilistically at small time steps. In each step, the work done for each cell is proportional to that cell's population. Since the populations of neighboring cells may vary by two orders of magnitude, some form of dynamic work allocation is needed to achieve efficiency. In a shared-memory control-parallel system, guided self-scheduling [PK87] is an appropriate technique. In a disjoint-memory control-parallel programming system, each of P processors can initially be made responsible for N/P contiguous cells. This keeps communication overhead to a minimum, since only boundary population values need to be exchanged at each time step. However, if the decomposition is static, it will result in very large load imbalance.

The solution is to shift cells dynamically from heavily-loaded processors to lightly-loaded neighbors. The implementation described in [SW91] did this by having each process include a measure of its current workload in each message sent to its neighbors. Every f_ℓ iterations, neighbors compared their relative execution times. If there was a great enough imbalance, a lightly-loaded worker would adopt one of its neighbors' cells. The protocol for effecting this exchange was included in the normal boundary value messages. Along with migrant predators and prey, each message included the population of the appropriate boundary cell, and the execution time of the last iteration.

This failed to achieve good load balance because high-valued cells thrashed back and forth between processes. A more sophisticated strategy, in which a process only relinquished the boundary cell with the lower population, was more successful. However, this required a complex multi-iteration protocol.

A very different data-parallel approach to the problem uses the parallel prefix (or scan) operator [Ble89]. This technique maintains several arrays, corresponding entries of which represent a single predator or prey. Populations are sorted by location index. In each iteration, one scan calculates and distributes the populations of each cell. Local calculations then determine which predators or prey die or produce offspring. The new populations are summed using a second scan, and the values in the arrays re-distributed. Migration calculations then increment or decrement the location index of each predator or prey. Values are then sorted to re-contiguize each cell's population.

The shared-memory and data-parallel are clearly the simplest. Further, they can be generalized to 2- and higher-dimensional meshes; there is no simple way to do this for the message-passing strategy, as it would be difficult to ensure that the repeated shifting of cells preserved mesh contiguity.

4 Skyline Matrix Solver

This problem is drawn directly from [Feo92], which describes implementations in Ada, C*, Scheme, PCN, Haskell, Miranda, and SISAL. It is included in order to test how easily programming systems can represent irregular matrix structures.

A skyline matrix is an $N \times N$ matrix for which there exist constants r_i and c_j, such that $1 \leq r_i \leq i$, $1 \leq c_j \leq j$, row i has non-zero values in columns r_i to i (i.e. the elements from column r_i to the left of the main diagonal are non-zero), and column j has non-zero values in rows c_j to j. Figure 2 shows an example of a skyline matrix.

Given a skyline matrix A and an N-vector b, we wish to solve the equation $Ax = b$ using LU-decomposition. The key to efficiency is to exploit the fact that many array elements are known to be zero. The solutions in [Feo92] fall into three categories: implicitly parallel (which we do not pursue), data parallel, and control parallel. The data-parallel solution stores non-zero matrix elements as triples $(i, j, a_{i,j})$, and constructs special whole-array operations on these. The control-parallel solutions represent the matrix as vectors of variable length, and construct customized scalar-vector and vector-vector functions to operate on these. In a shared-memory system, work can be allocated from a shared pool using guided self-scheduling. In disjoint-memory systems, row and column vectors can be allocated cyclically (blockwise decomposition would result in poor load balancing, as processors with low-indexed blocks would quickly fall idle). The only difference between this and the classic parallel LU-decomposition algorithm is that processors would frequently choose not to operate on their rows at all because of the presence of zero values.

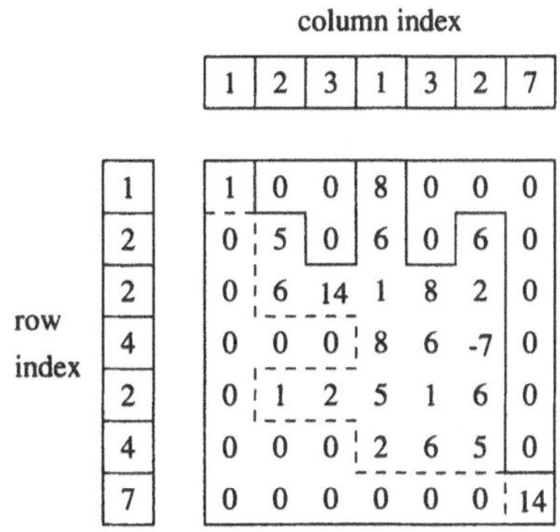

Figure 2

This problem combines the irregular workload of the Turing Ring with the non-local communication of dynamic programming. The complexity of the solutions presented in [Feo92] varies widely. Interestingly, the authors of the Occam section in [Feo92] chose not to exploit knowledge of the structure of A because their system would not allow them to create irregular data structures dynamically.

5 Image Thinning

This problem has been chosen because it consists of two distinct parts, and so tests the ease with which parallel programming clichès may be composed under a PPS. Partial implementations using Occam, procedural message-passing, and shared memory have been produced by Bill Austin of the Department of Computer Science, University of Edinburgh, Alasdair Bruce (now at Edinburgh Parallel Computing Centre), Kesavan Shanmugan (University of Oregon), and Isabella Urbanek (Australian National University).

The problem's input is a two- or three-dimensional image, which contains several straight line segments. Each segment may be several pixels in width, and the whole image may be corrupted by noise. The first task is to skeletonize the image, i.e. to attempt to reconstruct the original line segments of unit thickness (Figure 3); the second is to label the image's connected components.

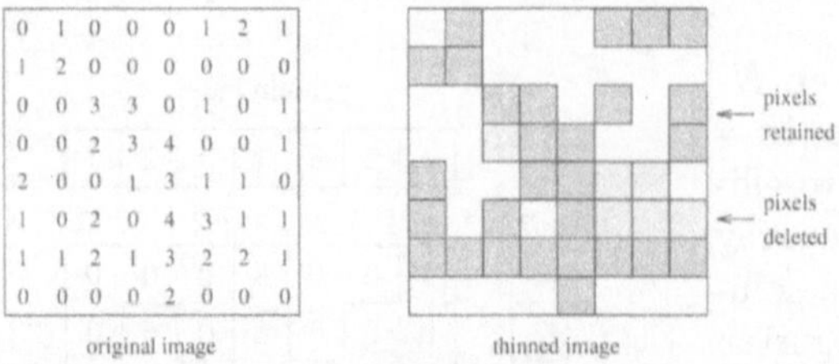

Figure 3

Skeletonization is done by making repeated passes over the data. In pass v, $1 \leq v \leq N$, a pixel with value v is removed unless (a) it is at the tip of a line segment, or (b) deleting it would disconnect a presently-connected image component. In some situations, either of two pixels may be removed, so long as the other is left. Serial implementations, resolve such ambiguities using sweeping order; parallel implementations must take care to ensure that exactly one pixel is retained in such cases.

The rules governing pixel removal can be implemented either using nested conditionals, or by encoding each pixel's surroundings and then using this to index a lookup table. The latter is typically used in data-parallel systems; however, as the connectivity neighborhood of the image is increased, the number of possible indices increases rapidly. Unless some degree of local indirection is permitted, both simplicity and performance may suffer.

A control-parallel system may tile the image, and have one process work on each patch. Processors' workloads can then be balanced by giving each many scattered patches [NS90]. However, this can be difficult to implement in connection-oriented systems which do not disguise the connectivity of the underlying hardware, in systems which do not support multi-tasking on each node, or in systems which deliver messages to processors, rather than processes.

Once the image has been thinned, its connected components must be found. Parallelizing this is more challenging. One technique uses "travelling sparks": each process asynchronously traces out the connected components within its region, and sends a message to a neighboring process whenever the tracing "spark" reaches a patch boundary. If the spark's value is lower than the value currently being used to trace that component, the component is re-traced; if the spark's value is higher, then a reply is sent telling the originator of the spark to re-trace its component.

An alternative technique is to have each process trace the components in its patch, and then construct a graph whose nodes represent points at which components overlap boundaries. A simple transitive closure algorithm can then be used to propagate coloring values between processes; each process can then re-label its part of each component.

6 Polygon Overlay and Display

This problem has been chosen because it exercises the I/O capabilities of systems, and because it may be formulated in terms of generating, filtering, and combining data streams.

Suppose we have been supplied with two maps, A and B. Each map covers the same geographical area, and is decomposed into a set of non-overlapping polygons. For simplicity, we require these polygons to be non-empty rectangles with vertices on an integer grid $[0 \ldots N] \times [0 \ldots N]$. We also require the input maps to have identical extents.

Our aim is to overlay the maps, i.e. to generate a new map consisting of the non-empty elements in the geometric intersection of A and B (Figure 4). This problem frequently arises in geographical information systems, in which the first map might represent soil type, and the second, vegetation. Their overlay then shows how combinations of soil type and vegetation are distributed.

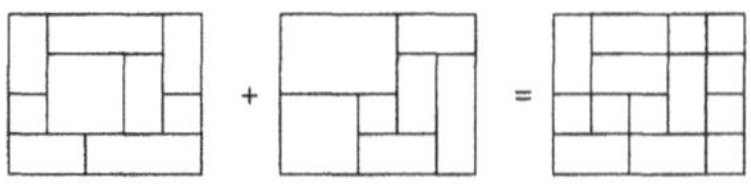

Figure 4

Implementations of this depend crucially upon whether each map's polygons are known, or required, to be sorted in some fashion. Parallel implementations on systems without virtual memory are also dependent on whether the whole of each map can fit into memory. If not, paging or multi-level sorting must be used. Again, we choose to simplify by assuming that both input maps, and the result map, can be held in memory at once.

One approach to parallelization of this problem is to decompose the map area into $M \times M$ patches, and create a list of the polygons in map A which intersect each patch. The polygons making up map B are then read in one at a time, broadcast to all processors, and tested against the polygons overlying each mesh patch. If the output map does not have to be sorted, its components are written out as they are found; otherwise, a second sorting pass is performed. This method may be used in both data- and control-parallel systems.

In a pipelined control-parallel implementation, each of P processes is allocated one or more of the N_A polygons of map A. The polygons of map B are then streamed through the pipeline; results are either passed through the same pipeline, stored locally for collection upon termination, or "bled off" as the pipeline executes.

The most interesting feature of parallel implementations of this problem will be the way in which I/O is managed. Many PPSs still do not provide adequate support for I/O; we therefore expect that the complexity of parallel implementations will be very dependent on the level of support for synchronized and unsynchronized I/O. As an optional part of this problem, implementations should display their inputs and output graphically. This is not only an acknowledgement of the growing importance of visualization in high-performance computing, but also a chance to determine whether a programming system has simply incorporated a sequential graphics library such as X, which does not include support for multi-writer windows, or whether a fully-parallel graphics library has been developed.

7 Constructing Crosswords

This problem has been included to test the ability of programming systems to support asynchronous, speculative search. The game we have chosen is *kece*. Given an ordered list of W words, two players construct crossword patterns on an $N \times N$ board. At any time, only the first T words in the list may be used. The score each player receives is equal to the number of letters which overlap when she places a new word. Figure 5 shows a game in progress; note that words may only be played left-to-right or top-to-bottom.

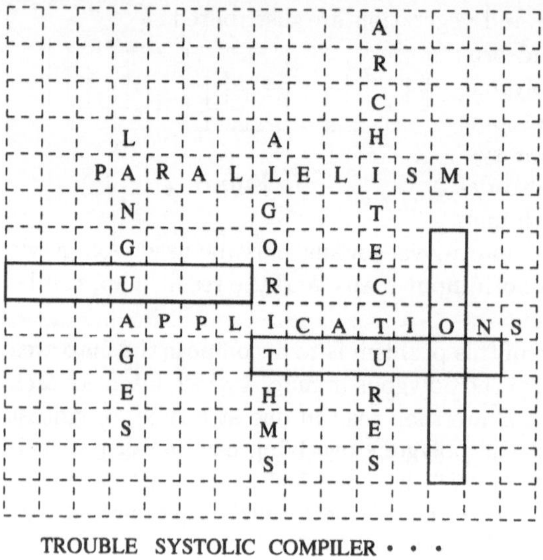

Figure 5

Most game programs use $\alpha\beta$ search [Lev88]. This guides search using two limit values α and β. If, during search, a position's score is below α, that branch can be pruned as unprofitable; if it is above β, it can also be pruned, as a rational opponent would never select it. $\alpha\beta$ is usually faster than full-width search. $\alpha\beta$ reduces the effective branching factor of a chess tree by approximately a factor of six. No other search algorithm returns an equivalent result with less effort [KM75].

$\alpha\beta$ search seems easy to parallelize. In a typical chess mid-game position, each player has approximately 40 moves. Since their values are independent, it would seem that each could be searched concurrently. However, this leads to an explosion of unnecessary work, since less pruning takes place.

One option is to pursue a functional decomposition, i.e. to make some processors responsible for generating moves, while others perform evaluation. This works on special-purpose hardware, but is unsuitable to general-purpose parallel computers because of synchronization and communication overheads. A better approach is to give have processors communicate partial scores as they search semi-independently. This was done by both Waycool [FO88], and Phoenix [Sch89]. Many variations on this theme, of ever-increasing complexity, are possible.

8 Active Chart Parsing

The last problem in the set is to parallelize the active chart parsing algorithm described in [Win83]. A first implementation was done by Felicity George using Meiko's CS Tools in 1989; another message-passing implementation, for the Fujitsu AP1000, has been done by Sam Taylor at the Australian National University.

Consider a sentence such as "Jane saw Fred in the park with the green telescope." Depending upon how it is parsed, it could mean (a) that Jane and Fred were both in the park, and Jane was using the telescope, (b) that Jane wasn't in the park, but Fred was, and Fred had the telescope, or (c) that Jane saw Fred in the park in which the telescope is located. Resolving this ambiguity is a semantic problem, but depends upon an ability to generate structures representing the different ways to parse this sentence.

A bottom-up approach to doing this is to insert a node between each word, and connect adjacent nodes with one arc for each of the categories to which the intervening word belongs. At each node, a program may the compare the arcs coming in on the left to the arcs going out on the right. Whenever a combination of arcs matches a grammar rule, the program may insert a new arc between the left and right nodes. This process continues until no further arcs can be added; any *Sentence* arcs spanning all nodes then represent complete parsings. Typically, this algorithm is implemented by maintaining three data structures: the arcs which have been installed, a reverse-lookup grammar table, and a list of arcs which have been generated by rule firings, but have not yet been installed. The algorithm terminates when this last structure is empty.

The obvious implementation in a disjoint-memory system is to create one process for each inter-word node. Each process is given the whole sentence, and told which words it lies between. It then simulates the operation of the original algorithm for its node alone. However, this begs an important question: how does the program know when to terminate? Since the pending arc list is not centralized, some technique must be used to determine when no more arcs are going to be added. It is not enough merely to know that all processes are idle at some instant, since messages could be in transit at that instant; some form of distributed termination detection algorithm must be used. The author believes that the extra burden of implementing this will indicate how well a PPS would support other fully-asynchronous applications, such as discrete event simulation.

9 Conclusion

The author believes that in order to be successful a control-parallel programming system must extend a current imperative programming language, permit efficient implementation, be relatively easy to learn, allow easy expression and composition of common clichés, and support large-scale software engineering. The seven problems in this suite will be used to quantify the last three of these issues. All seven are currently being re-written in ANSI C and Orca [Bal91] (an Algol-like language with explicit support for shared data-objects) by students at the Vrije Universiteit, Amsterdam. Once these implementations have been completed, tested, and analyzed, work will begin on implementations in other systems. Participation and comment from the wider community would be very welcome.

References

[Bal91] Henri Bal. *Programming Distributed Systems.* Prentice Hall, 1991.

[Ble89] Guy E. Blelloch. Scans as Primitive Parallel Operations. *IEEE Transactions on Computers*, 38(11), November 1989.

[BRH90] L. Bomans, D. Roose, and R. Hempel. The Argonne/GMD macros in FORTRAN for Portable Parallel Programming and Their Implementation on the Intel iPSC/2. *Parallel Computing*, 15:119–132, 1990.

[ECG93] Phil Edmonds, Eleanor Chu, and Alan George. Dynamic Programming on a Shared-Memory Multiprocessor. *Parallel Computing*, pages 9–22, 1993.

[Fen91] Norman E. Fenton. *Software Metrics: A Rigorous Approach.* Chapman and Hall, 1991.

[Feo92] John T. Feo, editor. *A Comparative Study of Parallel Programming Languages: The Salishan Problems.* North-Holland, 1992.

[FO88] E. W. Felten and S. W. Otto. A Highly Parallel Chess Program. In *Proc. International Conference on 5th Generation Computer Systems*, pages 1001–9, 1988.

[GS92] G. A. Geist and V. S. Sunderam. Network-Based Concurrent Computing on the PVM System. *Concurrency: Practice and Experience*, 4(4), June 1992.

[Hal75] Maurice H. Halstead. *Elements of Software Science.* Elsevier North-Holland, 1975.

[KM75] Donald Knuth and Ronald W. Moore. An Analysis of Alpha-Beta Pruning. *Artificial Intelligence*, 6, 1975.

[Lev88] David Levy, editor. *Computer Chess Compendium.* Batsford, 1988.

[McC76] Thomas J. McCabe. A Complexity Measure. *IEEE Transactions on Software Engineering*, 2(4):308–20, 1976.

[NS90] David M. Nicol and Joel H. Saltz. An Analysis of Scatter Decomposition. *IEEE Transactions on Computers*, 39(11):1337–45, November 1990.

[PK87] Constantine D. Polychronopoulos and David J. Kuck. Guided Self-Scheduling: A Practical Scheduling Scheme for Parallel Supercomputers. *IEEE Transactions on Computers*, 36(12), December 1987.

[Sch89] Jonathan Schaeffer. Distributed Game-Tree Searching. *Journal of Parallel and Distributed Computing*, 6:90–114, 1989.

[Smi93] Smith, Mark. Dynamic load-balancing strategies for data parallel implementations of reaction-evolution-migration systems. *International Journal of Modern Physics C*, 4(1):107–119, (1993).

[SS94] Duane Szafron and Jonathan Schaeffer. Experimentally Assessing the Usability of Parallel Programming Systems. In *Proceedings of the IFIP Working Conference on Programming Environments for Massively Parallel Distributed Systems*. Birkhaeuser Verlag AG, April 1994.

[SW91] Mark Smith and Greg Wilson. Dynamic Load Balancing on a One-Dimensional Mesh. Presented At Second European Distributed Memory Computing Conference, 1991.

[Tur52] Alan M. Turing. The Chemical Basis of Morphogenesis. *Transactions of the Royal Society of London*, 237, August 1952.

[WG92] Gregory V. Wilson and Felicity A. W. George. Using Dynamic Programming to Benchmark Communications on Parallel Computers. In *Proceedings of the Fifth North American Transputer Users' Group*. IOS Press, 1992.

[Win83] Terry Winograd. *Language as a Cognitive Process (Volume 1: Syntax)*. Addison-Wesley, 1983.

Programming Environments for Massively Parallel Distributed Systems, Monte Verità, Switzerland

Experimentally Assessing the Usability of Parallel Programming Systems

Duane Szafron* Jonathan Schaeffer †

Abstract

This paper discusses an experiment to compare the usability of two parallel programming systems (PPS). In this experiment, half of the students in a graduate parallel and distributed computing course solved a problem using the Enterprise PPS while the other half solved the same problem using a PVM-like library of message-passing routines. The feedback from such experiments is necessary to help narrow the gap between what parallel programmers want, and what current PPSs provide.

1 Introduction

A large number of software systems have been developed to simplify the task of developing parallel software. At one extreme, some of these systems support specialized programming models that allow programmers to quickly achieve high performance for selected applications. Unfortunately, this high performance cannot be matched across all classes of applications. Other systems provide a set of low-level primitives that allow the programmer to achieve high performance for many applications, but at the expense of drastically increased software development time.

There are many considerations that affect the assessment of parallel programming systems (PPSs), but the majority fall into three categories: performance, applicability and usability [7]. Since the performance and applicability issues are addressed in other papers, we do not elaborate on it further. Usability may be the most important since it influences the productivity of programmers. Given the extra complexity of debugging and testing parallel and distributed software, it is essential that a PPS eliminate, simplify, or at least mask the complexity.

Although there have been many human-factors studies of the productivity of sequential programmers [1], other than [4] we know of no comparable studies for programmers developing parallel software. In [7], we proposed two experiments

*Department of Computing Science,University of Alberta, Edmonton, Alberta, Canada, T6G 2H1. Email: duane@cs.ualberta.ca.

†Department of Computing Science, University of Alberta, Edmonton, Alberta, Canada, T6G 2H1. Email: jonathan@cs.ualberta.ca. Visiting professor, University of Limburg, Netherlands.

to assess the productivity of programmers using PPSs, one for novices and one for experts. This paper describes an experiment to measure the ease with which novices can learn the programming system and produce correct, but not necessarily efficient, programs.

A controlled experiment was conducted where half of the graduate students in a parallel/distributed computing class solved a problem using the Enterprise PPS [5] while the rest used a PPS consisting of a PVM-like library of message passing calls called NMP [3] [1]. The specific PPSs used in this experiment are not the focus of this paper. Instead, we argue that controlled experiments must be conducted so that PPS developers can determine which features should be included in PPSs.

2 The Programming Task

The problem chosen for the experiment was the computation of a transitive closure that iterates until all values in a set have been assigned a value. Each iteration must traverse a graph using the information from the previous iteration to resolve additional data values. This problem has an obvious solution, where each processor is responsible for a sub-graph, and the processes synchronize at the end of each iteration. It is possible to create a chaotic solution, where the processes do not synchronize, but this requires careful consideration of the termination conditions.

In Enterprise the interactions of processes in a parallel computation are described using an analogy based on the parallelism in a business organization [5]. Every sequential procedure that will execute concurrently is assigned an asset type (individual, line, department, etc.) that determines its parallel behavior. The user code for each of these procedures is sequential C, but a procedure call to such an asset is automatically translated into a message send by Enterprise. Consider the following user C code, assuming that `func` is an asset in the program:

```
result = func( x, y );
/* other C code */
a = result;
```

When Enterprise translates this code to run on a network of workstations, the parameters `x` and `y` are packed into a message and sent to the process that executes the asset `func`. The caller continues executing and only blocks and waits for the function result when it accesses the result (`a = result`). Allowing concurrent actions until the result of a previous computation is required has been called a *future*.

Enterprise has three components: an object-oriented graphical interface, a pre-compiler, and a run-time executive. The user specifies the application parallelism by drawing a hierarchical enterprise that consists of assets. At run-time, each asset corresponds to one or more processes. Sequential procedure calls in C are translated by the pre-compiler into message send/receives across a network.

[1] The experiment is described in more detail in [6].

The execution of the program (process/processor assignment, establishing communication links, monitoring network load) is done by the run-time executive.

The Network Multiprocessor Package (NMP) is a PVM-like message passing library [3]. Essentially it is a friendly interface to TCP and UDP. NMP provides the same basic facilities as PVM [2], except support for using heterogeneous processors and dynamic reconfiguration of processes and their communications paths. NMP was chosen over PVM for three reasons: 1) it is a subset of PVM and has less than 20 different library calls to learn, 2) the documentation for NMP is less than 20 pages, and 3) NMP has been used in a graduate course for the past 5 years.

3 Experiment Design

There are a number of considerations that must be taken into account in the design of a fair experiment to measure usability.

1. Prelude: We consulted a cognitive psychologist with expertise in designing experiments that involve human subjects. To eliminate biases, it was important that the students not know the exact nature of what was being measured.

2. Subjects: The students in a parallel programming graduate course were used as subjects. None of them had any previous parallel programming experience prior to taking this course. The 15 students were randomly divided into 2 groups: NMP (8 students) and Enterprise (7 students).

3. Instruction: For both Enterprise and NMP, the students were given a 50 minute classroom lecture, a 20 minute lab demonstration and documentation. In addition to the instructor, a teaching assistant who was familiar with both NMP and Enterprise was available to answer student questions.

4. Environment: Each student account was provided with a modified *zsh* shell that logged all commands executed by the students. The students were not told about the instrumentation. This is an important point since subjects who know about instrumentation may consciously or subconsciously modify their behavior. We had to be wary of ethical issues, and made sure the information gathered was comparable to that provided by the UNIX *lastcomm* facility. All programming was done on a network of 20 SUN 4s.

5. Epilogue: At the experiment's conclusion, students were asked to submit a two-page write-up commenting on their respective PPS.

4 Experiment Results

Our experiment measured five factors that seem to be indirect measures of usability as well as one factor (run-time performance) that may be sacrificed for increased usability. Figure 1 shows the six statistics that were analyzed:

1. Number of hours a student was logged in actively working on the assignment.
2. Number of lines of code in the solution program [2].
3. Number of editing sessions.
4. Number of compiles that attempted to link the program together (i.e., compiles which failed because of syntax errors were not included).
5. Number of times the students tested their parallel program by running it.
6. Execution times of their program.

In the first five cases, a lower number indicates higher usability, while in the sixth case, a lower number indicates better run-time performance. In each figure, the hollow circles represent NMP data points and the solid circles represent Enterprise data points. Each student is given a number, so the reader can compare an individual's performance across graphs. These graphs are ordered with the best performer on the left and the worst on the right. The right-hand side of each graph shows the average of the NMP students (dashed line) and the Enterprise students (solid line).

The statistics support our initial expectations that students would do less work (higher usability) with Enterprise, but get better run-time performance with NMP. Enterprise students did 14% fewer edits, wrote 66% fewer lines of code, did 34% fewer compiles and 13% fewer program test runs. However, perhaps surprisingly, they used 26% more login time. Why does this apparent anomaly exist? There are several reasons:

1. Enterprise compiles take roughly 5 times as long as NMP compiles. Enterprise must preprocess the user's code by making several passes over the input file before it produces a file that is compiled by the C compiler. From Figures 1a) and 1c), the average NMP user compiled 7.2 times per hour, while the average Enterprise user compiled only 3.5 times per hour.
2. Enterprise includes an option to replay a computation using animation. The user can see (and inspect) the messages being sent and monitor the status of each process. If the user watches an animation to completion using the default settings, it could take as long as 10 minutes. Each Enterprise user, on average, used this feature 25 times.

---

[2] Count included blank lines and comments. Students were given the sequential program (128 lines of code) and were expected to parallelize it. They were also given a library containing the parts of the program that did not have to be altered (over 1000 lines of code) during parallelization. The figure shows the parallel code written less the 128 lines of sequential code.

3. The students uncovered nine bugs in Enterprise; two of them serious errors that affected the student's progress. Although turnaround on bug fixes was rapid, most students assumed that the bug was in their program and not in Enterprise. We do not know how much time they devoted to solving these problems before reporting them.

4. Since the NMP performance was better, Enterprise students spent more time doing performance tuning to try to obtain better speed-ups.

As expected the NMP solutions (excluding the anomalous NMP-2 data point) had better run-time performance (27%). For this problem, the Enterprise communication time could be as high as 30% of the execution time depending on how the problem was solved. Since Enterprise has hidden manager processes that forward messages to replicated assets, there could be twice as many messages as in a hand-coded NMP solution. In addition, at least two of the Enterprise solutions had bugs in them whereby two futures overlapped, forcing sequential execution where concurrent execution was intended.

5 Conclusions

This paper has identified an area where the parallel/distributed computing community has been negligent in providing quantitative data. Hardware vendors are quick to cite measures that flatter the performance of their machines, but neglect to quantify the usability of their software. The growing base of parallel computing users could significantly benefit from an objective assessment of the usability of PPSs.

This experiment had four major results:

1. It demonstrated that the usability of PPSs can be measured.

2. It supported the claim that Enterprise is more usable than a message passing library.

3. It produced several direct benefits to the Enterprise PPS, including bug fixes, user-interface enhancements, extensions to the programming model and identified the need for faster compilation, more debugging tools and better documentation.

4. It identified some fundamental PPS independent concepts that are difficult for most novice parallel programmers to understand and indicated that these concepts should be stressed in the documentation for all PPSs. These include process startup, process termination and passing pointers between processes.

Although this is only a first attempt at measuring the usability of PPSs, the experiment nevertheless highlights the human factors issues that have been neglected to date. We propose that the above experiment (or variations on it) should

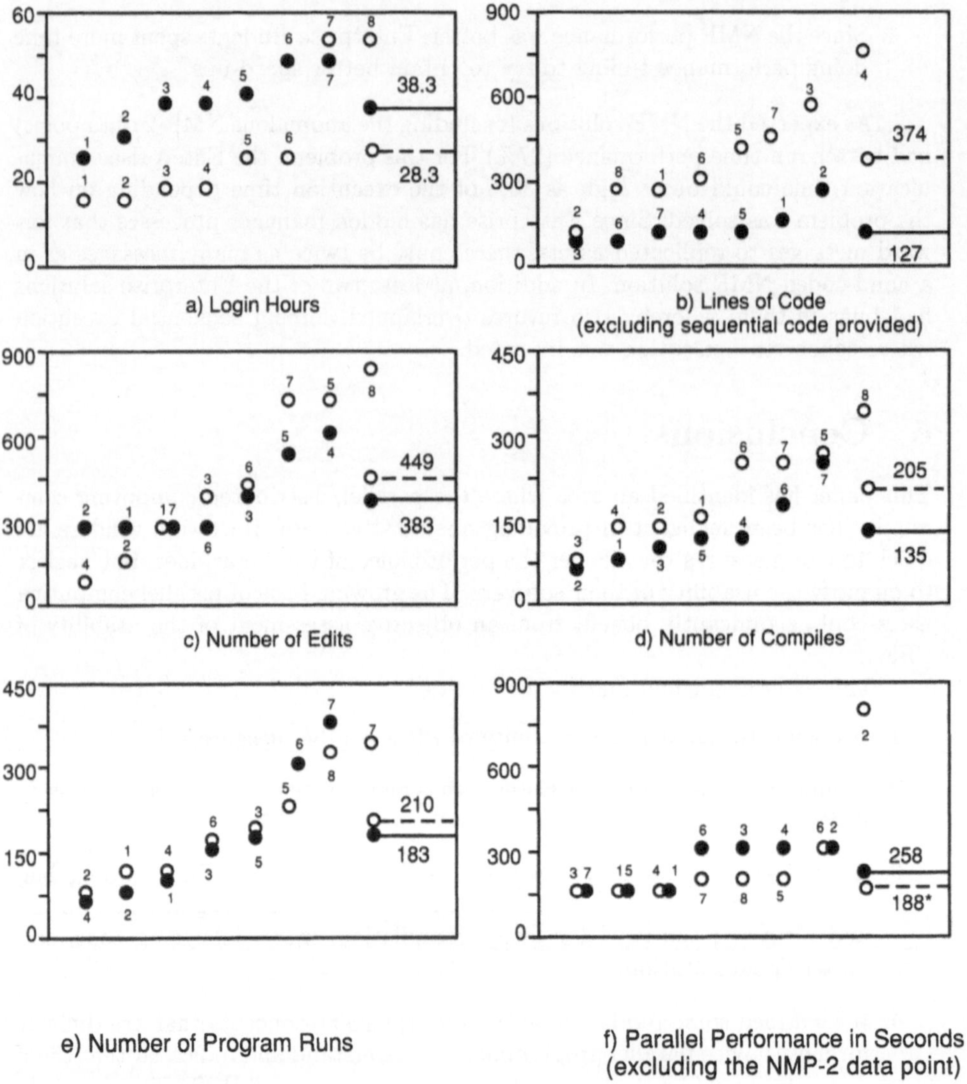

Figure 1: *Experimental Results*

be an integral part of the development cycle for parallel software tools. Given the diversity of programming systems available, researchers need more feedback as to what works well and why. We recognize that the cost of performing such quantitative measurements will be large. However, the cost of not performing them, as borne by a group which selects a low-usability PPS, will certainly be much larger.

Acknowledgements

Renee Elio, Randal Kornelson, Ian Parsons, Paul Iglinski, Robert Lake, Carol Smith and Bob Beck helped make this experiment possible. Many of the ideas in this paper originated from discussions with Greg Wilson. We would like to thank the CMPUT 507 class for their participation. This research has been funded in part, by NSERC grant OGP-8173 and a grant from IBM Canada Limited.

References

[1] R. Brooks. Studying Programmer Behavior Experimentally: The Problems of Proper Methodology. *CACM*, vol. 23, no. 4, pp. 207-213, 1980.

[2] G. Geist and V. Sunderam. Network-Based Concurrent Computing on the PVM System. *Concurrency: Practice and Experience*, vol. 4, no. 4, pp. 293-311, 1992.

[3] T. Marsland, T. Breitkreutz and S. Sutphen. A Network Multiprocessor for Experiments in Parallelism. *Concurrency: Practice and Experience*, vol. 3, no. 1, pp. 203-219, 1991.

[4] M. Rao, Z. Segall and D. Vrsalovic. Implementation Machine Paradigm for Parallel Processing. Supercomputing '90, ACM, New York, pp. 594-603, 1990.

[5] J. Schaeffer, D. Szafron, G. Lobe and I. Parsons. The Enterprise Model for Developing Distributed Applications. *IEEE Parallel and Distributed Technology*, vol. 1, no. 3, pp. 85-96, 1993.

[6] D. Szafron and J. Schaeffer. A Usability Study Comparing Two Parallel Programming Systems Technical Report 94-03, Department of Computing Science, University of Alberta. Available via anonymous ftp from ftp.cs.ualberta.ca.

[7] G. Wilson, J. Schaeffer and D. Szafron. Enterprise in Context: Assessing the Usability of Parallel Programming Environments. IBM CASCON, Toronto, pp. 999-1010, 1993.

Programming Environments for Massively Parallel Distributed Systems, Monte Verità, Switzerland

Experiences with Parallel Programming Tools

Fritz G. Wollenweber Saulo Barros David Dent
Lars Isaksen
Guy Robinson
European Centre for Medium Range Weather Forecasts,
Shinfield Park, Reading, RG2 9AX, United Kingdom
fwollenweber@ecmwf.co.uk

Abstract

The European Centre for Medium-Range Weather Forecasts (ECMWF) is well known as a high performance computing site with considerable computer power installed. Since 1983 ECMWF has been involved in parallel computing through early exposure to the Cray line of vector parallel processor machines. Since 1984 ECMWF has organized a biannual workshop on the use of parallel processing in meteorology, with an ever increasing attendance (the next workshop will be held in 1994). A way pursued to build up expertise in parallel processing is the continued participation in EC funded R&D projects, as e.g. GENESIS (1989-91), PPPE (1992-95) and GPMIMD2 (1993-95/96). In 1992 the European RAPS benchmarking effort was initiated and so far has turned out to be very successful. The efforts at ECMWF are aimed at all aspects of parallel programming which are of concern for an operational high performance computing centre This paper will briefly introduce the overall effort into parallel programming and then focus especially on the ongoing PPPE work. It demonstrates the usefulness of performance analysis and visualization tools by giving examples from our ongoing code parallelization effort.

1 Introduction

ECMWF has participated in a number of efforts in promoting parallel computing and is still actively engaged in a number of ongoing R&D efforts. The GENESIS project enabled ECMWF to investigate the feasibility of performing weather forecasts with a global spectral weather prediction model on a massively parallel computer. Different parallel approaches have been considered (parallel pipelines, 2D-decomposition, 3D- transposition) and the transposition approach chosen as the method with the most advantages [1]. Simplified versions of the model have been implemented and benchmarked on different platforms [2]. The conclusion we can draw from these tests is, that global spectral weather prediction models will run well on massively parallel computers, with good speed-ups and good performances as long as it is possible to achieve good single node performances. The EC funded GPMIMD2 project has several aspects. It tries to establish a European presence in the High Performance Computer market. It aims to demonstrate a large European MPP in a production environment tackling Grand Challenges problems, like weather prediction and climate modelling. For ECMWF the most significant achievement will be the gain of experience in operating a large MPP in a production like environment over considerable time doing real work, and exploring strategies for computer centres to provide balanced HPC services.

The RAPS benchmarking effort was initiated by a consortium of high performance computer sites in 1992. The idea is to ease the efforts necessary for vendors and potential buyers to benchmark the equipment by providing a suite of applications which are representative of a large class of application programs. Benchmarking all or parts of this suite should then help to make decisions about which hardware is most suited for particular problem areas and code types. A sound benchmark methodology is applied as described by [6].

2 PPPE - Portable Parallel Programming Environment

The acronym PPPE stands for Portable Parallel Programming Environment. It is an EC funded R&D project (ESPRIT project 6643). The objectives of this project are:

- provide tools to facilitate development, migration, debugging and performance tuning of large programs
- target architectures MIMD
- UNIX environment
- adhere to standards (European & open)
- incorporate application developers to ensure the tools meet the requirements
- define, publish and promote a layered programming model
- establish a FORTRAN based programming model for distributed memory architecture
- stimulate co-operation on research, development and production of tools and applications

How important adequate programming environments are has been stressed - especially from the users side [7] - in the past. The development of several vendor specific environments and also similar projects elsewhere [4] underlines the prime role these programming environments will play in the move towards the operational use of massively parallel computers at production sites. As PPPE aims at the scientific/engineering user community it is essential to support FORTRAN/F90 programming languages. At the beginning of the project a number of tools were already available. They originate partly from other EC-projects, e.g. PCTE, PATOOLS, VFCS, and in part from other sources like the public domain (Paragraph and PATOP). The Portable Common Tool Environment (PCTE) builds the integration platform of PPPE. PARMACS 5.1 are the GMD/ANL message passing macros [5] which build the basis for communication on the distributed memory machines envisioned. During the course of the project PARMACS 5.1 will be superseded by PARMACS 6.0, a library based approach for message passing, and ultimately replaced by MPI (Message Passing Interface) the upcoming standard for message passing. PATOOLS, PATOP and Paragraph are performance analysis tools. The Vienna Fortran Compilation System (VFCS) is an automatic parallelization tool. VFCS helps to convert FORTRAN 77 programs into parallel programs using F77 and message passing. It builds mainly on the data parallel paradigm.

3 Experiences

ECMWF's role in the PPPE effort is the role of an applications developer, providing information on specific needs for tools in the development process and as a tester of the resulting toolset for feedback and quality assurance reasons. The tools will be applied in the ongoing effort of ECMWF to parallelize its IFS (Integrated Forecasting System), a large scale weather prediction code [3].

3.1 The testbed - parallel IFS (Integrated Forecasting System)

The European Centre for Medium-Range Weather Forecasts operational model is a global spectral model, run with a resolution of T213L31 (triangular truncation, 213 waves around a great circle, 31 vertical layers). It is run operationally on a Cray C90/16, consuming about two hours wallclock time to produce a 10-day forecast. The parallel version of ECMWF's spectral model has been designed to enable the efficient utilization of up to a few thousand processors, at the current model resolution. Several points needed to be addressed in order to achieve this. The first is that the global dependencies inherent in spectral models create the need for global communication, no matter which data partitioning is employed. Our choice has been to use the transposition strategy, which involves data re-organizations between different computational stages. A closer look at the dependency patterns in the model shows that in any phase of the algorithm there is just one direction (coordinate) in which the computations are non locally coupled. The two remaining dimensions provide a large amount of parallelism that can be exploited. However, the coupling direction changes from phase to phase of the algorithm. A data transposition between two such phases is used to ensure that coupled data will reside on a single processor during every phase. For example, during physics computations all dependencies lie on vertical columns, while computations in different grid locations are independent. At this stage every column has to be allocated to a single processor, while we have complete freedom on how to divide the columns among the processors. Each time step of the algorithm requires six transposition steps. A second characteristic of the IFS model is that it employs semi-Lagrangian advection in the time-stepping scheme, which greatly improves the overall performance because longer time steps can be used. This creates data dependencies which are local in nature, but which change dynamically with the wind structures. Different strategies for the parallelization of this part of the model are being studied. Here, tools are of great help to ease the efforts necessary for investigating the different options.

3.2 PARMACS

In the ECMWF efforts - past and present - PARMACS has been used as a message passing standard. Currently we are moving from the macro based version 5.1 to the library based version 6.0. We have generally been happy with both the level of abstraction it provides and with the robustness of different PARMACS implementations.

3.3 Performance analysis tools

ECMWF has used PATOOLS and Paragraph as the main tools for looking at the parallel performance of its programs. Both packages have their advantages and specific weaknesses, but the overall conclusion is that they proved to be useful and even necessary to really understand what is happening and to detect areas for possible improvements. Using PATOOLS and Paragraph on a regular basis in an ongoing code development revealed that only a limited number of the different displays are really used. In particular, displays that enable the programmer to visualize the communication behaviour of the program are favourite. It is felt that more statistical type of tools are needed to provide information on program execution on larger machines or on longer runs. These might summarize, for example, the communication behaviour of the program, its requirement of resources and so on. Examples of these kind of tools can be found in some vendor specific toolsets, e.g PRISM of Thinking Machines or APPRENTICE of Cray Research. Within the PPPE program Intel will provide a considerably modified version of Paragraph as a basis for further development which will also improve on many of the current shortcomings of these performance analysis tools.

4 Examples

In this paragraph some examples on the use of the currently available performance analysis tools will be given. Unfortunately these tools really require colour displays so that it will not be possible to fully demonstrate their capabilities in this paper. The Paragraph toolset which forms the basis of the performance analysis tools, was originally developed for the public domain. It will be further enhanced and put on a more standardized graphical basis (Motif). The Feynman diagram of this tool is used to demonstrate some of the capabilities which are available. This is a time-process diagram with the host shown as node 0. Coloured time axes show the current activities of the different nodes (not shown here). The communication between the nodes shows as connecting lines between them, starting at the sending node and terminating at the receiving node (considering increasing time along the x-axis).

4.1 Example 1 - different transposition strategies

This example demonstrates the use of the Paragraph tool to investigate the communication for different transposition approaches. Figure 1 shows a data transposition between 8 processors. Each processor sends data to every other processor. This is organized in a stepwise manner. In the first step, a node sends data to the node below it (in the figure) and receives data from the node directly above it. In the second step the node sends data to the node below the one it send to in the first step (2 below) and receives data from the node directly above the node it received from in the first step (2 above). This continues until all the data is transferred.

Figure 2 shows the so called recursive transposition approach [1]. In this the processors are devided into two processor groups exchanging data. Then each group is subdivided into subgroups and so forth. This reduces the number of messages from n*(n-1) to n*log(n), but increases the message size per single message.

In Figure 3 each node sends all messages before it tries to receive from other nodes. The transposition in Figure 4 exploits bi-directional communication links. In each step it establishes communication between a pair of node processors and exchanges data between them. This pairwise communication pattern is then pursued until all the data is exchanged.

Although Paragraph does not easily allow to evaluate the performances of the different strategies, it nevertheless allows to check the communication between nodes.

4.2 Example 2 - performance bug in semi-Lagrangian communication

In Example 2, the code behaved in a serial manner when a certain number of processors was exceeded (Figure 5).

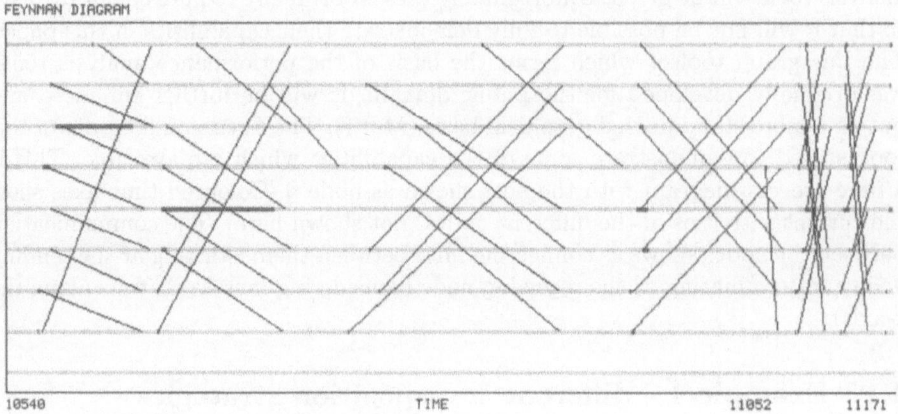

***Figure 1**: Communication for stepwise transposition*

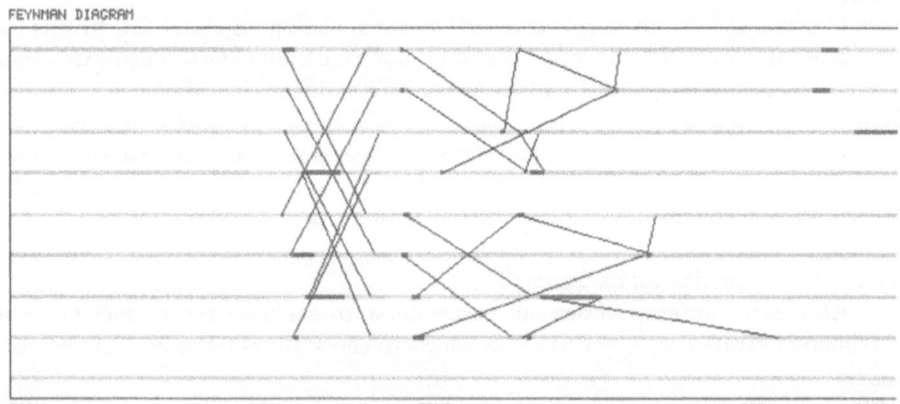

***Figure 2**: Communication for recursive transposition*

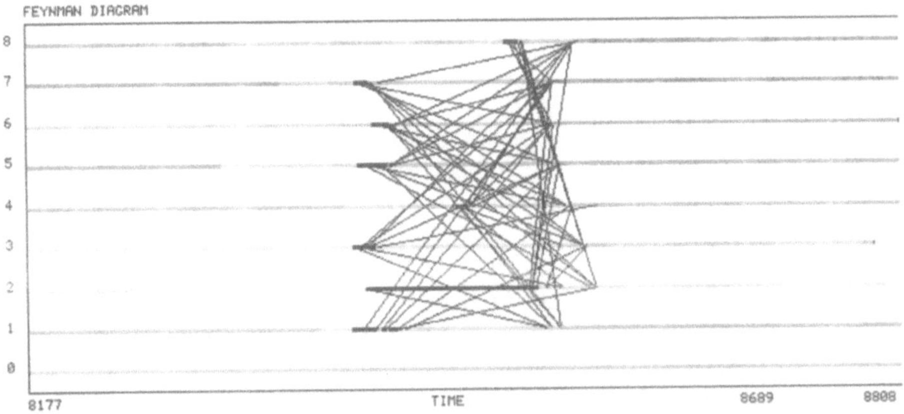

Figure 3: *Communication for send-all transposition*

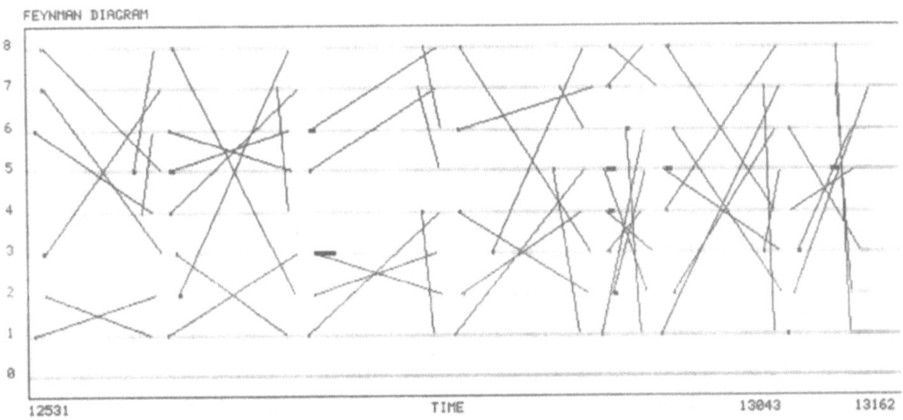

Figure 4: *Communication for bi-directional transposition*

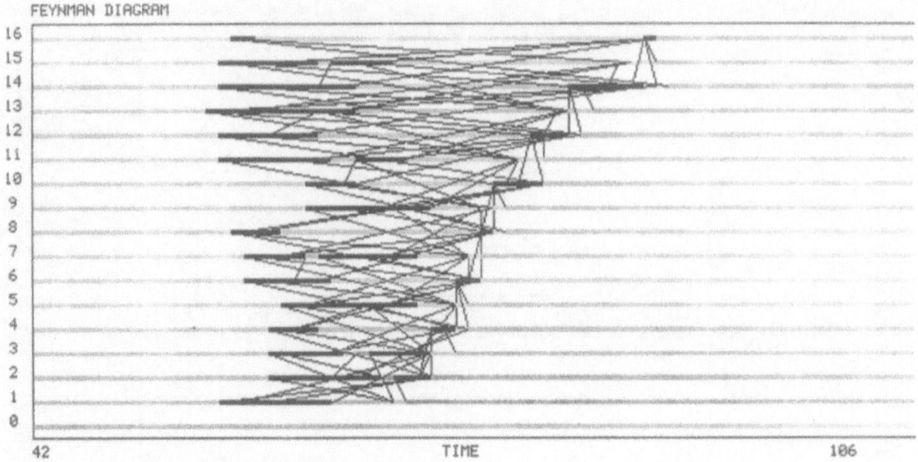

Figure 5: *Semi-Lagrangian communication with performance bug*

The numerical results of the calculation were correct, since the date was exchanged correctly. This feature of the code was detected, when the communication was examined using the Feynman display of Paragraph. Once the problem was detected it could be easily fixed by minor restructuring of the communication (Figure 6).

The impact on runtime for this example was minor. The real impact would only be seen with greater processor numbers. Figure 7 shows the scaling properties for real problem sizes as a function of the number of processors of the parallel system. For processor numbers below 100 the "bug" would pass undetected, since no significant impact could be found. Above 100 processors it would unexpectedly show in decreased performance of the parallel program.

5 Conclusion

The software development for an MPP system needs support and the PPPE project is targeted to provide this support. The examples show that tools like the PPPE tools are very helpful when dealing with large application codes like IFS. Parallelizing large applications for distributed memory computers creates new requirements to visualize distributed data and code and the need to handle communication between processors. This is a far bigger task to integrate into software development environments compared to the more conventional shared memory computers. Support aids do exist, usually addressing certain key issues like communication problems, portability across platforms, parallelization support for particular classes of problems and visualization of certain aspects of the program execution. These tools certainly add to the comfort of parallel programming and are needed to increase

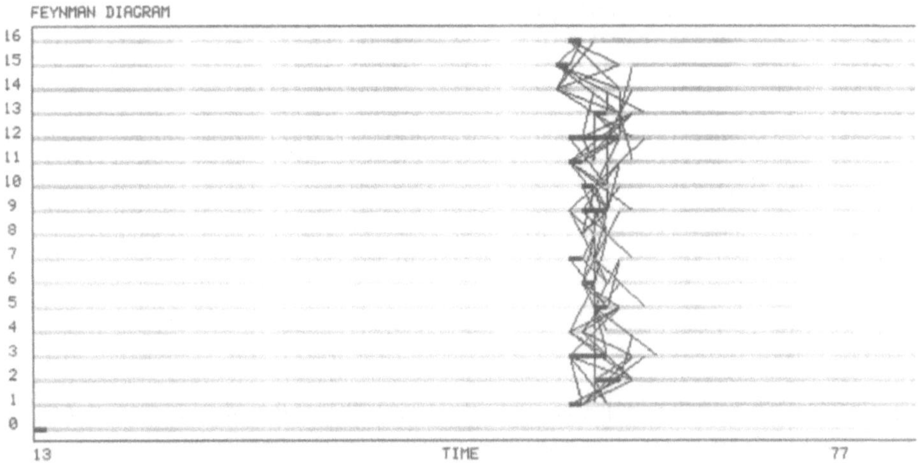

Figure 6: *Same as Figure 5 after restructuring the communication*

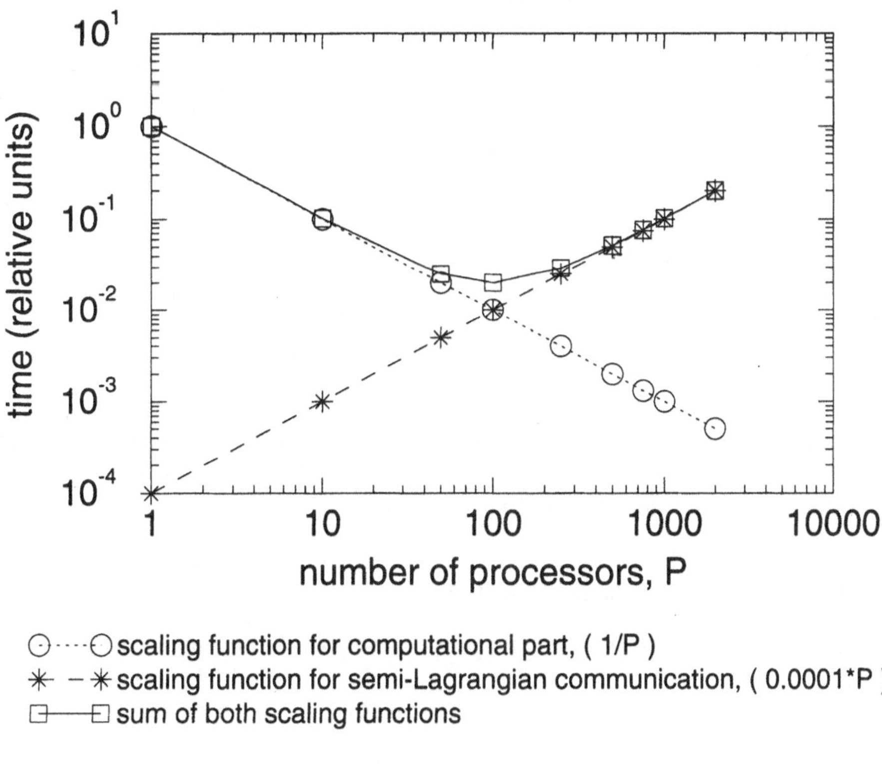

Figure 7: *Scaling properties of performance bug in S-L code*

acceptance of parallel computing in the scientific community.

Acknowledgements

The efforts described in this paper are the work of a number of people. Foremost to be mentioned are Geerd Hoffmann and Adrian Simmons who are managing the MPP efforts at ECMWF. Funding has been provided by the European Commission project number 6643 - PPPE (Portable Parallel Programming Environment) and 7255 - GPMIMD2 which the authors gratefully acknowledge.

References

[1] Barros, S. R. M. and Kauranne, T. (1990) *Spectral and multigrid spherical Helmholtz equation solvers on distributed memory parallel computers in Proceedings Fourth workshop on "Use of parallel processors in meteorology", 26-30 November 1990, ECMWF workshop proceedings, ECMWF, Shinfield Park, Reading RG2 9AX, UK.*

[2] Barros, S. R. M. and Kauranne, T. (1992) *On the parallelization of global spectral Eulerian shallow-water models in Proceedings of the Fifth ECMWF workshop on the Use of parallel processors in meteorology, 23-27 November 1992, Reading, UK G-R Hoffmann and T Kauranne (Eds.), 1993, World Scientific Publishers, 544 pp*

[3] Barros, S. R. M., Dent, D., Isaksen, L., Robinson, G. and Wollenweber, F. (1994) *The message passing version of ECMWF's weather forecast model to appear in Proceedings of HPCN '94, 18 - 20, April 1994, Munich.*

[4] Gao, G., Hendren, L., Panangaden, P., Feeley, M., Tao, L., Hancu, M., Hum, H., Lebensold, J., and Van Dongen, V. (1992) *Towards a Portable Parallel Programming Environment Proceedings of Supercomputing '92, Montreal, 7-10 June 1992*

[5] Bomans, L. and Hempel, R. (1990) *The Argonne/GMD macros in FORTRAN for portable parallel programming and their implementation on the Intel iPSC/2 Parallel Computing 15, 1990.*

[6] Hockney, R. (1992) *A Framework for Benchmark Performance Analysis Supercomputer, 48, IX-2, 1992, pp 9-22.*

[7] Willers, I. (1990) *State-of-the-art programming environments on parallel computers in Proceedings Fourth workshop on "Use of parallel processors in meteorology", 26-30 November 1990, ECMWF workshop proceedings, ECMWF, Shinfield Park, Reading RG2 9AX, UK.*

Programming Environments for Massively Parallel Distributed Systems, Monte Verità, Switzerland

The MPI Message Passing Interface Standard

Lyndon Clarke*
Edinburgh Parallel Computing Centre,
The University of Edinburgh,
Edinburgh EH9 3JZ, UK
lyndon@epcc.ed.ac.uk

Ian Glendinning†
Dep. of Elec. and Comp. Science,
University of Southampton,
Southampton, SO9 5NH, UK
igl@ecs.soton.ac.uk

Rolf Hempel†
GMD (German National Research Centre for Computer Science),
53731 Sankt Augustin, Germany
Rolf.Hempel@gmd.de

Abstract

The diverse message passing interfaces provided on parallel and distributed computing systems have caused difficulty in movement of application software from one system to another and have inhibited the commercial development of tools and libraries for these systems. The Message Passing Interface (MPI) Forum has developed a *de facto* interface standard which was finalised in Q1 of 1994. Major parallel system vendors and software developers were involved in the definition process, and the first implementations of MPI are already appearing. This article presents an overview of the MPI initiative and the standard interface, in particular those aspects which merge demonstrated research with common practice.

1 Introduction

The message passing paradigm is the most generally applicable and efficient programming model for parallel machines with distributed memory and has been used widely in parallel and distributed computing systems for some years. The development of parallel computing has been hindered by the absence of a standard message passing interface.

During 1992 the international Message Passing Interface (MPI) initiative was founded by Oak Ridge National Laboraory and the Center for Parallel Computing

*Work supported by the Science and Engineering Research Council NACC grant B/28667
†Work supported in part by CEC ESPRIT project 6643 (PPPE)

at Rice University [8]. The goal of this effort was to define a message passing interface wihch would be efficiently implemented on a wide range of parallel and distributed computing systems, this establishing a *de facto* standard and avoiding the overhead and delays associated with an official standardization process.

The procedures of the MPI Forum were modelled on those of the HPF Forum, in particular the process was open to all interested parties. Much of the technical discussion was conducted via electronic mail, and the forum met every six weeks in Dallas where formal decisions were made. The first complete draft [3] was presented in November 1993 at the Supercomputing Conference '93 in Portland, Oregon. Two further meetings were held early in 1994, the first at INRIA Sophia Antipolis, France and the second at Knoxville, Tennesee. These meetings considered public comment on the November draft which resulted in final changes and approval of the standard by the Forum. The finished interface document is planned to be released in April 1994.

2 Overview of MPI

MPI is intended to be the standard message passing interface for parallel application and library programming. The basic content of MPI is point–to–point communication between pairs of processes and collective communication within groups of processes. MPI also contains more advanced message passing features which allow the user to manipulate process groups, provide topological structure for process groups, and support the development and utilisation of parallel libraries.

The computing platforms for MPI comprise homogeneous and heterogeneous parallel and distributed systems. Every message whether in point–to–point or collective communication has an associated data type. The primitive data types of the host language, for example `INTEGER` and `REAL` in Fortran, are supported. MPI also provides very general facilities which can be used to describe `struct` types in C, and non-contiguous data in either C or Fortran, as "derived" data types. The data types of MPI provide all the information required for data conversion in heterogeneous environments, and do not preclude efficient implementation of MPI in homogeneous environments. They also allow the user to send and receive messages with complicated storage patterns without the need to copy data in to and out of message buffers, and allow an implementation to optimise communications with such storage patterns.

MPI does not make provision for process creation aside from requiring at least a basic SPMD process model from implementations. Other important issues such as parallel input/output and remote read/write were not included in MPI because the committee felt that research into these features is not yet mature enough for standardisation, or that there was insufficient time to establish concensus during this phase of MPI. The MPI Forum intends to cover further topics in a second phase which may commence as early as the second half of 1994.

3 Groups, contexts and communicators

Point–to–point and collective communications within MPI are performed within process groups. MPI defines a group as an ordered set of process identifiers, each of which is assigned a numerical rank within the group, between zero and the size of the group. Communications within MPI are also performed within a communication context which insulates messages in different parts of the program from one another. The defining property of a context is that a message sent in one context can only be received in that same context. The communication context is the primary mechanism for isolation of messages in different libraries and the user program from one another.

Process groups are user level objects in MPI but communication contexts are not directly visible. MPI bundles the process group and communication context concepts into a user level object called a *communicator* which provides communication services within a unique scope, as in the Zipcode [7] and CHIMP [5, 1] interfaces. MPI defines an initial communicator MPI_COMM_WORLD which has a group containing all processes of the program and a unique communication context.

MPI provides routines which allow the user to dynamically create new communicators, similar to the group routines of EUI [4]. MPI_COMM_DUP creates a duplicate of an existing communicator, i.e. a new communicator with the same group of processes and a different communication context. This routine is key to the construction of robust communicative parallel libraries. MPI_COMM_SPLIT creates one or more new communicators which contain distinct subgroups of an existing communicator and of course a different context. This routine is key to clear expression of task and control parallel programs. In the simplest use of MPI, which corresponds to a number of current communication libraries, MPI_COMM_WORLD is the only communicator used in the program.

4 Point-to-point communication

The point-to-point message-passing routines form the core of the MPI standard, the basic operations being *send* and *receive*. They allow messages to be sent between pairs of processes, with message selectivity based explicitly on message tag and source process, and implicitly on communication context. Each process can execute its own code, in MIMD style, and can be sequential or multithreaded. There is no explicit support for threads, but care has been taken to make MPI "thread safe", by avoiding the use of global state.

The send and receive primitives are provided in a blocking form in which the sender buffer can be reused immediately on return from send and the receiver buffer contains the complete message on return from receive. There is one blocking receive primitive MPI_RECV. There are four blocking send primitives corrspeonding to the four communication modes in MPI.

Standard The sender is blocked until the send buffer can be reused without altering the message. The receiver is blocked until the message has been copied into the receive buffer. Since the system is expected to copy the message subject to buffer resources, the send-recv pair does not guarantee synchronisation. This mode seems to best represent common practice. The send primitive is MPI_SEND.

Synchronous The sender is blocked until the receiver issues the corresponding receive. No system buffer is required and the message can be transferred without intermediate copies, at the expense of synchronisation. The send primitive is MPI_SSEND.

Ready-receive The program is in error if the send is issued before the matching receive has been issued. This allows a simple protocol where the message is sent "in hope" and dropped if there is no ready receive, but use demands special care. The send primitive is MPI_RSEND.

Buffered This mode allows the user to control the space available for buffering within a defined buffer model, providing guaranteed portability for programs that demand message buffering. The send primitive blocks until the message is copied into the buffer space or is in error if insufficient buffer space was available. The send primitive is MPI_BSEND.

MPI also provides primitives of the non-blocking, or immediate return, form, MPI_I?SEND and MPI_IRECV, in which the message buffer must not be used until the communication has completed, similar to the immediate routines in NX/2 [6]. There is a small but comprehensive set of routines to test and wait for completion of non-blocking functions. This functionality, which is semantically orthogonal to the four communication modes, allows the system to overlap communication with computation and allows the user to write programs which do not incur the overhead of copying message data into intermediate buffers.

5 Collective communication

Collective communications are provided where all processes in a process group are involved in a collective operation. A collective function is called as if it contained a group synchronisation, although this property is not mandated since efficient implementations may not synchronise. We now decribe a familiar selection of the collective routines.

MPI_BARRIER Synchronisation of every processes within a group.

MPI_BCAST Every process within a group receives data broadcast by a "root" process.

MPI_GATHER Every process within a group sends data to a "root" which stores the data in rank order.

MPI_SCATTER The inverse of MPI_GATHER, where a "root" process sends sections of data to every process within a group in rank order.

MPI_REDUCE Performs a parallel reduction over every group process within a group. The operation is selected from a set of defined arithmetic and logical operators or is described as a user function. The output is available to a "root" process, every process, or scattered over the processes.

MPI also contains collective routines for all-to-all global communication, all-to-all personal communication otherwise known as complete exchange, and inclusive parallel prefix otherwise known as scan.

6 Process topologies

Many numerical applications have a geometrical background. For example, the parallelization of a PDE solver on a three–dimensional grid leads to a corresponding arrangement of the processes. The most natural way of addressing those processes is to specify their coordinates in the grid, as opposed to their linear ranks in the group. MPI supports the setup of general Cartesian process structures, as well as arbitrary process graphs, similar to the PARMACS interface [2], Process topologies in MPI are assigned to process groups within communicators, and process ranks in the group are ordered by topological location. Topologies are created and deleted at run-time, and a process can exist within many topologies simultaneously.

Cartesian topologies are created by calling MPI_CART and can also be derived from higher dimension Cartesian topologies by calling MPI_CART_SUB. For example these functions can be used to create a two dimensional process grid group and the corresponding one dimensional process row and column groups. Since group boundaries limit the scope of collective operations the process topologies can easily be used for operations like broadcast and reduction in matrix columns.

Graph topologies are created by calling MPI_GRAPH which accepts an adjacency list as the description of the graph. This complements the Cartesian topology and is applicable in problems which are parallelised by the block structured domain decomposition approach where adjacent blocks are mapped to adjacent processors in the graph. Due to the locality principle of PDE methods, a process in a topology tends to exchange most messages with adjacent processes. Thus, the topology information can be used by an MPI implementation to minimize network congestion by mapping adjacent processes onto adjacent resources.

7 Conclusion

We have briefly described features of the MPI standard including the core point to point and collective communications, communication contexts and process groups, and process topologies. We have not described more advanced features such as the communicator cache facility, which allows the user to extend the collective communication and process topology capabilities of MPI, or provision for communication between processes in different groups, which makes MPI attractive for applications which contain internal parallel client-server or pipeline structures. The interested reader is referred to the interface document [3].

At the time of writing two implementations of MPI are known to be available in the public domain. The first of these has been authored by Argonne National Laboratory and Mississipi State University, and is based on a device interface which has been designed to allow rapid and reasonably efficient ports of MPI to parallel systems. The device interface has been implemented using Chameleon providing a range of platforms, and has also been ported directly to a small number of parallel systems. The second implementation has been authored by Edinburgh Parallel Computing Centre as a library running atop CHIMP, which also provides a range of parallel and distributed computing systems.

References

[1] R. Alasdair A. Bruce, James G. Mills, and A. Gordon Smith. Chimp version 2.0 interface. Technical Report EPCC-KTP-CHIMP-V2-IFACE, Edinburgh Parallel Computing Centre, University of Edinburgh, January 1993.

[2] Robin Calkin, Rolf Hempel, Hans-Christian Hoppe, and Peter Wypior. Portable programming with the PARMACS message–passing library. *Parallel Computing, special issue on message–passing interfaces*, to appear.

[3] Message Passing Interface Forum. Document for a standard message-passing interface. Technical Report CS-93-214, University of Tennessee, November 1993.

[4] D. Frye, R. Bryant, H. Ho, R. Lawrence, and M. Snir. An external user interface for scalable parallel systems. Technical report, IBM, May 1992.

[5] James G. Mills, Lyndon J. Clarke, and Arthur S. Trew. Chimp concepts. Technical Report EPCC-KTP-CHIMP-CONC, Edinburgh Parallel Computing Centre, University of Edinburgh, April 1991.

[6] Paul Pierce. The NX/2 operating system. In *Proceedings of the Third Conference of Hypercube Concurrent Computers and Applications*, pages 384–390. ACM Press, 1988.

[7] A. Skjellum, S. Smith, C. Still, A. Leung, and M. Morari. The Zipcode message passing system. Technical report, Lawrence Livermore National Laboratory, September 1992.

[8] D. Walker. Standards for message passing in a distributed memory environment. Technical Report TM-12147, Oak Ridge National Laboratory, August 1992.

Programming Environments for Massively Parallel Distributed Systems, Monte Verità, Switzerland

An Efficient Implementation of MPI

Hubertus Franke * Peter Hochschild Pratap Pattnaik
Marc Snir
IBM T.J. Watson Research Center

Abstract

MPI-F, a prototype high-performance implementation of MPI on the IBM SP1 is described and MPI-F communication performance is presented.

1 Introduction

During the past few years, there has been a significant growth in the availability of powerful massively parallel computers. Most of these computers, for various market driven reasons, are distributed memory computers. To support the users of these computers, vendors have developed proprietary message passing packages such as NX [11] on Intel Paragon, CMMD [13] on TMC CM-5 and EUI [7] on IBM SP1. In addition, portable message passing libraries have been developed by software vendors, such as Express [10] by Parasoft, or by research centers, such as PVM [4], P4 [2] and PARMACS [3]. These packages provide similar functionality, but are often incompatible at the application level. Proprietary libraries offer good performance on one platform, but inhibit portability; whereas portable, public domain libraries often compromise performance. Furthermore, currently available packages often lack important functions, such as good support for modular development of libraries. The lack of a standard message passing interface, which is implemented efficiently on a large variety of platforms, has been one of the most serious impediments to developing large scale parallel applications.

To remedy these deficiencies, an open work group was formed to propose a message passing interface (MPI) standard [6]. The group included participants from computer vendors (Convex, IBM, Intel, Meiko, Ncube, TMC, etc.), software vendors (Parasoft, KAI, etc.), Research centers (ANL, GMD, NOAA, ORNL, Sandia, etc.) and universities (Edinburgh, Maryland, Miss. State U., Southhampton, Syracuse, etc.) from various countries. After a year of extensive and open deliberation the final version of MPI was approved in early 1994. Vendors participating in the MPI forum have expressed their support for MPI, and both proprietary and

*contact: Hubertus Franke, IBM T.J. Watson Research Center, P.O. Box 218, Yorktown Heights, NY 10598, USA. email: frankeh@watson.ibm.com

public domain implementation of MPI are expected to become available within months.

MPI incorporates many features from existing message passing libraries, so that existing code will easily port to MPI. However, it also provides many novel features, in particular, in support of modular programming, and in order to allow enhanced performance on machines with intelligent communication hardware. MPI specifies a binding for Fortran77 and for C.

In this paper, we briefly sketch some of the key features of MPI and describe MPI-F, a prototype high-performance implementation of MPI on IBM SP1 [9].

2 Key Features in MPI

In this section we describe some of the key features of MPI as they relate to our implementation. For more detailed information on MPI functionality the user is referred to [6].

2.1 Point-to-Point Communication

MPI distinguishes between blocking and non-blocking send and receive operation. The (blocking) send operation MPI_SEND completes when data has been copied out of the send buffer, so that the communication buffer can be accessed again. A (blocking) receive operation MPI_RECV completes when an incoming message has been copied into the receive buffer and becomes available to the receiving process. However, the completion of a send operation does not necessarily indicate that a matching receive has occurred, or has even started. The outgoing message may be copied into an intermediary system buffer, thus allowing the sending process to proceed before a matching receive is posted.

The use of nonblocking operations allows a better overlap of communication and computation (on systems where hardware allows such overlap). Nonblocking operations immediately return a handle to the application which can be waited(MPI_WAIT) or queried(MPI_TEST) on later. Receives are generally more efficient if they are already posted when the message arrives: the incoming message may be moved immediately to user memory.

Both blocking and nonblocking sends come in three flavors:

- Standard Send - The send call can be invoked either before or after the corresponding receive has been posted, and completes as soon as the sender buffer is free to be reused.

- Ready Send - The send call can be invoked only after the corresponding receive has been posted, and completes as soon as the sender buffer is free to be reused.

- Synchronous Send - The send call can be invoked either before or after the corresponding receive has been posted, and completes only after the receive has been started at the receiving process.

2.2 Datatypes

In order to support heterogeneous environments and to ease programming, MPI provides, instead of the byte count, an explicit data_type parameter to communication routines. For both language bindings, a set of predefined datatypes (such as MPI_FLOAT, MPI_CHAR) exists, which is coherent with those defined in the language. In addition, the user can recursively define datatypes of arbitrary depth, such as multi-dimensional vectors with fixed or varying strides or C-like data structures. MPI also permits a send and corresponding receive to have different data_types, hence providing convenient means to perform data remapping, such as transpose of matrices etc. The overhead spent in defining these data_types can be amortized over multiple communications.

2.3 Communicator

One of the key features in MPI is the *communicator*, an object, supplied as an additional parameter to communication operations. Communicators provide modularity in the development of message passing code and, thus, provide important support for the development of libraries and of large codes. The use of communicators grew out of work done in Zipcode [12] and on collective communication in CCL [1].

Previous communication libraries used an absolute naming scheme for communicating processes. This is an impediment on modular development of code: all process names have to be shifted when two independent modules, each running on a disjoint set of processes, are combined together into one application. Instead, in MPI communication calls, processes are identified by their relative rank in a group. The communicator parameter identifies the group of communicating processes; communication using this communicator is restricted to this group of processes. Thus, a piece of parallel code that executes on a set of n processes, need not be changed when the set of executing processes is changed; one merely need to redefine the communicator used for internal communication by that piece of code.

Each communicator implicitly identifies a unique communication context. Each context is akin to an additional tag that differentiates messages. Contexts are managed in more restrictive ways by the system, e.g. they are hidden and can not be "wildcarded" in receive operations. Thus, each context provides a separate communication universe, and communication in one context cannot be confused or interfere with communication in another context. This significantly simplifies the design of libraries. MPI suggests the use of a different context (a different communicator) for any two independent computation activities that may concurrently send messages to the same destination. Message matching is restricted to a particular context and as such it is guaranteed that different library invocations do not interfere with each other when different communicators are used.

MPI provides a variety of mechanisms to create and manage communicators. An initial MPI_COMM_WORLD communicator is predefined at initialization time. The associated group includes all processes available at initialization time.

2.4 Collective Communications

MPI provides a rich set of collective communication functions. These include barrier synchronization, broadcast, scatter, gather and various reduction operations. All collective operations involve a group of processes and hence all calls have a communicator parameter which specifies the group involved. Thus, as in EUI [1], collective communication may involve an arbitrary, previously defined, subset of processes.

3 MPI-F Implementation

This section describes the approach taken towards implementing MPI on the IBM-SP1 and the various components of the MPI-F system.

3.1 SP1

The 9076 PowerPARALLEL System 1 (SP1) is a distributed memory multiprocessor that is marketed by IBM. Each SP1 node consists of an RS/6000 processor with up to 256 MBytes memory and up to 2 GBytes disk. Each node runs a full copy of the AIX Unix operating system. Fast communication is provided by the optional high performance switch. This is a multistage packet-switching network with a hardware capability for 40 Mbytes/s duplex transfers from each node, and a total latency which is below one microsecond. Due to limitations of the present SP1 communication adapter (a passive device attached on the Microchannel bus that provides a simple interface consisting of FIFO buffers for incoming and outgoing packets and control registers), the hardware cannot support more than 13 Mbytes/s Bandwidth. An implication of this hardware structure is that the entire communication protocol and all data transfers are currently executed in software.

3.2 System Architecture

In order to achieve a high performance version of MPI on the IBM-SP1 the entire communication stack is implemented in user space, as opposed to implementing it as a UNIX kernel extension. This presupposes that there is only one MPI user per processor, which is a reasonable assumption for high performance parallel computers. To accommodate the situation where there is more than one MPI user per processor, we have also implemented a version over IP/UDP. These two versions only differ in the packet layer described below.

MPI-F system evolved out of the EUI-F system (a high performance EUI implementation on SP1) and distinguishes different layers in its communication stack: *MPI Pt2Pt message layer*, *pipe layer* and *packet layer* (the latter two are shared between MPI-F and EUI-F). The functionalities of the different layers are as follows:

3.2.1 Packet Layer

The packet layer provides software point to point packet transport facility among processors by directly interacting with the communication network. Since the IBM-SP1 high performance switch network provides multiple paths among the processors, this layer is designed to use random routing by selecting routes from multiple tables. Hence, it is the responsibility of this layer to create appropriate packets, and insert appropriate routing information into each of the generated packets. To preserve the flexibility of choosing various routing strategies and simplify the error recovery, this layer, like IP-UDP, is not assumed to provide reliable transport or packet ordering. However, this layer is expected to provide uncorrupted packets, performing checksum on packets if necessary.

3.2.2 Pipe Layer

The pipe layer is built on top of the packet layer and provides a reliable, flow controlled, byte-stream oriented communication layer. Each process maintains a send and a receive buffer (called pipe) to every other process in the parallel job. These buffers perform functions similar to UNIX pipes and sockets (that is how their name evolved), yet they shall not be confused with them, as they are placed in user space to avoid the cost of a unix kernel access.

Task of the pipe layer is a reliable data transport from the send pipe to the corresponding receive pipe. This layer uses the typical mechanisms, such as, flow control, acknowledgements and retry after timeout etc. Flow control is achieved by associating tokens with the contents of the buffers. Tokens flow back when the message layer reads data from the receive pipe. Accordingly, the sending side is not permitted to enter new data into the send pipe if tokens are unavailable. The pipe layer provides the following *non-blocking* functional interface to the message layer (where # denotes a specific pipe number).

- *BytesFree(#):* tests how many bytes can be written to the pipe.
- *BytesAvail(#):* tests how many bytes can be read from the pipe.
- *WritePipe(#):* writes data into the pipe. The pipe maintains its internal status, i.e. buffer pointer, and takes care of wrap arounds etc.
- *ReadPipe(#):* Reads data from a pipe, i.e. from its next available position.
- *KickPipes():* Invokes the pipe scheduler.

MPI send mode	internal protocol	receive behavior
standard	if (size ≤ threshold) then eager else rendezvous	buffering if no match
ready	eager	error if no match
synchronous	rendezvous	

***Figure 1**: MPI Send Modes and Relationship to MPI-F Internal Protocol*

The pipe scheduler incorporates the following activities. Most importantly, it has to drain the packets from the network to avoid network congestion. Since packets may arrive out of order, it must place the incoming data at the correct position in the pipe-buffer and acknowledge the packet together with the appropriate number of tokens. When data arrives at the front of a receive pipe buffer, the *ReadFromPipe* callback function is called to notify the message layer that data can be read. Similarly, if acknowledge packets arrive, by which new send pipe buffer space is freed, the *ShoveIntoPipe* callback function will be called to allow the message layer to insert more data into the pipe. Since either the data packets or acknowledge packets can be lost, the pipe scheduler will resent unacknowledged data after a certain time-out, and consequently the pipe layer must recognize duplicate packets and drop them.

The pipes are scheduled in a fair manner to access the underlying network. Sending a large message will not prevent the delivery of pending sends on other pipes.

Since the scheduler does not run as a separate thread, but rather is invoked by the message layer in almost every pt2pt communication request (using *KickPipes*), progress must be guaranteed even in the situation that the application executes communication unrelated code for long periods of time. This is achieved by periodically invoking the scheduler asynchronously in the background using UNIX signal handling. An interrupt driven version also exists, which calls the scheduler when packets arrive from the high performance switch.

3.2.3 MPI Pt2Pt Message Layer

Task of the message layer is to implement the MPI point-to-point communication efficiently. This involves several tasks:

Message Delivery: With each destination the message layer maintains a message queue. When notified by the pipe layer via the ShoveIntoPipe callback the message layer will attempt to send a message along this pipe. A message is not guaranteed to fit completely into the pipe-buffer, therefore, a state must be maintained for each message to ensure correct delivery over several reentrant calls to ShoveIntoPipe. This is especially cumbersome for non-contiguous datatypes. Also MPI requires that messages to the same destination using different contexts (i.e.

different communicators) do not affect each other. To respect these MPI requirements and to implement the three different modes of send communication MPI-F uses two different internal protocols (see Figure 1):

eager: Messages are forced through the network. Hence, arriving messages, which do not have a matching receive posted yet, have to be pulled out of the pipe and temporarily buffered until the matching receive has been posted. This has the disadvantage that a sender can swamp a receiver hence leading to memory problems in temporary buffering.

rendezvous: A "request-to-send" is first send which will be acknowledged by the receiving side as soon as a matching receive has been posted. In the meantime other sends can proceed. Upon return of the acknowledge, the message reenters the send queue and is delivered. Though this method does not require any intermediate buffering for early arrival messages it requires an additional roundtrip which increases latency by a factor of 2.6 for zero-byte messages. For larger messages this overhead vanishes.

The current implementation tries to utilize the best of both worlds. The standard send uses the eager send protocol up to a threshold size. Above the threshold the rendezvous protocol is used. The threshold is configurable at job startup time, so to allow users to fine tune their applications. The case where a large number of small unmatched messages are send and have to be buffered on the receiving side can still lead to temporary buffer problems. Though this scenario is rare as most applications have some form of synchronous behavior, flow control can be enabled which limits the number of outstanding messages along one pipe at any given time, however has slightly worse latency.

Datatype Handling: The MPI point-to-point communication is required to deal with abritary non-contiguous datatypes. Rather than packing and unpacking the entire message and sending and receiving as a contiguous message, MPI-F incorporates mechanisms which efficiently packs and unpacks on the fly in and out the pipe buffers. This is cumbersome because simple recursive algorithms can not be used, due to the arbitrary reentrance requirements of the pipe layer. For this purpose MPI-F provides its internal stack object to emulate recursion under reentrance conditions. In the case of contiguous messages these objects are obsolete.

Object Management: The message layer creates and manages send and receive descriptors. A handle to this descriptor is returned as an opaque *MPI_Comm_request* object in non-blocking communication requests. The descriptors keep the information necessary to complete a communication request, even though the request might have been asynchronous and returned to the user. The object is transparent to the user.

Memory Management: Since the message layer callback functions *ReadFromPipe* and *ShoveIntoPipe* can be called asynchronously from the UNIX signal

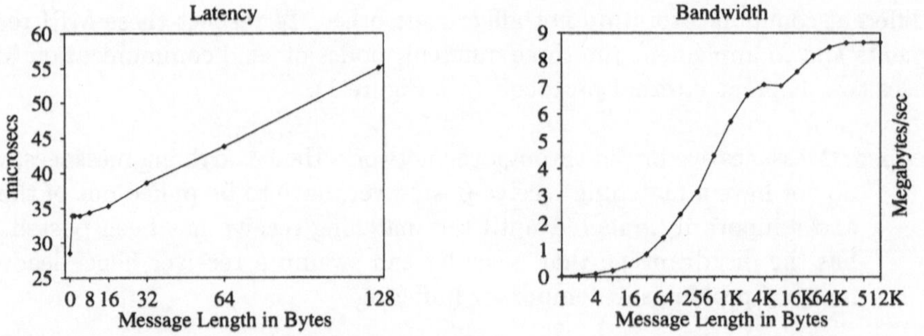

***Figure 2**: Latency and Bandwidth in MPI-F*

handler that ensures background message progress, message passing related objects, such as descriptors and temporary buffers can be allocated asynchronously. In order to avoid interference with the application's unprotected memory management calls as well as to provide high efficiency, the MPI-F Pt2Pt layer uses its own non-interfering memory management for message objects, buffers and stack objects. The used buffer space can be configured on a per job base.

3.2.4 Non Pt2Pt MPI Layer

The non-point-to-point functions of MPI, which include group and communicator management, collective communication and virtual topologies, are either implemented independently or above the MPI point-to-point message layer. For this upper layer we have utilized the emerging public domain version of MPI provided by Argonne National Laboratory and Mississippi State University [5]. We have closely collaborated with them to ensure a smooth and efficient interface between device dependent and device independent code [8].

3.3 Status and Performance

The MPI-F system implements the entire MPI standard, with the exception of interprocess communicators. It provides a C and a Fortran77 interface. To our knowledge this is the only full and efficient native MPI implementation on any parallel machine.

To determine the latency and bandwidth for MPI point-to-point communication we have measured the time of a simple ping-pong program using MPI_Send and MPI_Recv for various message sizes.

The resulting latency and bandwidth as a function of message size is shown in Figure 2. The 0-byte latency of the MPI_Send/MPI_Recv pair is $28.5\mu secs$ and the effective bandwidth is 8.7 MBytes/sec (1KByte $== 2^{10}$ and 1MByte $== 2^{20}$). The irregularity in the Bandwidth between 4 and 8KBytes is attributed to the default rendezvous setting of 4KBytes. It can be shifted by modifying the threshold.

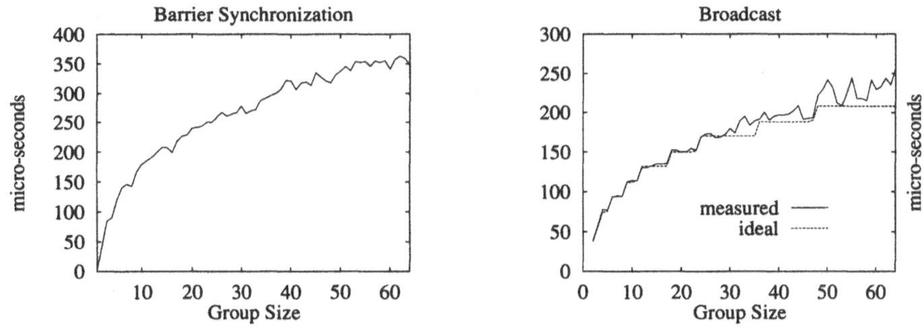

Figure 3: *Barrier Sync and Broadcast Performance in MPI-F*

Communication time in μsec as a function of msgsize n can be approximated by $T_{comm}(n) \approx T_{start} + 0.15 \times n$, where T_{start} is either $33.5\mu secs$ for eager or $77\mu secs$ for rendezvous based communication.

Figure 3 shows the latency for the collective operations "barrier synchronization" and "broadcast" as a function of the participating group size. The logarithmic shape of both the curves demonstrates the scalability of these collective operations under MPI.

The achievable bandwidth for a 3D character vector $A[d_2][d_1][d_0]$ as a function of d_0 and d_1 ($d_2 := 16Meg/(d_1 * d_0)$) is shown in Figure 4. As can be expected for small d_0 the overhead is large and hence the bandwidth is limited. However, the contour projections in the $\prec d_0, d_1 \succ$ plane reveal, that (1) the bandwidth basically depends only on the size d_0 of the inner block and (b) 85% of the maximum achievable bandwidth of 8.3 Mbytes (small and non-contiguous messages can not achieve 8.7 Mbytes) is already reached at $d_0 = 64bytes$.

MPI-F can not take advantage of some of the opportunities for communication optimization in MPI, due to current limitations of the communication adapter in SP1. In particular, since all communication is executed in software, communication and computation cannot be overlapped. MPI offers interesting opportunities and challenges when implemented on a machine with an advanced communication adapter, in terms of protocol offload and communication and computation overlapping. We expect to explore some of these issues on future generations of the SP1 product.

4 Conclusion

The large number of functions in MPI, and the added functionality in the basic communication functions may lead one to suspect that MPI is difficult to implement, and will not be efficient. Our experience dismisses this suspicion. MPI-F was implemented by a small number of people in a few months. This was possible because MPI functions can be implemented by composing a small number of prim-

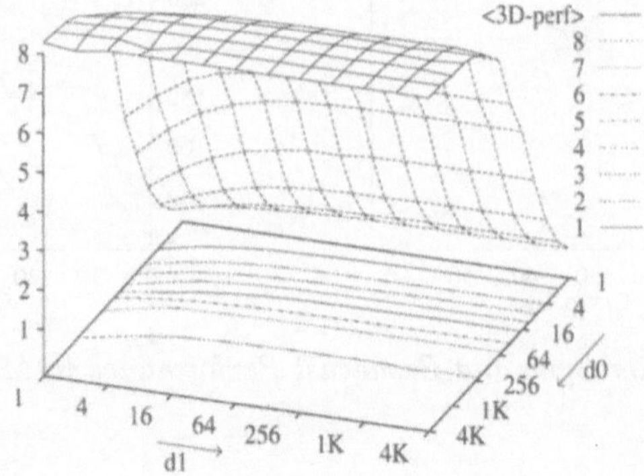

***Figure 4**: Bandwidth for 3-D Vectors in MPI-F*

itive functions; low-level layers of existing communication libraries can be reused, although care has to be exercised not to lose performance, as MPI requires more multiplexing of independent communications. MPI-F is as efficient as the most efficient communication library currently available on SP1, when executing the same type of communication. Overheads are higher when more advanced features are exercised, e.g. when complex derived data_types are used. It is our experience that the higher level of abstraction of MPI as compared to other similar message-passing libraries lead to cleaner and better integrated implementation, ultimately resulting in improved performance.

An efficient implementation of MPI is only the first step towards a usable MPI-based programming environment. We are currently working on interfacing debugging and performance tuning tools with the MPI library. Work on an MPI interface to a parallel file system is also in progress. We expect that MPI will be quickly available on a large variety of platforms, both with native, high-performance implementations and with portable, public domain implementations. This, and the convenient support of libraries in MPI, is likely to lead to the fast proliferation of libraries and tools that enhance MPI useability.

References

[1] V. Bala, J. Bruck, R. Cypher, P. Elustondo, A. Ho, C.-T. Ho, S. Kipnis, and M. Snir. Ccl: A portable and tunable collective communication library for scalable parallel computers. *IEEE Transactions on Parallel and Distributed Computing*, to appear.

[2] R. Butler and E. Lusk. User's guide to the P4 programming system. Technical Report TM-ANL-92/17, Argonne National Laboratory, 1992.

[3] R. Calkin, R. Hempel, H.-C. Hoppe, and P. Wypior. Portable programming with the parmacs message–passing library. *Parallel Computing, special issue on message–passing interfaces*, to appear.

[4] J. Dongarra, A. Geist, R. Manchek, and V. Sunderam. Integrated PVM framework supports heterogeneous network computing. *Computers in Physics*, 7(2):166–75, April 1993.

[5] N. Doss, W. Gropp, E. Lusk, and A. Skjellum. An initial implementation of mpi. Technical Report MCS-P393-1193, Mathematics and Computer Science Division, Argonne National Laboratory, December 1993.

[6] M. P. I. Forum. Document for a standard message-passing interface. Technical Report CS-93-214, University of Tennessee, November 1993.

[7] D. Frye, R. Bryant, H. Ho, R. Lawrence, and M. Snir. An external user interface for scalable parallel systems. Technical report, IBM, May 1992.

[8] W. Gropp and E. Lusk. An abstract device definition to support the implementation of a high-level point-to-point message-passing interface. Technical report, Mathematics and Computer Science Division, Argonne National Laboratory, December 1993.

[9] IBM. *IBM 9076 Scalable POWERparallel 1, General Information*, Feb 1993.

[10] Parasoft Corporation. *Express Version 1.0: A Communication Environment for Parallel Computers*, 1988.

[11] P. Pierce. The NX/2 operating system. In *Proceedings of the Third Conference on Hypercube Concurrent Computers and Applications*, pages 384–390. ACM Press, 1988.

[12] A. Skjellum, S. Smith, C. Still, A. Leung, and M. Morari. The Zipcode message passing system. Technical report, Lawrence Livermore National Laboratory, September 1992.

[13] Thinking Machines Corporation. *CMMD Reference Manual*, December 1992.

Programming Environments for Massively Parallel Distributed Systems, Monte Verità, Switzerland

Post: A New Postal Delivery Model

Marc Aguilar Béat Hirsbrunner
IIUF-Institute of Informatics, University of Fribourg,
Ch. du Musée 3, CH-1700 Fribourg, (Switzerland)
Aguilar@CfrUni52.Bitnet

Abstract

We present in this paper a new communication and dynamic migration technique which is based on a postal delivery model providing transparent mail management and routing facilities for the implementation of dynamic load balancing strategies. Protocols are defined by concepts such as a finite state machine and a distributed address book. This postal delivery model is actually used for the design and development of Cola, a new coordination language.

1 Introduction

In order to support dynamic migration and load balancing strategies, we present in this paper a new postal delivery model for message passing systems which provides flexible, dynamic and transparent communication techniques for mail and address management. Our objective is to guarantee that the designers of distributed applications have no longer to deal with machine dependent communication, addressing and routing mechanisms, even if the processes migrate dynamically during the execution of the application.

At each site of the system, routing information and mail management will be handled by a Post, cf. figure 1. Within the context of the Pact project [Agu93], an environment for parallel heuristic programming on MIMD machines, we implemented different dynamic migration protocols and tested the robustness of the Posts. For a detailed discussion about related work [AF89] [BL90] [Roz+90], we refer to [Agu93]. Another very interesting postal mail delivery model has been introduced by [Bur93] in the Remote Objects' Message Exchange (ROME) abstraction.

This paper is organized as follows. Section 2 focuses on the definition and description of dynamic migration and communication protocols. Section 3 presents a prototype and some results concerning routing information, pending mail, rerouted messages and execution time. Section 4 contains the concluding remarks and describes some future research areas we expect to benefit from our approach. Finally,

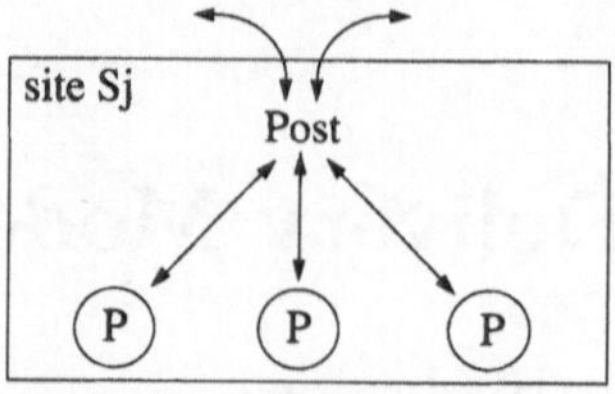

Figure 1. Postal delivery model

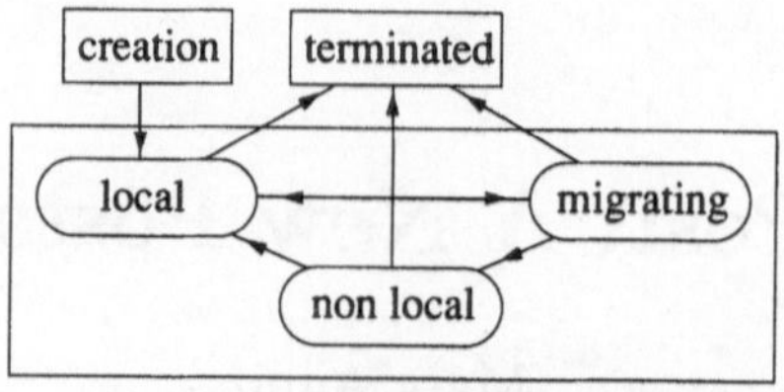

Figure 2. Abstract finite state machine

formal protocol definitions are given in the appendix.

2 Dynamic migration and communication

Three basic design concepts define the specification of the Post: (a) an abstract finite state machine which defines the different states a process can take on a site; (b) a fully distributed address book which contains all necessary routing information; (c) a new high level identification concept for distributed processes, representing communicating processes as correspondents.

While designing the migration protocols, two other important characteristics have been taken into account: (a) the dynamic migration of a process can take place more than once during the runtime of an application; (b) the anticipated termination of a process is possible.

2.1 Abstract finite state machine

The Post of a site Sj delivers the mail to a process P with respect to the current state P has on site Sj. Transitions between states are raised by asynchronous events, i.e. the creation, the termination and the migration of a process. For any site Sj of the distributed system, the state of a process P is defined to be (see figure 2): (1) local, if P is physically located on Sj; (2) migrating, if the current location of P is unknown to the Post of Sj; (3) non local, if the Post of Sj has the information that P is local to another site Sk; (4) terminated, if P has terminated its execution.

2.2 Dynamic migration protocols A and B

Protocol A: When process P migrates from site Sj to site Sk, protocol A sets up in the local address book of site Sj the following routing information : (1) the unique identifier of P; (2) the current state of P; (3) the forward chaining address. A copy of P's correspondents routing information will be memorized in the local address book of site Sk if the allocation strategy at site Sk allows P to execute locally. A formal definition of protocol A is given in the appendix.

```
-- On the reception of a message m for process P
case current state of P is
   local:        deliver m to P;
   migrating:    cash m as pending mail;
   non local:    reroute m to the Post designated by the forward chaining address;
   terminated:   destroy m;
end case;
```

Figure 3. Communication protocol

Protocol A has one major drawback: each migration of P involves the transfer of all P's correspondents routing information known at site Sj. This technique is very expensive in memory and transmission time. Therefore we suggest protocol B which reduces considerably the routing information to transmit.

Protocol B: For any migration of process P from site Sj to site Sk, protocol B sets up at site Sj the same routing information as protocol A but does not transmit the routing information of P's correspondents. Mail addressed by P's correspondents will be routed from site Sj to site Sk by using the forward chaining address at site Sj. But if P sends messages to its correspondents, Post Sk cannot compute the corresponding routing paths. Therefore, protocol B memorizes at site Sk the expedition site address Sj to reach P's correspondents by back chaining. If necessary, this technique will be repeated by the different Posts. A formal definition of protocol B is given in the appendix.

Optimizations: Routing path information can be dynamically updated, if intermediate Posts add to the mail the *current* used routing path. While delivering the mail, the optimized protocols (denoted by A* et B*) update their local routing information by snooping the added path information.

2.3 Communication protocol

For the migration protocol A, the communication protocol is given by the pseudocode of figure 3. For the migration protocol B, it is possible that no routing information of the addressed correspondent is available; in this case mail has to be sent to the Post designated by the back chaining address.

3 Prototype and results

In this section, we present some results obtained by implementing the communication and dynamic migration protocols on an iPSC/2 MIMD computer. For our tests, migration techniques are restricted to passive objects.

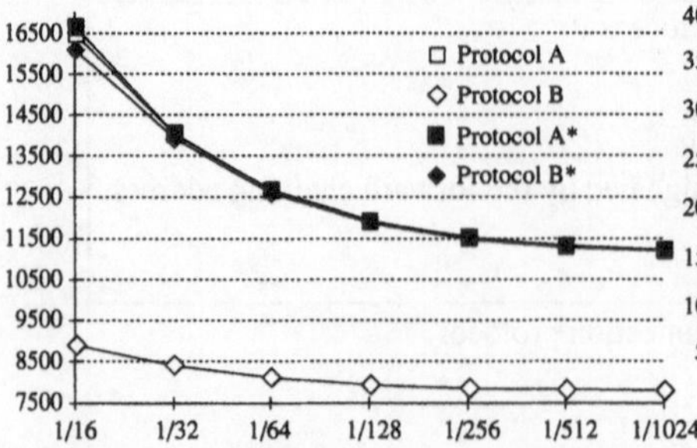

Figure 4. Amount of routing information

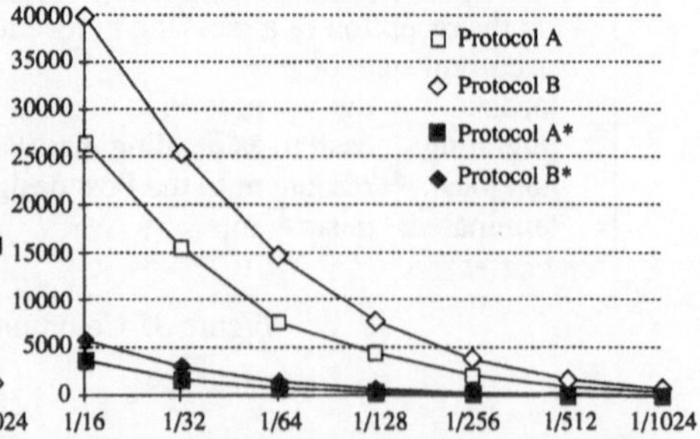

Figure 5. Amount of rerouted mail

3.1 Prototype

The four protocols described in section 2.2 have been implemented on a iPSC/2 with 8 sites. To test the protocols, we computed a tree of depth 5 and branch factor 5, i.e. 3906 nodes or objects. Each object has 6 correspondents, its father and its 5 children. The initial placement guarantees that all the correspondents of an object are placed on a different site. This strategy produces a maximum number of intersite communications. During the runtime of the application, the objects are randomly migrated among the resources of the system with a frequency $f(n) = 1/n$, where n defines the number of local events before a migration occurs. An event is defined to be a random object activation and a message send operation to all of its correspondents. On each site of the system, the execution of the application stops after 10'000 events.

3.2 Results

Routing information: Figure 4 shows the influence of the migration frequency upon the number of routing information stored at the Posts. For this criteria protocol B is optimal. By comparing the number of routing information generated by the protocols A, A* and B*, Figure 4 illustrates that protocol B cuts down the number of routing information closely to a factor 2 for high migration frequencies and to a factor of 1.5 for low migration frequencies.

Rerouted messages: Figure 5 shows the influence of the migration frequency upon the number of rerouted messages in the system. The optimized protocols A* and B* cut down the number of rerouted messages by a factor between 6 and 10.

Pending mail: Figure 6 illustrates the amount of pending mail produced during the runtime of the application. Our tests showed that pending mail depends on the distributed allocation strategy and the time it takes to migrate an object P. If the allocation strategy is poor in the sense that P is shifted around among several sites until P can execute, the amount of pending mail will raise.

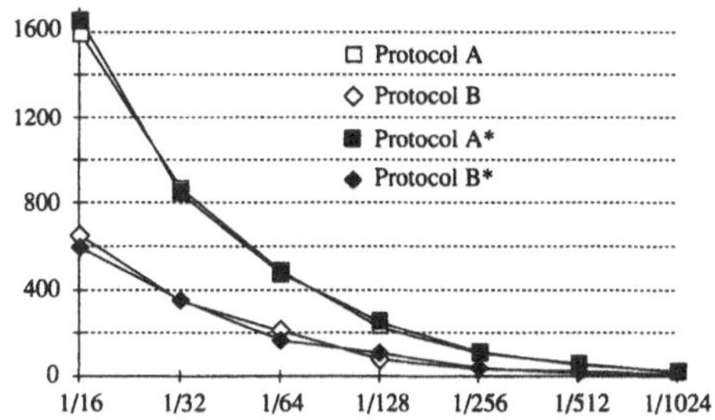

Figure 6. Pending mail

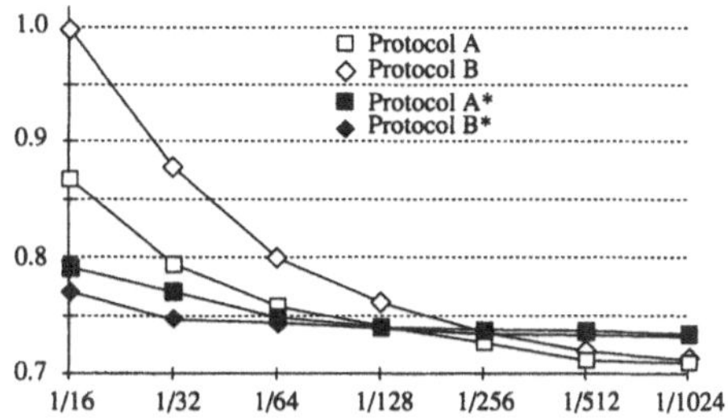

Figure 7. Normalized execution time

Execution time: Figure 7 outlines the normalized execution time of the application. For high migration frequencies, B* is best whereas A does best for low frequencies. The optimized protocols don't improve the performance for low frequencies because of the overhead for updating the routing information. The most interesting phenomenon of this study is that the optimized protocols use approximately the same execution time for migration frequencies in the interval [1/1024, 1/128]. For more detailed experimental results, consult [Agu93].

4 Conclusions and future work

The post delivery concept we presented in this paper offers transparent communication tools for dynamic load balancing strategies. This new approach is based on the definition of an abstract finite state machine, a fully distributed address book and the new identification concept of representing communicating processes as correspondents. The new tool of postal mail management makes massively parallel computers much easier to use and allows the programmer to abstract from technical and physical details related to the target machine. Our prototypes show that in a massively parallel environment the classical available communication and synchronization tools are neither adequate for a clever specification nor for an efficient implementation of the postal mail management.

In future works, we will concentrate on the development of a new coordination language called Cola [HAK94]. Cola uses the new postal delivery concept presented in this paper as a platform for the design and the implementation of new communication and synchronization mechanisms between correspondents. Relations between correspondents are only logically defined and dynamically computed by declarative rules. Cola supports a higher level of abstraction because the programmer: (a) computes the related communicating processes in terms of an application oriented communication topology; (b) uses the postal mail delivery model for efficient and transparent message passing.

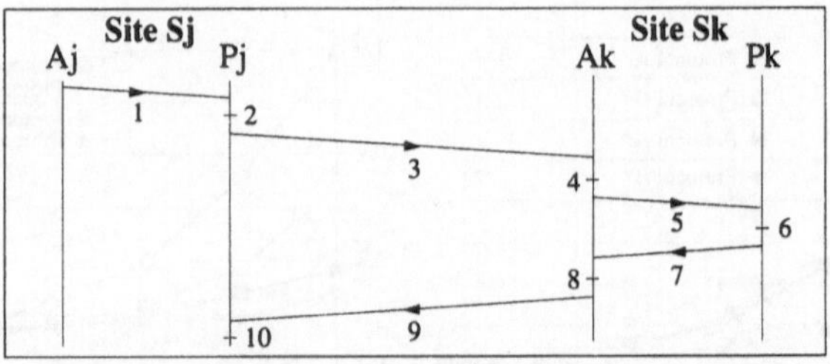

Figure 8. Diagram of the migration protocols A and B

Appendix: Formal definition of protocols

Protocol A: (1) Post Pj receives from the local allocator Aj a process P which has to be migrated to site Sk; (2) Post Pj switches the current state of process P from *local* to *migrating* and sets up P's correspondents routing information. For the special case where a correspondent Cj is in state *migrating*, Post Pj adds address Sj as routing information for Cj; (3) Process P and its correspondents routing information are sent to site Sk; (4) Post Pk memorizes P's correspondents routing information; (5) Post Pk transmits P to the local allocator Ak; (6) Allocator Ak receives P and decides if P can be executed locally; (7) If P can run on site Sk, Ak announces the establishment of P to his local Post Pk, else Ak determines a new destination site Sl and sends P back to Pk; (8) If P stays at site Sk, Post Pk switches the state of P to *local*, else Pk sets up P's correspondents routing information. In the latter case, Pk keeps any routing information of P's correspondents; (9) If P is *local* to site Sk, the Post Pk informs the Post Pj that P is *local* to site Sk, else P and its correspondents routing information are sent to site Sl; (10) Post Pj switches the state of P from *migrating* to *non local* and adds address Sk to the routing information of P.

Protocol B: The formal specification of protocol B is identical to protocol A, with the following differences: the routing information related to correspondents is no longer transmitted and in step (8) of figure 8, if P remains local to site Sk, the Post Pk memorizes only the address of the expedition site Sj.

References

[AF89] Y. Artsy and R. Finkel. Designing a process migration facility: The charlotte experience. *IEEE Computer*, 22(9):47–56, September 1989.

[Agu93] Marc Aguilar. *Communication et migration dynamique dans Pact, un environnement pour la programmation heuristique parallèle.* PhD thesis, Université de Fribourg, Chemin du Musée 3, CH-1700 Fribourg, Switzerland, April 1993.

[BL90] Th. Bemmerl and Th. Ludwig. Mmk: A distributed operating system kernel with integrated dynamic load balancing. In H. Burkhart, editor, *Compar90 - VAPP IV, Joint Conference on Vector and Parallel Processing*, pages 744–755. Springer-Verlag, September 1990.

[Bur93] S. Burleigh. Rome: Distributing c++ object systems. *IEEE Parallel and Distributed Technology*, 1(2):21–32, May 1993.

[Roz+90] M. Rozier et al. Overview of the chorus distributed operating system. Technical Report CS/TR-90-25, Chorus Systems, 6, avenue Gustave-Eiffel, F-78182 Saint Quentin Yvelines Cedex, France, 1990. 45 pages.

[HAK94] B. Hirsbrunner, M. Aguilar, and O. Krone. Cola: a coordination language for massively parallel systems. Submitted to 13th ACM Symposium on Principles of Distributed Computing, Los Angelos, 14-17 August 1994.

Programming Environments for Massively Parallel Distributed Systems, Monte Verità, Switzerland

Asynchronous Backtrackable Communications in the SLOOP Object-Oriented Language

N. Signès, J.-P. Bodeveix, D. Plaindoux, F. Cabestre, C. Percebois
Institut de Recherche en Informatique de Toulouse
31062 Toulouse - France
{signes, bodeveix, plaindoux, cabestre, perceboi}@irit.fr

Abstract

In this paper, we present the resolution algorithm of an extension of the Prolog language to backtrackable communications. This algorithm is based on a dependency graph recording the connections between communication points. An example illustrates the use of backtrackable communications into the SLOOP object-oriented language.

1 Introduction

SLOOP [CPPB93] is a multi-paradigm language combining object-oriented programming, logic programming and parallelism. Parallelism is supported by threads executing a Prolog goal. Communication and synchronization between threads are supported by explicit message passing or by updates of shared objects.

In this paper, we focus our attention on explicit message sending and more precisely on the interaction between communication and resolution. In SLOOP, we consider asynchronous point to point communications where a choice done by the transmitter process has an effect on the receiver process. A failure over the receipt of a message may lead to a backtrack on the transmitter process.

Compared to existing models, our approach differs from CS-Prolog approach [FF92] which uses non-deterministic N to 1 blackboard based communications. Our primitives are closely related to Δ-Prolog [CMCP92] except that asynchronous and backtrackable capabilities are available.

2 The Resolution Algorithm

We present the resolution algorithm of our Prolog extension in a more general non-logical framework wherein we consider a set of non-deterministic threads cooperating via asynchronous communications.

2.1 The Abstract Language

Each thread i is defined by an internal state `state`(i) initially set to r_i, and by an action `action`(i) defined by the following abstract syntax:

action ::=	exec(f), action	*apply the function f to the current state*
	| alt(action,action)	*don't know non-deterministic choice (OR-node)*
	| send(j), action	*send the internal state to thread j*
	| recv(j,f), action	*receive a state from j and merge it with f*
	| abort	*global failure*
	| exit	*local successful termination*

Running a program made of a set of threads consists in looking for a sequence of applications of actions leading each thread from its initial state to a successful state. This search is implemented by a concurrent depth-first traversal of the graph of reachable states with backtracking. Backtracking may influence the execution of a thread which communicates with another thread leading to a failure.

2.2 The Dependency Graph

Backtrackable communications link (initially independent) threads: the success of the receiver thread depends on the success of the sender thread and conversely. The implementation of these communication primitives ensures the search of a *coherent* solution for the set of communicating threads: a term received in the branch leading to the success of the receiver thread must be the same as the term sent in the branch leading to the success of the sender thread.

Solving a failure is based on a simplified analysis of its reasons; more complex analysis leads to intelligent backtracking algorithms [BB93]. A failure depends on the previous choices it is subsequent to. This algorithm ensures that all the alternatives of these choice points are tried and that the search is complete in a finite space.

The execution builds a dependency graph over the choice points introduced by the execution of `alt` instructions: a dependency link connects an old choice point to a newly created choice point. To take into account dependencies induced by communications, we complete this dependency relation by a link from the transmission point to the receiver point. Thus, we define a partial order relation over the nodes of the whole application. A failure is only subsequent to the choices made on the (distant or local) points the current node depends on. These dependencies are recorded in a *dependency graph* denoted by the binary relation $\rightarrow$.

2.3 The Resolution Algorithm

The resolution algorithm updates a set of backtrackable states indexed by thread numbers: `bstate`(i). They are compound by the state of the thread (`state`(i)), the current backtrack point (cp(i)), the action to be performed (`action`(i)) and two families of pointers on message queues (`in`(i)(j) and `out`(i)(j)) respectively defining the index of the first message to be received from the thread j in the queue ji and of the last message sent to the thread j in the queue ij. Thus, restoring the state of a thread also restores the messages sent and received by the thread.

```
-- execution of a family of threads running act(i) from the state r_i
∀i ∈ Threads , bstate(i) :=< r_i, bstate(i), alt(act(i), abort), empty_in, empty_out >;
→:= ∅;
par i in Threads loop -- parallel execution
  loop
    if ¬ failure(i) and action(i) ≠ exit then -- Forward Resolution
      switch action(i):
        case send(j), a => -- send to j and execute the next action a
-- add a message (the state) into the queue ij at the index out(i)(j)
          add-queue(queue(i,j), out(i)(j),bstate(i)); action(i) := a;
        case recv(j,f), a => -- receive from j and merge the state with f
          if in(i)(j) < out(j)(i) then -- a message is ready to be read
-- get a message of the queue ji at the index in(i)(j)
            mess := get(queue(j,i),in(i)(j));
-- get the most recent of the current cp and the received cp
            new_cp := max(cp(i),cp(mess)); -- with respect to →
            →:=→ ∪{mess → bstate(i), min(cp(i), cp(mess)) → new_cp};
            state(i) := f(state(i),state(mess)); cp(i) := new_cp;
          -- else wait for a message
          end if;
        case alt(a1,a2) => -- create a choice point and update the graph
          →:=→ ∪{cp(i) → bstate(i)};
          cp(i) := bstate(i); action(i) := a1;
        case exec(f), a => update the local state
          state(i) := f(state(i)); action(i) := a;
        case abort => exit(global failure);
      end case;
    else -- Backward Resolution
      if (∀j action(j) = exit and the i^th thread is selected for backtracking)
        -- look for the next solution
        or (failure(i)) then -- the i^th thread fails
        for k in Threads loop
          if k = thread(cp(i)) then -- Backtrack to cp(i)
            P_i := {maximal ascendant of cp(i) for →};
            choose p in P_i;
-- graph updating to visit all points the failure depends on
            →:=→ ∪{q → p | q ∈ P_i − {p}};
            bstate(k) := <state(cp(i)),p,alt_action(cp(i)),in(cp(i)),out(cp(i))>;
          elsif k depends on cp(i) then
-- restart the dependent thread k
            state(k) := the older local ancestor that depends on cp(i);
          end if;
        end for;
      end if;
    end if;
  end loop;
end loop;
```

The forward algorithm extends the Prolog algorithm by updating the dependency graph each time a thread executes an `alt` or `recv` action and each time the choice point is selected for backtracking. The backward resolution algorithm is activated each time a failure leads to the backtrack on the choice points associated with the defined primitive.

2.4 Synchronization of the threads after a failure

During its backward resolution, a thread has to interrupt the computation of dependent threads. For this purpose, we have introduced two signals: the BACKTRACK signal enforces the failure of the destination point; the RESTART signal enforces the resumption of the computation from the destination point.

A BACKTRACK signal is sent to the selected choice point, a maximal ancestor of the failing point in the dependency graph, and execution goes on after the completion of the distant backtrack request. This synchronization between the failing thread and the thread selected for backtracking is required to ensure that messages which remain valid after the completion of the backtracking algorithm and messages invalidated by the backtrack are not together in use.

On receiving a BACKTRACK signal, the thread undoes the computations that are more recent than the addressed choice point and fails. All computations done by any thread and which depend on the selected node for backtracking must be undone. For this purpose, if backward processing comes over a source of some dependency links, RESTART signals are sent to extremity choice points associated with these links. When a receipt point is reached, the previously received message is sent back to the communication buffer. Thus, the message does not need computing and transmitting again.

On receiving a RESTART signal, forward execution starts again from the addressed choice point as if the choice point were newly created. Backward processing is the same as for a BACKTRACK signal.

3 Integration into the SLOOP Language

In order to integrate the proposed extensions into SLOOP, communications are embodied into classes. Methods of basic classes are defined by directly calling Prolog predicates while methods of higher level classes are defined in the SLOOP language. This distinction is only based on implementation considerations.

Basic classes include the `thread` class which allows the creation of a thread executing a user's Prolog goal, the `port` class which supports backtrackable communications via `send` and `recv` methods and the `cluster` class which creates a list of mutually dependent threads.

At a higher level, we have defined two types of synchronization constraints between the threads of a `cluster` class instance:

- The `conjunction` class connects a set of threads with an *and* operator. The `wait` method of the `conjunction` class guarantees that son threads have all successfully exited before an answer is returned.

- Likewise, the `disjunction` class connects a set of threads with an *or* operator. The method `wait` waits for and returns the exit value of one of the threads.

3.1 The Map Coloring Problem

Solving the famous map coloring problem consists in giving a color to each region of a map such that any two neighbour regions have different colors. This example illustrates the use of *asynchronous* backtrackable communications. Our solution couldn't be directly transcribed in Δ-Prolog which only defines *synchronous* backtrackable communications.

In SLOOP, we have specified this problem with two classes:

- The `region` class inherits from the `thread` class and contains an attribute associated with the list of adjacent regions. This class defines the behaviour of the thread attached to a `region`. The thread chooses a color, sends the selected color to its neighbourhood, receives the color of each neighbour and checks if it differs from its own color.

- The `map` class creates a `conjunction` from the regions which define the map and waits for a compatible solution for each region.

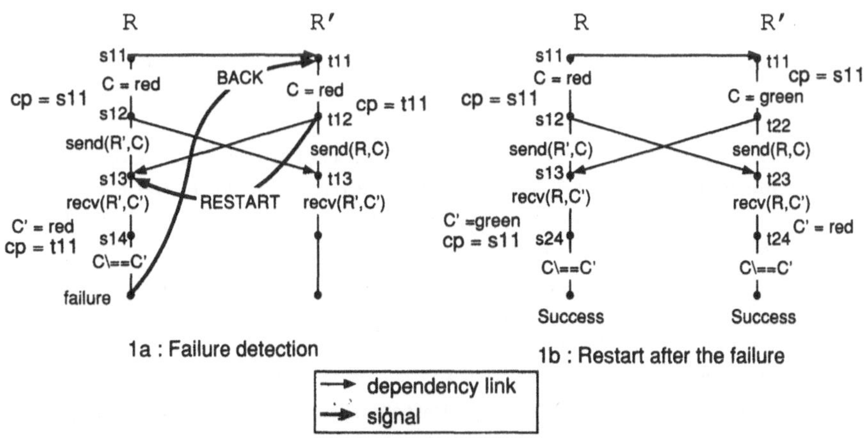

***Figure 1**: Execution of the map coloring problem*

The figure (*figure 1*) illustrates the execution of the map coloring problem with two regions R and R'. A first run leads to a failure (*figure 1*a) on the state

$s14$ of the thread R: the backward algorithm is then activated. A BACKTRACK signal is sent to the current choice point of the region R computed by the forward resolution: the node $t11$. When undoing all computations done after the state $t11$, the region R' cross away the state $t12$ and sends a RESTART signal to the state $s13$ of the region R. Then both threads continue their execution (*figure 1*b) from the state $s13$ for the region R and from the state $t11$ for the region R'; a success occurs.

4 Conclusion

The SLOOP language combines object-oriented programming, logic programming and parallelism. In this paper, we have presented asynchronous one to one backtrackable communications between Prolog threads. These primitives are implemented on top of the IC-Prolog [CC93] multi-threaded language. In addition, these tools are integrated into the SLOOP object-oriented language and have been validated. Backtracking primitives widen the object-oriented paradigms towards the prototyping of extensible applications which require the co-ordination of concurrent actors. However, the use of these primitives must be limited to applications where completeness is the main issue because distributed backtracking induces an important overhead. A first prototype implementation of the SLOOP language with backtracking communications is available on a mono-processor workstation. We now plan to work on a version suited for distributed architectures.

References

[BB93] J.-P. Bodeveix and E. Bizouarn. A Parallel Execution Model - Theroretical Approach and Experimental Results. In IEEE Computer Society Press, editor, *procs. of the* 7th *International Parallel Processing Symposium*, pages 7–15, Apr 1993.

[CC93] D. Chu and K. Clark. I.C. Prolog II : a Multi-Threaded Prolog System. In Giancarlo Succi and Giancarlo Colla, editors, *Procs. of the ICLP'93 workshop on Concurrent, Distributed, & Parallel Implementations of Logic Programming Systems*, pages 115–136, Jun. 1993.

[CMCP92] J.C. Cunha, P.D. Medeiros, M.B. Carvalhosa, and L.M. Pereira. Delta Prolog: A Distributed Programming Language and its Implementation on Distributed Memory Multiprocessors. In Peter Kacsuk and Michael J. Wyse, editors, *Implementation of Distributed Prolog*, pages 335–356. J. Wiley & Sons, 1992.

[CPPB93] F. Cabestre, D. Plaindoux, C. Percebois, and J.-P. Bodeveix. SLOOP: Une extension de Prolog aux objets concurrents. In Equipe ArMen, editor, *procs. des* 5èmes *rencontres sur le parallélisme*, pages 115–119, May 1993.

[FF92] Sz. Ferenczi and I. Futó. CS-Prolog: A Communicating Sequential Prolog. In Peter Kacsuk and Michael J. Wyse, editors, *Implementation of Distributed Prolog*, pages 357–378. J. Wiley & Sons, 1992.

Programming Environments for Massively Parallel Distributed Systems, Monte Verità, Switzerland

A Parallel I/O System for High-Performance Distributed Computing*

Steven A. Moyer
V. S. Sunderam

Department of Mathematics and Computer Science
Emory University, Atlanta, GA 30322, U.S.A.
{moyer, vss}@mathcs.emory.edu

Abstract

PIOUS is a parallel file system architecture for providing process groups access to permanent storage within a heterogeneous network computing environment. PIOUS supports parallel application development by providing coordinated access to *parafile* file objects with guaranteed consistency semantics and a dynamically-selectable fault tolerance level. For performance, PIOUS declusters files to exploit the combined file I/O and buffer cache capacities of multiple interconnected computer systems.

1 Introduction

Programming environments for developing distributed applications with groups of cooperating processes are becoming increasingly important for cost-effective, high-performance computing. Existing parallel-distributed computing environments, such as PVM [Sun90b] and Linda [ABC$^+$90], provide interprocess communication, synchronization and concurrency control, fault tolerance, and process management. However, many parallel applications require or could benefit from a unified parallel I/O system that such environments generally lack.

PIOUS, the Parallel Input/OUtput System, is a parallel file system that provides process groups access to permanent storage within a heterogeneous network computing environment. This paper focuses on the PIOUS architecture and programming model.

*Research supported by the National Science Foundation, under Award No. CCR-9118787, U. S. Department of Energy, under Grant No. DE-FG05-91ER25105, and the Office of Naval Research under grant N00014-93-1-0278.

2 Basic Architecture Principles

The PIOUS architecture embodies a number of principles that we feel are essential to developing a flexible, reliable, and high-performance network parallel file system:

- transport and native file system independence to enhance portability; PIOUS assumes only that mechanisms exist to reliably transport data between cooperating machines, and to access data on permanent storage from a subset of those machines;
- an asynchronous model of operation to increase system parallelism; components of the PIOUS architecture operate independently without the need for explicit synchronization;
- data declustering for cost-effective scalable performance; PIOUS declusters files over multiple interconnected systems to aggregate transfer rate and buffer cache capacities and load-balance access requests;
- integrated concurrency control and fault tolerance mechanisms for guaranteed consistency semantics and reliability; PIOUS provides sequential consistency of access and tolerance of system failures by requiring components of the architecture to interoperate via transaction-based protocols;
- access mechanism and policy independence to facilitate experimentation in file structure and user interface design; components of the PIOUS architecture that provide consistent and reliable data access are separate from components that implement the file system model.

3 PIOUS Software Architecture

The PIOUS software architecture is depicted in Figure 1. PIOUS consists of a set of data servers, a service coordinator, and library routines linked with client processes. An underlying transport mechanism is assumed to carry messages between client processes and components of the PIOUS architecture. PIOUS data servers are assumed to access permanent storage via a native file system.

A PIOUS Data Server (PDS) resides on each machine over which files are declustered. Each PDS provides transaction-based access to the local files that represent a portion of a declustered file. PDS do not interpret the global structure of a file, however, thus separating file access mechanisms from policies. PDS are independent and hence do not communicate, enhancing system parallelism and scalability. Though ideally each PDS accesses a file system local to the machine on which it resides, two PDS may share a file system via a network file service.

A single PIOUS Service Coordinator (PSC) initiates activities within the system. For example, when a process opens a file the PSC is contacted to obtain file meta-data and to ensure that the requested file access semantics are consistent

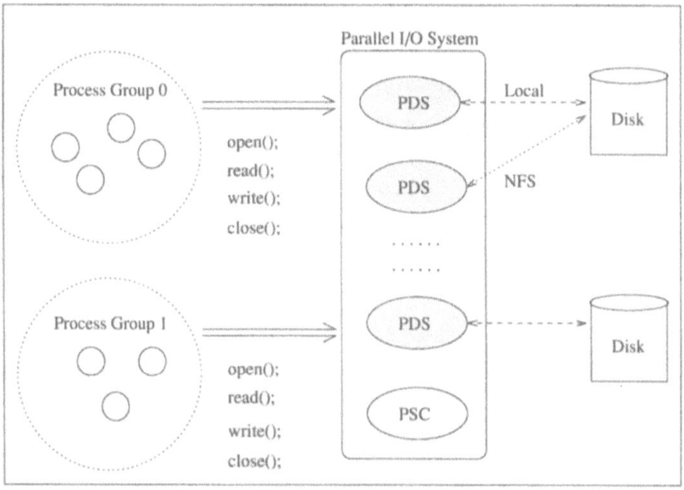

Figure 1: *PIOUS software architecture*

with those of other processes in the group. Note that the PSC only participates in major system events and not general file access, thus it does not represent a system bottleneck.

Finally, each PIOUS client process is linked with library routines that translate file operations into PDS/PSC service requests. Global file structure and access policies are implemented at this level, facilitating experimentation in user interface design without requiring re-implementation of the PDS or PSC.

The PIOUS architecture emphasizes asynchronous operation and scalable performance via the independence of parallel data servers, the interpretation of global file structure in client library routines, and the lack of a centralized manager for all but major events. Furthermore, the architecture is relatively free of assumptions concerning the underlying transport and storage subsystems.

4 Transactions in PIOUS

Parallel I/O operations in PIOUS are performed within the context of transactions [BHG87], transparently to the user, to provide sequential consistency [Lam79] of access and tolerance of system failures. Referring to Figure 1, client library routines act as transaction managers for the data servers participating in a distributed transaction satisfying a user request.

The PIOUS architecture defines two distinct transaction types: *stable* and *volatile*. Both transaction types guarantee serializability of access. A stable transaction is a "traditional" transaction that employs logging and synchronous disk write operations to also guarantee that coherence is maintained in the event of a system failure. A volatile transaction is a "light-weight" transaction that does not guarantee fault tolerance. Providing two distinct transaction types allows user-selectable levels of fault tolerance to be implemented.

Specifying that PIOUS components interoperate via transaction-based protocols might seem to be an implementation detail rather than an architectural issue. However, employing transaction-based protocols allows elements of the PIOUS architecture to operate independently and obviates the need for special concurrency control and fault tolerance components.

5 PIOUS File Structure and User Interface

A PIOUS file structure and interface design are presented below. To better support parallel applications, our file system model is based on a parallel access file object, called a *parafile*, and a user interface that directly supports the coordinated interaction of cooperating processes.

For the remainder of this text the term PIOUS refers to our particular implementation of the PIOUS architecture. Thus we discuss features of PIOUS not directly specified by the architectural description; e.g. file structure details.

5.1 Parafile Objects

Parafiles are implemented in PIOUS to facilitate parallel data mapping. Parafiles are logically single files composed of one or more physically disjoint segments. Each segment is composed of a linear sequence of zero or more bytes. The number of segments in a parafile is set at the time of creation and does not change for the life of the file.

Each parafile segment resides on a single PIOUS data server. If the number of parafile segments exceeds the maximum number of PDS for declustering the file, then segments are mapped to data servers in a round-robin fashion.

Figure 2 illustrates a parafile object with four segments declustered over two data servers. At each data server a directory contains file entries that represent parafile segments and associated meta-data; the directory path name is the logical file path name at the given server. Implementing parafiles on top of a conventional file system necessitates representing each parafile segment as a separate file.

Because parafiles are two-dimensional, array and tabular data map naturally. Thus developing parallel scientific, database, and sorting applications, among others, should be greatly simplified. Parafiles are based on Kotz's *multifiles* [Kot93] and McElrath's *virtual files* [McE93], two segmented file schemes proposed independently. The terms *file* and *parafile* are used interchangeably for the remainder of this text, as a parafile is the only file object implemented in PIOUS.

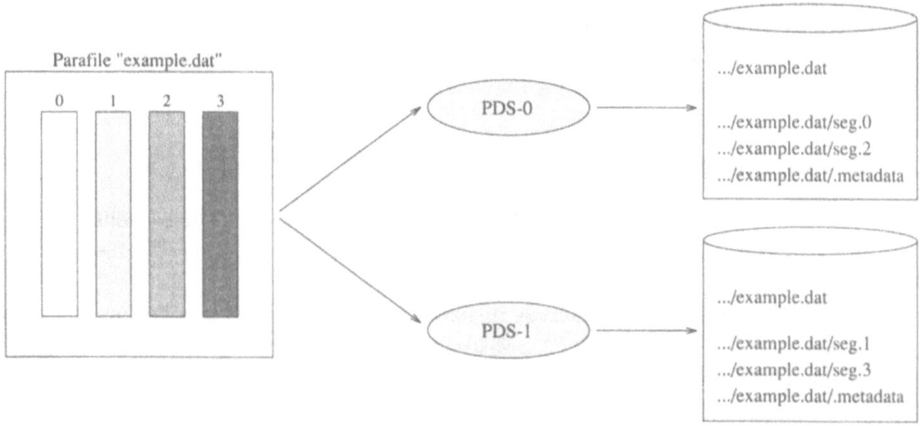

Figure 2: *Parafile object*

5.2 Parafile Access Semantics

The PIOUS interface provides a process group with three *views* of a parafile object: global, independent, and segmented. Each parafile view provides a process group with a distinct set of access semantics, as defined below:

global A file appears as a linear sequence of data bytes; all processes in a group share a single file pointer; datum access and file pointer update are atomic.

independent A file appears as a linear sequence of data bytes; each process in a group maintains a local file pointer; datum access is atomic.

segmented The segmented structure of a parafile is exposed; each process accesses a segment via a local pointer; datum access is atomic.

Under the views defined, parafiles are either accessed by segment or logically mapped to a linear sequence of bytes. A linear byte sequence is defined by ordering the bytes in a parafile by fixed size blocks taken round-robin from each segment. Thus for a block size of b, the first b bytes in the linear sequence are the first b bytes in the lowest numbered segment, the next b bytes in the linear sequence are the first b bytes in the next segment, and so on.

Note that a view only defines the way a parafile is accessed and does not alter the physical representation. Thus a given parafile can always be opened with any view. All processes in a group open a file with the same view.

Parallel file systems are relatively new and an area of active research. Currently no particular file structure or user interface has been embraced as being clearly superior; in fact, most commercial parallel file systems implement a traditional Unix[1] model. The set of file views currently supported in PIOUS is limited,

[1]Unix is a registered trademark of X/Open Company Ltd.

though sufficient to implement a super-set of the common parallel file access patterns identified by Crockett [Cro89]. We feel that until further experience is gained with the system, development of a more sophisticated interface is premature.

5.3 Consistency and Fault Tolerance Semantics

PIOUS provides all processes sequential consistency of access to files opened under any view. Between processes of different groups, some form of flexible file locking is being considered as well.

PIOUS provides parafile access in two user-selectable fault tolerance modes: *volatile* and *stable*. Stable mode guarantees file consistency in the event of a system failure; volatile mode does not. Volatile mode is intended for non-critical applications that require high-performance. Applications requiring fault tolerance can access files in the lower-performance, but guaranteed consistent, stable mode.

The current PIOUS implementation does not provide applications with fault tolerance of media failures. Media fault tolerance is achieved by data replication on independent devices, either as multiple file copies [BHG87] or as computed parity information [PGK88]. Such techniques are independent of the file system architecture, provided that multiple independent storage devices can be accessed.

5.4 PIOUS Interface Definition

A PIOUS user interface can now be defined that supports the file model and usage semantics discussed above. For portability of sequential programs, a subset of the PIOUS interface is POSIX [Ins88] equivalent. Interface definitions use C-language bindings, though Fortran language bindings will be implemented as well.

5.4.1 File Primitives

Prior to performing input-output operations, a file must be opened with one of the following functions:

int pious_pfopen(*group*, *path*, *view*, *map*, *faultmode*, *oflag* [, *mode* [, *seg*]])
int pious_pfopens(*servers*, *group*, *path*, *view*, *map*, *faultmode*, *oflag* [, *mode* [, *seg*]])
int pious_open(*path*, *oflag* [, *mode*])

char ***servers*, **group*, **path*;
int *view*, *map*, *faultmode*, *oflag*, *seg*;
pious_modet *mode*;

Pious_pfopen() opens for a process in group *group* the parafile *path* with view *view* and returns a file descriptor for subsequent I/O operations. If the file view specifies a linear mapping, i.e. is global or independent, then the number of bytes taken round-robin from each segment is specified by *map*; otherwise, if the view is segmented, *map* determines which segment is to be accessed. Fault tolerance mode is specified by *faultmode* as either stable or volatile. File access mode is specified via *oflag* as one of read-only, write-only, or read-write; a file creation flag determines if the file is to be created if it does not exist. Upon file creation, *mode* specifies the file permission bits, in accordance with the standard Unix access control mechanism, and the number of parafile segments is determined by *seg*, with a default value equal to the number of data servers. Data is declustered over a predefined set of default data servers.

Pious_pfopens() is identical to pious_pfopen() except that the set of data servers over which the file is declustered is specified via the *servers* argument. This feature allows the user to choose the set of data servers that best meet the needs of the application; e.g. a set of RAID [PGK88] servers for media fault tolerance.

Pious_open() is a POSIX equivalent open function that results in Unix file semantics in most cases. Pious_open(*path*, *oflag*, *mode*) is equivalent to pious_pfopen(NULL, *path*, INDEPENDENT, MAPDEFAULT, VOLATILE, *oflag*, *mode*).

Functions are also provided to close a file and to query file status and configuration; e.g. to determine the number of data servers on which a file is declustered.

5.4.2 Input-Output Primitives

Once a file has been opened, data may be read or written using the following functions:

pious_ssizet pious_read(*fildes*, *buf*, *nbyte*)
pious_ssizet pious_reado(*fildes*, *buf*, *nbyte*, *offset*)
pious_ssizet pious_write(*fildes*, *buf*, *nbyte*)
pious_ssizet pious_writeo(*fildes*, *buf*, *nbyte*, *offset*)
pious_offt pious_lseek(*fildes*, *offset*, *whence*)

int *fildes*, *whence*;
char **buf*;
pious_sizet *nbyte*;
pious_offt *offset*;

Pious_read() attempts to read *nbyte* bytes from file *fildes* into the buffer *buf*. The read operation starts at the file position indicated by the appropriate file pointer, as determined by the view; the file pointer is incremented accordingly.

Pious_reado() performs the same function as pious_read(), except that reading starts at the file position *offset*, relative to the file view, and does not alter any file pointer.

The pious_write() and pious_writeo() functions are the obvious extensions of the corresponding read operations, with data moved from the user buffer to the indicated file.

Finally, the pious_lseek() function repositions the appropriate file pointer for the given view relative to either the current file pointer position or the beginning of the file, as indicated by *whence*.

5.4.3 Maintenance Primitives

In addition to file access primitives, the following basic parafile maintenance primitives are defined to provide a more complete environment:

```
int pious_chmod( path, mode)
int pious_chmods( servers, path, mode)
int pious_unlink( path)
int pious_unlinks( servers, path)
int pious_mkdir( path, mode)
int pious_mkdirs( servers, path, mode)
int pious_rmdir( path)
int pious_rmdirs( servers, path)

char **servers, *path;
pious_modet mode;
```

The maintenance functions extend standard Unix functions to parafiles in the PIOUS environment. Pious_chmod() sets the file access control bits of file *path* to *mode*. Pious_unlink() removes parafile *path*. Pious_mkdir() and pious_rmdir() create and remove directory *path*, respectively, at each data server.

All PIOUS maintenance functions have a "standard" version, that refers to the default data servers, and a "server" version, that refers to specific data servers.

5.4.4 Transaction Primitives

The PIOUS I/O operations of section 5.4.2 are performed within the context of a transaction, transparently to the user, as discussed in section 4. For most applications, the programming model is simplified by hiding the mechanism that is providing concurrency control and fault tolerance. However certain applications may desire to perform multiple access operations all within the context of a single transaction. This functionality is supported in PIOUS via the following functions:

```
int pious_tbegin( faultmode)
int pious_tabort()
int pious_tend()

int faultmode;
```

Pious_tbegin() and pious_tend() mark the beginning and end of a transaction, respectively. All PIOUS access operations that occur between a transaction begin and end point are part of that transaction. The transaction fault tolerance mode is specified by *faultmode* as either stable or volatile, as defined in section 4. An application can abort the current transaction at any time via pious_tabort().

5.4.5 Record Support

As defined, PIOUS read-write operations operate on uninterpreted blocks of bytes. While this is sufficient in an environment with a homogeneous data representation, in a heterogeneous data environment the burden is placed on the application to convert data to some universal format such as XDR [Sun90a].

In a later version of the PIOUS interface we intend to explore record support to address this issue. A solution will probably involve a form of record descriptor, such as employed in the MPI [Mes93] environment.

6 Related Work

The PIOUS architecture has roots in a number of network and parallel computer file systems. A brief overview of this related work is presented below.

Parallel machines commonly provide a parallel file system interface; familiar examples include the Intel CFS [Pie89] and nCUBE Parallel I/O System [DdR92]. Such systems provide parallel applications with varying degrees of file access coordination and control and often employ data declustering to increase aggregate performance. The IBM Vesta [CFPB93] multicomputer file system implements two-dimensional files and a unique stencil-based logical partitioning operator to coordinate parallel file access.

Swift [CL91] and Zebra [HO93] are research network file systems that implement disk striping across multiple servers with RAID-4/5 [PGK88] fault tolerance of media failures. Zebra is unique in that a log-structured file system is employed to allow striping on a per client basis. However, Swift and Zebra are not parallel file systems as they lack support for parallel application development.

Express is a CUBIX-model [Sal87] parallel computing environment that implements a parallel file system interface. However, in network environments, Express does not employ data declustering to aggregate the performance of distributed resources.

PIOUS extends the work of existing parallel file systems by incorporating transactions as a generalized concurrency control and fault tolerance mechanism. Consequently, PIOUS provides parallel applications with guaranteed consistency semantics, asynchronous file operations, and dynamically-selectable fault tolerance modes. Furthermore, to our knowledge PIOUS is the first network parallel file system to employ data declustering for scalable performance.

7 Conclusions

PIOUS is a parallel file system architecture for providing process groups access to permanent storage within a heterogeneous network computing environment. The PIOUS file structure and interface implement a programming model that supports the coordinated interaction of cooperating processes, thereby simplifying parallel applications development. The PIOUS software architecture employs data declustering to exploit distributed resources transparently to the user.

A PIOUS prototype has been implemented and benchmarked [MS94], however space limitations prevent us from presenting performance results in this paper. To summarize, the overhead introduced by the PIOUS software is minimal for modest size data transfers. Aggregate system performance for volatile mode access is limited by the latency and bandwidth of our transport mechanism for two or more data servers; thus we are unable to measure scalability in this mode. Aggregate system performance for stable mode access is disk bandwidth limited; performance scales proportional to the number of disks employed.

8 Acknowledgements

The authors wish to thank the referees for their advice on improving this paper to better meet the conference objectives.

References

[ABC+90] M. Arango, D. Berndt, N. Carriero, D. Gelernter, and D. Gilmore. Adventures with network Linda. *Supercomputer Review*, 10(3):42–46, October 1990.

[BHG87] Philip Bernstein, Vassos Hadzilacos, and Nathan Goodman. *Concurrency Control and Recovery in Database Systems*. Addison-Wesley Publishing Company, 1987.

[CFPB93] Peter F. Corbett, Dror G. Feitelson, Jean-Pierre Prost, and Sandra J. Baylor. Parallel access to files in the Vesta file system. In *Proceedings of Supercomputing '93*, pages 472–481, November 1993.

[CL91] Luis-Felipe Cabrera and Darrell D. E. Long. Swift: Using distributed disk striping to provide high I/O data rates. *Computing Systems*, 4(4), Fall 1991.

[Cro89] Thomas W. Crockett. File concepts for parallel I/O. In *Proceedings of Supercomputing '89*, pages 574–579, 1989.

[DdR92] Erik DeBenedictis and Juan Miguel del Rosario. nCUBE parallel I/O software. In *Eleventh Annual IEEE International Phoenix Conference on Computers and Communications (IPCCC)*, pages 0117–0124, April 1992.

[HO93] John H. Hartman and John K. Ousterhout. The Zebra striped network file system. In *Proceedings of the Fourteenth ACM Symposium on Operating Systems Principles*, pages 29–43, December 1993.

[Ins88] The Institute of Electrical and Electronics Engineers, Inc. *POSIX: IEEE Standard Portable Operating System Interface for Computer Environments*, 1988. IEEE Std 1003.1-1988.

[Kot93] David Kotz. Multiprocessor file system interfaces. In *Proceedings of the Second International Conference on Parallel and Distributed Information Systems*, pages 194–201, 1993.

[Lam79] Leslie Lamport. How to make a multiprocessor computer that correctly executes multiprocess programs. *IEEE Transactions on Computers*, C-28(9):690–691, September 1979.

[McE93] Rodney McElrath. MRJ Inc., Personal Communication, June 1993.

[Mes93] The Message Passing Interface Forum. *Document for a Standard Message-Passing Interface (Draft)*, November 1993.

[MS94] Steven A. Moyer and V. S. Sunderam. PIOUS: A scalable parallel I/O system for distributed computing environments. In *1994 Scalable High Performance Computing Conference*. May, 1994. To appear.

[PGK88] David Patterson, Garth Gibson, and Randy Katz. A case for redundant arrays of inexpensive disks (RAID). In *ACM SIGMOD Conference*, pages 109–116, June 1988.

[Pie89] Paul Pierce. A concurrent file system for a highly parallel mass storage system. In *Fourth Conference on Hypercube Concurrent Computers and Applications*, pages 155–160, 1989.

[Sal87] John Salmon. CUBIX: Programming hypercubes without programming hosts. In *Proceedings of the Second Conference on Hypercube Multiprocessors*, pages 3–9, 1987.

[Sun90a] Sun Microsystems, Inc. *Network Programming Guide*, 1990. External Data Representation Standard: Protocol Specification.

[Sun90b] V. S. Sunderam. PVM: A framework for parallel distributed computing. *Concurrency: Practice and Experience*, 2(4):315–339, December 1990.

Programming Environments for Massively Parallel Distributed Systems, Monte Verità, Switzerland

Language and Compiler Support for Parallel I/O

Rajesh Bordawekar Alok Choudhary
ECE Dept. & NPAC, Syracuse Univ., Syracuse, NY 13244
rajesh,choudhar@npac.syr.edu *

Abstract

This paper addresses the problem of performing parallel input-output in data parallel computations. Specifically, we present language support (as extensions to HPF), and initial compiler implementation in the Fortran90D/HPF compiler for distributed memory machines. In this paper we only address the problem of reading and writing data in parallel. We suggest a set of compiler directives for parallel I/O which can be used in addition to standard HPF directives. The runtime primitives along with the compiler directives provide a common I/O platform for parallel languages like HPF.

1 Introduction

Parallel computers have become the preferred computational instrument of the scientific community due to their immense processing capacities. As scientists expand their models to describe physical phenomena of increasingly large extent, the memory capacity of parallel machines, although immense, become insufficient to contain all the required computational data, and I/O becomes important.

In recent years, data distribution is used by several languages to map the arrays on the distributed memory machines. Important among these languages are HPF Fortran [6], Vienna Fortran [2] and Fortran D [4]. Data decomposition often requires data to be accessed (read/written) from the disks in a distributed manner. The inconvenience of having to explicitly specify and control file access for a given data distribution has prompted recent proposals for the inclusion of parallel I/O support primitives into parallel programming languages such us HPF Fortran [6] and Vienna Fortran [2].

*This work was sponsored by ARPA under contract # DABT63-91-C-0028 and by an NSF Young Investigator Award CCR-9357840 (Alok Choudhary) with matching support from Intel SSD.

However these languages donot take into account the cost of data distribution. Parallel file systems vary in their level of support for data distribution; some provide no support whatsoever. The cost of distributing data from the disks depends on both the disk mapping and processor mapping. We have proposed an efficient strategy - two phase strategy - to perform optimal I/O [3].

1.1 Organization

In this paper we only consider input and output of data (and not out-of-core computations). The paper has the following organization. In Section 2, we present an overview of current parallel language support for data distribution. Section 3 describes the design of the language directives introduced to provide the necessary information to the runtime I/O library. Section 4 presents a sample HPF code that uses the I/O directives. Corresponding compiler generated F77+MP code with appropriate parallel I/O calls is also explained. In Section 5, we present experimental performance results for the runtime primitives. Finally, we summarize in Section 6.

2 Languages Supporting Data Distribution

We concentrate on parallel programs which use the Single Program Multiple Data (SPMD) programming paradigm for MIMD machines. This is the most widely used model for large-scale scientific and engineering applications. In such applications, parallelism is exploited by a decomposition of the data domain. To achieve load-balance, express locality of access, reduce communication, and to achieve other optimizations, several decompositions and data alignment strategies are often used (e.g., block, cyclic, along rows, columns, etc.). To enable such decompositions to be expressed in a parallel program, several parallel programming languages or language extensions have emerged. These languages provide intrinsics that permit the expression of mappings from the problem domain to the processing domain, allow a user to decompose, distribute and align arrays in the most appropriate fashion for the underlying computation. An example of parallel languages which support data distribution includes Vienna Fortran [2], Fortran D [4] and High Performance Fortran or (HPF) [6].

In order to address the I/O bottleneck problem, these languages propose to provide some support for parallel I/O operations. Important examples include Vienna Fortran [2] and High Performance Fortran [6, 5].

3 Parallel I/O Directives

Currently, we are addressing two parallel I/O problems; 1) parallel reads/writes from files, and 2) support for out-of-core computations. A brief description of the directives to support these problems is as follows.

• **DISKS**: This directive is used for describing the logical mapping of disks over which one or more files may be distributed and/or which are used to distribute scratch files for out-of-core computations. The syntax for this directive is similar to the **PROCESSORS** directive in HPF.

For example,

DISKS D(8,8)

indicates that disks are logically arranged as a two-dimensional logical grid of size 8×8. This directive aids a compiler associate a disk (or a set of disks) with processors for file distributions and out-of-core computations. Many processors are allowed to be associated with one disk and many disks are allowed to be associated with one processor. For example, if processor grid size id 16×16, each disk can be associated to maintain scratch files of a 2×2 processor sub-array.

• **FILEPROC**: This directive is also similar to the **PROCESSORS** directive in HPF except that it specifies the processors which really participate in performing I/O. From our earlier studies [3], we observed that the best performance need not necessarily be obtained when all processors performing computations also perform I/O. Thus, this provides the user the flexibility to specify a set of processors to perform I/O. This directive is optional, and if not specified, the default is the number of processors specified in the **PROCESSORS** directives.

For example,

FILEPROC FP(2,2)

specifies that a 2×2 array of processors participates in I/O.

• **FILEDISTR**: This directive declares a file-template and distributes it over the specified number of disks declared in the **DISK** directive. It also uses the optional FILEPROC parameter. This directive uses names declared in **DISKS** and **FILEPRC** as pointers to the corresponding topologies. For example,

FILEDISTR F(D,[FP])

declares a file-template F which is distributed over D disks, and it associates this template with the processors declared in FP. Thus a file distributed over a set of disks can be associated with different sets of processors by using this directive. For example, when declared together,

FILEDISTR F(D, FP1)
FILEDISTR F(D, FP2)

permit two different processor configurations to access files on the same set of disks.

• **FILEALIGN**: This directive is similar to the **ALIGN** directive of HPF. **FILEALIGN** aligns the list of associated files to the template declared using

FILEDISTR directive. However, there is a fundamental difference between **ALIGN** and **FILEALIGN**. File may not have a size at declaration time. Thus the same file may be aligned to more than one file-templates as illustrated above. This is quite logical since a file can be opened by two different processor grids. Following example illustrates the **FILEALIGN** directive.

FILEALIGN F :: F1, F2, F3

• **ASSOCIATE**: This directive describes the relationships between an array's and the corresponding file's mapping. That is, the **ASSOCIATE** directive **associates** a file-template with the corresponding array template. **ASSOCIATE** directive has the following form

ASSOCIATE :: (file-template, array-template)

For example,

ASSOCIATE :: (F,A),(,),...

associates the file-template F with the array-template A.

Thus, this directive provides an HPF compiler a list of files to be used for I/O for a set of arrays aligned to the corresponding array template.

• **OUT_OF_CORE**: This directive declares an array as an out-of-core array. Following example declares array A as an out-of-core array.

OUT_OF_CORE :: C

Figure 1 illustrates the relationships between these directives. File-template declares an abstract template (F), which is distributed over (logical) disks (D) and processors (FP). Note that FP specifies a set of processors which may be a subset of processors declared in the processor directive or a may be a different set (e.g., I/O nodes). Implementation, therefore, may vary from one architecture to another. Files to be accessed in the HPF program are aligned to this template F. Array template, to which arrays C and D are aligned, is distributed over a set of processors (PROCS). As illustrated, the array template A and file template F are associated using the associate directive. Thus a set of files mapped to the a file-template will have a set of arrays (may have different sizes) associated with them. As a result, a compiler can optimize the parallel accesses (e.g., read/write) of distributed arrays from/to the associated files using various strategies (e.g., [3]).

4 Compiler and Runtime Support for Parallel I/O

Information provided by the compiler directives is used to extract parameters about array and file distributions, which in turn are used in the runtime primitives.

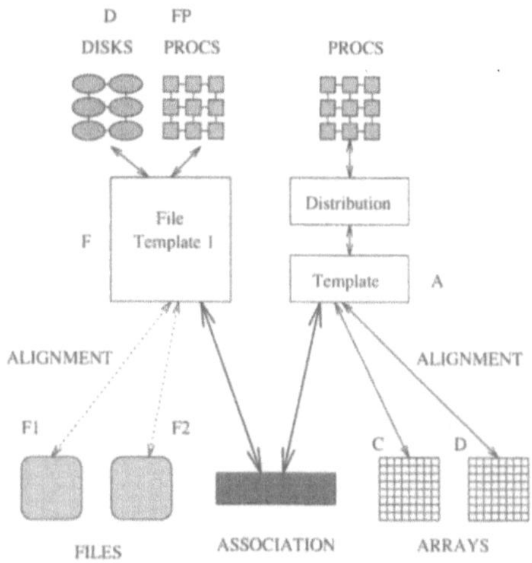

Figure 1: *File Distribution and Association in HPF*

In the following we briefly discuss the primitives and how they are used by the compiler.

Input and output operations include reading/writing arrays from/to files. The cost of reading/writing files in parallel may vary tremendously as a function of the distribution of data on compute nodes [3].

We have developed a set of runtime primitives to perform parallel read and write operations [3]. These primitives provide consistent (and high) performance independent of the type of distribution [3]. The parallel I/O primitives include parallel read (pread), parallel write operation (pwrite) and several supporting primitives including popen, pclose, array_map and proc_map.

We have developed compiler support in our HPF compiler [5] to automatically embed the runtime primitives in the compiler code (F77+MP+I/O) using the directives and constructs specified in the source HPF program. Figure 2 illustrates a set of directives and HPF code fragment as well as the corresponding compiled code in F77+MP+I/O. We only show the pertinent code for the sake of brevity. Note that in the source HPF code, the user uses very simple constructs called pread and pwrite (figure 2(I)) which are automatically converted into the appropriate calls to the runtime routines. Also, the compiler performs all the necessary transformations.

5 Experimental Results

In this section we present performance results for the runtime primitives when used in conjunction with a variety of data distributions. The tables below contain Best

(I) HPF Program

```
real A(64,64),B(64,64),C(64,64)
CHPF$ processors p(1,4)
CHPF$ template R(64,64)
CHPF$ distribute R(block,block)
CHPF$ align (I,J) with R(I,J) :: A,B
CHPF$ disks d(8,8)
CHPF$ fileproc H(1,4)
CHPF$ filedistr F(H,d)
CHPF$ filealign F :: F1,F2
CHPF$ associate :: F,R
CHPF$ out_of_core :: A
call popen(3,'F1',SEQUENTIAL,UNFORMATTED,OLD)
call pread (A,3)
call pwrite(A,3)
```

(II) F77+MP+I/0 Program

```
REAL A (64, 16), B (64, 16), C (64, 64)
INTEGER array_map,map_info(1536)
INTEGER size_info(7),proc_info(7),distr_info(7),block_size(7)
COMMON /INFO/F_INFO, P_INFO, A_INFO
[Initialize the data structures]
CALL popen (3,'F1', 0, 0, 1, disks, procs)
TT3temp = array_map (A, size_info, distr_info, block_size, proc_info, proclist)
CALL pread (A, 64, 16, TT3temp, 3, TT2temp, 1024, 1024)
CALL pwrite (A, 64, 16, TT3temp, 3, TT4temp, 1024, 1024)
```

Figure 2: *(I) shows a sample HPF program fragment which uses the proposed I/O directives. Disks are logically arranged as an 8×8 logical grid (D) and I/O processors are arranged as 1×4 grid (H). File-template F is distributed over H and D. Files F1 and F2 are aligned to the file-template F. Finally, file-template F is associated with array template A. Array A is declared out_of_core. HPF compiler automatically generates F77+MP+IO code (Shown in (II)).*

Table 1: *Comparing Direct Access with Two-phase Access (64 Processors, 10K*10K Array, time in msec)*

Distr. Mode	Best Read	Re Distr.	Total Read	Direct Read	Speedup
1	11395	-	**11395**	**11395**	**1**
2	11395	2478	**13873**	**63400**	**4.57**
3	11395	1028	**11623**	**78767**	**6.78**
4	11395	3092	**14487**	*	> 248

Read, Redistribute, Total Read, and Direct Read times for the four 1-dimensional distributions considered in this paper.

For a given array size, the Best Read time represents the minimum of the read times of the four distributions; the Best Read time is derived from the distribution that most closely conforms to the disk storage distribution for the given file. The Redistribution time is the time it takes to redistribute data from the conforming distribution to the one desired by the application. The Total Read time is the sum of the Best Read and Redistribution times; it denotes the time it takes for the data to be read using the optimal Read access and then be redistributed (two-phase access). The Direct Read time is the time it takes to read the data with the selected distribution using direct access. The last row of each table shows the speedup obtained from using the two-phase access strategy over the direct access strategy. Note that the Block-Block distribution is not supported by CFS, hence Table 2 do not present any performance numbers for direct access. (1 denotes Column Block access, 2 column cyclic access, 3 denotes Row Block and 4 represents Row cyclic access.)

Table 1 shows access times for 10Kx10K array, read and distributed over 64 processors. The reduction in cost ranged from 11.4 secs, to over 60 minutes for the 10Kx10K Row-Cyclic case. Note that the variation in Total Read time is again very small (at most a factor of 1.27). However, for all the four types of distribution, the total read time is nearly consistent (of the same order). Thus using the two-phase access we are able to get the data distribution performance which is independent of both the disk distribution and the processor distribution.

Tables 2 show access times for arrays distributed in the Block-Block fashion 64 processors. Again, note that the read time is consistent with the times obtained for other distributions.

The results above show that for every case, regardless of the desired data distribution, performance is improved to within a factor of 2 of the Best Read Time performance for all distributions. Further, the cost of redistribution is small compared with the Total Read Times. This indicates an effective exploitation of the additional degree of connectivity available within the interconnection network of the computational array. Further, the results also show that by using the runtime

Table 2: Block-Block Distribution over 64 Processors using the Runtime Primitives(time in msec)

Size	Best Read	Redistr.	Total Read
1K*1K	350	82	432
2K*2K	1100	186	1286
4K*4K	2462	577	3039

primitives, the data can be distributed in Block-Block fashion effectively.

6 Summary

The main goal of this paper was to describe directives which, based on our experience, are useful to perform parallel I/O from HPF programs. We also described how these directives are used to embed parallel I/O runtime primitives in the generated code.

We have also developed runtime primitives for out-of-core computations. These include communication and the corresponding optimizations for out-of-core data as well as read and write routines to perform accesses to scratch files. One of the important features of these routines in the they use access pattern information (to be provided by the compiler) to enhance the I/O performance.

References

[1] Juan Miguel del Rosario, and Alok Choudhary. High Performance I/O for Parallel Computers: Problems and Prospects. To appear in IEEE Computer.

[2] S. Benkner, B. Chapman, and H. Zima. Vienna Fortran 90. *Scalable High Performance Computing Conference*, April 1992.

[3] Rajesh Bordawekar. Issues in Software Support for Parallel I/O. Master's Thesis, ECE. Dept., Syracuse University, May 1993.

[4] Geoffrey Fox, Seema Hiranandani, Ken Kennedy, C. Koelbel, Uli Kremer, and Chau-Wen Tseng. Fortran D Language Specification. Technical Report Rice COMP TR90-141. Rice University, December 1990.

[5] Zeki Bozkus, Alok Choudhary, Geoffrey Fox, Tomasz Haupt, and Sanjay Ranka. Fortran 90D/HPF Compiler for Distributed Memory MIMD Computers: Design, Implementation, and Performance Results. *Supercomputing'93*, November 1993.

[6] High Performance Fortran Forum. High Performance Fortran Language Specification Version 1.0. Technical Report CRPC-TR92225. CRPC, Rice University, January 1993.

Programming Environments for Massively Parallel Distributed Systems, Monte Verità, Switzerland

Locality in Scheduling Models of Parallel Computation

Peter Thanisch* Michael G. Norman Cristina Boeres
Susanna Pelagatti
Department of Computer Science, University of Edinburgh,
Mayfield Road, Edinburgh EH9 3JZ, Scotland
{pt, mgn, cbx}@dcs.ed.ac.uk, susanna@di.unipi.it

Abstract

Effective tools for the design of parallel algorithms must be based on a computational model for parallel computing that is a trade-off between realism and simplicity. Where the underlying programming model requires the mapping and scheduling of tasks, the computational model should incorporate some notion of interprocessor communication delay. If the target architecture is massively parallel then a more complex model, including some notion of locality, may be required.

When working with locality-ignoring computational models, researchers on the mapping problem have been able to discover efficient approximation techniques that are guaranteed to find a mapping with a near-optimal makespan. However, techniques with such good performance bounds have so far eluded researchers investigating locality-based computational models. In an initial attempt to explain this difference, we show that estimating the minimum makespan in locality-based models is problematic because processor requirements may become unreasonable.

1 Introduction

A major obstacle preventing the wider acceptance of massively parallel computers has been the lack of systems which are easy to program yet give reasonable performance on different target architectures [NT93b]. In such systems, programmers must have the ability to express their algorithms in a high-level, machine-independent way, and the system itself determines how to configure the available hardware resources. Papadimitriou and Yannakakis [PY90] observed that, for the *sequential* programmer, the algorithm development process has two stages: (a)

*To whom correspondence may be addressed.

choose an algorithm and (b) analyse it, whereas for the *parallel* programmer, there are four stages; (1) choose the algorithm (say an acyclic directed graph (dag), indicating the elementary computations and their interdependence), (2) choose an architecture, (3) find a schedule and (4) analyse the performance. They identified combining stages (2), (3) and (4) as being critical in programmming and computational models for parallel computing, if such models are to boost the productivity of parallel programmers. To this end, they proposed an approach to the architecture-independent design and analysis of parallel algorithms. Underlying this approach is a computational model of parallel computer architecture in which interprocessor communication delay, i.e. the ratio of the message delivery time to the instruction cycle time, is the sole architectural parameter. In their model, delay is independent of the pair of processors that perform the communication. Consequently, they are able to model delay as a constant, τ. They assume that there is an unlimited number of processors available. Although Papadimitriou and Yannakakis proved that finding an optimal schedule is NP-complete, they also proposed a polynomial time complexity, heuristic scheduling algorithm which is guaranteed to find a schedule with a makespan that is no worse than a factor of two longer than the makespan of an optimum schedule. Furthermore, Jung *et al.* [JKS93] have given an algorithm which finds a minimum-makespan schedule in an amount of time that is polynomial in the (constant) communication delay, τ, for Papadimitriou and Yannakakis' model.

One of the advantages of this model of parallel computation is that the issue of *recomputation* is brought within the province of the mapping technique: there is no incentive to recompute if, in the underlying computational model, the communication of a result is assumed to be instantaneous. The critical importance of recomputation in the mapping problem has been established by Jung *et al.* [JKS93] who proved that, for a given dag algorithm, the optimal schedule that ignores recomputation may be worse than the true optimal schedule by a multiplicative factor which is a function of τ.

Although Papadimitriou and Yannakakis ignore the number of processors as a parameter to the problem, their scheduling technique is not outrageously processor wasteful, using no more processors than there are tasks. Furthermore, Thurimella and Yesha [TY92] have adapted the scheduling principle of Brent [Bre74] to re-map a schedule onto a fixed number of processors.

Massively parallel architectures are built out of a large number of processing nodes together with an interconnection network that may be either configurable or in some fixed topology. Each processor has a limited number, called the *arity*, of physical links through which it may communicate with "neighbouring" processors. If a task, mapped to a particular processor, sends a message to another task that has been mapped to a non-neighbouring processor, that message must be routed through the interconnection network. In other words non-neighbouring communication may be more expensive, in terms of delay, than communication between neighbouring processors. If this extra delay for non-neighbouring communication is negligible, then the assumption that there is a uniform delay, τ, is a convenient fiction, since the interconnection network behaves as if it were fully connected. This has the major advantage that the mapping technique only has to make the two-way decision about whether or not two tasks should be executed on the same processor. If, however, non-neighbouring communication is significantly more expensive, then the uniform delay assumption becomes a less realistic assumption. The mapping problem becomes harder because the relative placement of tasks becomes significant. Thus some notion of locality must be incorporated into the architectural model.

In the manner of Papadimitriou and Yannakakis [PY90] we wish to frame a scheduling problem which puts no bounds upon the number of processors used by the computation. However, we wish to introduce some notion of locality within the set of processors on which the computation is scheduled. The natural way of achieving this would be to specify the arrangement of the processors in some sort of graph, with the delay between a pair of processors dependent upon their relative distance in this graph, but this graph would then have to form part of our problem instance. A more attractive alternative would be to consider scheduling to an indexed family of graphs such as the k-ary n cubes, where k and n, as indices of the graph, would form part of our problem instance.

In order to avoid loss of generality we choose simply to state that each processor will incur a unit delay in communicating with a fixed number, α of processors, and a larger delay, τ in communicating with any other processor. The processors with which it has unit communication delay are said to be *adjacent* to it, and may be thought of as being connected in some processor network. Our model is intended to capture the essence of hardware limits on connectivity in parallel computer systems.

In models where communication delay is uniform (τ is a constant) there is no performance improvement to be gained from using more processors than there are tasks to be scheduled [NT93a]. In the present paper, we show that in order to achieve optimal performance in model introduced here, an *exponential* number of processors may be required.

2 The Locality Model

We can define a scheduling problem in terms of an acyclic directed graph ("dag") of tasks and their dependencies, say $G = (V, E)$, a set, P, of processors and a communication delay function for P, $d : P \times P \rightarrow Z_0^+$. We assume that there is no delay for intraprocessor communication and that adjacent processors can communicate in unit time. A problem instance specifies an adjacency bound, α: each processor is adjacent to at most α other processors. For non-adjacent processors, communication delay is given by a second parameter, $\tau \geq 1$. More formally, the conditions may be stated as follows.

1. $\forall p \in P$, $d(p,p) = 0$.
2. $\forall p \in P$, where $Q_p = \{q \in P : d(p,q) = 1\}$, $| Q_p | \leq \alpha$ and $\forall q \in P - Q_p - \{p\}$, $d(p,q) = \tau$.
3. $\forall p, q \in P$, $d(p,q) = d(q,p)$.

A schedule of $G = (V, E)$ onto P is a set, say S, of 3-tuples such that for each $(v,p,t) \in S$, $v \in V$, $p \in P$ and $t \in Z_0^+$. $(v,p,t) \in S$ indicates that task v is executed on processor p at time t by schedule S.

A schedule S will be said to have *makespan* M if

$$max_{(v,p,t) \in S} t = M - 1 .$$

A schedule S will be said to be *valid* for G, P, d if all tasks are executed at least once, if no task is executed at the same time as any other task on the same processor and if for any execution of a task, the predecessors of a task have been executed in time for data to be transferred to the processor on which the task is being executed. More formally the conditions are as follows.

1. $\forall v \in V$, $\exists p \in P$ and $t \in Z_0^+$ such that $(v,p,t) \in S$.
2. $\forall (v,p,t) \in S$, $\nexists w \in V$ such that $(w,p,t) \in S - \{(v,p,t)\}$
3. $\forall (v,p,t) \in S$, $\forall (w,v) \in E$, $\exists p' \in P$, $t' \in Z_0^+$ such that $t' + d(p',p) < t$ and $(w,p',t') \in S$.

2.1 Scheduling with limited processor adjacency

We define an instance of scheduling with limited processor adjacency as follows.

Instance An acyclic directed graph $G = (V, E)$, a non-negative integer communication delay τ, a positive integer limit on adjacency, α and a non-negative integer time limit k.

Question Let P be a set of processors of unbounded cardinality. Does there exist a communication delay function d for P that has adjacency limit α and non-adjacent delay τ, such that there exists a valid schedule for G, P, d with makespan at most k ?

Theorem 1 *Scheduling with limited processor adjacency is NP hard.*

Proof
If we let $\alpha = 0$ then our scheduling model becomes identical to that of Papadimitriou and Yannakakis [PY90] and NP hardness follows from their Theorem 1.
□

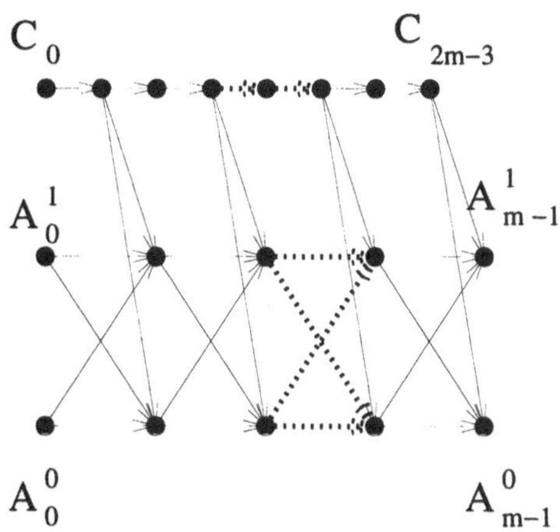

Figure 1: *The Toblerone Dag*

3 Exponential Processor Requirements

We now construct an instance of scheduling with limited processor adjacency for which we will show that the accompanying question can be answered in the affirmative if and only if the number of processors available is exponential in the size of the dag being scheduled. This would cast doubt upon whether the limited adjacency scheduling problem is in NP. We refer to the dag that forms part of our instance as the Toblerone dag since it looks vaguely like that particular brand of Swiss confectionery.

Definition 1 ***Toblerone Dag.***

Let m be a positive integer. A Toblerone dag $G = (V, E)$ with index $m >= 2$ is constructed as follows:

$$\begin{aligned}
A &= \{A_i^j : i = 0, \ldots, m-1, j = 0, 1\} \\
C &= \{C_i : i = 0, \ldots, 2m-3\} \\
V &= A \cup C \\
E^A &= \{(A_{i-1}^j, A_i^k) : i = 1, \ldots, m-1, j = 0, 1, k = 0, 1\} \\
E^C &= \{(C_{i-1}, C_i) : i = 1, \ldots, 2m-3\} \\
F &= \{(C_{2i-1}, A_i^j) : i = 1, \ldots, m-1, j = 0, 1\} \\
E &= E^A \cup E^C \cup F
\end{aligned}$$

Figure 1 illustrates this construction.

The following pair of Lemmas establish earliest start times for the tasks in the sets C and A, respectively. We note that this pair of Lemmas hold regardless of the values of τ and α.

Lemma 1 *For $i = 0, 1, \ldots, 2m-3$, task C_i must be executed at, or after, time i.*

Proof
For $i = 0, 1, \ldots, 2m-3$, the *depth* of task C_i is i, i.e. C_i has i predecessors that must execute sequentially before C_i can execute. Thus i is the earliest time step at which C_i can execute. □

Lemma 2 *For all tasks A_i^j, $0 \leq i < m$, $0 \leq j < 2$, A_i^j must be executed at, or after, time $2i$.*

Proof
The lemma clearly holds for $i = 0$. For $i = 1, 2, \ldots, m-1$, the task A_i^j, $0 \leq j \leq 1$, depends on task C_{2i-1} which, by Lemma 1 cannot be executed until time $2i-1$, and so A_i^j, cannot be executed until at or after time $2i$. □

From now on, we consider the case in which $\tau = 2$ and $\alpha = 3$. First, we establish that it is possible to achieve the makespan $2m-1$.

Theorem 2 *Let G be the Toblerone dag with index m and let $\alpha = 3$ and $\tau = 2$. Then there exists a schedule for G, α, τ with makespan $k = 2m-1$.*

Proof
Firstly, we define our set of processors and the adjacency pattern in the processor graph. For $a = 1, 2, \ldots, m$, let $P_a = \{p_a^1, p_a^2, \ldots, p_a^{2^a}\}$. Then our set of processors is $P = \cup_{a=1}^{m} P_a$. For each $p_a^b \in P$, let $d(p_a^b, p_a^b) = 0$. For $a = 2, 3, \ldots, m$, we let $d(p_a^b, p_{a-1}^{\lceil b/2 \rceil}) = 1$ and for $a = 1, 2, \ldots, m-1$, $d(p_a^b, p_{a+1}^{2b-1}) = 1$ and $d(p_a^b, p_{a+1}^{2b}) = 1$. For all other pairs of processors p, q let $d(p, q) = \tau$. We construct the schedule, S, and delay function, d, as follows. If we consider those pairs of processors which are adjacent in d as being edges in an undirected processor graph then that graph forms a pair of disjoint binary trees rooted at p_1^1 and p_1^2.
We schedule task A_i^0, $i = 0, \ldots, m-1$ on each processor P_{m-i}^b, $b = 1, 3, \ldots, 2^{m-i}-1$ at time $2i$ along with its $2i$ predecessors in C preceding it, and similarly each task A_i^1 $i = 0, \ldots, m-1$ on each processor P_{m-i}^b, $b = 2, 4, \ldots, 2^{m-i}$ at time $2i$ along with its $2i$ predecessors in C preceding it. □

We note that the function d in effect "wires up" some of the processors in the form of a pair of complete binary trees, each tree rooted at the processor that computes a sink task. Both trees have depth $m-1$ (where the depth of the root node is defined to be zero). Thus the schedule uses 2^m processors. Next, we establish that any schedule with a makespan no greater than $2m-1$ will also require a number of processors that is exponential in m. Of course the size of the representation of a problem instance is polynomial in m.

The following four lemmas refer to our instance. The next pair of lemmas establish that, if a processor executes a task at the above earliest start times, then it will have been busy throughout the duration of the computation executing predecessor tasks in the set C.

Lemma 3 *In any valid schedule, say S, for G, if there exists $p \in P$ such that $(C_i, p, i) \in S$, $0 \leq i \leq 2m-3$, then for $t = 0, 1, \ldots, i$, $(C_t, p, t) \in S$.*

Proof

The method of proof is by induction on i.

Base The hypothesis is clearly true for $i = 0$.

Induction Suppose that the hypothesis has been proved for $i = 0, 1, \ldots, h$ and suppose that $(C_{h+1}, p, h+1) \in S$. C_h must execute before C_{h+1}, which executes at time $h+1$. By Lemma 1, C_h cannot execute before time step h. Thus C_h must execute at time h on the same processor, i.e. p, as C_{h+1}. By inductive hypothesis, $C_0, C_1, \ldots, C_{h-1}$ also execute on p at time steps $0, 1, \ldots, h-1$. □

Lemma 4 *For any valid schedule, say S, such that for some task, $A_i^j \in A$ and processor $p \in P$, $(A_i^j, p, 2i) \in S$, then for $t = 0, 1, \ldots, 2i-1$, $(C_t, p, t) \in S$.*

Proof

From the definition of G, $(C_{2i-1}, A_i^j) \in E$. By Lemma 1, C_{2i-1} cannot execute before time step $2i-1$. But by Lemma 2, A_i^j executes at time step $2i$, so C_{2i-1} executes at time $2i-1$ and, furthermore, C_{2i-1} must execute on processor p. Thus, by Lemma 3, tasks $C_0, C_1, \ldots, C_{2i-1}$ execute on processor p at time steps $0, 1, \ldots, 2i-1$. □

Again assuming that the earliest start time for a task in A is achieved on some processor, say p, in a schedule, the next lemma establishes that predecessor tasks in A must be executed at *their* earliest start times on processors that are adjacent to p.

Lemma 5 *In any valid schedule, say S, if $\exists A_i^j \in A$, $1 \leq i \leq m-1$, such that from some processor $p \in P$, $(A_i^j, p, 2i) \in S$, then $\exists q, r \in P$, $q \neq r$, such that $(A_{i-1}^0, q, 2(i-1)) \in S$, $(A_{i-1}^1, r, 2(i-1)) \in S$, $d(p, q) = 1$ and $d(p, r) = 1$.*

Proof

(A_{i-1}^0, A_i^j), $(A_{i-1}^1, A_i^j) \in E$, so the results of A_{i-1}^0 and A_{i-1}^1 must be available on processor p at time $2i$. By Lemma 4, processor p is busy executing task C_j at time steps $j = 0, 1, \ldots, 2i-1$, thus neither A_{i-1}^0 nor A_{i-1}^1 can execute on processor p before time $2i$. By Lemma 2, neither A_{i-1}^0 nor A_{i-1}^1 can execute before time $2i-2$, thus both tasks must execute at time step $2i-2$, since otherwise the results will neither be available for task A_i^0, nor for task A_i^1, on processor p by time $2i$. From the definition of a valid schedule, a processor may only execute one task at a time. Thus there must exist distinct processors, q and r, such that $(A^0_{i-1}, q, 2i-2) \in S$ and $(A^1_{i-1}, r, 2i-2) \in S$. Since the results of these execution must be available at time $2i$, it follows that $d(p,q) = d(p,r) = 1$. □

Lemma 6 *In any valid schedule, say S, such that for some $A^j_i \in A$, $0 \le j \le 1$ and $1 \le i \le m-1$, $(A^j_i, p, 2i) \in S$, the triples of S imply the existence of a complete binary sub-tree of processors with depth $i-1$, rooted at p.*

Proof
The method of proof is by induction on the depth, g, of a task in the subdag $G^A = (A, E^A)$.

Base If $g = 0$ then clearly a processor, say p, such that $(A^j_0, p, 2) \in S$, $0 \le j \le 1$, is at the root of a binary sub-tree of depth zero.

Induction Suppose that the lemma has been proved for $i = 0, 1, \ldots, g$. Let $(A^0_{g+1}, p, 2(g+1)) \in S$ and $(A^1_{g+1}, p', 2(g+1)) \in S$. By Lemma 5, $\exists q, r \in P$, $q \neq r$, such that $(A^0_g, q, 2g) \in S$ and $(A^1_g, r, 2g) \in S$. Thus, by inductive hypothesis, there are complete binary trees of depth g rooted at q and r. Furthermore, by Lemma 5, $d(p,q) = 1$ and $d(p,r) = 1$.

Again by Lemma 5, we can state that there exist processors w, x, y, z such that $d(q,w) = d(q,x) = 1$ and $d(r,y) = d(r,z) = 1$ and the following tuples are in S: $(A^0_{g-1}, w, 2(g-1))$, $(A^1_{g-1}, x, 2(g-1))$, $(A^0_{g-1}, y, 2(g-1))$ and $(A^1_{g-1}, z, 2(g-1))$. Both processors w and x are different from r, otherwise r would execute both tasks A^0_{g-1} and A^1_g or both tasks A^1_{g-1} and A^1_g, contradicting Lemma 4. Similarly, processors y and z are different from q.

Let us suppose now that $w = y$, so that we have $d(q,w) = d(r,w) = 1$. By Lemma 5 that there exists two distinct processors k and l such that $d(w,k) = d(w,l) = 1$. Thus, there exists a processor with arity 4, contradicting the definition of our model, where $\alpha = 3$. Thus, w, x, y, z are distinct processors.

We conclude that there is a complete binary tree of depth $g+1$ rooted at p. □

We are now in a position to state our main result

Theorem 3 *Any valid schedule for the Toblerone dag with index m that has a makespan no greater than $2(m-1)$ requires at least 2^{m-1} processors.*

Proof
If the tasks A^0_{m-1} and A^1_{m-1} are executed at time $2(m-1)$ then, by Lemma 6, the schedule requires two complete binary trees of processors, each with depth $m-2$. The number of processors in each such tree is thus 2^{m-2}. Thus at least 2^{m-1} processors are required by a schedule to achieve the makespan $2(m-1)$. □

We have established that the Toblerone dag of index m, the limit on adjacency 3, the communication delay 2 and the time limit $2m-1$ represent a family of instances of *scheduling with limited processor adjacency* for which there exists a valid, minimal makespan schedule if and only if the cardinality of that schedule and the number of processors needed to execute the schedule is exponential in the size of the instance.

4 Discussion and concluding remarks

Although the Toblerone dag is contrived, it is not "pathological". In general, to achieve the optimum makespan in the Locality model, it may be necessary to have a distinct processor for each *path* in the dag from the sources to the sinks. By contrast, in Papadimitriou and Yannakakis' model, it is never necessary to have more processors than tasks in order to achieve the optimum makespan. Indeed, in a sense, the Toblerone dag represents a relatively "easy" mapping problem because the optimum makespan is obtained from a mapping in which only nearest-neighbour communications occur.

It should also be noted that our result holds for any real value of non-neighbouring communication delay greater than one, given that neighbouring communication takes unit time. For the original Papadimitriou and Yannakakis model, the scheduling technique proposed by Jung *et al.* [JKS93] has a running time that is polynomial in the delay. This indicates the extra complexity of incorporating locality into the scheduling model.

We can also identify the extra computational problem in finding approximate solutions. Papadimitriou and Yannakakis define a function, e, that gives an estimate of a task's earliest start time in any valid schedule. Although it might be an optimistic estimate, the function e has the useful property that it is easy to find a schedule in which each task, say v, may then be scheduled to start at time $2e(v)$ and the resulting schedule is guaranteed to have a makespan no worse than twice that of the optimal schedule. The function, e, is easily computed by a greedy algorithm: given a task, say v, once $e(w)$ has been computed for each ancestor, w of v, then $e(v)$ can be computed. However, in the Locality model, it is harder to identify a function that has similar characteristics to e. It seems unlikely that an algorithm which computes a "good" estimate of the earliest start times could ignore mapping issues.

Hwang *et al.*[HCAL89] proposed a model that takes locality into account, by specifying a communication cost function τ, the value of which depends on the distance between two processors. They also defined a heuristic algorithm called Earliest Task First (ETF). The evaluated upper bound on the performance of ETF is a multiplicative factor that depends on the maximum communication requirements on *all* the chains of the input graph and, thus, it is not constant as in the Papadimitriou and Yannakakis model.

In conclusion Papadimitriou and Yannakakis' model seems very promising and achieves a tight bound, but fails to take locality into consideration. The model proposed by Hwang *et al.* [HCAL89] accounts for locality, but it is unable to achieve a good bound on performance. We observe that locality-ignoring scheduling models lead to approximation algorithms guaranteed to produce schedules with makespans that are within a constant factor of the optimum, whereas for models that incorporate a notion of locality, approximation algorithms have data dependent performance bounds. We hope that the results represented here may help to explain this difference.

Acknowledgements

Cristina Boeres is on leave from Universidade Federal Fluminense(UFF), supported by grant 1553/91-8 from CAPES, Ministry of Education, Brazil. Susanna Pelagatti is supported by a grant of the "Progetto Finalizzato Sistemi Informatici e Calcolo Parallelo" subproject *Architetture Parallele* funded by the Italian National Research Council (CNR).

References

[Bre74] R.P. Brent. The parallel evaluation of general arithmetic expressions. *J. ACM*, 21:201–206, 1974.

[HCAL89] J-J. Hwang, Y-C. Chow, F.D. Anger, and C-Y. Lee. Scheduling precedence graphs in systems with interprocessor communication times. *SIAM J. Comput.*, 18(2):244–257, 1989.

[JKS93] H. Jung, L. Kirousis, and P. Spirakis. Lower bounds and efficient algorithms for multiprocessor scheduling of directed acyclic graphs with communication delays. *Information and Computation*, 105:94–104, 1993.

[NT93a] M.G. Norman and P. Thanisch. Bounds beyond which there are no performance gains from adding processors to scheduling models. Technical Report EPCC-TR-93-06, Edinburgh Parallel Computing Centre, 1993.

[NT93b] M.G. Norman and P. Thanisch. Models of machines and computations for mapping in multicomputers. *ACM Computing Surveys*, 25(3), 1993.

[PY90] C.H. Papadimitriou and M. Yannakakis. Towards an architecture-independent analysis of parallel algorithms. *SIAM J. Comput.*, 19:322–328, 1990.

[TY92] R. Thurimella and Y. Yesha. A scheduling principle for precedence graphs with communication delay. In Q.F. Stout, editor, *Proceedings of the INternational Conference on Parallel Processing*, pages III–229 – III–236. CRC Press, 1992.

Programming Environments for Massively Parallel Distributed Systems, Monte Verità, Switzerland

A Load Balancing Algorithm for Massively Parallel Systems

Mario Cannataro Giandomenico Spezzano
Domenico Talia
CRAI
Località S. Stefano, 87036 Rende, Italy
{mario,gds,dot}@crai.it

Abstract

Load balancing for massively parallel computers is very significant. This paper describes a new load balancing algorithm for massively parallel computers called Probabilistic strategy with Neighbourhood Synchronization. This algorithm uses only status information from neighbour nodes and takes into account the information lags in message-passing systems for estimating the system load. The proposed strategy differs from fully distributed approaches which require a high inter-processor communication overhead when the number of processors becomes large. After the description of the algorithm, experimental results obtained from a real implementation on a Transputer-based multicomputer are discussed.

1 Introduction

During the last years several massively parallel computers ranging from hundreds to thousands nodes became commercially available. They continue to gain recognition as powerful tools for scientific research, information management, and engineering applications. This trend must be powered by software tools and parallel algorithms which contribute to make massively parallel computers useful to implement a broad range of applications. Algorithms and tools for high-level programming, communication handling, monitoring, task scheduling, load balancing, and debugging are essential components in supporting users in the software development on parallel systems.

Among these tools, scheduling and load balancing algorithms may play an important role to achieve an effective use of the computing power offered by massively parallel computers. Load balancing algorithms provide a distribution of tasks (processes) to the computing nodes of a parallel computer attempting to balance the load on all nodes such that the whole throughput of the system is maximized [ELZ86]. They allow an effective use of resources of the nodes composing a parallel computer, avoiding heavily and lightly loaded nodes.

Load balancing may be *static* or *dynamic*, depending on the time at which the task assignment decisions are taken. In static load balancing all processes composing a concurrent program are available before the program execution and at that time each of them is assigned to a computing node. A concurrent program is represented by a weighted graph which must be mapped on the processor network. The process mapping is a NP-hard problem. Many heuristics and techniques based on mathematical programming [Chu69], graph theoretic [CA82], and queuing theory [NH85] can be used to find an acceptable solution.

Dynamic load balancing provides the process-to-processor mapping during the program execution each time a process must be spawned (*process placement*) or after a process has been spawned (*process migration*). Process migration strategies are not widely used because of the high implementation overhead they incur.

Static load balancing algorithms cannot be used when sufficient information about the parallel program is not available at compile time. In particular, this occurs when the number of processes to be created is not known a priori since the nondeterminism of computation or the data dependencies and the computational cost of subprocesses cannot be predicted before the execution (e.g., divide-and-conquer, ray tracing, parallel logic/functional languages). In all these cases a dynamic strategy must be used, where the more realistic hypothesis is made that none or very little a priori knowledge is available about the resource needs of a process [CH88].

The implementation of load balancing strategies on distributed-memory massively parallel computers (*multicomputers*) is very critical due to the large number of computing nodes and the overhead resulting from communications necessary to accomplish the application load balancing. Furthermore, most of the strategies which have been proposed are designed for distributed systems with few computing nodes (e.g., LANs). They cannot easily be adapted to multicomputers composed of a large number of medium/fine-grain processors which support the execution of thousands of fine-grain processes.

In some cases load balancing may result in a large increase of the execution time of parallel applications. Obviously, it is not possible to collect maximal state information with minimal communications. Load balancing strategies must make a compromise to solve this two-criteria problem.

Randomized load balancing algorithms belong to strategies which use none status information. These strategies do not introduce large overhead, but they are not able to adapt to variations which can occur in the system and do not guarantee any predictable locality degree in workload distribution. On the other hand, fully distributed strategies may become too expensive and not scalable on parallel computers, especially if a large number of computing nodes is used.

This paper presents a new load balancing strategy for distributed memory parallel computers. This load balancing strategy is called Probabilistic strategy with Neighbourhood Synchronization (PNS) [CSS93].

The proposed strategy differs from fully distributed approaches which require a high inter-processor communication overhead when the number of processors becomes large. The PNS strategy

- reduces the high interprocessor communication overhead resulted from information exchange by restricting communication between a node and its neighborhood, and
- takes into account in the load balancing decision the likelihood of the workload information about a node being obsolete by sending tasks to processors about which has more updated workload information.

After the description of the algorithm, experimental results obtained from a real implementation of the load balancing strategy on a Transputer-based multicomputer are discussed and compared with a random strategy.

2 Load balancing on multicomputers

Most of the proposed load-balancing strategies use centralized [CK82,LR92] or fully distributed [BS85,WM85] models for taking the task assignment decision. In a centralized model, a special node collects the global information about the state of the system and assigns tasks to individual nodes. In a fully distributed model, each node executes a scheduling algorithm by exchanging information with all the other nodes. For multicomputers consisting of a large number of nodes, centralized and fully distributed load-balancing strategies are not very suitable for many reasons.

Centralized strategies are based on a central scheduler running on a special node. In a multicomputer system composed of a large number of computing nodes, a central scheduler becomes a bottleneck and may abate the performance. Moreover, the memory requirements for storing the state information about all the nodes may become excessively high. Due to these reasons centralized strategies are not scalable. Finally, these strategies are not fault tolerant. The failure of any component of the central scheduler will stop the whole system.

On the other hand, fully distributed strategies incur large communication overhead due to the information exchange among all the nodes of a multicomputer. This communication overhead on each node increases with the system size (number of nodes), degrading the multicomputer performance [SC89]. To solve this problem small state information might be collected from every node. In multicomputers with a large number of nodes this limited information may result in a complex and inaccurate operation to establish the suitable node on which a process may be scheduled.

Another problem in fully distributed strategies is due to the control overhead. The control overhead depends on the load of the whole system. Thus when the load is heavy this overhead may be very high producing an overwhelming effect on the system performance.

In a multicomputer system the computing nodes are not fully connected. That is, each node n is directly connected with a small number of other nodes. These nodes constitute the neighbourhood of n. Thus, communication cost and delay between two nodes depend on the distance over the network between these nodes. Furthermore, neighbour nodes have more up-to-date information about one another.

The degree of obsolescence of information is affected by the frequency of information exchanges as well as by the communication delay between nodes. The cost of exchanging state information between nodes puts a limit on the frequency of exchanges. In a non-fully connected network the state information about each polled node may be obsolete due to the communication delay. Each node has a perfect knowledge of its state, but its information about the state of other nodes has different degree of obsolescence (*information lags*). Therefore information obsolescence must be taken into consideration when taking decision in a multicomputer system [LY91,MTS89].

Due to the reasons discussed, a load-balancing algorithm for a multicomputer should take into account these requirements using a locality-based or semi-distributed scheduling strategy and preferring local distribution of work over global distribution when possible. The PNS strategy follows this approach like other load balancing algorithms for multicomputers described in references [AG91, LK87, SK89].

3 The PNS algorithm

This new load balancing algorithm uses only load information from neighbours and takes into account the effect of information lags in distributed systems for task assignment. This effect means that dynamic status information of processors among which we choose one for executing a new task is not immediately available because a status information measured at time t on a node i will arrive an a node j at time $t + t'$, where t' is a time required to pass the distance between i and j. Thus, a status information collected by a node producing the load balancing decision may be obsolete. Then, if the flow of task arrivals has no regularity (or we don't know it) decision taken on the basis of currently available information will be non optimal. To cope with this problem we defined a probabilistic strategy based on the combination of two simple ideas:

i) A new task must be sent with a higher probability to a processor with a short task queue and with lower probability to a processor with a long queue.

ii) A new task must be sent with higher probability to a processor about which we have more updated state information and with lower probability to a processor which we have more obsolete information about.

To describe PNS let us introduce the following notation and definitions:

- P, the number of processors (nodes) in the multicomputer.
- A, the node where a decision about the assignment of a new task to a node must be taken.
- $W(A)$, the neighbourhood of A such that $A \in W(A)$. The neighbourhood may be defined in different ways depending on the structure and topology of the system we use.
- $N = N(W(A))$, the number of processors belonging to $W(A)$, $N \leq P$.
- $M = N - 1$, the number of neighbours belonging to $W(A)$ without A.
- $\tau(i)$, $1 \leq i \leq P$, the period at which every node i sends its load information to all nodes belonging to $W(i)$.
- $T(i)$, $1 \leq i \leq M$, the time of the last arrival onto the node A of the message with an information about load of node i. For node A, we define $T(N) = T(A)$ as the starting time of the load balancing procedure (i.e., node A is identified by the number N in $W(A)$).
- $l(i)$, $1 \leq i \leq M$, the length of task queue on the processor i (it is contained in a message sent from a node i to the node A), $l(A) = l(N)$.
- $t_m(i)$, $1 \leq i \leq M$, the time required to pass the message containing $l(i)$ from a node i to node A.
- $t_a(i)$, $1 \leq i \leq M$, the time required to activate a task from the node A to a generic node i, if the node i will be obtained as a result of the load balancing procedure. $t_a(i)$ may depend from the size of the task to be activated.
- $t(i) = T(A) - (T(i) - t_m(i) - t_a(i))$, $1 \leq i \leq M$, the time of synchronization of node A with a node $i \in W(A)$. It represents the obsolescence of $l(i)$ on node A. It is obtained as the difference between the time of $l(i)$ measurement on a node i and the time of arrival of a task from the node A to the node i, if this one will be obtained as a result of load balancing procedure executed on the node A. It is obvious that $t(A) = t(N) = 0$.
- $\alpha(i)$, $1 \leq i \leq N$, the degree of utilization of synchronized times, $0 \leq \alpha(i) \leq 1$.
- $\Delta l(i)$, $1 \leq i \leq N$, the difference between the maximum queue length and the length $l(i)$ taking into account the obsolescence of $l(i)$.
- $p(i)$, $1 \leq i \leq N$, the probability to assign a task to the processor i.

Each time on a node a new task must be scheduled, the scheduler performs the steps as follows:

Step 1. Calculate the times of synchronization $t(i)$ for each node i such that $1 \leq i \leq M$.

Step 2. Calculate the values

$$l_{max} = \max\{l(i) : 1 \leq i \leq N\} \quad \text{and}$$

$$t_{max} = \max\{t(i) : 1 \leq i \leq N\},$$

Step 3. For each node i such that $1 \leq i \leq N$, calculate the difference between the maximum queue length and its queue length $l(i)$ taking into account the obsolescence of $l(i)$

$$\Delta l(i) = (l_{max} - l(i))(1 - a(i)t(i)/t_{max}) \qquad \text{where} \quad 0 \leq \alpha(i) \leq 1.$$

Step 4. For each node i such that $1 \leq i \leq N$, compute the probability

$$p(i) = \Delta l(i)/S,$$

$$\text{where} \quad S = \sum_{k=1}^{N} \Delta l(k),$$

$$\text{if} \quad S = 0, \text{ then set} \quad p(A) = 1.$$

Step 5. The result of the load balancing procedure is obtained by a randomized choice with probabilities $p(i)$ computed on Step 4, on a random variable $X \in 1 \ldots N$.

In the proposed algorithm the synchronization between node A and its neighbourhood is carried out using the synchronization times $t(i)$. When the queue information is not obsolete (there exists at least one such case - when we take load balancing decision on the node A, so $t(A) = 0$), the synchronized queue length calculated on Step 3 represents precisely the difference between the maximal queue length taking place in $W(A)$ and the length $l(i)$.

When the information about the load state of a node i is obsolete ($t(i) > 0$), we decrease the probability to send a task to the node i (see Steps 3, 4). Obviously, the probability of the assignment of a task to a processor with queue length equal to l_{max} is zero. By means of the $\alpha(i)$ parameter it is possible to adjust the degree of influence of synchronization times on the result of the load balancing procedure. In case $\alpha(i) = 0$, $1 \leq i \leq N$, we use no information about the times of the load measurement. In case $\alpha(i) = 1 \leq i \leq N$, we use this information in the strongest manner.

On Step 4 we use a simple probabilistic mechanism to avoid the following situation. Suppose that a node i has the smallest queue length in the system. During an interval, at least a period $\tau(i)$, all its neighbours send new tasks to this node and its load increases rapidly. At the same time the load of the neighbours

remains the same or decreases (because of termination of some task). Thus, we have an unbalanced situation again. Introducing Step 4 permits to distribute new tasks more uniformly.
The five steps of the PNS algorithm may be implemented using three different schemes, as follows.

- The *one-hop scheme*. According to this scheme the load balancing procedure takes the assignment decision only one time, so a task is sent to be executed in the target node.

- The *multi-hop scheme*. In this scheme PNS works using the parameters *min_hops* and *max_hops* as the Adaptive Contracting within Neighbourhood algorithm [SK89]. Every hop of the multi-hop scheme is executed using the one-hop PNS and a new assignment decision may be taken. The notion of $W(A)$ may be changed from hop to hop (for example, the cardinality of $W(A)$ can be decreased depending on the number of hops traveled);

- The *scheme with saturation control*. The main idea of this scheme is to forbid task assignment to processors with a load greater than a saturation threshold known a priori. This approach may be combined with each of the two schemes described above. It may be applied in different ways.

4 Performance evaluation

The effectiveness of the one-hop scheme of PNS has been evaluated on PALM (PArallel Logic Machine), a parallel interpreter of logic programs [CST91]. The PNS algorithm has been implemented in the run-time support of PALM. The multicomputer we used is a Transputer-based system composed of 32 Inmos T800 processors connected in a toroidal mesh.

For this system we defined the neighbourhood $W(A)$ as $W(r, A)$. It contains all processors with a distance lower or equal to r links from processor A.
The one-hop PNS strategy has been evaluated on the known problem of $N-$*queens* on a chessboard with $N = 6$. We have compared the PNS strategy with a randomized strategy. The number of processes activated in PALM to solve the problem is equal to 6140.
The experiments on PALM have revealed that only a small subset of the cooperating processes exchange a large amount of data, whereas the rest of processes has a very short lifetime. This very dynamic behavior represents a worst case for load balancing strategies which use collected status information. The major problem of these strategies is the overhead to collect and process data. On the other hand, the advantage is a better allocation of processes and the decreasing of the execution time of the application. As mentioned before, for the $N -$ *queens* problem only a small subset of the processes will take advantage of a good allocation, thus this will not result in a proportional decreasing of the response time. We have chosen

this test problem as a worst case. In fact, if the application processes has a longer lifetime, a greater improvement in response time will be obtained.
In the experiments we have measured the following characteristics:

- the response time and
- the maximum length of the process queue during the resolution of the problem.

We have run the experiments varying the following parameters of PNS: $\alpha(i)$, $\tau(i)$ and r. As mentioned before, the parameter $\alpha(i)$ measures the utilization degree of the synchronized times. Here we have chosen $\alpha(i) = 0$, $1 \leq ileP$, (no use of synchronized times), versus $\alpha(i) = 1$, $1 \leq i \leq P$, (full use of synchronized times). The period of the data exchange $\tau(i)$, $1 \leq i \leq P$, has been varied from 0.1 to 0.5 time units. The radius r has been varied between 1 and 3 links. We present the average values obtained by four experiments.

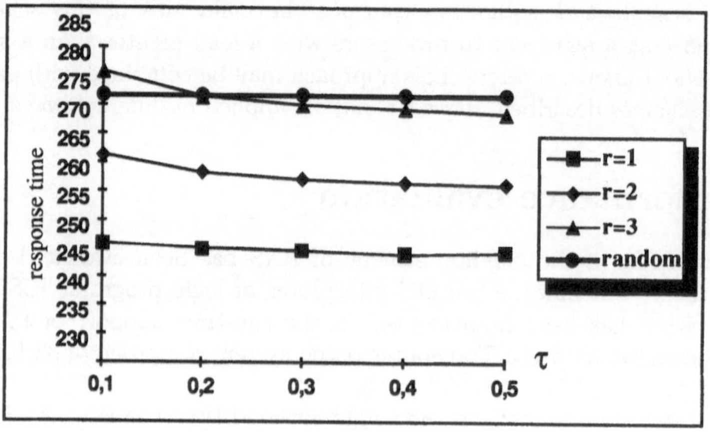

Figure 1: *PNS versus random response time.*

The response time obtained using the random strategy is 276.6 time units. Fig. 1 shows the response time obtained using the PNS strategy varying the period τ and defining three different neighborhoods (three values of the radius).

The average length of the maximum process queue for the random strategy is 9.25. The results for the PNS strategy are shown in Fig. 2. For both figures the value of α is 1. With respect to the random strategy, the PNS response time is preferable when the radius is less than 3, for every value of τ. In particular it decreases when increasing τ. This effect is due to the lower frequency of data exchange that reduces the communication overhead. For the maximum process queue, the PNS values are still better for all values of τ when the radius is greater than one, and also for radius equal to one if a sufficiently short period is chosen.

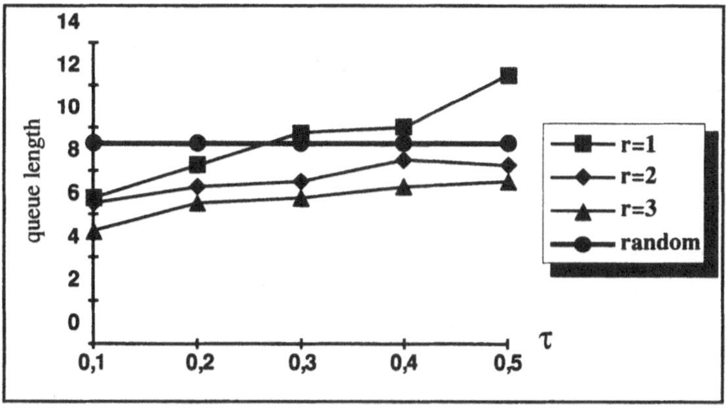

Figure 2: *PNS versus Random process queue length.*

Obviously, reducing the period improves the knowledge of the system load and then results in a better task distribution.

Comparing Fig.s 1 and 2 it is possible to note a trade-off between the response time and the maximum queue length both respect to the period and the radius. Increasing the system knowledge (reducing the period) improves the task distribution, but an overhead must be paid in terms of communication time. Vice versa reducing the communication overhead by augmenting the period, the response time decreases, but this requires a larger quantity of busy resources.

Increasing the radius results in a significant rise in the response time and a decrease in the maximum queue length. The first effect is due to the larger data exchange, the second one is due to the knowledge of the load on a wider part of the network. In fact, varying the radius it is possible to enlarge or contract the neighbourhood of a processor.

With respect to the maximum queue length, the use of the synchronized times ($\alpha = 1$) improves the load balancing. This occurs because the information are managed by PNS according to their obsolescence. However, the response time is not very sensitive respect to the use of the synchronized times, even if we noticed an insignificant increase due to the overhead to process a larger amount of data. Finally, the major factors of the application that we have to consider to choose the PNS parameter α, τ, r are:

- the amount of resources on each processor (i.e., the number of available processes),
- the grain size and lifetime of processes composing the application, and
- the requested locality degree.

The choice will be a trade-off between the necessity to have the shortest response time, usually when a single-user machine is used and the best use of resources, usually when balancing the load on a multi-user machine.

5 Conclusions

This paper discussed a new dynamic load balancing algorithm for multicomputer systems called PNS. This strategy uses a locality-based approach. On each node of a multicomputer only status information collected from its neighbour nodes are used and the information lags due to message passing are taken into account for estimating the system load.

The performance figures show that the PNS strategy schedules the processes guarantying a locality-based computation. This results in a better response time and a more balanced load distribution of our strategy respect to the randomized strategy. In particular, the PNS strategy yields a good performance when medium grained processes must be scheduled.

The behavior of the load balancing algorithm can be tuned varying the dimension of the neighbourhood, the period of information exchange and the utilization degree of the information obsolescence. This feature allows to realize an adaptive strategy if these parameters are dynamically changed in accordance with the system workload change.

Acknowledgments

This research has been partially supported by "Progetto Finalizzato Sistemi Informatici e Calcolo Parallelo" of C.N.R. under grant no. 93.01687.69. We thank Ya. D. Sergeyev for its contribution to the algorithm design.

References

[AG91] I. Ahmad and A. Ghafoor. Semi-distributed Load Balancing for Massively Parallel Multicomputer Systems. *IEEE Transactions on Software Engineering*, SE-17(10):987–1004, October 1991.

[BS85] A. Barak and A. Shiloh. A Distributed Load Balancing Policy for a Multicomputer. *Software Practice and Experience*, 15(9):901–913, September, 1985.

[CST91] M. Cannataro, G. Spezzano, and D. Talia. A Parallel Logic System on a Multicomputer Architecture. *Future Generation Computer Systems*, 6(4):317–331, 1991.

[CSS93] M. Cannataro, Ya. D. Sergeyev, G. Spezzano, and D. Talia. A Dynamic Load Balancing Strategy for Massively Parallel Computers. in *PARLE'93 Parallel Architectures and Languages Europe*, LNCS 694, pages 664–667. Springer Verlag, 1993.

[CK88] T.L. Casavant and J.G. Kuhl. A Taxonomy of Scheduling in General-Purpose Distributed Computing Systems. *IEEE Transactions on Software Engineering*, SE-14(2):141–154, February 1988.

[CA82] T.C.K. Chow and J.A. Abraham. Load Balancing in Distributed Systems. *IEEE Transactions on Software Engineering*, SE-8(4):401–412, July 1982.

[CK82] Y.-C. Chow and W.H. Kohler. Models for Dynamic Load Balancing in Homogeneous Multiple Processor Systems. *IEEE Transactions on Computers*, C-36(5):667–679, May 1982.

[Chu69] W. Chu. Optimal File Allocation in a Multiple Computing System. *IEEE Transactions on Computers*, C-18(10):885–889, October 1969.

[ELZ86] D.L. Eager, E.D. Lazowska, and J. Zahorjan. Adaptive Load Sharing in Homogeneous Distributed Systems. *IEEE Transactions on Software Engineering*, SE-12(5):662–675, May 1986.

[LY91] A. Leff and P.S. Yu. An Adaptive Strategy for Load Sharing in Distributed Database Environments with Information Lags. *Journal of Parallel and Distributed Computing*, 13:91–103, 1991.

[LK87] F. C. H. Lin and R. M. Keller. The Gradient Model Load Balancing Method. *IEEE Transactions on Software Engineering*, SE-13(1):101–112, January 1987.

[LR92] H.-C. Lin and C. S. Raghavendra. A Dynamic Load-Balancing Policy with a Central Job Dispatcher (LBC). *IEEE Transactions on Software Engineering*, SE-18(2):148–158, February 1992.

[MTS89] R. Mirchandaney, D. Towsley, and J. A. Stankovic. Analysis of the Effects of Delays on Load Sharing. *IEEE Transactions on Computers*, C-38(11):1513–1525, August 1989.

[SH86] V. Sarkar and J. Hennessy. Compile-Time Partitioning and Scheduling of Parallel Programs. in *Proc. SIGPLAN '86 Symp. on Compiler Construction*, pages 17–26, 1986.

[SC89] K.G. Shin, and Y.-C. Chang. Load Sharing in Distributed Real-Time Systems with State-Change Broadcast. *IEEE Transactions on Computers*, C-38(8):1124–1142, August 1989.

[SK89] W. Shu, and L.V. Kalé. Dynamic Scheduling of Medium-Grained Processes on Multicomputers. Technical Report, Dept. of Computer Science, Univ. of Illinois at Urbana-Champaign, 1989.

[WM85] Y.-T. Wang, and J.T. Morris. Load Sharing in Distributed Systems. *IEEE Transactions on Computers*, C-34(3):204–217, March 1985.

Programming Environments for Massively Parallel Distributed Systems, Monte Verità, Switzerland

Static Performance Prediction in PCASE: A Programming Environment for Parallel Supercomputers

Yoshiki Seo*
(seo@csl.cl.nec.co.jp)

Tsunehiko Kamachi*
(kamachi@csl.cl.nec.co.jp)

Yukimitsu Watanabe†
(yukimi.nsis.cl.nec.co.jp)

Kazuhiro Kusano*
(kusano@csl.cl.nec.co.jp)

Kenji Suehiro*
(suehiro@csl.cl.nec.co.jp)

Yukimasa Shiroto†
(shiroto@nsis.cl.nec.co.jp)

Abstract

This paper presents a performance estimator, a prototype of which is implemented within the parallel programming environment PCASE. The estimation is based on static performance prediction, using not only the design information of target machines but also benchmarking results. Additionally, communication costs are estimated based on a hierarchical memory machine model, which enables users to understand all the underlying communication costs on distributed memory machines for each parallel loop. With this performance suggestion, it is possible to interactively optimize data distribution and appropriately select vectorized or parallelized loops. Moreover, the *skeleton profiling* method is presented. It makes high speed trace (execution count of each statement) generation possible by deleting statements which do not affect the execution path of a program.

1 Introduction

The importance of performance prediction capability is rapidly increasing, as the architecture of parallel machines becomes more sophisticated and complicated. It is very difficult for users to understand how their programs run on parallel machines, or to correctly select optimization choices. Automatic performance estimation helps users to tune their programs without studying the details of the machine architecture.

*C&C Research Laboratories, NEC Corporation
†NEC Scientific Information System Development, Ltd.

Using dynamic information such as performance monitoring results is also important, but it alone does not help users to fully understand the behavior of programs, because it is not realistic to run individual versions of possible optimization choices. Especially, optimization for data distribution has a variety of choices, because the distribution of one data object affects the distribution effectiveness of others. Moreover, monitoring the behavior of parallel programs itself has some problems, such as the difficulty in implementing a high resolution timer, the probe effect and handling the huge amount of trace data.

In order to address these difficulties, an experimental system is developed for static performance prediction within the parallel programming environment PCASE[5]. The design considerations are: (1)the estimation time should be small enough to be easily used for large scale problems, and to be included in the compiler's optimization phase, (2)it should help users to judge the scalability of programs, and to select the best optimization candidates, and (3)it should work on workstations without using the target machine.

This paper presents the static prediction prediction and a trace generation method which enables high-speed trace generation for the prediction.

2 Overview of the PCASE System

PCASE is an interactive programming environment which translates sequential FORTRAN programs into their parallel form. Programmers can control the parallelization through a graphical user interface as well as browse through program information related to parallelization. Figure 1 shows the configuration of PCASE.

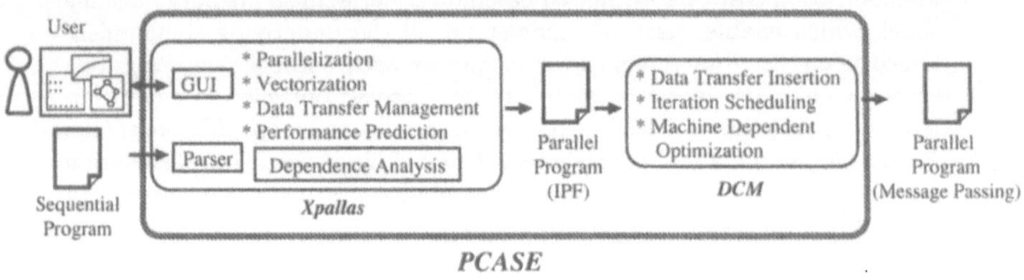

***Figure 1**: Configuration of PCASE*

PCASE consists of two parts, namely, *Xpallas*, an interactive parallelizer which generates IPF (Intermediate Parallel Fortran) programs, and *DCM* (Data distribution & Communication Manager), which translates the IPF programs into parallel programs for a target machine.

The IPF interface is designed to allow specification of parallelization in a machine independent form by introducing an abstract machine model, where each processing node is a scalar processor which may be equipped with a vector processing unit (VU), because PCASE has both vectorization and parallelization capabilities.

The interface is defined based on simplified SX-3 microtasking directives[6], with LOCAL and DISTRIBUTE directives added. The LOCAL directive plays the role of variable privatization as is used in some of conventional vector supercomputers, and specifies the access range and attributes of shared variables inside a DO loop. Data placement on distributed memories is specified by the DISTRIBUTE directive[4] [3] [2].

PCASE models memory architecture with three different types of memory area: local area, shared area and distributed area. Using these three kinds of memory area, Xpallas provides programmers with two memory paradigms, namely, *the hierarchical memory paradigm (HMP)* and *the distributed memory paradigm (DMP)*. In HMP, using local and shared areas, users can parallelize programs assuming a hierarchical memory machine, where the data transfer can be controlled by the LOCAL directive . On the other hand, DMP provides local and distributed areas. If a programmer wants to take advantage of memory access locality, he can specify data distribution on the memories using DMP.

3 Static Performance Prediction

The performance prediction module (PPM) estimates the parallelized program's efficiency quantitatively. The estimation is based on static performance analysis which can be performed at compile time. We adopt the 'training set' approach[1] for generating the performance data of synchronizations and communications. The performance data for other instructions such as *addition* and *load* are prepared from the hardware design information. Figure 2 shows the blockdiagram of PPM.

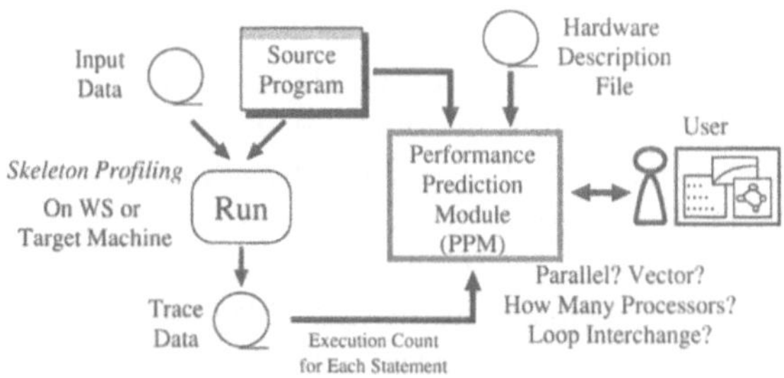

Figure 2: *Blockdiagram of Static Performance Prediction*

The inputs for PPM are a source program, a hardware description file and trace data. The trace data contains an execution count (frequency) for each basic block of the program, which is generated using a skeleton profiling technique descibed in Section 4. First, PPM lists up basic operations for executing each statement, then, it estimates execution cost for each loop or basic block according to the optimization pattern, using the other two inputs. When the trace data is not available, PPM assumes dummy execution counts which are calculated using compile-time information, such as constant propagation results and array declarations.

3.1 Performance Estimation

Basically, PPM calculates the cost (time) for each statement using the number of machine cycles required for basic instructions, such as *addition*, *multiply*, *load*, *store*, *branch*, intrinsic functions (SQRT, ABS, etc.), data transfer, synchronizations, and so on[7]. In a hardware description file, the costs for scalar and vector instructions are prepared using hardware design information, and communication/synchronization costs are prepared using measured results on the target machine. For vector instructions, the *start-up* time is an execution time when vector length equals to 1. *Throughput* is the number of elements which can be calculated in a clock cycle.

These hardware description data are prepared for target machines, and stored in a file in advance. Then, PPM sums up this for all the statements in the range of a loop or a procedure by the following method.

(1)Scalar Execution Cost For the scalar computation part, the execution cost of a statement is calculated by simply summing up all the basic operation costs in the statement. Then the result is multiplied by the execution count of the statement. Here, multiple appearances of load/store operations for the same variable in a basic block are reduced to one appearance, considering the register allocation optimization by a compiler.

(2)Vector Execution Cost First of all, the average loop length n of a vectorized loop is calculated by simply dividing the execution count of the statement just after the DO statement by that of the DO statement. Then, the strip mining iteration frequency l is computed by $l = n/m$ as well as its remainder r $(= l - (n/m) * m)$. Here, m is the maximum length of a vector register.

The cost of a vector operation in the case of length $i(i <= m)$ is calculated by $s + i/t$. Here, s and t are the start up time and the throughput for the operation, respectively. Then, the costs when vector length is $m(COSTm)$ and $r(COSTr)$are calculated for each appearance of operations in the DO loop. Finally, the cost for the DO loop of length n is calculated by summing up $l \times COSTm$ and $COSTr$ for all the operations in the loop.

Currently, we do not take chaining effect into account. However, it can be considered by preparing a list of paired operations which can be executed in a chain, for example ($add \rightarrow multiply$), and substracting start up time for the corresponding operations using the data dependence informaton.

(3)Parallel Execution Cost First of all, the average loop length n of a parallelized loop is calculated in the same manner as for the vectorized loops. Then, the number of iterations assigned to one processing element l is calculated by $\lceil n/np \rceil$, where np is the number of processors (np=1,2,4,...,the max number of PEs). Next, the cost for l iterations of the DO loop is calculated using the scalar and vector execution cost estimation described above. Finally, the parallel loop execution cost is computed by adding the synchronization and communication costs.

The communication cost is calculated using the information in the LOCAL directives which are inserted by PCASE. If variables with unknown values are used in the directives, these values are presumed using average loop length n or declaration of variables. In this way, parallel loop execution costs using various numbers of PEs are simultaneously calculated. At the moment, PPM does not consider the load imbalance effect.

3.2 Measurement Results

We carried out performance evaluation using Cenju2, a R3000 based parallel machine system. The sample program is a 3-D ($60 \times 60 \times 60$) Poisson equation solver discretized using FDM. The generated linear system is solved by the SCG (scaled conjugate gradient) method.

Figure 3 shows the measured and predicted results for a SCG simulation program on Cenju2 with three data transfer optimization levels: a) no optimization, b) interactively optimized with HMP and c) optimized with DMP by data distribution specification. The results show that the predicted performance collectly reflects performance inprovement throughout the communication optimization process.

By introducing the performance estimation based on HMP, users can understand all the underlying communication costs for each parallel loop. With this performance suggestion, it is possible to interactively optimize data distribution and appropriately select vectorized or parallelized loops.

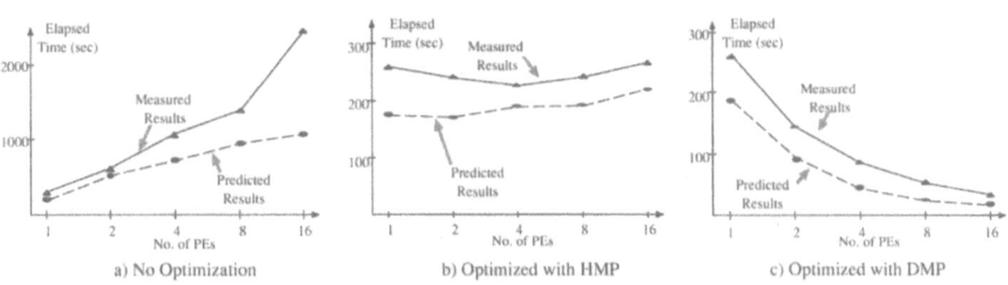

***Figure 3**: Measured and Predicted Performance with three Data Transfer Optimization Levels*

Major factors which cause the estimator's inaccuracy are: (1)cache effect,

(2)chaining effect for vector instructions, (3)memory bank conflict effect, (4)changing loop length or true ratio of IF statements, (5)network conflict effect and (6)load imbalance effect.

Of course, some of these effects can be taken into account by paying additional estimation costs. However, we believe that 50% accuracy is sufficient for checking the scalability of parallelized loops, and for determining data distributions or parallelized loops. The prediction goal is performance which is practical and cheap enough to use in a real-time optimization support tool. For this purpose, the above results proved the feasibility of our approach.

4 Efficient Execution Count Generation

As described in the previous section, the execution count for each statement is indispensable for statically predicting effective performance of a program. We developed an efficient execution count generation technique, called *skeleton profiling.* Its basic idea is that computational results are not necessarily calculated just for the purpose of trace generation. Therefore, statements which do not affect the control flow can be eliminated. Additionally, users do not have to prepare input data for the programs when it does not affect the execution path of the program.

Figure 4 shows an example. Program *example*2 is a profiling program for *example*1. A counter increment statement is inserted to every basic block. In this example, the most time consuming part is a DO 10 loop, and its computational result *sum* does not affect any control flows. Therefore, the statement inside the loop can be eliminated, as well as the DO statement itself. Then the final program *example*3 results.

Original Program

```
   program example1
   real*8 a(10000),sum
   read(5,*) n
   read(10,*) a
   sum=0.0d0
   do 10 i=1,n
    sum=sum+a(i)
10 continue
   write(6,*) sum
   stop
   end
```

Conventional Profiling Program

```
   program example2
-> real*8 a(10000),sum
   ic1=0  )
   ic2=0  ) Counter Initialization
   ic3=0  )
   ic1=ic1+1   <- Counter Increment
   read(5,*) n
-> read(10,*) a
-> sum=0.0d0
-> do 10 i=1,n
    ic2=ic2+1  <- Counter Increment
->  sum=sum+a(i)
->10 continue
   ic3=ic3+1   <- Counter Increment
-> write(6,*) sum
   write(6,*) ic1,ic2,ic3   Counter Output
   stop
   end
```

Skeleton Profiling Program

```
   program example3
   ic1=0
   ic2=0
   ic3=0
   ic1=ic1+1
   read(5,*) n
   ic2=ic2+n
   ic3=ic3+1
   write(6,*) ic1,ic2,ic3
   stop
   end
```

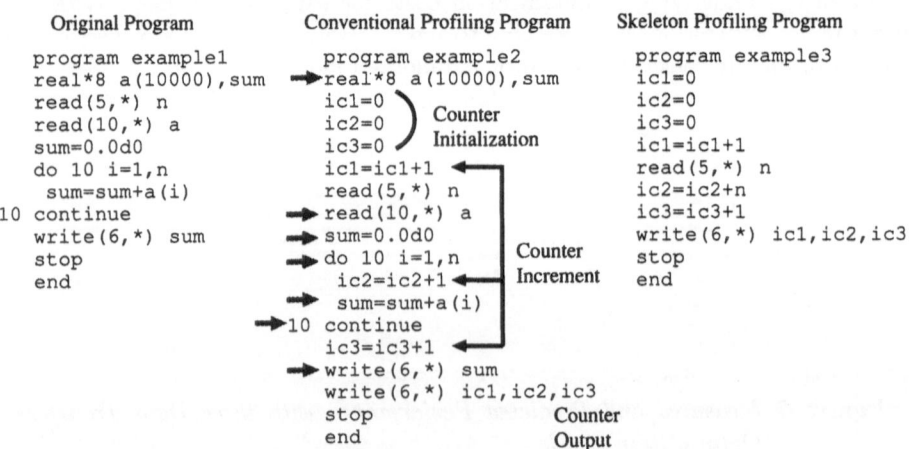

Figure 4: An Example of Skeleton Profiling

For this program transformation, first, variables which affect the control flow of a program are examined. Then, statements which have nothing to do with execution path are computed using the USE-DEF relation of variables. Note that the computation without inter-procedural analysis does not work well, because almost all the variables used in the main computation part are usually passed between procedures.

4.1 Intra-procedural Analysis

The generator translates a source program in the following steps:
(1) Create USE-DEF chain[8].
(2)List variables which directly affect the execution path. We call them *control variables*, which include the variables, such as: a)variables which appear in logical expressions of IF statements, b)variables which appear in assigned GOTO and computed GOTO statements, c)variables which control DO loop iteration and d)variables which appear in I/O statements, where statements for write only or read only files are excluded.
(3)Mark all the control statements (including I/O control statements) and statement label assignment statements.
(4)Tracing USE-DEF chain from the variables shown above and mark necessary statements.
(5)Eliminate unmarked statements. Note that when a statement to be eliminated has a statement label, the statement is replaced with a CONTINUE statement with the same label.
(6)Insert count accumulating statements for each basic block.

With this algorithm, a high speed count generation program can be created, when time consuming computation parts do not use global data.

4.2 Inter-procedural Analysis

For this kind of analysis, interprocedural analysis is indispensable. This is because, assuming that all the COMMON variables and formal parameters affect the control flow, almost none of the statements can be eliminated. However, directly applying the above argorithm through procedures in a target program requires much computation time. Therefore, we use a flow-insensitive analysis to reduce the analysis cost. In the analysis, control flow inside a procedure is not considered to handle interprocedural relations. More precisely, if there exists a control flow along which variable s affects the value of variable t, all the statements which define the value of s are considered to affect the value of t.

In the following algorithm, procedures in the CALL graph are visited twice in bottom-up and top-down order. In the bottom-up traversal, information about control variables and those defined is propagated upward. Then, information about control flow variables is propagated downward in the top-down traversal. In these two traversals, the three types of relation between a variable's definition and its use in statements, which affect control flow shown in Fig.5, are guaranteed to be examined. We assume that all the COMMON variables are made visible from each procedure, for simplicity.

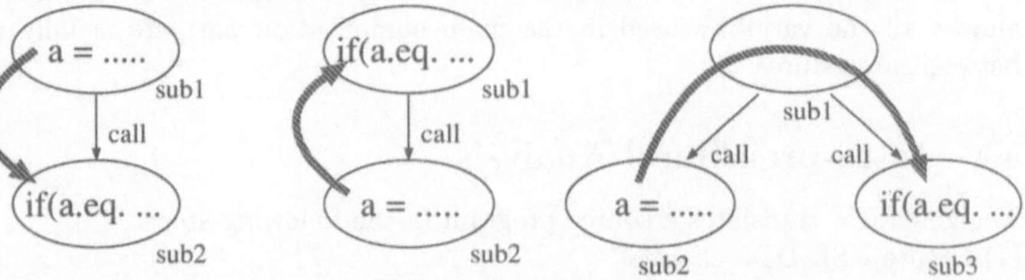

***Figure 5**: Three Types of USE-DEF Relation across Procedures*

Definition $V(p)$: a set of variables which are visible in procedure p
$C(p)$: a set of variables in $V(p)$ which affect control flows in the whole program
$C_{self}(p)$: a set of variables which affect control flows in procedure p
$C_{succ}(p)$: a set of variables which affect control flows in procedure p or its successor procedures
$D_{self}(p)$: a set of variables which are defined in procedure p
$D_{succ}(p)$: a set of variables in $V(p)$ of which values are defined in procedure p or its successor procedures
$R_{succ}(v,p)$: a set of variables in $V(p)$ which are (directly or indirectly) referred to in procedure p or its successor procedures to define the value of variable v
$Child(p)$: a set of procedures which are directly referred to in procedure p
$Parent(p)$: a set of procedures which directly refer to procedure p

Algorithm for interprocedural analysis Visit p in the bottom-up order (from leaf to root) in the call graph, and compute $C_{succ}(p)$, $D_{succ}(p)$ and $R_{succ}(v,p)$ for each procedure p by the following Steps (1) and (2).

(1) Create a Use-Def chain of p, after virtually replacing each procedure reference of q ($\in Child(p)$) with a statement in which elements of $D_{succ}(q) \cap V(p)$ are defined ,$C_{succ}(q) \cap V(p)$ is used in a logical expression for conditional branch, and $R_{succ}(q) \cap V(p)$ is used to define v ($\in D_{succ}(q)$).

(2) Determine $C_{succ}(p)$, $D_{succ}(p)$, $R_{succ}(v,p)$(for each $v \in D_{succ}(p)$) by intra-procedural analysis, as follows.

- Compute a temporary control variable set $C_{tmp}(p)$ by

$$C_{tmp}(p) \leftarrow (C_{self}(p) \cup \bigcup_{q \in Child(p)} C_{succ}(q)) \cap V(p)$$

- A set of variables $C_{ref}(v,p)$ which affect the value of v is determined by traversing the Use-Def chain, starting from each temporary control variable $v \in C_{tmp}(p)$. Then, compute $C_{succ}(p)$ by the following equation.

$$C_{succ}(p) \leftarrow C_{tmp}(p) \cup \bigcup_{q \in C_{tmp}(p)} C_{ref}(v,p)$$

- Compute $D_{succ}(p)$ by

$$D_{succ}(p) \leftarrow (D_{self}(p) \cup \bigcup_{q \in Child(p)} D_{succ}(q)) \cap V(p)$$

- Compute $R_{succ}(v,p)$ by traversing the Use-Def chain, starting from each variable $v \in D_{succ}(p)$ determined above.

Then, visit p in top-down order (from root to leaf) in the call graph, and compute $C_{succ}(p)$. $TMP(p)$ means a temporary set including variables in $D_{succ}(p)$ which are determined to affect control flow.

(3)

$$TMP(p) \leftarrow \bigcup_{q \in Parent(p)} (D_{succ}(p) \cap C(q))$$

(4)

$$C(p) \leftarrow C_{succ}(p) \cup TMP(p) \cup (\bigcup_{r \in TMP(p)} R_{succ}(r,p) \cap D_{succ}(p))$$

With this algorithm, a variable set $C(p)$ is calculated for each procedure p. Then, all the statements which set a value of $C(p)$ are marked as necessary statements for each p.

4.3 Effect of Skeleton Profiling

Figure 6 shows measurement results on some real applications. SPIN is a spin glass simulation using the transfer matrix method. We got good results for SPIN, FFT and LU, but in the case of SCG program, no speed up was obtained. This is because the main part of SCG is a convergence calculation, where no statements can be eliminated. However, these cases can be covered by creating a program of one iteration, because the target for parallel or vector optimizations is usualy one iteration in simulations with an iterative algorithm.

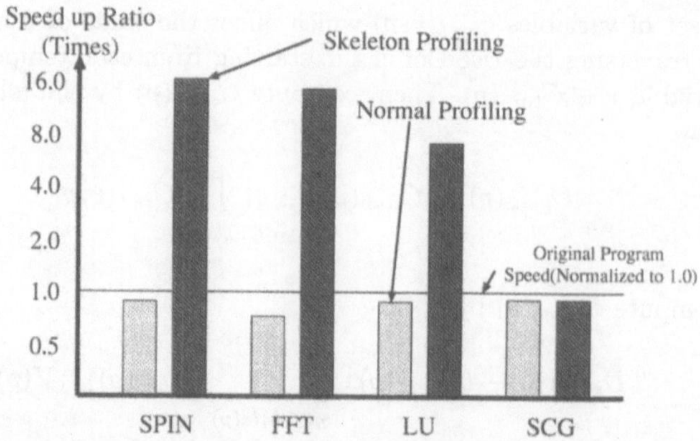

Figure 6: *Speed Up Ratio of Count Accumulating Programs Produced by the Count Generator (measured on EWS 4800/220)*

5 Conclusions

We have proposed a method for statically predicting the effective performance of parallel programs by using benchmarking results as well as design information of target machines. Performance for communications among processing elements is estimated based on a hierarchical memory model, in order to make it possible for users to understand all the underlying communication costs for each parallel loop on distributed memory machines. The comparison between the measured and estimated results proved that the estimator can correctly guide data transfer optimization in two steps: optimizing data transfers assuming hierarchical memories, and determining data distribution. Furthermore, skeleton profiling effectively reduced the cost of preparing the trace information for performance prediction, which makes it possible to optimize real programs.

We believe that the methodology presented in this paper, to statically predict the performance of parallel programs, will help fully utilize highly parallel machines.

References

[1] V. Balasundaram, G. Fox, K. Kennedy, U. Kremer:*A Static Performance Estimator to Gide Data Partitioning Decisions*, ACM SIGPLAN Symposium on Principle & Practice of Parallel Programmig(PPoPP), pp.213-223, 1991.

[2] B. Chapman, P.Mehrotra, H. Moritsch, H. Zima: *Dynamic Data Distributions in Vienna Fortran*, in Proc. of Supercomputing '93, pp.284-293, 1993.

[3] G. Fox, S. Hiranandani, K. Kennedy, C. Koelbel, U. Kremer, C. Tseng, M. Wu: *Fortran D Language Specification*, Tech. Report TR90-141, Rice University, 1990.

[4] *High Performance FORTRAN Language Specification*, Technical report, Rice University, 1993

[5] T. Kamachi, Y. Seo, S. Matsuno: *Data Distribution Management for Distributed Memory Machines in Parallel Programming Environment PCASE* (In Japanese), In Proc. of Joint Symposium on Parallel Processing (JSPP) '93, pp.31-38, 1993.

[6] *FORTRAN77/SX User's Manual*, NEC Corporation, 1992.

[7] V. Sarkar: *Determining Average Program Execution Times and their Variance*, In Proc. of ACM SIGPLAN '89 Symposium on Programming Language Design and Implementation (PLDI), pp.298-312, 1989.

[8] H. Zima, B. Chapman: *Supercompilers for Parallel and Vector Computers*, ACM Press, Addison-Wesley, New York, 1990.

Programming Environments for Massively Parallel Distributed Systems, Monte Verità, Switzerland

A Performance Tool for High-Level Parallel Programming Languages *

R. Bruce Irvin Barton P. Miller

rbi@cs.wisc.edu bart@cs.wisc.edu

Computer Sciences Department
University of Wisconsin
Madison, WI USA 53706-1685

Abstract

Users of high-level parallel programming languages require accurate performance information that is relevant to their source code. Furthermore, when their programs experience performance problems at the lowest levels of their hardware and software systems, programmers need to be able to peel back layers of abstraction to examine low-level problems while maintaining references to the high-level source code that ultimately caused the problem. In this paper, we present NV, a model for the explanation of performance information for programs built on multiple levels of abstraction. In NV, a level of abstraction includes a collection of nouns (code and data objects), verbs (activities), and performance information measured for the nouns and verbs. Performance information is mapped from level to level to maintain the relationships between low-level activities and high-level code, even when such relationships are implicit.

We have used the NV model to build ParaMap, a performance tool for the CM Fortran language that has, in practice, guided us to substantial improvements in real CM Fortran applications. We describe the design and implementation of our tool and show how its simple tabular and graphical performance displays helped us to find performance problems in two applications. In each case, we found that performance information at all levels was most useful when related to parallel CM Fortran arrays, and that we could subsequently reduce each application's execution time by more than half.

*This research was supported in part by Department of Energy grant DE-FG02-93ER25176, Office of Naval Research grant N00014-89-J-1222, and National Science Foundation grants CCR-9100968 and CDA-9024618.

1 Introduction

High-level parallel programming languages promise to make programmers' lives easier. They offer portable, conceptually compact notations for specifying parallel programs, and their compilers automatically map programs onto complex parallel machines, freeing programmers from the difficult, error-prone, and sometimes ineffective task of specifying parallel computations explicitly. Unfortunately, effective performance measurement tools for high-level parallel programming languages are difficult to build because they must account for implicit low-level activities created by compilers and must present performance information about those activities in terms of the source code language.

In this paper we present NV, a new model for the explanation of performance measurements of high-level parallel applications. With NV, we organize a high-level parallel application into a set of abstraction layers that corresponds to the set of layers of software on which the application is built. Each layer of abstraction consists of a collection of nouns (representing code and data elements) and verbs (runtime actions). In NV, mapping functions relate nouns and verbs of a given layer of abstraction to nouns and verbs of other layers of abstraction. Mapping functions preserve the relationships between low-level system-dependent activities that are performed on behalf of high-level system-independent code constructs. These mapping functions allow us to get performance information not easily obtained from current tools.

Using NV as a guide, we have designed and implemented ParaMap, a performance tool for CM Fortran programs running on CM–5 systems. ParaMap has allowed us to study large and long running applications and significantly improve their execution times (73% in one case). ParaMap summarizes system performance at the source code level in terms of CM Fortran arrays, array subsections, and statements. However, if performance problems cannot be fully understood at the source code level, ParaMap allows the user to peel back layers of abstraction to view the runtime system and processor activity while retaining mappings to the appropriate CM Fortran constructs.

We first describe the NV model using CM Fortran as an example language. We then describe the design of ParaMap, and demonstrate its use with example CM Fortran programs. We briefly discuss the related problem of debugging optimized code before summarizing and concluding with a discussion of how NV based tools can utilize dynamic instrumentation and automated bottleneck searching within the context of next generation performance tools [3].

2 The NV Model

A major goal of our research is to identify performance characteristics that are common across programming models. To help achieve this goal, we have developed a framework within which we can discuss performance characteristics of programming models. This section provides an informal description of the Noun–Verb (NV) model for parallel program performance explanation. In the NV model, *nouns* are the structural elements of a particular program, and *verbs* are the actions taken by the nouns or performed on the nouns. [1]

A collection of nouns and verbs from a particular software or hardware layer is called a *level of abstraction.* Nouns and verbs from one level of abstraction are related to nouns and verbs from other levels of abstraction with *mappings.* A mapping expresses the notion that high-level language constructs are implemented with low-level software and hardware. With mappings, performance information collected at lower levels can be related to language level nouns and verbs. A mapping may be *static*, meaning that it is determined before runtime, or *dynamic*, meaning that it is determined at runtime and possibly changes over the course of program execution.

In describing the NV model, we use the data-parallel language CM Fortran [7] as our example language because its characteristics are representative of many high-level parallel programming languages, including HPF [2]. The NV model, however, is applicable to many other parallel programming models.

2.1 Nouns and Verbs

A *noun* is any program element about which performance measurements can be made, and a *verb* is any potential action that might be taken by a noun or performed on a noun. We will use the example CM Fortran program in Figure 1 to describe some of the nouns and verbs of the CM Fortran language. The example program declares two multi-dimensional arrays (line 3), initializes all elements of array A with a parallel assignment statement (line 5), assigns values to a subsection of array A (line 7), computes the sum of the array (line 8), and computes a function of the upper left quadrant of array A and assigns it to array B (line 9).

A particular execution instance of the program construct described by a verb is called a *sentence.* A sentence consists of a verb, a set of participating nouns, and a cost. The cost of a sentence may be measured in time, memory, channel bandwidth, etc. Finally, *performance information* consists of the aggregated costs measured from the execution of a collection of sentences. For example, performance information for array `A` in Figure 1 might include measurements of the assignments of lines 5, 7, and 9, and the reduction on line 8. Performance information for array `B`, however, would include only measurements of the assignment on line 9.

2.2 Levels of Abstraction and Mapping

In the NV model, each level of abstraction for which performance may be measured is represented by a distinct set of nouns and verbs. Furthermore, nouns, verbs, and

[1] An alternate terminology could be *objects* and *methods.* However, we feel that these terms have been overused, so we have chosen *nouns* and *verbs.*

```
      PROGRAM EXAMPLE
      PARAMETER (N=1000)
      INTEGER A(N+1,N+1), B(N,N), ASUM

      A = 0
      DO K = 1,10
         FORALL (I=2:N+1, J=2:N+1)  A(J,I) = K*(I+J)
         ASUM = SUM(A)
         FORALL (I=1:N/2, J=1:N/2)  B(J,I) = A(J,I) + A(J+1,I+1)
      END DO
      END
```

***Figure 1**: Example CM Fortran Program*

performance information of one level may be mapped to nouns and verbs of other levels.

For CM-5 systems, a CM Fortran program is compiled into a sequential program and a set of node routines. [2]

The sequential program executes on the CM-5 Control Processor and makes calls to the parallel node routines and to parallel system routines through the CM Runtime System (CMRTS). The CMRTS creates arrays, maps arrays to processors, implements CM Fortran intrinsic functions (e.g. SUM, MAX, MIN, SHIFT, and ROTATE) and coordinates the processor nodes. Each parallel CM Fortran array is divided into subgrids, and each subgrid is assigned to a separate node. Each node performs computations with its local array subgrids; if non-local data are needed, then they are retrieved before computation proceeds.

We model the CM-5 with three levels of abstraction. The highest level, called the CMF level, contains the nouns and verbs from the CM Fortran language. The middle level is the RTS level. RTS level nouns include all of the arrays allocated during the course of execution. This set of arrays includes all of the arrays that correspond to CMF level arrays as well as the arrays generated by the compiler for holding intermediate values. Verbs of the RTS level include array manipulations such as *Shift*, *Rotate*, *Get*, *Put*, and *Copy*. The lowest level of abstraction is the node level. Node level nouns include the processor nodes, and verbs include *Compute*, *Wait*, *Broadcast Communication*, and *Point-to-Point Communication*.

A *mapping* is a relationship between nouns (verbs) from one level of abstraction and nouns (verbs) of another level. NV mappings are either *static* or *dynamic*. Static mappings are independent of time or context. For example, the mapping between node level routines and CMF level statements is a static mapping that is determined at compile time. Dynamic mappings are determined at execution time.

[2]In this discussion, we do not consider the nodal style of execution for CM Fortran programs in which each CM-5 node executes a separate CM Fortran program.

For example, CM Fortran arrays are mapped to processor nodes as the arrays are allocated.

Verb mappings are either *explicit* or *implicit*. An explicit mapping indicates that a high level verb is directly implemented by a lower level verb. For example, a SUM reduction (line 8 of Figure 1) is directly implemented by node level additions, so the mapping from CMF level SUM operations to node level additions is explicit. Implicit mappings indicate that a lower level verb helps to maintain the semantics of a higher level verb. For example, a SUM reduction is implemented on a CM-5 system with partial reductions on each processor node and a final reduction of the partial results using the CM-5 broadcast network. The creation of parallelism and broadcast communication caused by such a reduction is implicit because neither is specified directly by the CMF level SUM statement. Therefore, the NV mapping from CMF level SUM operations to creation of parallelism and broadcast communication is an implicit mapping.

3 The ParaMap Tool

The NV model can be used as a guide for the design and implementation of performance measurement systems for high-level parallel languages. To evaluate the NV model in this role and to gain experience with mapping in an actual parallel language system, we have built a performance measurement tool for CM Fortran. The tool, called ParaMap, measures performance information for nouns and verbs at three levels of abstraction and maps performance information between levels.

3.1 Overview

Measured nouns at the CMF level of abstraction include subroutines, statements, and arrays, while verbs include array assignment and reduction, subroutine execution, and statement execution. At the RTS level, ParaMap measures the cost of array manipulations such as Shift, Copy, and Move. At the node level, ParaMap measures computation (CPU time), waiting, and broadcast communication. Point-to-point communication at the node level is difficult to measure directly, so we instead measure process time in node-level routines that perform point-to-point communications.

ParaMap gives users a simple command line interface to performance information. The user constructs sentences from nouns and verbs and asks the tool for the measured cost of the constructed sentences. Costs are provided in three formats: a count of the number of times the sentence was recorded, the total time cost of the sentence, and a time plot showing the cost of the sentence graphed over time.

ParaMap uses NV mappings to compute the costs of high-level sentences. When a user asks for the cost of a sentence, ParaMap automatically maps the noun and verb to lower levels and aggregates the lower level costs before returning the cost to the user. For example, if the user asks for the cost of using a particular array in assignment statements, ParaMap will map the request to explicit computations in PN code blocks as well as implicit runtime system activities such as shifting or broadcasting the array. If the user selects a sub-region of the array, then ParaMap will only provide information from the processors on which the elements of the selected subregion are stored.

ParaMap allows users to constrain low-level performance information with *contexts.*. A context is simply a set of nouns and verbs selected by the user that specifies how to limit low-level information. For example, a ParaMap user may select the noun *Array A* and the verb *Reduction* at the CMF level and ask the tool to create a context. Then, when the user peels back layers of abstraction by moving to the RTS or node level, ParaMap will will constrain the set of nouns and verbs visible to the user; only the nouns and verbs that map to reduction of array A will be available for constructing sentences. Furthermore, ParaMap also constrains the available performance information to that collected during reductions of array A. In this way, contexts allow users to evaluate the low-level performance impact of high-level nouns and verbs.

3.2 Implementation

A user instruments their application by compiling with the ParaMap compiler driver. The driver uses the standard CM Fortran compiler, but also automatically inserts probes at subroutine boundaries of the sequential user object code and links the application with an instrumented version of the CM Runtime System (CMRTS). The instrumented CMRTS monitors RTS level sentences on the control processor and node level sentences on the processor nodes.

Performance information for each noun and verb is gathered in three formats: count, time, and time histogram. A time histogram is a discrete representation of a performance metric over time. Because counters, timers, and time histograms are constant size formats, ParaMap can record long running executions in the same amount of space as short executions.

In addition to performance data, ParaMap collects mapping information so that node and RTS level sentences can be explained at the language level and so that CM Fortran nouns and verbs can be mapped to lower levels. Static mappings such as symbol tables and line number maps are collected during compilation, and dynamic mappings for array layouts are collected during execution.

Compiler optimizations often obscure the mappings between CM Fortran statements and PN code blocks. The CM Fortran compiler compiles each statement into several individual code blocks and co-optimizes the resulting code blocks to reduce the total cost of execution. As a result, a single PN code block may correspond to several CM Fortran statements, and performance information gathered for a particular code block must be mapped to the corresponding statements.

One way to map between CM Fortran statements and co-optimized PN code blocks is to divide an individual code block's costs among the corresponding CM

Fortran statements [6]. However, this method assumes that an equal portion of a code block's computations are performed on behalf of each statement. This assumption may not hold for all optimization techniques. Instead, ParaMap joins groups of co-optimized statements into inseparable statement lists. A statement list is simply a group of statements whose corresponding PN code blocks have been optimized together. ParaMap users may not select an individual statement as a noun if it has been co-optimized with other statements; only statement lists may be selected.

One unique feature of Paramap is its ability to provide performance information for parallel CM Fortran arrays. ParaMap users may request costs for entire arrays or rectangular subgrids of arrays. The tool maps subgrids to the corresponding processor nodes. ParaMap records internal CMRTS array distribution data structures to map array subgrids to processor nodes.

On the processor nodes, each measurement of computation, waiting, or communication cost is tagged with the memory location of the routine that is executed and with the memory location of the CMF arrays being processed. The tags create a vector of performance information, one set of values for each routine executed and for each array processed on each node. ParaMap maps the node routine tags to routine names using the application's symbol table, and maps the array tags to array names with an associative table that is updated each time the control processor allocates an array.

The tags implement mappings that allow ParaMap to satisfy sentence queries that contain one noun and one verb. For example, the user can ask for node level computation that maps to array assignments involving array B. However, tag combinations are not supported because the memory required to keep counters, timers, and time histograms for all tag combinations is too large. In the final section of this paper, we discuss how selective, dynamic instrumentation could be used to support arbitrarily complex sentence mappings.

As an application executes, the instrumentation probes update the counters, timers, and time histograms in memory until the application exits. When the application exits, the instrumented CMRTS collects the performance and mapping data from all of the processors and stores it in a file for post mortem analysis.

4 Experience

In this section we present results from using ParaMap to study the performance of two CM Fortran applications. The first study examines a toy example and illustrates a common CM Fortran performance problem. The second study examines a real chemical engineering code and demonstrates the benefit of attributing performance information to arrays. In each case, we compiled the application with maximum compiler optimizations, linked it with ParaMap instrumentation, executed it on a 32 node CM-5, studied performance information at multiple levels of abstraction, and finally changed the source code to reduce execution time.

Version	Execution Time
Initial Parallel (uninstrumented)	4 min 54.5 sec
Initial Parallel (instrumented)	9 min 12.0 sec
Serial (uninstrumented)	20.3 sec
Final Parallel (uninstrumented)	4.8 sec

Table 1: *Execution times for small example*

MAIN/A:Assignment -- Cost Breakdown

COMPONENT	COUNT	TIME
Explicit Computation(Compute)	11	1.297 sec
Implicit Communication(Broadcast)	5000000	45 min 0.412 sec
Implicit Computation(MemoryManagement)	1	0.001 sec
	Total Time:	45 min 1.712 sec

Figure 2: *Costs of assignments involving* **A**. *Costs are summed over all processor nodes that map to the array.*

4.1 Simple Example

In our first example, we use ParaMap to analyze the program shown in Figure 1. This simple example is useful because it exhibits a significant performance problem that is common in programs written by novice CM Fortran programmers. The first row in Table 1 shows the execution time of the initial version of the program. When compared with the runtime of a serial version of the program (third row of Table 1), measured on a single processor Sun Sparc 10/30, the initial parallel program appears to be very slow.

To analyze the example program, we used ParaMap to determine the noun costs at the CMF level. The tool told us that array **A** was responsible for a majority of the total CPU time. Figure 2 shows a cost breakdown for array assignments involving array **A**. A cost breakdown maps the noun and verb of a given sentence (in this case, the sentence **MAIN/A:Assignment**, i.e. assignment operations involving array **MAIN/A**) to lower levels and summarizes the lower level costs by the type of mapping and the purpose of the lower level activity. In this case, assignments involving **A** map to small amounts of explicit and implicit computation, and a large amount of implicit communication. The explicit computation costs include the time spent computing values for assignments involving **A**. The implicit computation costs include time spent in the runtime system managing memory for **A**.

To investigate the implicit communications, we created a context for the sentence **MAIN/A:Assignment** and moved to the NODE level. At the node level, we

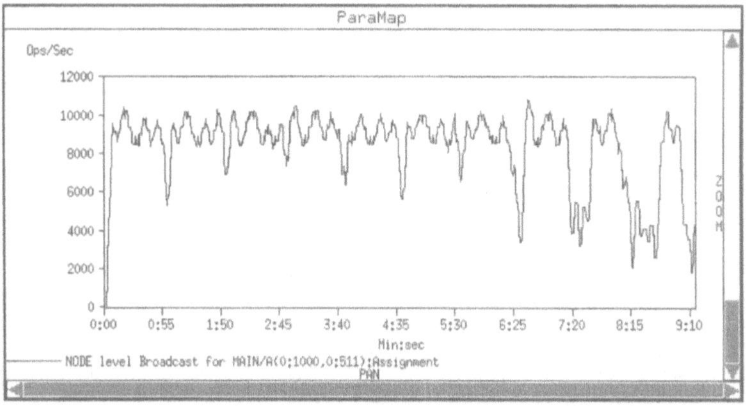

Figure 3: *Time plot of Broadcasts that map to an array sub-region. Only events from the nodes that map to the selected sub-region are shown.*

found that five million node broadcasts mapped to the sentence `MAIN/A:Assignment`. Since we knew that exactly five million elements of `A` were used to compute `B`, we investigated whether the broadcasts were caused by transfers of `A` to `B`. We asked the tool to refine the context to the upper left quadrant of `A` because assignments to `B` use only elements from the upper left quadrant of `A` (line 9 of Figure 1). However, the tool told us that we could only shrink our subregion to the left half of `A` (subregion [0:1000, 0:511]) because the runtime system had not distributed the row axis of `A` across processors. Nevertheless, we found that all five million broadcasts mapped to the left half of `A`. Since all of the broadcasts mapped to the left half of `A` and since five million elements of `A` were used to compute `B`, we concluded that all of the broadcasts of `A` were used to send elements to the control processor for computation of `B`. Figure 3 shows a time plot of broadcasts that mapped to the selected subregion of `A`. The display shows that broadcasting of subregion [0:1000, 0:511] of array `A` occurred during nearly the entire execution of the program.

5 Dual Reciprocity Boundary Element Method

Our second application is a parallel implementation of the Dual Reciprocity Boundary Element Method (DRBEM) [5], a non-linear solution technique used for heat transfer, and vibration analysis applications. The full DRBEM application is comprised of 2200 lines of code spread over 18 source files. The application reads initial conditions from a file, sets up a system of linear equations, solves the equations for a series of time steps, and finally writes the results to file. We ran the program on a problem involving 1000 boundary points, 250 interior points, and 200 time steps. The runtime of the initial parallel version is shown in the first row of Table

Version	Time	Improvement
Initial	66 min 16 sec	
Initial (instrumented)	71 min 31 sec	
CMSSL Gaussian Elimination (uninstrumented)	48 min 17 sec	27.1%
Eliminate Unused Arrays (uninstrumented)	65 min 12 sec	1.6%
CMSSL Solver (uninstrumented)	43 min 35 sec	34.2%
CMSSL Inverse (uninstrumented)	56 min 52 sec	14.2%
All Changes Together (uninstrumented)	17 min 37 sec	73.4%

Table 2: *Runtimes for Parallel DRBEM. Rows 3-6 show the results of implementing each improvement separately, while the last row shows the result of applying all improvements at once.*

2.

We began our analysis of the DRBEM application by examining CMF level profiles of the verbs Statement_Execution and Assignment (Figures 4 and 5). The verb Statement_Execution maps to the execution of PN code blocks generated by the compiler to implement CM Fortran statements. The verb Assignment maps to both execution of PN code blocks and to implicit runtime system activities such as allocation, shifting, and rotating arrays. Each profile lists all nouns that participated in sentences involving the given verb. The nouns are sorted by the cumulative costs measured for the sentences. The cumulative costs for statement executions include only explicit node-level computations that map to each execution; mapping of implicit costs to statement executions is not yet supported. The cumulative costs for array assignments include the costs of both implicit and explicit lower level activities that map to each assignment.

The execution and assignment profiles illustrate why it is necessary to examine different types of nouns to best localize performance problems. The statement execution profile (see Figure 4) shows that 6 different statements in the file decomp.fcm are responsible for most of the explicit node-level computation in the application. By examining the code in decomp.fcm, we found that the top array shown in the assignment profile (`MAIN/H` in Figure 5) was accessed in every statement listed in the execution profile. Therefore, we decided to concentrate on how array `MAIN/H` was accessed rather than concentrate on the code of any particular line.

The code in decomp.fcm that processed `MAIN/H` was an implementation of Gaussian elimination factorization. A cost breakdown of `MAIN/H` (not shown, but similar to Figure 2) showed us that two-thirds of the node-level time that mapped to the array was spent in point-to-point communication routines. Therefore, we concluded that the Gaussian elimination implementation had caused the point-to-point communications as well as the node-level computations. We decided that

CMF Profile -- *:Statement_Execution

NOUN	COUNT	TIME
decomp.fcm<92,96>	1249	1 hr 0 min 12.063 sec
inverse.fcm<100,102>	1250	36 min 33.571 sec
decomp.fcm<81,83,82>	1249	29 min 56.119 sec
decomp.fcm<61>	1249	14 min 8.491 sec
inverse.fcm<92,83,93>	1250	12 min 16.351 sec
inverse.fcm<144,145>	1250	10 min 27.330 sec
inverse.fcm<149>	1250	6 min 26.298 sec
inverse.fcm<141,147>	1250	6 min 21.923 sec
hg.fcm<105>	1000	3 min 14.325 sec
pack.fcm<88,88>	200	1 min 42.361 sec

Figure 4: *Statement Execution Profile for DRBEM. Line numbers listed within angle brackets represent groups of statements that were merged during compiler optimization.*

since Gaussian elimination is a well understood method that has been implemented in many linear algebra libraries, we could simply replace the entire subroutine with a call to a library routine. Therefore, we replaced the routine with a call to the vendor provided CM Scientific Software Library (CMSSL) Gaussian elimination routine. The improvement reduced the runtime of the application by 27.1% as shown in the third row of Table 2.

Figure 4 also shows large explicit computation costs for 10 lines in the file inverse.fcm. When we examined the listed lines, we found that array `MAIN/F` (listed third in the assignment profile) was accessed on 8 of the 10 lines. Again, it seemed more important to study the processing of `MAIN/F` rather than examine any particular line. We displayed a Cost Breakdown table (see Figure 6) and found that more than 50% of the costs of assignments involving `MAIN/F` were due to point-to-point communication of elements of `MAIN/F` and spreading subsections of `MAIN/F` across processors. We examined the use of `MAIN/F` on the 8 lines and identified the operations that cause point-to-point communications and spreading of array elements. The code lines were part of a routine that computed the inverse of matrix `MAIN/F`. The routine took advantage of symmetries in the matrix, but we found that by employing a CMSSL routine for general matrix inversion, we improved the execution time of the entire application by 14.2% as shown in the sixth row of Table 2.

Array assignment profiles are also useful for locating unused arrays. Unused arrays are arrays that are specified by the programmer, allocated by the runtime system, but never used by the program. In ParaMap they appear as CMF-level nouns, but they are not recorded in any assignment sentences. Therefore, an array assignment profile lists unused arrays at the bottom showing no cumulative cost.

CMF Profile -- *:Assignment

NOUN	COUNT	TIME
MAIN/H	9996	2 hr 57 min 11.215 sec
decomp/TMP	2499	1 hr 44 min 19.918 sec
MAIN/F	7501	1 hr 7 min 2.516 sec
inverse/AI	11280	53 min 31.442 sec
MAIN/G	3702	28 min 9.189 sec
pack/CH	5804	15 min 44.178 sec
back2/ROW	10362	14 min 56.545 sec
elim2/TMP	6253	1 min 50.018 sec
decomp/PVT	2898	49.640 sec
MAIN/DFI	400	48.631 sec

Figure 5: *Array Assignment Profile for DRBEM. This table sorts CM Fortran Arrays by their cumulative explicit and implicit costs.*

MAIN/F:Assignment -- Cost Breakdown

COMPONENT	COUNT	TIME
Explicit Computation(Compute)	5004	28 min 51.634 sec
Implicit Communication(Broadcast)	2500	2.627 sec
Implicit Communication(Point-to-Point)	1250	23 min 46.354 sec
Implicit Communication(Spread)	3750	14 min 21.902 sec
	Total Time:	1 hr 7 min 2.516 sec

Figure 6: *Cost Breakdown for assignment operations involving* **MAIN/F**. *The table shows that most low-level operations involving the array were implicit and caused communication*

For the DRBEM application we found 16 unused arrays and improved the program by eliminating them from the code. The runtime savings (shown in the fourth row of Table 2) were minimal, but the memory savings amounted to 32 Megabytes (5% of the total).

A final major performance problem involved sequential subroutine execution time. Subroutine execution time is measured as process time on the control processor and is measured for each subroutine in the application. We displayed a profile of subroutine execution and found that 27 minutes were spent in the subroutine `solve2`. The subroutine implemented the solution phase of the application and apparently had not been parallelized. We decided that the vendor provided CMSSL parallel linear system solver could be used to improve runtime performance, and inserted the CMSSL solver in place of `solve2`. This change reduced the overall runtime of the program by 34.2% as shown in the fourth row of Table 2.

Figure 7 illustrates key aspects of the behavior of the DRBEM application

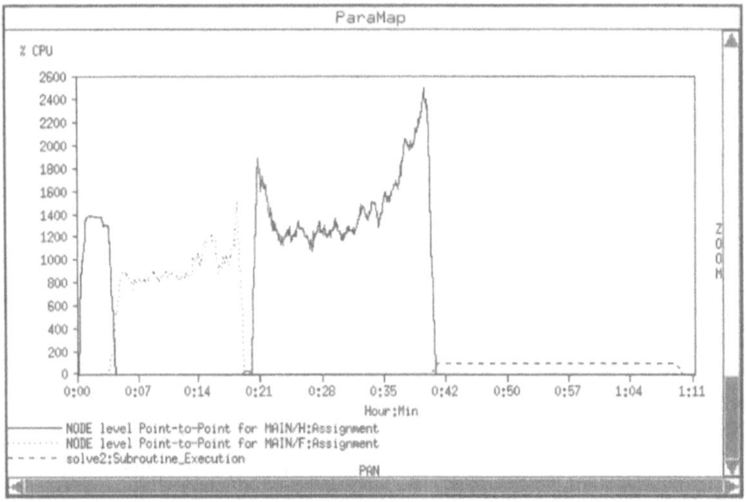

Figure 7: *Time plot of CPU Time for the entire initial parallel DRBEM application. The display shows three primary runtime contributors: Point-to-Point communications that map to arrays* ***MAIN/H*** *and* ***MAIN/F****, and sequential execution in the routine* ***solve2****.*

over time. The figure presents the process time spent performing point-to-point communications of elements of arrays `MAIN/H` and `MAIN/F`,and serial time spent in subroutine **solve2**. The figure shows that the implicit communications and the serial computations degraded the performance of the application by using a significant amount of the parallel processing resources of the machine. In particular, during the 27 minutes in which **solve2** executed on the control processor, all of the processor nodes remained idle. The final line of Table 2 presents the total savings achieved by incorporating all of the improvements listed above.

6 Related Work

Performance measurement of programs written in high-level languages bears some resemblance to the problem of debugging optimized code [1, 8]. In the latter problem, a symbolic debugger must present a view of an optimized program that is consistent with the original source code and must hide the effects of optimizations that have reordered statements, eliminated variables, or otherwise altered the steps of a computation. Performance measurement of parallel programs written in high-level languages is fundamentally simpler than the debugging of optimized code because performance measurement tools need not reconstruct the instantaneous state of a computation. A symbolic debugger must be able to stop the execution of a program at any instruction, identify the corresponding location in the source code, and provide access to variables in the original program. A performance measurement tool, on the other hand, is generally concerned with the cumulative activity of program elements (code constructs and data objects). Performance measurement tools must identify the program elements that are active at a given point but rarely need access to the values of variables.

7 Conclusions

We claim that even a simple tool based on the NV model can have great advantages when studying the performance of programs written in high-level parallel languages. With ParaMap, we answered performance questions that could not easily be answered with other tools. In particular, by displaying performance data for CM Fortran parallel arrays we quickly located primary performance problems, and by examining runtime system and processor activities (while maintaining references to high-level arrays and sub-sections of arrays) we evaluated the low-level results of array operations. Specific examples of this type of analysis include the localization of broadcasts to a particular portion of an array and attribution of point-to-point messages to a few important arrays.

We have found that providing performance information for the fundamental constructs of a language (e.g. parallel arrays in CM Fortran) provides a good first step in understanding any application's performance. However, when we have located an array with high performance costs, we have used ParaMap to drop down to the runtime system or node level to evaluate the object's impact on the system and to determine whether the cumulative costs are due to the programmer's explicit requests for computation or whether the programmer has implicitly and perhaps unknowingly caused extra runtime activity. This type of analysis represents a departure from high-level language tools that provide information exclusively at the language level.

We intend to address important performance questions that ParaMap does not yet answer. For example, we have often wanted to cross reference performance information for arrays by performance information for statements, because arrays are assigned using CM Fortran statements. With our present instrumentation system, such a cross-product of information would be very expensive to gather. Therefore, we will employ a dynamic instrumentation system [4] that will allow us to selectively insert measurement probes to measure arbitrary noun and verb combinations without measuring all combinations at all times.

High-level parallel language systems are often intricate and sorting through all possible performance information for all nouns and verbs at all levels of abstraction can be an arduous task, even for simple applications. Therefore, we will employ automated search techniques [3] to assist in the evaluation of real applications. Automated searching for performance bottlenecks in high-level parallel language applications will require NV style mapping for locating and explaining performance bottlenecks to programmers.

Acknowledgements

We thank Jens Christoph Maetzig for the original serial DRBEM code, and Bruce Davis and Brad Richards for the initial CM Fortran version.

References

[1] J. L. Hennessy. Symbolic debugging of optimized code. *ACM TOPLAS*, 4(3):323–344, July 1982.

[2] High Performance Fortran Forum. *High Performance Fortran Language Specification - Version 1.0*, January 1993.

[3] Jeffrey K. Hollingsworth and Barton P. Miller. Dynamic control of performance monitoring on large scale parallel systems. In *7th ACM International Conference on Supercomputing*, pages 185–194, July 1993.

[4] Jeffrey K. Hollingsworth, Barton P. Miller, and Jon Cargille. Dynamic program instrumentation for scalable performance tools. In *Scalable High Performance Computing Conference*, May 1994.

[5] D. Nardini and C. A. Brebbia. A new approach for free vibration analysis using boundary elements. *Boundary Element Methods in Engineering*, 1982.

[6] Steve Sistare, Don Allen, Rich Bowker, Karen Jourdenais, Josh Simons, and Rich Title. Data visualization and performance analysis in the Prism programming environment. In *Programming Environments for Parallel Computing*, pages 37–52. North-Holland, 1992.

[7] Thinking Machines Corporation, Cambridge MA. *CM Fortran Reference Manual*, January 1991.

[8] Polle T. Zellweger. An interactive high-level debugger for control-flow optimized programs. *ACM SIGPLAN Notices*, 18(8):159–172, March 1983.

Programming Environments for Massively Parallel Distributed Systems, Monte Verità, Switzerland

Implementation of a Scalable Trace Analysis Tool*

Xavier-François Vigouroux†
Laboratoire de l'Informatique du Parallélisme,
Unité de Recherche Associée 1398 du CNRS
Ecole Normale Supérieure de Lyon,
69364 Lyon Cedex 07, France.
vigourou@lip.ens-lyon.fr

Abstract

Monitoring is a way to understand a parallel program. It consists in generating and gathering the information concerning a parallel execution. This method has the drawbacks of being intrusive, greedy for memory and furthermore, the amount of generated data is at least linear in the processor number. With the massively parallel machines the management of the data become impossible, and the traditional and sequential treatment is no more feasible. In this paper, I present a tool for analyzing the large amount of data with a scalable approach. This tool is called PIMSY (for Parallel Implementation of a Monitoring SYstem). It gives as fast as possible the information asked by clients and must be scalable and extensible. To be scalable, PIMSY is composed of a collection of trace servers that deal with a part of the information. To be extensible, each trace server communicates with the others to gather the total information and to give it back to the clients. Our first step does not take care of the generation of trace data, but the future versions of PIMSY will include this feature.

1 Introduction

Passing from the sequential programming to the parallel (or distributed) one, brings much more power, but also a lot of new problems. [CBM90] presents the different new ways to debug parallel programs. One of them is the **monitoring**. It consists in generating a TF (Trace File) containing the information related to one execution. Once, the information is generated, the monitoring tool has to bring

*This work was supported by the Ministère de la Recherche et de l'Espace under grant MRE-974

†supported by ARCHIPEL SA and CIFRE under contract 920-335

it outside of the parallel machine to allow analysis on workstations. These three phases (generation, transport and analysis) compose the monitoring.

For the sake of intrusiveness, The designers of monitoring tools must choose between a lot of strategies: the information to generate, the grammar (Pablo [Ayd93] or SIMPLE and its Trace Description Language [HKM+92]), the approach (adaptative as in Pablo, or dynamic), etc. A lot of strategies are explained in [vRT91].

Concerning the analysis, many tools exist: ParaGraph [HE91], IPS-2 [IM93], SIMPLE, PIE [LSV+89], Pablo, etc. They have been designed before the birth of massively parallel machines. Thus, their conception is not scalable: the number of nodes can not be more than one hundred because they can not efficiently handle the amount of generated information. To reduce this information, we have two main methods, but the data management is still enormous: "Clumping" (grouping recursively the nodes to obtain arity constant groups), "filtering" (limiting the treatment by keeping interesting events).

2 The goals

The aim of PIMSY is to give as fast as possible and in a scalable way the traced information to a trace analyzer. The only way to succeed is to design it as a multi-process task. Each task deals with a part of the information and exchange data with the other ones. At the top of PIMSY is a set of clients (VisT for Visualization Tools). These clients interact with the TSs (Trace Servers) of PIMSY thanks to a protocol. They also may synchronize themselves to display multiple views on the same instant of a trace file. The number of clients and their kind are not fixed. If a user wants a new view, he picks it up from a standard set or create new one thanks to a library. The clients must also be scalable by using the clumping and filtering methods.

3 The model

As we have seen, PIMSY is a distributed system, and can be executed on a MIMD parallel machine. Furthermore, we have the basic hypothesis that the TFs are also distributed to allow multiple concurrent reads. Figure 2 shows a distribution which follows the partition of the machine. This hypothesis is true at the generation, but after, the TFs are usually merged into one. If we have only one disk, we have only one reader, and PIMSY architecture becomes more classic, even if all components are executed concurrently.

Actually, due to the use of screens and keyboard, we do not use a real parallel machine but a network of SPARCstations connected by EtherNet. This network communicates using PVM 3.2.x. After this first phase of implementation, the system will be executed on a real parallel machine (HPC for "High Performance

Computer", constructed by Archipel; at the present time, made of 48 nodes [i860 and T800]; in the future, 1024 nodes), obviously, any computer running PVM can hold PIMSY.

The communication graph between the TSs (Trace Servers) and the clients is very simple: a client communicates only with one TS and a TS reachs any other TSsTo make the interface between the user and PIMSY, a process is created: TSF (Trace Server Front). To summarize (see Figure 2, each TS has 4 I/O ports: ↔ TSF, ↔ Clients, ↔ TS, ← Hard disks. To be efficient, the number of TSs must be a function of the number of nodes. Then, when the power of the machine is raised by doubling the number of nodes, PIMSY becomes also more powerful.

4 Protocol

This section describes the protocol between the different parts of the PIMSY. it is close to classical client-server protocol, and data base request management. Thus, the server is always waiting for the clients, and the client is always initiated and destroyed by the server.

4.1 Initialization

The initialization starts from the TSF, it creates as many TSs as disks, then it initiates each one by broadcasting the context (the list of TSs, where the data are stored, the name of the screen, etc.). When the user wants to add a new client (for instance a Space-Time), he asks the TSF to create it. The TS that handles the new client is then chosen by the user. As this initialization is managed by the TSF, it knows the global situation, thus it will be able to balance the load of the global system. As soon as the client is created, it receives a message from its TS to determine which screen must be used, its name, and some other small data. Then, the client and the TS knows each other. Usually, a client is interested in one type of events and their evolution along the time. Thus, the filter associated to each client may be chosen as soon as the client is created. Consequently, the client sends a message to its TS in which the filter is described. Then the client may ask for the list of available trace. Then, the client may choose one of the TF and ask for further information (the name of programmer, the number of timestamps per second, etc.)

4.2 Request for Trace Information

When the source client emits a request in direction of its *source trace server*, it has to specify the list of destination clients and some information concerning the request itself. The selection of the TSs that may have the information is done thanks to a table indicating the partition of the machine. Thanks to a filter on the nodes id, we can select the working TSs and then order them (to optimize the gathering

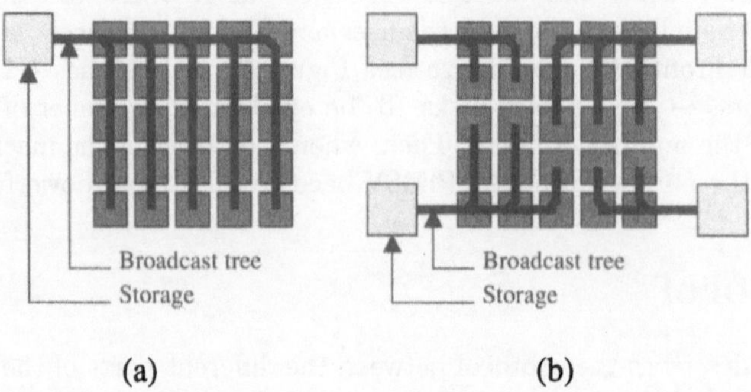

Figure 1: *Link between the node and the disk with (a) one storage place and (b) multiple storage places.*

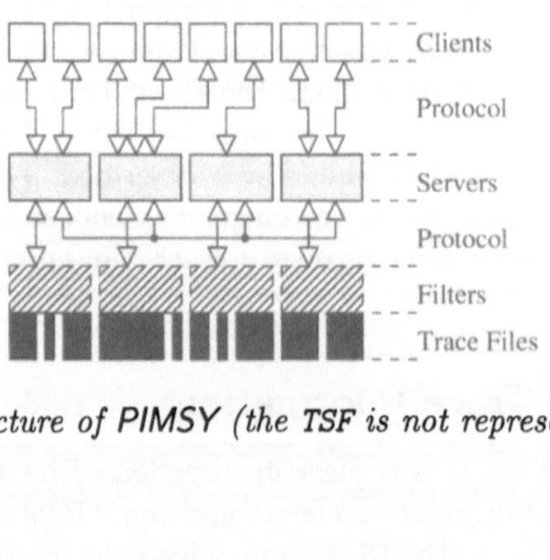

Figure 2: *Architecture of PIMSY (the TSF is not represented here).*

of the local information). The source TS broadcasts the request to each working TS. The broadcast message contains only the filter and the information to identify the request. When each working TS reads the information and filters it, they have to gather it. An optimal algorithm is the odd-even; it allows to merge each parts as fast as possible in the source TS. Then it knows when is the end of the treatment, and can reply to the request by sending the slice to the destination TSs which forward it to the destination clients. Each client in the destination list receives the information it really need (this implies a personnal filtering, but anyway, they would ask for this filtering). Obviously, the clients must handle responses they did not ask: changing their context if they were on a totally different slice, sending an acknowledgment ("End Of Work"). Indeed, When a source client wants to synchronize several clients, the group speed is limited by the slowest client. This limitation is done by waiting for all "End Of Work" before asking for a new slice. To avoid a work overhead for the source client, the source TS accumulates the number of "End Of Work" received, before forwarding a global one to the source TS.

5 Client Samples

At the top of PIMSY, we have built some clients to test it. At the present time, some other clients are in progress. From this clients, we have tried to extract a library. This library contains routines for the communication. Furthermore, we have designed the prototype of a client to make the creation of new ones easier.

Two real clients have been programmed in C. They implement the clumping method on the communication and on the efficiency of a process. By clicking on a group, the user explodes it and see its components. A tree will be added to visualize the position of the group displayed and it will permit fast moves.

We have also worked on sound, and how to generate them thanks to a SPARC-station. The result has been 3 small programs that "auralize" the communications in a TF.

6 Future Works and conclusion

We are continuing an implementation of PIMSY. A prototype has already been implemented on a LAN of SPARCstations using PVM package. This version shows the efficiency of our approach. The next prototype will be implemented on another distributed memory multi-computer called Volvox manufactured by Archipel. This implementation will show the portability of our approach. A real-time implementation of the trace server is also under study. Such a trace-server will store the runtime information in local memory and be able to serve client requests in a real-time fashion. Furthermore, the load balancing is not yet implemented, but all the necessary stuff is available to do it soon.

We will implement several others tools to read a sufficient set of representations (i.e. visualization and auralization). The existing set of tool is limited but exists.

In this paper, we have first presented our client-server based approach to massively parallel monitoring. In order to avoid the traditional bottleneck of parallel monitoring, we have designed a monitoring system in which not only the generation of the runtime information is distributed, but also the storage and the processing of this information.

References

[Ayd93] Ruth A. Aydt. The pablo self-defining data format. Department of Computer Science, University of Illinois at Urbana-Champaign, March 1993. available by ftp anonymous bugle.cs.uiuc.edu:pub/Release-1.1/Documentation/SDDF.ps.Z.

[CBM90] W. Cheung, J. Black, and E. Manning. A framework for distributed debugging. *IEEE Software*, 7:106–115, January 1990.

[HE91] M. Heath and J. Etheridge. Visualizing performance of parallel programs. TR TM-11813, Oak Ridge National Laboratory, TN, May 1991.

[HKM+92] R. Hofmann, R. Klar, B. Mohr, A. Quick, and M. Sigle. Distributed performance monitoring : Methods, tools and application. TR 8/92, Universität Erlangen–Nürnberg, IMMD VII, August 1992.

[IM93] R. Irvin and P. B. Miller. Multi-application support in a parallel program performance tool. TR 1135, University of Wisconsin-Madison, 1210 W Dayton Street, Madison, Wisconsin 53706, 1993. accessible as grilled.cs.wisc.edu:technical_papers/multiapp.ps.Z.

[LSV+89] T. Lehr, Z. Segall, D. F. Vrsalovic, E. Caplan, A. L. Chung, and C.E. Fineman. Visualizing performance debugging computer. *IEEE*, pages 38–51, October 1989.

[vRT91] M. van Riek and B. Tourancheau. A general approach to the monitoring of distributed memory machines. Research Report 91-28, LIP – Ecole Normale Supérieure de Lyon, 1991.

Programming Environments for Massively Parallel Distributed Systems, Monte Verità, Switzerland

The Design of a Tool for Parallel Program Performance Analysis and Tuning

Anna Hondroudakis Rob Procter
Department of Computer Science
Edinburgh University, Mayfield Road
Edinburgh EH9 3JZ, Scotland
ah@dcs.ed.ac.uk

Abstract

The implementation of efficient parallel programs can be very difficult, and numerous computer-based tools have been developed to help with the task of performance analysis and tuning. We describe the initial steps in the design of such a tool. Our aim is to show how its design has evolved out of an explicit attempt to understand the human factors issues in parallel program implementation. By adopting this approach, we seek to look beyond the current fashion for graphical user interfaces and data visualization techniques. Our emphasis is on gaining a better understanding of the problems inherent in program analysis and tuning and using this as a foundation for developing more usable tools.

1 Introduction

Parallel program performance analysis and tuning is concerned with achieving efficient utilisation of system resources. One common technique is to collect trace data and then analyse it for possible causes of poor performance. The program source code is then modified in the light of the analysis. In practice, tuning is much more difficult than this brief sketch suggests.

The amount of trace data produced may be very large, particularly in the case of massively parallel systems. For this data to be useful, the tuner needs appropriate tools to process and present it in a comprehensible form. It can often be very difficult to relate the low-level account of program behaviour provided by the trace data to the source code. Compounding this problem is the tendency for parallel programming environments to provide progressively higher-level programming facilities [CG88, RC89, DFH+93]. Whilst this is of great assistance in the design and coding stages of program implementation, it often makes tuning more difficult, with the tuner having to relate low-level events to increasingly abstract program representations. The tuner faces equally difficult problems due to the fact that desired levels of performance may only be achieved after many iterations of the unit tuning cycle.

This paper describes VISPAT (**VIS**ualization for **P**erformance **A**nalysis and **T**uning), a tool for parallel program performance analysis and tuning. Numerous examples of such tools already exist, many of which employ the latest graphical techniques for user interface design and visualization of trace data [RAM+92, HE91, HIM91, Moh91, MHJ91, Sto88, BB92, FR92]. In spite of this, however, their design often appears to rest upon largely unstated assumptions concerning the nature of the tuning task, and evidence for their effectiveness is often lacking. Graphical user interfaces are not a panacea for usability problems and, in fact, their use can increase the scope for poor design [Bro94]. In contrast, our approach to the design of VISPAT has been to seek a better understanding of the nature of the tuning task and the needs of tuners through the application of user-centered design methodologies.

The results of this investigation highlighted the importance of two specific user requirements. The first was for the tool to provide help in achieving source code reference. It reflects the difficulties of tuning *in the small*, i.e. the detection, diagnosis and remedying of a specific instance of inefficiency as the outcome of the unit tuning cycle. The tuner should be able to visualize the trace data in ways which significantly reduce the effort necessary to relate the observed behaviour to the program's source code. The second requirement was for the tool to provide assistance in the management of tuning *in the large*, i.e. the lengthy series of repetitions of the unit tuning cycle that may be required to achieve the desired overall level of performance. The typical tuning problem is associated with a number of inter-dependent program performance parameters for which some 'optimum' set of values has to be found. Tuning *in the large* may be thought of as a heuristic search through the multi-dimensional performance space defined by these parameters. As a consequence, the tuner must evaluate and compare the results of a succession of unit tuning cycles. To expedite the outcome, the tuner may need help in managing the search process.

The first section briefly describes the programming environment within which VISPAT is to be used. The second gives an overview of how the tool's requirements were elicited from users and evolved into a specification, and the third section describes the design of VISPAT in some detail. Finally, we discuss the next stage in its development.

2 The Programming Environment

The Common High-Level Interface to Message Passing (CHIMP) library was developed at the Edinburgh Parallel Computer Centre (EPCC) and is available on a number of parallel and distributed platforms [BCMT93]. It provides for the transfer of messages between processes on a MIMD parallel computer. Blocking, non-blocking and multi-casting communications are available. CHIMP has a two-level naming scheme for processes, consisting of symbolic and numeric components. Each process has a number of Service Access Points (SAPs) through which it can receive and send messages. Processes with common algorithmic features are functionally grouped. Every functional group (SAP group) has a name and each process's SAP in the SAP group is identified by a membership number.

The Parallel Utilities Library (PUL) is a collection of reusable basic parallel utilities that support program development [BCMT93]. PUL is built on top of CHIMP to take advantage of its portability. The utilities of PUL fall into three different classes: modules that implement generic functionality independent of the underlying mapping; modules that follow a certain programming paradigm e.g. for decomposition or mapping, and modules that are application-specific. Some of the utilities have a procedural interface which encloses data flow and some can have, in addition, a skeletal interface which encloses control flow. Example modules are PUL-EM (extended message passing), PUL-TF (task farm paradigm) and PUL-RD (regular domain decomposition).

3 User Requirements Capture

To maximise the usability and effectiveness of a new tool, it is essential for the designer to explore users' requirements thoroughly and to gain a sound understanding of the nature of the task that they wish to perform. These goals can only be achieved if designer and users work in partnership within the framework of a user-centred design methodology [Bro94]. Where there is uncertainty about user requirements, the designer must be prepared to follow an iterative approach based upon successive cycles of requirements capture, design and evaluation.

As the first step in the design of VISPAT, a series of meetings was held with CHIMP and PUL users, beginning with "brainstorming sessions" in which the participants were simply encouraged to voice their ideas. These were subsequently ranked in importance by the participants and further categorised as being either high- or low-level requirements. The requirements thus defined were used in a second series of meetings as the basis for an initial design. This was then presented to prospective users in the form of a set of paper-based mock-ups of the user interface. At each meeting, the mock-ups were examined page by page and comments solicited from the group. In this way, requirements and specifications were generated, elaborated and refined, eventually leading to the point where they were deemed by the group to be a sufficient basis for the implementation of a first prototype.

At the same time, the nature of the tuning task was explored through group discussion and through the examination of individual tuning case studies. The unit tuning cycle, or tuning *in the small*, is shown in Figure 1. The upper half of the figure represents those aspects of the task as it is directly supported by VISPAT. The instrumented program is executed and the trace data then is passed to graphical displays through a series of abstraction and filtering mechanisms. Each display may render a different aspect of the program's behaviour. The lower half of the figure represents those aspects of the task which are indirectly supported by VISPAT. The tuner examines the visualized trace data and considers its relevance in the context of the emerging understanding of the program's behaviour. This in turn guides the tuner in the generation of a *hypothesis* concerning the relationship of parameters to performance, and the specification of an *experiment* in which parameter values are manipulated in accordance with the *hypothesis*. Finally, the tuner begins a fresh new iteration of the unit tuning cycle by re-executing the program with the new parameter values and another set of trace data is collected. It is this repetition of the unit tuning cycle which underlies the notion of tuning *in the large*.

The outputs of the requirements capture process were eventually categorised into one of four fundamental design issues: trace data format; filtering mechanisms; display options, and the management of the tuning task over time. The first three are concerned with tuning *in the small* in that they reflect tuners' needs within the unit tuning cycle. The last issue relates to tuning *in the large* which will be the subject of a future paper.

Within each of these categories, requirements were further classified as either low- or high-level. Low-level requirements include the spatial arrangement of displays on the screen, and the precise ways in which the tuner might interact with them. High-level requirements reflect issues that define the character and scope of VISPAT. Three of the principal high-level requirements will now be discussed in more detail.

3.1 Trace Data Format

The trace data format requirements are largely determined by the programming model and the requirement for source code reference. The control flow of each process's code consists of time-grouped sequences of interesting events, or *phases*. A *phase* occupies a part of the program's execution time and corresponds either to a call of a library function or to a programmer-defined logical part of the source code. A phase is identified by the name of the function, together with a number which distinguishes each unique occurrence of it within the trace data file. It is also characterized by its class which can be either CHIMP, PUL-EM, PUL-TF, PUL-RD or Application (if the phase is programmer-defined).

Groupings cover many layers of abstractions, with the most abstract layer concerned with phases evident in the execution of almost any parallel program — initialization, computation and closing. Each of these top level phases consists of a series of sub-phases, which can have sub-phases of their own and so on. Figure 2 depicts the hierarchy of phases in a program written with PUL. Functions whose names begin with CHIMP, RD and EM are respectively functions of the CHIMP, PUL-RD and PUL-EM Libraries. There is a one-to-one relationship between the structure of phases in a program and the structure of the trace files. This is car-

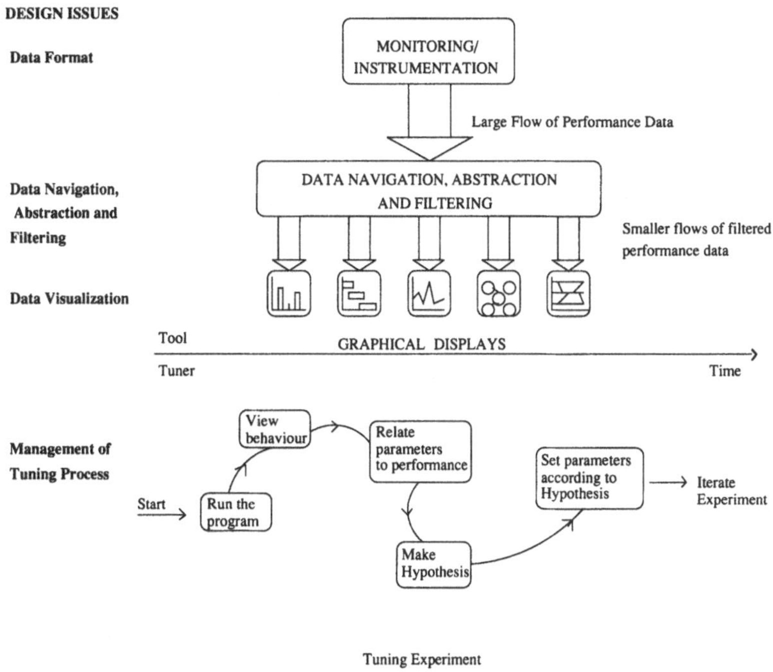

Figure 1: *The Tuning Model*

ried through into VISPAT's data visualization facilities. By this means, VISPAT enables the tuner to relate the behaviour of the program to the source code — a facility found in few other tools ([SAB+92] being one notable exception).

3.2 Data Navigation and Filtering

In this hierarchical presentation of events and phases, a mechanism to help the tuner identify events of interest is important. Data navigation provides the tuner with a means of determining what data will be subsequently visualized by the performance displays. More specifically, the requirements investigation emphasised that the tuner should be able to determine interactively: a region of the trace file (pan over the data); the time grain (zoom in or out of the chosen region); which events will be visible (filter out unwanted events) and, finally, control the level of abstraction (fold or unfold phases).

These requirements were realised through a single user interface mechanism — the **Navigation** display — a form of Gantt chart (see Figure 3). The Navigation display determines the context of data visualization. It has a central role because VISPAT's other displays render data only over the time period and parts of the program that are currently visible within it. In the figure, the early phases of

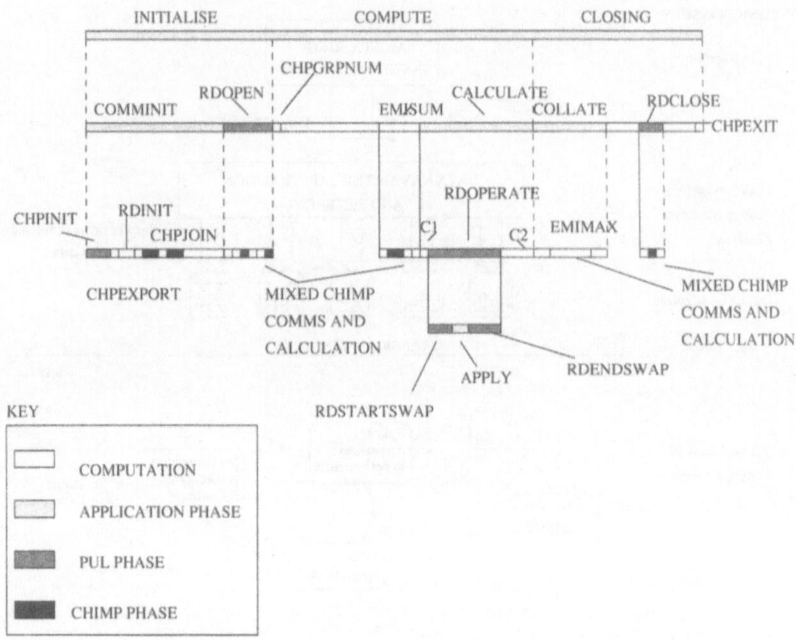

Figure 2: *The phase hierarchy.*

a program computing the Optimal Matrix Multiplication Order (OMMO) of 4 matrices [Sed90, WG92] are shown. The program has three types of processes: four workers which calculate costs and store them in a cost matrix; eight matrix line managers, which store and update rows and columns of the cost matrix, and one barrier synchronization manager to allow workers to co-operate in determining the value of a particular cost matrix entry.

3.3 Data Visualization

Another high-level requirement is the need for a number of distinct types of visualization format for presenting detailed information relating to program performance.

The Single Event display is a special case of the Navigation display. As its name implies, it shows one particular phase over the program execution time, allowing the tuner to compare relative timings of the phase across processes.

The Animation display (see Figure 4) presents a two dimensional image of the program, depicting significant events such as communication between processes. Incoming arrowheads indicate where processes have initiated a blocking receive. Outgoing arrowheads on the uppermost process indicate that it has initiated blocking sends. The presence of an arrow body indicates that a communication is in progress.

The Membership Matrix display (see Figure 4) provides access to SAP group membership information for each of the processes in the program. Information about SAP group membership is essential if the tuner is to be able to interpret program behaviour. SAP group membership defines the way processes communicate, and corresponds to an algorithmic view of the program. SAP group names are shown in the first column and processes along the top row. In the example program, the first SAP group is called **synch** and consists of the barrier synchronization manager process. This process has the SAP group membership number zero.

The Statistics display consists of a number of tabular displays providing summary performance data. An instance of the Statistics display is given in Figure 5. The metrics are colour coded and the user can access the actual values of these metrics by interacting with the display.

Together, the Navigation and data visualization displays constitute the principal parts of VISPAT's user interface. They are the means by which the tuner is able to reduce a large volume of trace data into a more manageable form, and use it to extract meaningful information about program behaviour.

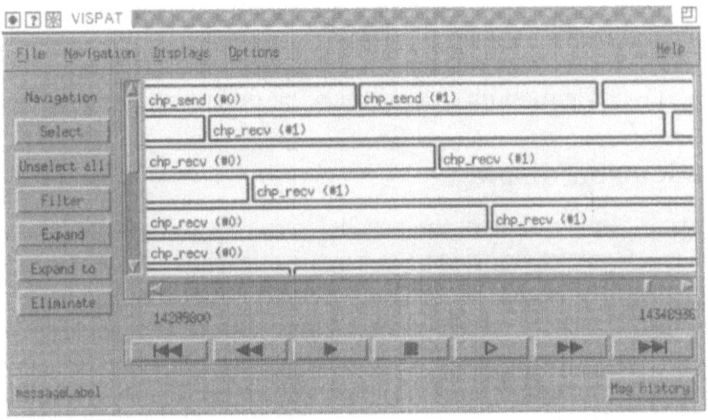

Figure 3: *The Navigation display.*

4 Implementation of VISPAT

VISPAT is a postmortem visualization tool for the analysis of parallel programs written with the CHIMP message passing system and the PUL utilities libraries

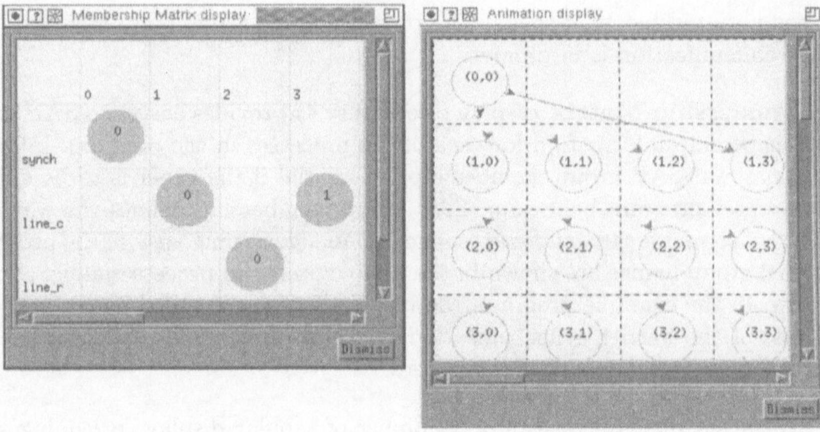

***Figure 4**: Membership Matrix and Animation displays*

[TW92]. It processes and visualizes trace files that have been produced by instrumented versions of CHIMP and PUL. Trace files are read in by a pre-processor and passed on to the visualizer which then renders the data using the displays described in the previous section.

The current display repertoire consists of the Navigation, Animation and Membership Matrix displays. Plans for future work include development of the single event display and a suite of statistics displays. The tool has been built in a modular way so that new displays can be added easily. Because of its central importance, the Navigation display will now be described in some detail.

4.1 Navigation display

The Navigation display renders the parallel event histories of the processes in the program. It is a Gantt chart where the time line is depicted on the horizontal axis and the set of processes on the vertical axis. Each process occupies a horizontal strip of the display where all the interesting events of that process are depicted as they take place in time. The Navigation display provides the context for the visualization of trace and performance data. When used in combination with VISPAT's abstraction mechanisms, this context also provides the means for achieving source code reference.

The Navigation display enables the tuner to move around within the space of program phases. Navigation can be performed in both a horizontal fashion, i.e. forwards and backwards in time, or in a vertical fashion, i.e. up and down the phase hierarchy. Two event trace 'playback' modes are provided, *logical* and *temporal*. The requirement for different playback modes arises from the effect of non-blocking communications on phase sequencing. In logical playback, a non-blocking communication finishes when the function initiating it returns. Logical

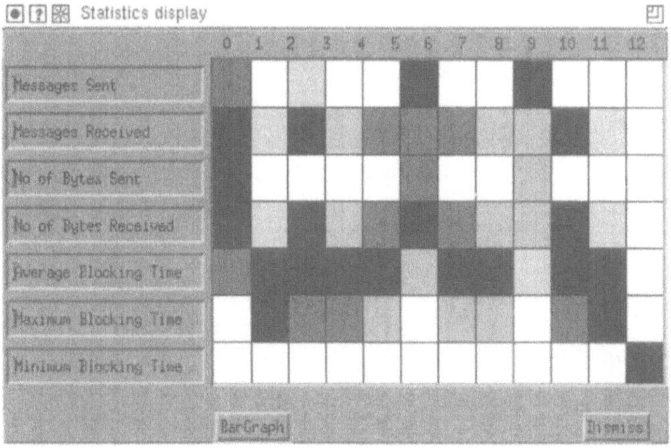

***Figure 5**: An example of the Statistics display*

playback is more coarse-grained and hides some timing information. Temporal playback takes into account the completion times of non-blocking communications, and so allows phases to be interleaved on the process time line.

Traversing the various levels of the phase hierarchy is achieved through unfolding and folding, with the additional option of filtering. This not only allows for the transfer of the focus of visualization to a higher or lower level of abstraction, but also for the view to be limited to specified phases. The data visualization displays show events only for those phases visible on the Navigation display after all filterings and abstractions have been applied. In this way the tuner is able to relate trace data to specific parts of the program.

The design of the Navigation display is driven by the requirement for flexible abstractions over the trace data. Tuners need to be able to view the phases at different levels of abstraction in order to be able to hide irrelevant information, and distinguish the most interesting events. Such abstraction mechanisms [BW83] are found in other tuning environments where, in a 'bottom up' way, low-level events are abstracted to higher level ones. Event abstraction in VISPAT is more extensive and higher-level events are defined automatically by the PUL and CHIMP library functions. The hierarchical grouping of events in VISPAT reflects the hierarchical grouping of the library functions in the program and in this way provides the abstractions necessary to limit the focus to the areas of interest whilst maintaining a close link to the structure of the source code.

The function of the current version of the Navigation display can be categorised into three distinct groups: operations on phases; operations on processes, and user interface operations. The first group consists of the **Selection**, **Unfolding/Folding** and **Filtering** mechanisms:

Selection — when phases are chosen for expansion or filtering. A selection can

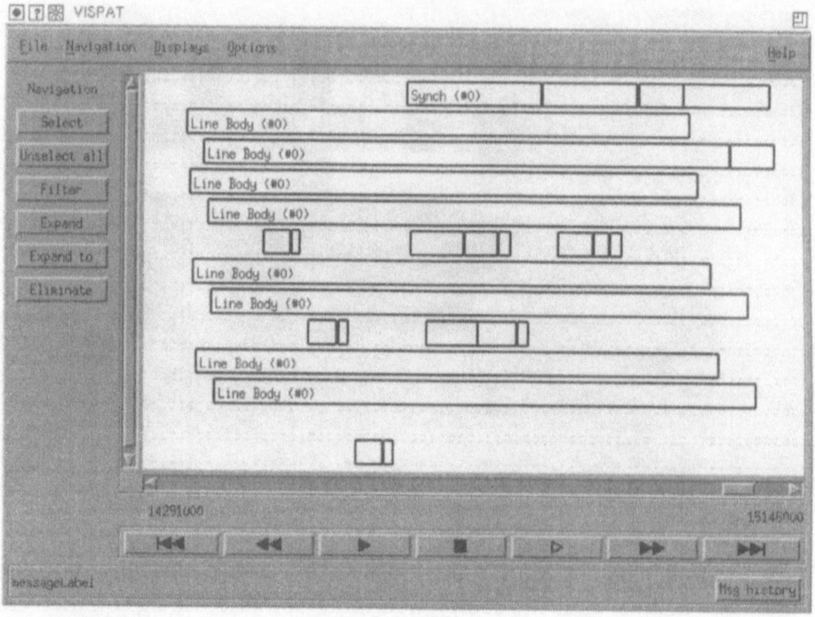

Figure 6: *Programmer-defined phases in the Navigation display*

be global or local. Global selection of a phase ensures that not only the current instance but all subsequent instances of a phase will be selected. Local selection means that only the current instance of a phase is selected. The view of selected phases can then be either enhanced or removed.

Unfolding/Folding — where selected phases can be unfolded into their sub-phases (or sub-phases folded into their parent phases). There are two ways of unfolding a phase. Unfolding is either *simple* or it is *specific*. In the former, a phase can be unfolded into all its sub-phases independently of the class to which they belong. In the latter, the parent phase is unfolded only into phases of a nominated class. This class may be one of the pre-defined CHIMP or PUL classes, or a programmer-defined Application class. In this manner, the trace data can be abstracted in two orthogonal directions and the phase hierarchy traversed horizontally and vertically.

Filtering — which realises a more immediate abstraction mechanism by enabling the user to remove selected phases from the display. The Navigation display in Figure 6 shows the user-defined phases of the OMMO program after filtering has excluded all other phases from Figure 3. It is clear from this that one worker process in the penultimate row has no work to do.

The second category of Navigation display operations focuses on process abstractions:

Elimination — whereby those processes whose behaviour is not currently of interest can be removed from the screen.

User interface operations are provided to make the Navigation display more interactive. Apart from the means of changing the time unit and the scale width of the display, the user can hide uninteresting sequences, or the periods where the behaviour of the program has already been analysed.

5 Conclusions and Future Work

A prototype tuning tool has been implemented which, through the principle of hierarchical phases, enables the tuner to relate low-level events in trace data to program source code. There is a one-to-one correspondence between the structure of program phases, the structure of the trace files, and visualization mechanisms.

A user-centered requirements capture methodology has been employed as a means of identifying the major user requirements of performance analysis and tuning tools. This has enabled the gaining of valuable insights into tuners' needs and the nature of the tuning task itself. Future versions of VISPAT will be implemented in the light of full-scale user evaluation of the prototype. It is expected that this will lead to the refinement of existing requirements and perhaps also the identification of new ones. For example, more data visualization options may be added and the functionality of others improved. Special attention will be given to the provision of scalable representations to cater for programs which run on massively parallel systems.

CHIMP will be replaced in the near future by EPCC's own implementation of the Message Passing Interface standard (MPI) [For93]. A feasibility study is being conducted to indicate the necessary changes for VISPAT to be used for tuning programs which use MPI.

Subsequent iterations in the design and evaluation process will also serve as a vehicle for a more detailed investigation of the nature of the tuning task. This will focus on the kinds of task management issues that arise within the context of tuning in the large.

References

[BB92] J. D. Becher and K. L. Beck. Profiling on a massively parallel computer. In *Second Joint International Conference on Vector and Parallel Processing*, pages 97–102, September 1992.

[BCMT93] R. A. A. Bruce, S. R. Chapple, N. B. MacDonald, and A. S. Trew. Chimp and pul: Support for portable parallel computing. Technical Report EPCC–TR93–07, Edinburgh Parallel Computing Centre, 1993.

[Bro94] Dermot Browne. *STructured User-interface Design for Interaction Optimization.* Prentice Hall, 1994.

[BW83] P. C. Bates and J. C. Wileden. High level debugging of distributed systems: The behavioral abstraction approach. *The Journal of Systems and Software*, (3):255–264, 1983.

[CG88] N. Carriero and D. Gelernter. Applications experience with linda. In *Proceedings of the ACM Symposium on Parallel Programming*, New Haven, July 1988.

[DFH+93] J. Darlington, A. J. Field, P. G. Harisson, P. H. J Kelly, D. W. N. Sharp, Q. Wu, and R. L. White. Parallel programming using skeleton functions. In *Proceedings of the 2nd Abstract Machines Workshop*, Leeds, April 1993.

[For93] Message Passing Interface Forum. *Document for a Standard Message–Passing Interface.* University of Tennessee, November 1993. Presented in Supercomputing 93.

[FR92] J. M. Francioni and D. T. Rover. Visual–aural representations of performance for a scalable application program. In *Proceedings of the Scalable High Performance Computing Conference, SHPCC'92.*, pages 433–440, Williamsburg, Virginia, April 1992.

[HE91] M. T. Heath and J. A. Etheridge. Visualizing the performance of parallel programs. *IEEE Software*, 8(5):29–39, September 1991.

[HIM91] J. K. Hollingsworth, R. B. Irvin, and B. P. Miller. The integration of application and system based metrics in a parallel program performance tool. In *ACM Symposium on Principles and Practice of Parallel Processing*, May 1991.

[MHJ91] A. D. Mallony, D. H. Hammerslag, and D. J. Jablonowski. Traceview: A trace visualization tool. *IEEE Software*, 8(5):27–39, 1991.

[Moh91] B. Mohr. Simple: a performance evaluation tool environment for parallel and distributed systems. In *Proceedings of the 2nd European Distributed Memory Computing Conference, EDMCC2*, pages 80–89. Springer, April 1991.

[RAM+92] D. A. Reed, R. A. Aydt, T. M. Madhyastha, R. J. Noe, K. A. Shields, and B. W. Schwarts. An overview of the pablo performance analysis environment. Technical report, Deparment of Computer Science, University of Illinois, Urbana, Illinois 61801, November 1992.

[RC89] G. C. Roman and K. C. Cox. A declarative approach to visualizing concurrent computations. *IEEE Computer*, 22(10):25–36, October 1989.

[SAB+92] S. Sistare, D. Allen, R. Bowker, K.Jourdaneis, J. Simons, and R. Title. Data visualization and performance analysis in the prism programming environment. In *Working Conference on Programming Environments for Parallel Computing*, pages 37–52, Edinburgh, April 1992. North Holland.

[Sto88] J. M. Stone. A graphical representation of concurrent processes. In *Workshop on Parallel and Distributed Debugging*, pages 226–235, Wisconcin, January 1988. SIGPLAN Notices 24(1).

[TW92] N. Tomov and K. Wierenga. Application engineering tools for chimp and pul. Technical report, Edinburgh Parallel Computing Centre, 1992.

Programming Environments for Massively Parallel Distributed Systems, Monte Verità, Switzerland

The MPP Apprentice™ Performance Tool: Delivering the Performance of the Cray T3D®

Winifred Williams, Timothy Hoel, Douglas Pase
Cray Research, Inc.
655-F Lone Oak Drive
Eagan, Minnesota 55121
ww@cray.com

Abstract

The MPP Apprentice™ performance tool is designed to help users tune the performance of their Cray T3D, applications. By presenting performance information from the perspective of the user's original source code, the MPP Apprentice tool helps users rapidly identify the location and cause of the most significant performance problems. Unlike many trace-based performance tools, the data collection mechanism permits fine-grained performance statistics to be collected with a low level of intrusion for work sharing, data parallel, and message passing codes. The low level of intrusion also permits the mechanism to scale to permit performance analysis on long running codes on thousands of processors. Information displayed within the tool includes total time through regions of code, instruction counts, time spent in overheads related to shared memory, time spent in message passing routines, calling tree information, and performance measures. We will demonstrate the benefits of the data collection mechanism of the MPP Apprentice tool and how it guides the user's identification of performance problems using application examples from benchmarks and industry.

1 Introduction

Fast hardware, system software, and libraries are a great starting point, but what really matters is the performance that the end user is able to attain. MPPs have been notoriously difficult to program. It has been even harder to approach the peak performance of the systems. Cray's MPP Fortran programming model [5], along with hardware support from the Cray T3D [1], attacks the programming issue by letting the user program a distributed memory system as though the memory were shared, while achieving significant performance. But whether the user is programming in the Fortran programming model or using Parallel Virtual Machine (PVM) message passing calls, there is always more the user can do to improve the performance of a program. The difficulty users face with MPP systems is understanding what is happening in thousands of processors at a given time and how that relates to their source code.

Strong tool support can reduce the user's time-to-solution and time-to-performance. The focus of the MPP Apprentice tool is to deliver the performance of the Cray T3D to the user. The MPP Apprentice tool assists the user in the location, identification, and resolution of performance problems on the Cray T3D. Its instrumentation and displays scale to handle long running programs on thousands of processors, and support work-sharing, data parallel, and message passing programming models. Performance characteristics are related back to the user's original source code and are available for the entire program, or a subroutine, or even small code blocks.

2 Possible approaches

Many performance tools today collect a time stamped record of user and system specified events, more commonly called event traces. AIMS [8], GMAT [6], Paragraph [2], and TraceView [4] are examples of event trace based tools. These tools present information from the perspective of time, and try to give the user an idea of what was happening in every processor in the system at any given moment. Event trace tools have traditionally been used on distributed memory machines. Other tools record and summarize pass counts and elapsed times through sections of code, and will be called "stopwatch" tools for the purposes of this paper. Cray's ATExpert [6,7] and MPP Apprentice performance tools are examples of these tools. Stopwatch tools present information from the perspective of the user's program and provide the user with performance characteristics at a particular point in the program. Profiling tools, such as prof [6], collect information very differently, but attempt to present information similar to stopwatch tools. Stopwatch and profiling tools have traditionally been used on shared memory machines.

Event traces have great potential to help the user understand program behavior, but also have some serious disadvantages. One of the strengths is that judiciously chosen events can identify most performance problems, and some correctness problems. Task schedules may be directly obtained from trace files, and an immense amount of flexibility is available in assigning and interpreting time-stamped events. But, the volume of data, which is proportional to the number of processors, the frequency of trace points, and the length of program execution, creates a number of difficulties. Keeping all the trace data in processor memory is prohibitive, so the volume of data is typically managed by limiting the size of the trace buffer and periodically writing the buffer on each processor out to a file, usually when one processor's buffer fills. Writing the data out to a file causes a disruption that would not occur in an uninstrumented run of the user's program.

Tools that try to compensate for this disruption require the processors to synchronize when writing out their data. The additional I/O and synchronization also degrade network performance and impact interprocessor communication and I/O. When post-processing, the data volume is also difficult to manage. The full set of data can be displayed and the user left to interpret all the events happening on thousands of processors, or the post-processing tool can summarize the data for the user. With continued increases in the number of processors and the size of the applications they are able to address, event traces as they exist today are not a solution that scales well.

Stopwatch tools require far less data to be collected, stored, displayed, and interpreted. The summarization that occurs during data collection gives the tools less information from which to work, but the reduced data volume requires fewer resources and intrudes less on program behavior. While some data is not available, e.g. to generate a global schedule and high and low peaks within a processor, the lower level of intrusion permits the collection of much finer grained statistics. And, because the data volume is proportional to the size of the program, stopwatch tools scale well to continuously growing numbers of processors in MPPs. The lower data volume is more manageable for a tool to postprocess and for a user to interpret.

To highlight the differences between event trace tools and stopwatch tools, consider the problem of trying to determine whether there is a load imbalance in a message passing code. With event trace tools, trace points are used to collect all the message send and message receive events at run-time. A post-processing tool needs to pair the sends and receives together by time stamp and destination processor. If the clocks are not synchronized, the time stamps must be adjusted. Then the timings must be subtracted, summarized, and compared across processors to determine if a load imbalance occurred. With stopwatch tools, for every message receive site in the source code, the total amount of time spent waiting and the number of calls is recorded. A sum of the square of the time could also be kept to compute the variance later. The volume of data and time spent postprocessing is significantly less, but most of the story remains.

Collection of data may be done by subroutine calls inserted into the source code or by modifying the compiler directly. Inserted by hand or via a pre-processor, subroutine calls to a data collection library provide a portable method of instrumentation and do not require compiler support. But the use of subroutine calls substantially distorts the optimizations that would otherwise occur if the subroutine calls were not present. The user ends up tuning something other than a fully optimized program. The cost of a subroutine call and return prohibits the collection of fine-grained data. Although it is more difficult to directly modify the compiler itself, the resulting system can collect fine-grained data on a fully optimized program with much less overhead than a subroutine call and return. Hardware supported performance monitoring or a post-compilation filter are other instrumentation possibilities. While hardware supported performance monitoring is probably the most accurate and least intrusive, the additional hardware adds significant expense and is therefore frequently prohibitive, particularly on systems with large numbers of processors. A post-compilation filter is another viable option but less information is available to a post-compilation filter than to instrumentation done within the compiler itself, e.g. progenitor source lines and the purpose of specific instructions.

3 MPP Apprentice method

The MPP Apprentice performance tool is a stopwatch tool. It collects statistics for each section of code, summarizes this data on each processor, and displays data that has been summarized across all processors. During program execution, timings and pass counts for each code block are summed within each processor and kept locally in each processor's memory, enabling the MPP Apprentice tool to handle very long-running codes without any increase in the use of processor memory. At the end of program execution, or when requested by the user, the power of the Cray T3D is used to do a global reduction of the statistics for each code object across the processors, keeping high and low peaks, and a run-time information file (RIF) is created.

MPP Apprentice instrumentation is built into the compiler. The instructions generated for the user's code are analyzed in order to strategically add data collection instructions to obtain the required data while minimizing the impact on the user's program. Unavoidably, instruction and data cache are affected, but less than they would be affected by subroutine calls.

A compile time flag turns on MPP Apprentice instrumentation, and produces a compiler information file (CIF) for each source file. A CIF contains a description of the source code from the front end of the compiler and encapsulates some of the knowledge of the user's code from the back end of the compiler, such as instructions to be executed and estimated timings. The MPP Apprentice tool post-processes the RIF, the CIFs, and the user's source files.

4 Visualization of data

When a user initially runs the MPP Apprentice tool on a run-time output file, the tool provides a summary of the statistics for the program and all subroutines, sorting them from the most to the least critical. The list of subroutines includes both instrumented as well as uninstrumented subroutines, such as math and scientific library functions. The tool defines long running routines as "critical", and permits the user to redefine "critical" if desired. The summary breaks down the total time for each instrumented subroutine into time spent in overhead, parallel work, I/O, and called routines. For uninstrumented subroutines, only the total time is available. Overhead is defined as time that would not occur in a single processor version of the program, and includes PVM communication, explicit synchronization constructs (such as barriers), and implicit synchronization constructs (such as time spent waiting on data, or implicit barriers at the end of shared loops). The MPP Apprentice tool details the exact amount and specific types of overhead.

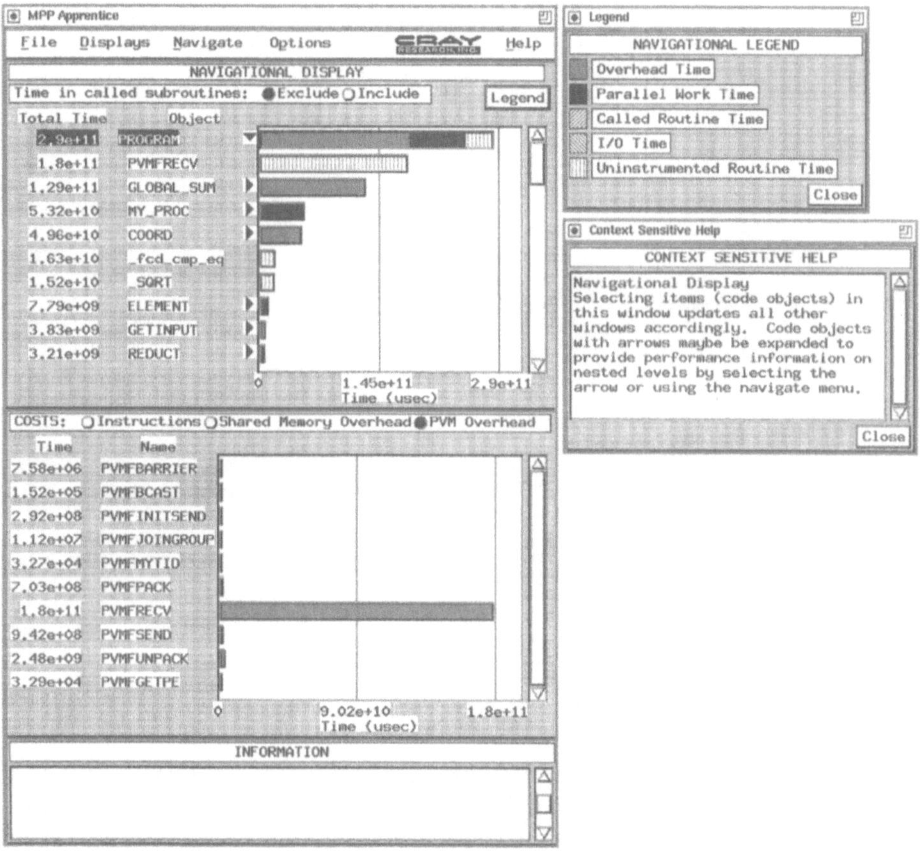

***Figure 1**: Main window of the MPP Apprentice tool*

Figure 1 shows a sample main window of the MPP Apprentice tool. The upper panel of the window, or navigational display, shows summarized statistics for the program and each of its subroutines. The small legend window identifies the breakdown of the total time for each code object. A small arrow to the right of a subroutine name indicates that the subroutine has been instrumented and that it may be expanded to see performance characteristics of nested levels. All of the detailed information available for the program and subroutines is also available for nested levels. Nested code objects are identified by a name identifying the code construct, e.g. If or Do, and a line number from the original source code. The user may ask to see the full source code for a code object. A source code request invokes Cray's xbrowse source code browse, loads the appropriate file automatically, and highlights the corresponding lines of source code. (See Figure 2.)

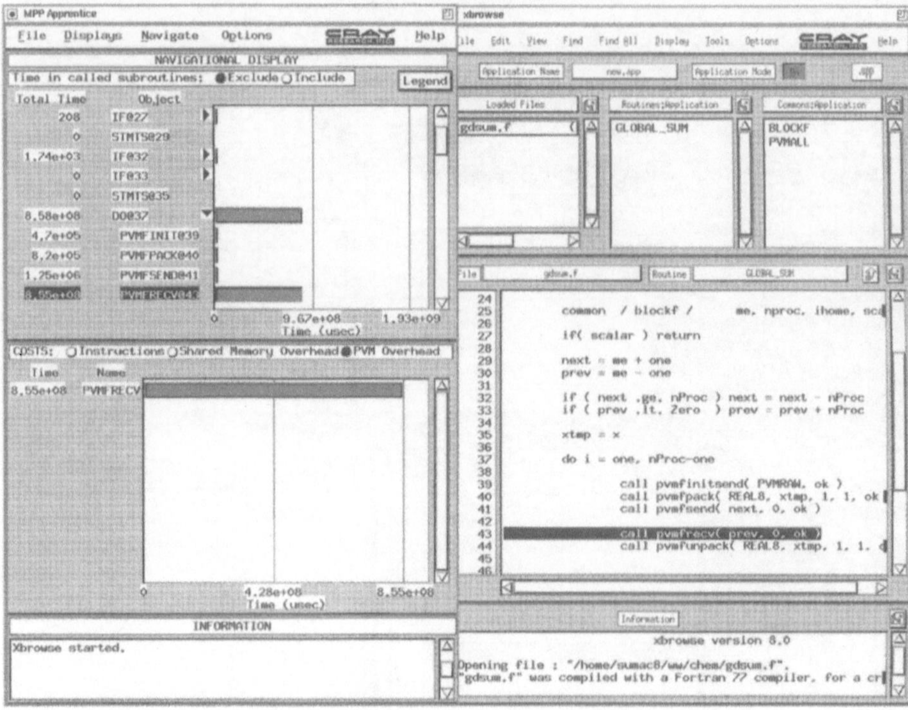

***Figure 2**: MPP Apprentice tool working cooperatively with Xbrowse*

The middle panel of the MPP Apprentice tool details the costs for the code object selected in the navigational display. It toggles between providing information on instruction counts, shared memory overheads, and PVM overheads. When displaying instruction counts, the exact number of each type of floating point and integer instruction is available, as well as the number of local, local shared, and global memory loads and stores. These values assist the user in balancing the use of the integer and floating point functional units and maximizing local memory accesses to fully utilize the power of the T3D. The shared memory overheads display gives the amount of time spent in each type of synchronization construct as well as time spent waiting on the arrival of data. The PVM overheads display gives the amount of time spent in each type of PVM call. Samples of each of these displays is available in Section 5.

By default, the timings shown in the MPP Apprentice tool are exclusive of time spent in called subroutines. This brings problems that are easily fixed to the user's attention first. An inclusive mode is available within the tool to look at algorithmic problems with the way subroutines are called from one another. A call sites display helps look at these types of problems as well. It lets the user see all the sites from which a selected subroutine was called, and all the subroutines to which the selected subroutine makes calls. Timings and pass counts are available with this information.

A knowledge base built into the MPP Apprentice tool derives secondary statistics from the measured values. It provides the user with performance measures (such as MFLOPs ratings), analyzes the program's use of cache, makes observations about the user's code, and suggests ways to pursue performance improvements. It attempts to put the knowledge of experienced users into the hands of novices. Since the T3D is a relatively new machine, even experienced users have a lot to learn, so the knowledge base is expected to grow.

5 Identification of Performance Problems

Many of the commercial and benchmark codes optimized with the MPP Apprentice tool so far have had a large amount of time spent on a synchronization construct as their primary performance bottleneck. Time at synchronization constructs indicates some type of imbalance in the code, a problem that is typical of MPP codes in general. The interconnection topology of the T3D [1] is much faster than other commercially available MPPs, but these performance problems while reduced substantially, still exist. In the next few sections we will demonstrate, with MPP Apprentice output, the identification of different types of performance problems from real applications.

5.1 Load imbalance with a message passing code

Figure 1 shows the initial MPP Apprentice output for a chemical code. With the subroutines sorted in order of decreasing total time, it is evident that PVMFRECV, a blocking message receive function, is consuming the most time, more than half of the total time of the program. Intuitively it seems undesirable to spend more than half of program execution time waiting for messages. This time could be caused by a large volume of communication, network contention, or a load imbalance. If the problem were a large volume of communication, it could be caused by many small messages or a few very large messages. Either way, by selecting subroutine PVMFRECV in the Navigational Display and taking a look at the call sites display, we can see each call to PVMFRECV and the amount of time spent in it.

In Figure 3 we can see all of the calls to PVMRECV. There are not many of them, but two calls are taking substantially more time than the others. There are a number of ways a user might approach this problem. The developer working on this code inserted a PVMFBARRIER just before the loop in which PVMFRECV was called to determine whether the load imbalance existed before the call to PVMFRECV or at the call itself. When the code was rerun, all the time accumulated on the PVMFBARRIER indicating the load imbalance existed prior to

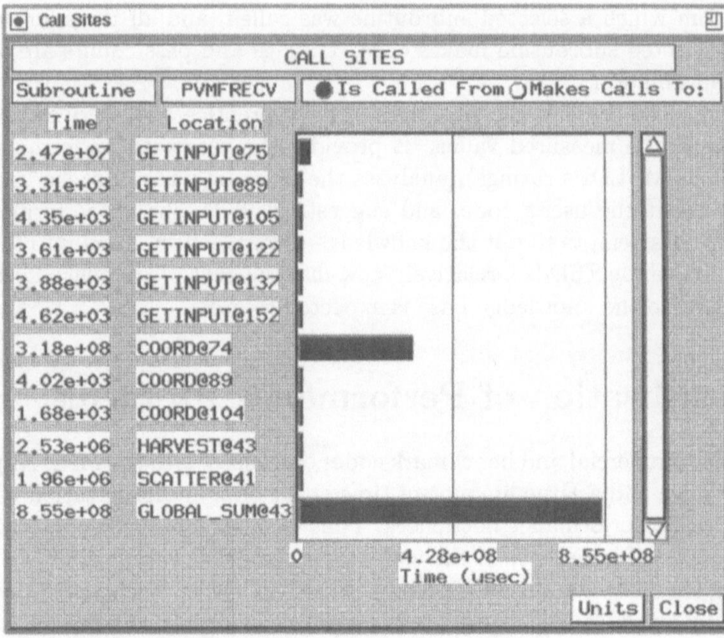

Figure 3: *Call sites display for PVMFRECV*

the loop calling PVMFRECV. The developer was then able to properly focus his attention, quickly resolved the problem, and achieved a speedup of 3 1/2 times.

5.2 Load imbalance with Fortran programming model code

The main window in Figure 4 is from the NAS SP benchmark code. This code uses one of the synchronization constructs available as part of Cray's Fortran Programming Model, a barrier. The navigational display makes it evident that the barrier is the most critical subroutine in the user's program. With the middle panel toggled to show shared memory overheads, the time spent in the barrier shows up as a type of overhead. Since a barrier is a subroutine call, we can approach this problem similarly to the PVM problem by using the call sites display to let us view the locations from which the barrier was called, and the time spent at each location. From Figure 5 we can see that at two call sites, `trans231@16` and `trans321@16`, significantly more time was spent at the barrier. `trans231@16` indicates that subroutine `trans231` made a call to the barrier at line 16 in the file where subroutine `trans231` is defined. This time could be caused by many calls to the barrier, or by a load imbalance at the time it was called. The units menu of the display permits us to toggle to view pass counts instead of timings. If we were to do this we would see that subroutines `trans231` and `trans321` make fewer

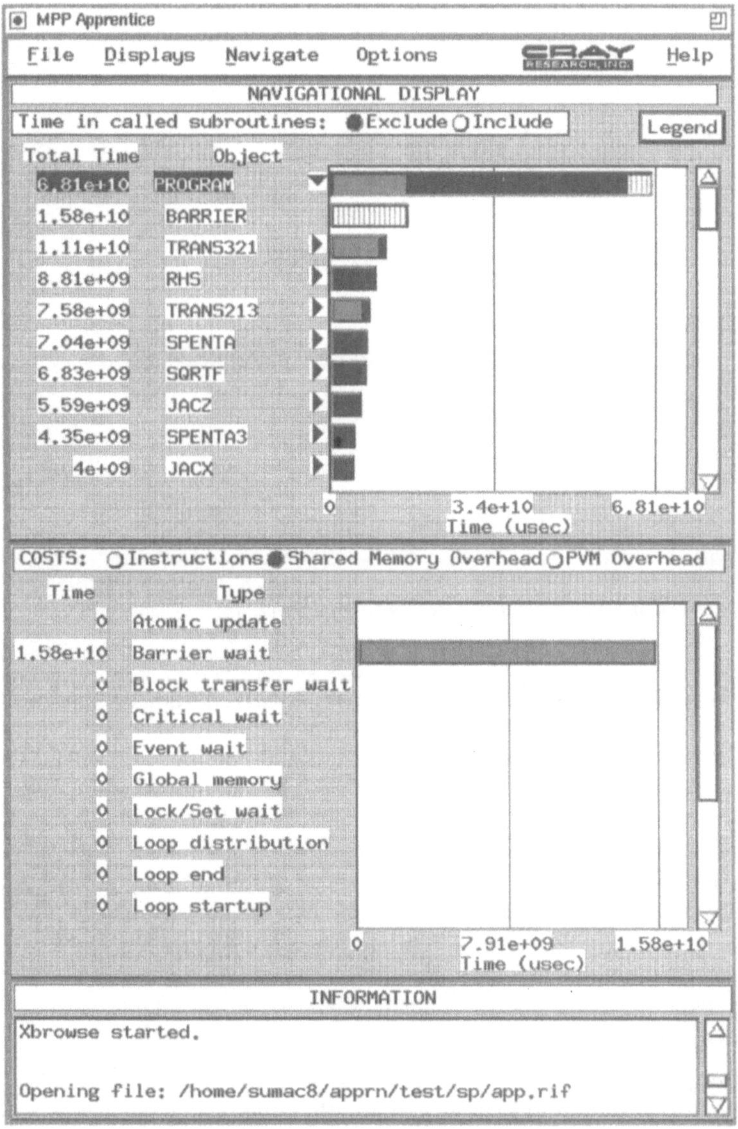

***Figure 4**: Main window of CRAFT code with a barrier*

calls to the barrier than any other call sites. The larger timings combined with the smaller pass counts is an indication of a load imbalance for the user to pursue, and the user knows at precisely which locations to pursue it.

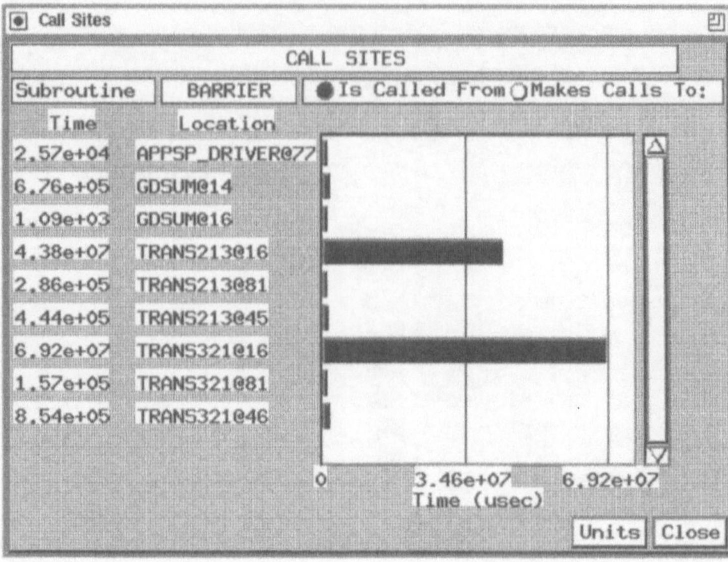

Figure 5: *Time spent at each call site of the barrier*

5.3 Poor balance of floating point and integer calculations

Figure 6 shows the main window for a hydrodynamics code. The most critical subroutine is an uninstrumented subroutine called **$sldiv**. If the user were to search the source code, **$sldiv** would not be found. As a user, it can be very difficult and immensely frustrating to resolve a performance problem with a subroutine that can not be identified. This is just one of many situations where the MPP Apprentice analysis and observations engine can offer assistance.

The observations window in Figure 7 notes and explains the time spent in **$sldiv**. Since there is no integer divide functional unit on the alpha chip used in the Cray T3D, a subroutine call must be made to do the divide. Since the cost to call a subroutine is significantly greater than the direct use of a functional unit, the program performance will benefit by limiting the number of integer divides. If we return to Figure 6, and look at the middle panel which is currently displaying instruction counts, we will note a large number of integer instructions relative to floating point instructions. Since there are both integer and floating point functional units which may be used simultaneously, it is desirable to balance their use. The instructions display indicates an underutilized floating point unit. When this is combined with the large amount of time spent in **$sldiv**, a strong case could be made for converting some integers to floats.

The observations window also provides a number of performance measures derived from the measured statistics, works to focus the user's attention on points of interest, and offers suggestions on how to pursue performance problems.

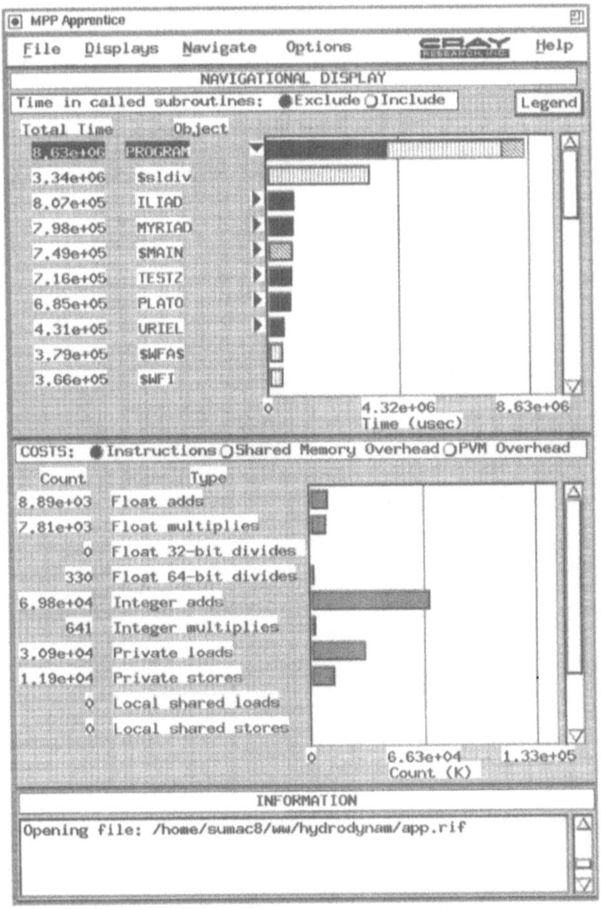

Figure 6: *Main window of hydrodynamics code*

6 Conclusion

Initial users have had a tremendous amount of success with the MPP Apprentice tool on substantial codes. The speedup achieved by resolving one performance problem on the chemical code example, was already mentioned. Several developers working on an electromagnetics benchmark were surprised to find that the routines they had been working to optimize were the two running most efficiently, and their biggest bottleneck was elsewhere. Another user was able to take his code from 29.1 MFLOPs to 491 MFLOPS in a short period of time by resolving problems with PVM communication and barriers that the tool pointed out. These are just a few success stories from a large initial user base.

The method of data collection, and the choice of the data being collected,

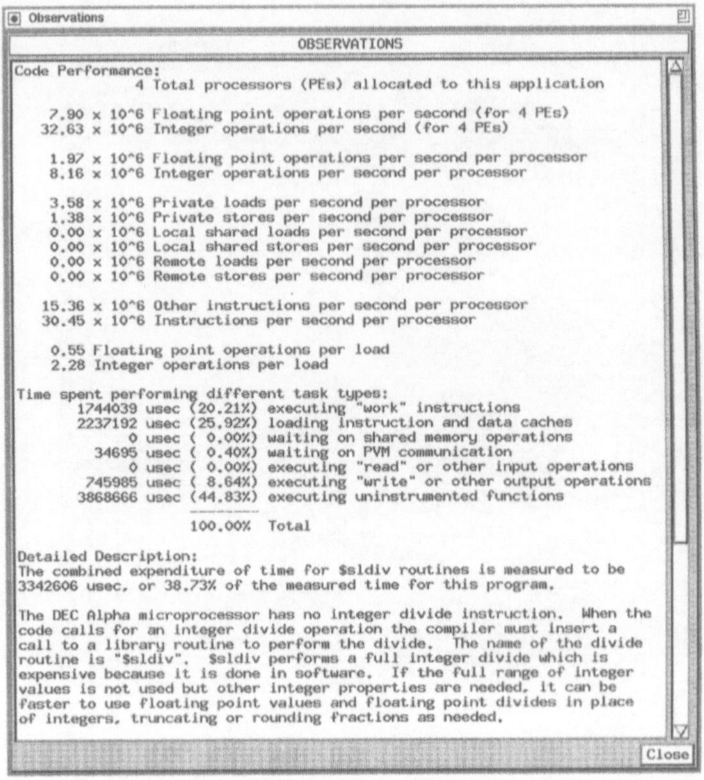

***Figure 7**: Observations for the hydrodynamics code*

permits the MPP Apprentice tool to scale well to long-running programs on large numbers of processors. By presenting data from the perspective of the user's original source code, the user is able to quickly identify the location of performance problems. Detailed information on instructions, shared memory overheads, and PVM communication allow a user to quickly identify the cause of performance problems. The knowledge base encapsulated in observations provides performance numbers and helps the user identify and resolve more difficult problems. As demonstrated above, the identification of problems in Cray T3D codes today can be achieved efficiently using the MPP Apprentice performance tool.

References

[1] *Cray T3D System Architecture Overview.* HR-04033, Cray Research, Inc., Eagan, Minnesota, 1993.

[2] Heath, M. and Etheridge, J. Visualizing the Performance of Parallel Programs. *Software.* IEEE Computer Society, Silver Spring, MD, September 1991, Volume 8(5), pp. 28–39.

[3] *Introducing the MPP Apprentice Tool.* IN-2511 1.0, Cray Research, Inc., Eagan, Minnesota, 1993.

[4] Maloney, A., Hammerslag, D., and Jablonowski, D. Traceview: A Trace Visualization Tool. *Software.* IEEE Computer Society, Silver Spring, MD, September 1991, Volume 8(5), pp.19–28.

[5] Pase, D. MacDonald, T. and Meltzer, A. MPP Fortran Programming Model. CRAY Internal Report, February 1993. To appear in "Scientific Programming," John Wiley and Sons.

[6] *Unicos Performance Utilities Reference Manual.* SR-2040 6.0, Cray Research, Inc., Eagan, Minnesota, 1991.

[7] Williams, W.and Kohn, *J. ATExpert,* Winifred Williams and James Kohn. *The Journal of Parallel and Distributed Computing* 18, Academic Press, June 1993, pp. 205-222.

[8] Yan, Jerry C. Performance Tuning with AIMS – An Automated Instrumentation and Monitoring System for Multicomputers. HICSS 27, Hawaii, Jan 1994.

Programming Environments for Massively Parallel Distributed Systems, Monte Verità, Switzerland

Optimized Record-Replay Mechanism for RPC-based Parallel Programming*

Alain Fagot Jacques Chassin de Kergommeaux
LGI — IMAG
46 avenue Félix Viallet
F-38031 Grenoble Cedex 1, France.
{Alain.Fagot,Jacques.Chassin-de-Kergommeaux}@imag.fr

Abstract

This paper presents a mechanism for record-replay of parallel programs written in a remote procedure call (RPC) based parallel programming model. This mechanism, which will serve as a basis for implementing a user-level debugger, exploits properties of the programming model to limit drastically the volume of records that need to be done. This reduction can be applied to other programming models.

1 Introduction

This paper presents a mechanism allowing programmers to cope with the inherent non-determinism of parallel executions, when debugging programs written in a remote procedure call (RPC) based programming model, designed for massively parallel multiprocessors.

Many parallel programs present a non-deterministic behavior, even if they produce deterministic computation results. Non-deterministic execution behaviors originate mainly in the execution environment of the program. This environment depends on a large number of factors that cannot be controlled by the programmer, such as the initial contents of cache memories, the initial state of the operating system or the simultaneous execution of daemon processes on the same multiprocessor. Programs adapting to the execution environment for efficiency reasons, using dynamic load balancing techniques, for example, are very prone to exhibit non-deterministic execution behaviors. Non-deterministic execution behavior of erroneous parallel programs may result in transient errors which appear very unfrequently or vanish when debugging tools are used, because of changes introduced by these tools in the causal relationship between parallel processes.

*This work has been partially supported by the French Ministery of Research under the inter-PRC project TRACE.

The most classical technique used to catch transient errors appearing during executions of parallel programs is to *record* an initial execution and to *force* subsequent executions to be deterministic with respect to the initial execution, using the recorded information. Debugging an erroneous program then amounts to record an erroneous execution and to apply cyclic debugging techniques during subsequent replayed executions. In order for this technique to be effective, the perturbation resulting from the recording operation ought to be kept sufficiently low so that errors appearing in un-recorded executions do not vanish in recorded ones and vice-versa. If this overhead is low enough, recording can be left active during each execution of a parallel program, so that an error occurring unfrequently can be captured and subsequently reproduced.

Efficient record-replay techniques are mostly based upon the "Instant Replay" mechanism of LeBlanc and Mellor-Crummey [LMC87]. The efficiency of the instant replay comes from the observation that it is sufficient to record the order of accesses to shared objects to be able to reproduce "indistinguishable" executions. A version number is associated to each shared object. During an initial recording, each process accessing a shared object records its version number on a *history tape*. During replayed executions, history tapes are used to force processes to access the same versions of shared objects. For programs using shared-memory, shared objects may be semaphores, locks, monitors, etc. The instant replay mechanism was adapted to message passing programming models [LSZ90], where each process records on a tape the identifiers of received messages. The replay system forces reexecuting processes to treat incoming messages in the same order as during the initial recording. This mechanism was used as a basis for the implementation of parallel debuggers [MC89, LS92, HPR92, Jam93].

This paper describes an optimized record-replay mechanism for ATHAPASCAN[1], the programming model of the APACHE research project. APACHE aims at designing and implementing a parallel programming environment for massively parallel computers, providing both static and dynamic load balancing facilities [Pla93]. ATHAPASCAN consists essentially of blocking and non blocking Remote Procedure Calls (RPC), each RPC resulting in the computation of a light-weight process (or thread). The mechanism described in the sequel of this paper, exploits the characteristics of remote procedure calls to reduce drastically the volume of traces that need to be recorded in order to be able to replay programs deterministically with respect to the original recorded computation.

This introduction is followed by a presentation of the ATHAPASCAN programming model. The record-replay mechanism, optimized for ATHAPASCAN is then explained. The paper terminates with a conclusion sketching future work.

---

[1] ATHAPASCAN is the language of the Apaches.

2 The Athapascan programming model

In ATHAPASCAN, the execution of parallel programs is performed by a set of identical virtual processors operating asynchronously. Expression of parallelism is achieved by blocking and non-blocking remote procedure calls (requests), thereby hiding the underlying communication protocols under the parameters and results transmission mechanisms. Thus the ATHAPASCAN model is well suited for expressing *control parallelism.* Each virtual processor includes several *Entry Points*, which are the targets of remote procedure calls (see Figure 1). No other communications are available in ATHAPASCAN.

A remote procedure call results in the execution of a light-weight process (thread) within the virtual processor holding the target entry point. This thread may in turn create new threads by issuing remote procedure calls. Several light-weight processes execute concurrently within each virtual processor to hide the latency of communications in massively parallel systems. ATHAPASCAN offers two types of remote procedure calls:

- blocking (*Call*): control is returned to the caller after receiving the result of the called procedure,
- non blocking (*Spawn*): control is returned to the caller after the creation of the remote thread. Two operators are provided to test (*TestSpawn*) or wait (*WaitSpawn*) for the completion of non-blocking remote procedure calls.

A prototype of ATHAPASCAN was implemented as a set of operators used from a host language (currently C) using PVM as communication library and several thread libraries.

3 Minimal trace recording

The non-deterministic behavior of an ATHAPASCAN program execution is due to the variable order in which requests are handled by entry points and to the results of non-deterministic primitives which are related to the current state of the system. The two causes can be tracked down separately.

Basic mechanism The principle of the control driven replay is to record the order of accesses to shared resources. Classical implementations of Instant Replay record the order of system-level primitives for passing messages [LS92] or accessing shared variables [LMC87]. In the ATHAPASCAN model, shared resources are entry points, accessed by requests. Our record-replay mechanism uses an intermediate level of abstraction where several system-level events can be abstracted in one, thereby reducing the number of records while being independent of the underlying communication system.

Each call to an entry point results in a typical sequence of such "abstract" events. Figure 1 represents a complete sequence of events generated by a call to an entry point, from the request emission (event **a**) to the result receipt (event **d**) passing through the request receipt (event **b**) and the result emission (event **c**). A replay can be driven by forcing the execution order of request receipts (event **b**). Since an entry point controls racing requests, it can be responsible for recording the order in which it serves incoming requests.

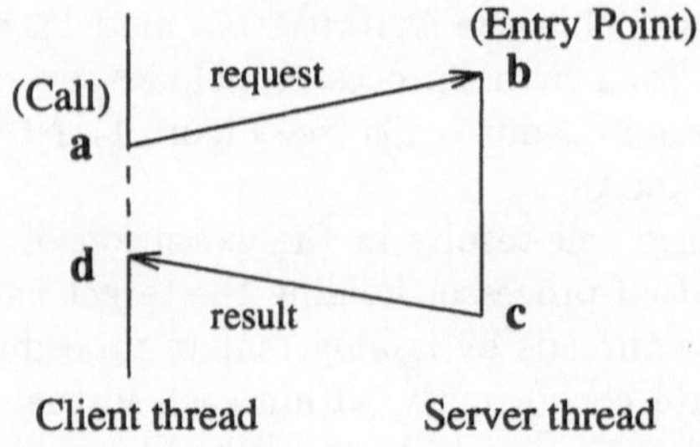

Figure 1: *Sequence of events for a call to an entry point.*

The order of request emissions (event **a**) is not recorded since an emitting thread will reproduce this order if all its non deterministic operations produce the same values. However, this order may not be significant since the ATHAPASCAN model does not impose this order to be followed by the request receipts.

The order of request receipts (event **b**) is the order in which incoming requests are processed by an entry point. This fundamental order represents the order in which access is granted to shared resources and is recorded by each entry point.

The order of result emissions (event **c**) is not significant since a single result is emitted by a thread and this occurs at the end of its execution.

The order of result receipts (event **d**) is not visible from the point of view of the client thread. A client thread is informed of the presence of the result only through primitives *TestSpawn* and *WaitSpawn* in the case of a non blocking call or implicitly in the case of a blocking call.

Each entry point is responsible for recording its request receipt history (event **b**). This history contains the order of request unique identifiers. A request identifier is constructed independently by the client thread emitting the request in a deterministic way: in particular, it is independent of the other threads sharing the same virtual processor. For the ATHAPASCAN model, it has the following form: ⟨VirtualProcessorID, EntryPointID, ThreadID, RequestID⟩.

Indeterministic primitives Indeterministic primitives may be considered as predefined indeterministic entry points of the ATHAPASCAN kernel. For this type of entry points, results cannot be computed during replayed executions as during a recorded execution. Therefore, the instant replay mechanism must record the result computed for the request along with the request identifier in order to provide the same result to the same request during the replay. This technique mixes data driven replay with the general control driven strategy.

Interest of the proposed model The simplifications brought to the classical models result from the communication simplicity of the ATHAPASCAN model. Processes obey a Client-Server protocol which is a sub-class of the model of communicating processes. To each request corresponds a result and a result is emitted only after a request was received.

The ATHAPASCAN request and result transmissions can be implemented in several different ways without consequences on the design of the record-replay mechanism. This independence leads to a reduction of the number of trace-points for some implementations, up to a factor of 6 relative to the classical solution of implementing the record-replay at the system level. This reduction factor is obtained at low cost since no additional information is appended to the messages, except the small request identifier.

The proposed model can easily be adapted to object-oriented parallel programming models for active objects as well as for passive ones. Adapting this model to the active object model consists in translating the ATHAPASCAN model entities into entities of an object model. For example, ATHAPASCAN virtual processor instances and ATHAPASCAN entry points are respectively equivalent to object instances and methods. When considering a model with passive objects, extensions of the request mechanism should be considered. The proposed model can also be applied to applications structured according to a Client-Server architecture.

4 Conclusion and future work

This paper describes an adaptation of the Instant Replay mechanism to ATHAPASCAN, a hierarchical, RPC-based programming model, where parallel programs are executed by a potentially high number of light-weight processes, grouped in (potentially many) virtual processors. This adaptation was optimized by exploiting the characteristics of the programming model, resulting in an important reduction of the number of records necessary to replay programs deterministically. A demonstration that executions of any Athapascan program, recorded and replayed with the mechanism defined above, are equivalent is given in [FdK94]. Two executions of the same program are *equivalent* if each process performs the same sequence of requests (same order, same parameters) in both executions. The techniques described in the paper can be used for any RPC-based parallel programming model or adapted to object-oriented parallel programming models.

A prototype implementation of the RPC-based ATHAPASCAN programming model including record-replay techniques was implemented on the top of PVM [Sun90] and several thread libraries available for different hardware architectures. This prototype was tested with highly non deterministic programs, creating many threads competing to access shared resources. Preliminary measurements indicate that the cost of recording –time overhead and volume of recorded traces–, remains limited enough to use the recording mode as a normal execution mode for ATHAPASCAN and therefore be able to record even unfrequent errors.

The implementation of this instant replay mechanism will serve as a basis for the development of an ATHAPASCAN debugger. If measurement results confirm the efficiency of the preliminary experiments, the recording mode will become the normal ATHAPASCAN execution mode, so that unfrequent errors can be captured as soon as they occur and later debugged using a cyclic method like in sequential debugging. Execution replay will be connected to a visualization tool providing a high-level view of the execution of parallel programs. This approach is similar to the approach of Leu and Schiper in [LS92]. Another track of research currently under consideration is to extend the record-replay mechanism to do performance measurements, as does Mellor-Crummey in [MC89].

References

[FdK94] A. Fagot and J. Chassin de Kergommeaux. Optimized record-replay for debugging Athapascan programs. Rapport APACHE in preparation, IMAG Institute.

[HPR92] M. Hurfin, N. Plouzeau, and M. Raynal. EREBUS A debugger for asynchronous distributed computing systems. *3rd IEEE Workshop on Future Trends in Distributed Computing Systems*, Taiwan, April 1992.

[Jam93] H. Jamrozik. *Aide à la Mise au Point des Applications Parallèles et Réparties à base d'Objets Persistants.* PhD thesis, Université Joseph Fourier, Grenoble, May 1993.

[LMC87] T.J. LeBlanc and J.M. Mellor-Crummey. Debugging Parallel Programs with Instant Replay. *IEEE Transactions on Computers*, C-36(4):471–481, April 1987.

[LS92] E. Leu and A. Schiper. Execution replay : a mechanism for integrating a visualization tool with a symbolic debugger. *CONPAR 92 - VAPP V.*, volume 634 of *Lectures Notes in Computer Science*, Springer-Verlag.

[LSZ90] E. Leu, A. Schiper, and A. Zramdini. Execution Replay on Distributed Memory Architectures. In *Proceedings of the 2nd IEEE Symposium on Parallel and Distributed Processing*, pages 106–112, December 1990.

[MC89] J.M. Mellor-Crummey. Debugging and Analysis of Large-Scale Parallel Programs. Technical Report 312, University of Rochester, 1989.

[Pla93] B. Plateau et al. Présentation d'APACHE. Rapport APACHE 1, IMAG Institute, October 1993.

[Sun90] V.S. Sunderam. PVM: A Framework for Parallel Distributed Computing. *Concurrency: Practice and Experience*, 2(4):315–339, 1990.

Programming Environments for Massively Parallel Distributed Systems, Monte Verità, Switzerland

Abstract Debugging of Distributed Applications

Thomas Kunz
Inst. für Theoret. Informatik
Technische Hochschule Darmstadt
Darmstadt, Germany
kunz@iti.informatik.th-darmstadt.de

James P. Black
Dept. of Computer Science
University of Waterloo
Ontario, Canada
jpblack@uwaterloo.ca

Abstract

Distributed applications are highly complex and consequently difficult to debug. In particular, applications with hundreds of processes produce great quantities of information during debugging, easily overwhelming a human user. This paper uses a faulty implementation of a distributed simulation to present a debugging approach addressing this complexity problem. Using various abstract visualizations of an execution, the likely cause of an error is identified iteratively. The approach presented facilitates the debugging of distributed applications by enabling a user to gradually and selectively increase the level of detail, keeping the overall amount of information manageable.

1 Introduction

Despite a long and ongoing effort to write *provable* programs, real applications still contain errors. The detection and correction of the underlying cause (i.e., the debugging effort) consumes significant resources: manpower, time, and system utilization.

One architecture that has recently come into widespread use is that of distributed systems. These systems offer a number of potential advantages over a traditional von Neumann architecture, such as parallelism, fault tolerance, scalability, etc. One specific problem in debugging applications running on these architectures is their complexity. Applications with a large number of processes typically produce a huge amount of (irrelevant) information during the debugging process, easily overwhelming a human user. Our research tries to solve this problem by following a *top-down*, *inductive* debugging method. The execution of an application is examined at various levels of abstraction. By starting with a high-level abstraction, the amount of information collected is small enough to be manageable. The likely cause of an error is detected by successively identifying the erroneous part of an execution and reexamining this part at a lower level of abstraction, until the cause of an observed error is determined and can be fixed.

To support top-down debugging, suitable abstractions have to be defined. Existing debuggers either provide a fixed set of abstractions [HC88] or require a manual bottom-up definition of these abstractions [Bat88]. Given the complexity of distributed applications, this task is tedious as well as error-prone. Typically, proponents of the manual derivation of abstractions claim that they do not intend to model an application completely, but rather that they allow a tool user to quickly and easily create small, succinct behaviour models and investigate application behaviour from that perspective. Formulating such small, succinct behaviour models, however, requires some general understanding of the application at hand. A global understanding has to be gained first by examining the faulty application at higher levels of an abstraction hierarchy [KCC89].

This paper discusses the abstract debugging of *distributed applications*, using a sample application. In the following, distributed applications are considered to consist of a number of sequential processes, cooperating to achieve a common goal. Cooperation includes both communication and synchronization, and is achieved by the exchange of messages. Processes may be created and destroyed dynamically. The execution of distributed applications can be depicted graphically in figures similar to Figure 1.

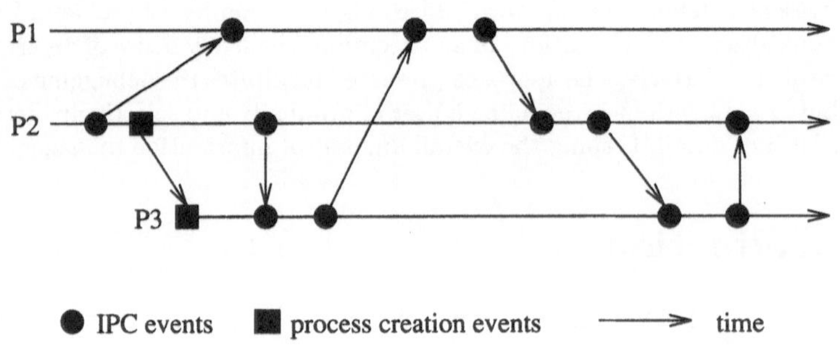

Figure 1: *Model of the Execution of a Distributed Application*

In these *process-time* diagrams, one dimension represents processes and the other dimension represents time. In Figure 1, time flows from left to right. In each process, a number of relevant events occurs. These primitive events constitute the lowest level of observable behaviour. In distributed debugging, the events of interest are typically events related to process creation and termination as well as interprocess communication events. Messages are drawn as arrows, connecting the corresponding send and receive events. Asynchronous message passing is depicted by slanted arrows, indicating that sending a message occurs before it is received. Synchronous message passing is drawn as a vertical arrow to indicate that sending and receipt of a message occur at the same moment.

2 Abstract Distributed Debugging

We present our concept of *abstract* debugging in the context of a real debugging situation. The distributed application used is a simulation of an airport shuttle system described in [KMF90]. This airport shuttle system transports passengers between four terminals. Passengers signal their travel request by pushing a destination button at the control panel of their station. The system can support up to three different trains running in parallel, controlled by a distributed computer system. Passenger requests are serviced on a first-come-first-served basis.

The sample application is a simulation of this shuttle system. Train movements are represented by messages exchanged between track segments. The track layout is split into seven segments. Each track segment and each point (or switch) of the physical system is modelled by an application process. Furthermore, the control panels at each station are simulated by `button` processes. The complete application consists of these processes plus further processes necessary to organize and control the flow of trains, for a total of 16 processes.

In a first implementation, trains sometimes collided, depending on the initial location of trains and the set of passenger requests. One such case occurred when the simulation was executed with two trains, one train in the `SouthEast` station and one train in the `NorthWest` station. Furthermore, two passenger requests were issued, one passenger travelling from `SouthEast` to `NorthWest` and the other passenger travelling from `NorthWest` to `SouthWest`. The execution terminates with the following error message: `Trains 2 and 1 collided`.

To examine the likely cause for this collision, an existing distributed debugger [Tay92] for our target environment was used. This debugger graphically displays the execution in a process-time diagram similar to Figure 1.

Given the number of primitive events in the event stream, it is impossible to display the whole execution at once. A first abstract view of the application uses process clusters. Frequently, nothing is known in advance about the process structure of an application. A first step to gain an overview could be to write down all processes and to connect communicating processes by an arrow. Though the number of processes is very small (only 16), such a diagram quickly becomes unreadable. By rearranging and grouping the processes, one essentially clusters them. The result of such a grouping effort reveals the following structure. The shuttle system simulation consists of two symmetrical groups of processes, reflecting the physical track layout. These two clusters will be called `EASTSECTOR` and `WESTSECTOR` in the following. Each group of track segments is managed by a section `controller`, these `controllers` communicate with the central `scheduler` process and share access to one common track segment.

The debugger offers the possibility to display the execution sequence using process clusters. All communication internal to a cluster is omitted from the display, and so only messages that cross cluster boundaries are displayed. Figure 2 shows the high-level view of the execution. Uppercase names represent process clusters, lowercase names indicate individual processes. The cluster `SYSTEM` contains all the runtime system processes created during the application execution.

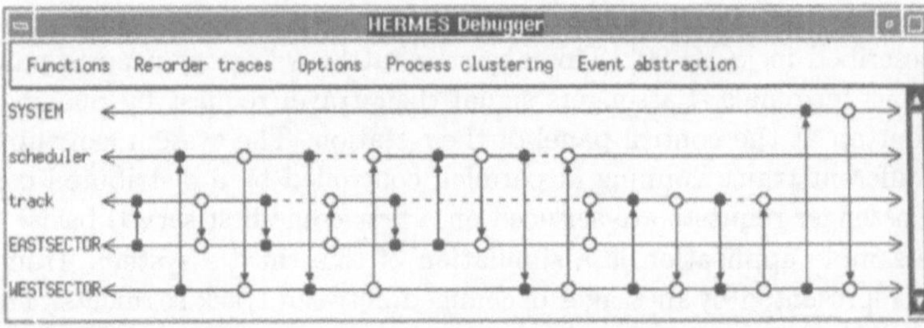

Figure 2: *A high-level View using Process Clusters*

Figure 2 illustrates that the collision occurred in the **WESTSECTOR** process cluster. One process in this cluster communicates with processes in the **SYSTEM** cluster to report the collision. While this display contains fewer processes and events than a low-level process-time diagram, it is still difficult to identify the sequence of actions leading to the train collision. The primitive events in this figure are not grouped in any meaningful way, showing too low-level a view of the execution behaviour.

A second abstract view is obtained by grouping primitive events into abstract events, reducing the number of events to be examined. Ideally, these abstract events should encapsulate meaningful *units of work*. Figure 3 displays the execution of the faulty execution, using both event abstractions and process clusters. The process cluster **WESTSECTOR**, containing the track segment where the train collision occurred, is displayed at a low abstraction level, showing all its constituent processes. The less interesting process clusters **SYSTEM** and **EASTSECTOR** are displayed at a higher abstraction level, showing only those messages that cross the cluster boundaries.

Abstract events generally involve primitive events from a number of different processes. Therefore, they are displayed as vertical rectangles, stretching over the range of all processes involved. The intersection of this open rectangle with a process is drawn as a black square if events from this process are part of the abstract event. Figure 3 depicts nearly the complete execution. It shows how the processes inside the **WESTSECTOR** cluster are created and initialized by the first message sent to a process from its creator. The activities forming the body of the simulation are displayed as various abstract events. The first two abstract events, for example, involving processes from the **EASTSECTOR** process cluster as well as the process `scheduler`, group all primitive events that correspond to the forwarding of a passenger request to the global `scheduler` (the first abstract event) and one resulting scheduling action (the second abstract event). The train collision is reported by the last process on the display. The two abstract events involving

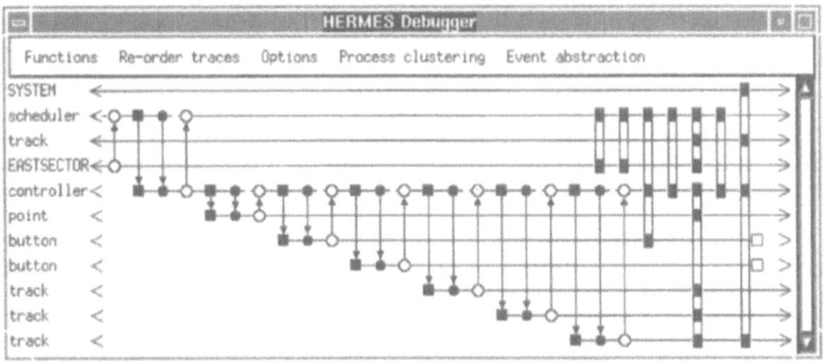

Figure 3: *A high-level View combining Process Clusters and Event Abstractions*

events from this process represent two independent train movements in this execution. The first train movement is local to the `WESTSECTOR` cluster, involving all three `track` processes, the `point` process, and the section `controller`. The second train movement involves the track segment connecting the two sections, the local `controller`, and the track segment where the two trains collide. The train arriving from the shared track segment is advanced to the "collision" track segment without ensuring that it is empty. In this specific execution, the second train is currently occupying this segment, resulting in the collision reported.

3 Conclusions and Future Work

The preceding section described the analysis of a faulty distributed application using abstract visualizations. The debugging approach presented relies on the existence of suitable abstraction hierarchies. Given the complexity of distributed applications, it is unrealistic to expect that such abstraction hierarchies be derived manually. Instead, we are currently working on two tools to derive such abstraction hierarchies automatically. For a description of these tools, see [Kun93, Kun94].

Both abstraction tools are implemented and we are currently in the process of experimenting with them. The process cluster hierarchy presented here, for example, was originally derived by the clustering tool and then modified slightly by hand. This reflects the global philosophy behind our abstraction tools. We do not expect them to derive *perfect* cluster or event abstraction hierarchies, but rather aim at providing good initial abstractions, doing the bulk of work for a complex application. As soon as a user gains some insight into the application at hand, he or she can manually modify the abstraction hierarchies to better correspond to his or her understanding. Such manually modified abstraction hierarchies can be saved for later re-use. The abstract events displayed in Figure 3, on the other hand, were derived directly by our event abstraction tool: no manual modifications were necessary.

The experience collected with the abstraction tools to date shows that it is possible to assign meaningful interpretations to the abstractions derived. It therefore appears that these tools do in fact derive good abstractions. But a more comprehensive exploration of such derived abstraction hierarchies is still missing.

It is our belief that the tools and the debugging approach presented here complement each other to successfully cope with the debugging complexity of distributed applications. Furthermore, we expect the approach presented here to generalize to other software maintenance tasks where understanding the behaviour of complex applications is an essential first step.

References

[Bat88] Peter Bates. Distributed Debugging Tools for Heterogeneous Distributed Systems. In *Proc. of the 8th Int. Conf. on Distributed Computing Systems*, pages 308–315, San Jose, California, June 1988.

[HC88] Alfred A. Hough and Janice E. Cuny. Initial Experiences with a Pattern–Oriented Parallel Debugger. In *Proc. of the ACM SIGPLAN/SIGOPS Workshop on Parallel and Distributed Debugging*, pages 195–205, Madison, Wisconsin, May 1988.

[KCC89] David W. Krumme, Alva L. Couch, and George Cybenko. Debugging Support for Parallel Programs. In Jack Dongarra et al., *Vector and Parallel Computing: Issues in Applied Research and Development*, pages 205–214. Ellis Horwood Limited, Chichester, 1989.

[KMF90] Jeff Kramer, Jeff Magee, and Anthony Finkelstein. A Constructive Approach to the Design of Distributed Systems. In *Proc. of the 10th Int. Conf. on Distributed Computing Systems*, pages 580–587, Paris, France, May 1990.

[Kun93] Thomas Kunz. Process Clustering for Distributed Debugging. In *Proc. of the ACM/ONR Workshop on Parallel and Distributed Debugging*, pages 75–84, San Diego, California, May 1993.

[Kun94] Thomas Kunz. An Event Abstraction Tool: Theory, Design, and Results. Technical Report TI–1/94, Technical University Darmstadt, January 1994.

[Tay92] David J. Taylor. A Prototype Debugger for Hermes. In *Proc. of the 1992 CAS Conference, Volume I*, pages 29–42, Toronto, Ont., Canada, November 1992.

Programming Environments for Massively Parallel Distributed Systems, Monte Verità, Switzerland

Design of a Parallel Object-Oriented Linear Algebra Library

F. Guidec J.-M. Jézéquel
I.R.I.S.A. Campus de Beaulieu
F-35042 RENNES CEDEX, FRANCE
{guidec,jezequel}@irisa.fr

Abstract

Scientific programmers are eager to exploit the computational power offered by Distributed Memory Parallel Computers (DMPCs), but are generally reluctant to undertake the manual porting of their application programs onto such machines. We demonstrate that a purely sequential object-oriented language can be used to build parallel libraries that permit an efficient and transparent use of DMPCs. As an illustration, we discuss the design of an extensible object-oriented parallel linear algebra library.

1 Introduction

It is our conviction that object-oriented techniques can ease the programming of DMPCs. In this paper, we demonstrate that a purely sequential object-oriented language can be used to build an extensible linear algebra library that permits an efficient and transparent use of DMPCs. This library is implemented within EPEE, our Eiffel Parallel Execution Environment [Jez93]. EPEE combines a data-parallelism model together with a SPMD (Single Program Multiple Data) mode of execution. This combination is attractive because it offers the conceptual simplicity of the sequential instruction flow, while exploiting the fact that most of the problems that may advantageously run on DMPCs involve large amounts of data.

Two levels of programming are considered in EPEE: the user (or *client*) level and the designer (or *provider*) level. At client level, nothing but performance improvements appears when replacing a sequential library by a parallel counterpart. The parallelization thus remains transparent to the user who still views an application program as a purely sequential one, even though it uses parallel classes instead of sequential ones and runs concurrently on a DMPC.

EPEE is based on Eiffel [Mey92] because this language features strong encapsulation with static type checking, multiple inheritance, dynamic binding and genericity. However, any other object-oriented language featuring these mechanisms could be used as well. An EPEE prototype based on Eiffel 2.3 is available for Intel iPSC computers (iPSC/2 and iPSC/860), Paragon XP/S and clusters of workstations above TCP/IP. New implementations are in progress to deal with Eiffel 3.

Our parallel linear algebra library is quite similar to ScaLapack++ [DPW93], except that ScaLapack++ relies on a pre-existent non object-oriented numerical kernel [LHKK89]. Our approach is slightly different, since it encourages the design of stand-alone fully object-oriented parallel libraries.

2 The Parallel Linear Algebra Library

2.1 Overview

The specifications of the basic entities of linear algebra are encapsulated in the classes MATRIX (see figure 1) and VECTOR, which are both generic and partially

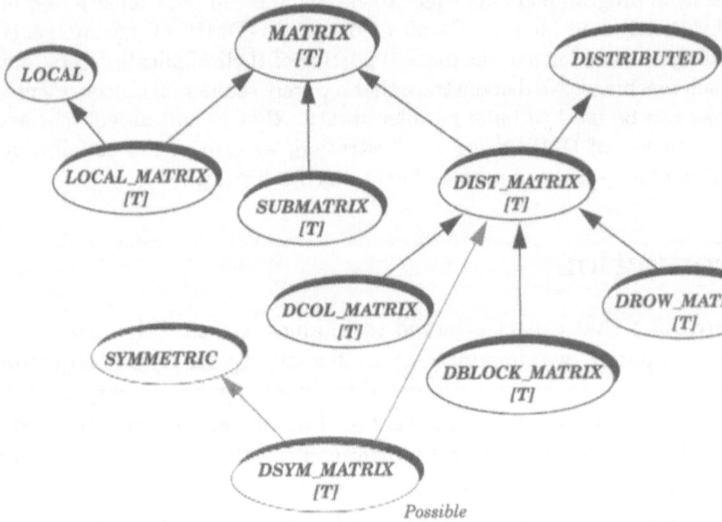

Figure 1: *Class hierarchy for matrix entities*

deferred: they provide no details about the way an instance shall be represented in memory. Several alternative implementation layouts can thus be defined in descendant classes.

The methods in MATRIX and VECTOR are divided in two categories: accessors and operators. Accessors are methods used for accessing the matrix in read or write mode. Operators are high level methods used for performing computations that imply a matrix or a vector as a whole, and possibly other arguments. Typical operators perform scalar-vector, scalar-matrix, vector-matrix and matrix-matrix

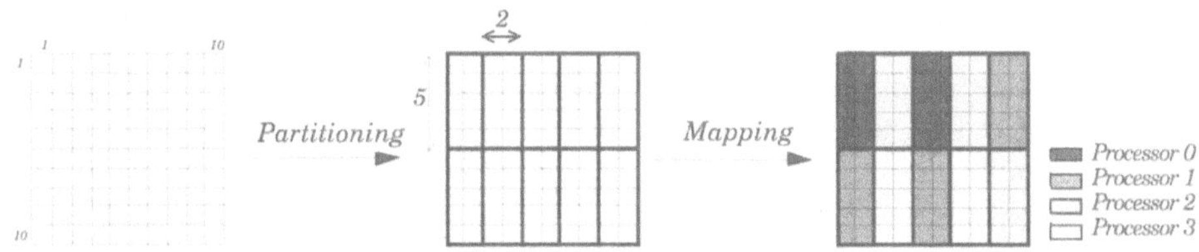

***Figure 2**: Partition of a* 10×10 *matrix into* 5×2 *blocks and mapping over 4 processors*

operations. The library also provides operators for performing *Cholesky*, LDL^T or *LU* factorizations, for solving triangular systems, etc. Unlike accessors, which are representation-dependent and must be kept deferred in MATRIX and VECTOR[1], operators can usually be given a *default* implementation. All descendant classes inherit this default implementation, but any descendant can still redefine an operator if necessary (*e.g.* for optimizing this operator).

A matrix is either local or distributed. Distributed matrices are decomposed into partitions, which are mapped over the processors of the target DMPC (figure 2 shows the distribution of a 10×10 matrix over 4 processors). For creating a new matrix, the user needs to specify at creation time whether this matrix is to be local, distributed by blocks, by rows, or by columns, and invoke the creation routine with the appropriate parameters (the parameterization for creating a distributed matrix is inspired from the syntax of the HPF [For93] directive DISTRIBUTE). The various implementations for matrices are encapsulated in classes LOCAL_MATRIX, DBLOCK_MATRIX, DROW_MATRIX and DCOL_MATRIX (see figure 1).

2.2 Extensibility of the Library

To date our demonstrator library only permits the creation of dense matrices and vectors, but it may easily be augmented with new classes describing other representation variants, such as sparse matrices and vectors, or symmetric, lower triangular and upper triangular matrices, etc. We may also provide more "exotic" distribution patterns, such as diagonal-wise distributions, or even distributions with irregular patterns (blocks of various sizes or various shapes, etc.).

Providing a new representation variant simply comes down to adding a new class in the library. Moreover, a new class is rarely built from scratch, but usually inherits from already existing classes. For example, a distributed symmetric matrix may combine features inherited from such classes as MATRIX, SYMMETRIC and DISTRIBUTED. Hence, providing a new representation variant for a matrix or a vector usually consists in assembling existing classes to produce a new one. Most of the time, this process does not imply any development of new code.

[1]A *deferred* method in Eiffel is equivalent to a pure virtual function in C++.

2.3 Interoperability of Representation Variants

A major advantage of the library is that, as far as the user is concerned, all matrices are handled the same way, except at creation time. For creating a new matrix, the user simply needs to specify the name of the class that corresponds to the desired representation format and provide creation parameters accordingly. After the matrix has been created, its use does not depend on whether it is distributed or local, sparse or dense, symmetric or triangular.

In the library, we therefore ensure the interoperability of all matrices and vectors, whatever their internal representation. A method defined in MATRIX or VECTOR is inherited by all the descendants of the class. Hence a method such as *cholesky*, which is defined in MATRIX and performs a Cholesky factorization, can operate on any matrix that satisfies the preconditions of the method: the matrix must be square symmetric definite positive. The same method operates on a local matrix as well as on a sparse or distributed one. An optimized version of the Cholesky factorization is actually for distributed matrices, but this optimization remains absolutely transparent to the user who keeps invoking method *cholesky* on a matrix M with the dot notation call $M.cholesky$.

Interoperability also goes for algorithms that admit several arguments. For example the class MATRIX provides an infix operator "+" that computes the sum of two matrices A and B and returns the resulting matrix R. The user may write an expression such as $R := A+B$ while matrix R is duplicated on all processors, A is distributed by rows and B is distributed by columns. Interoperability guarantees that all internal representations can be combined transparently.

Complementary to the interoperability of representation variants, a conversion mechanism is available for adapting the representation of a matrix or vector to the requirements of the computation. This mechanism also plays the role of a redistribution facility. A local matrix, for example, can be transformed dynamically into a distributed one, assuming that this new representation is likely to lead to better performances. For the designer of the library, the conversion facility is a convenient tool for parallelizing algorithms, most notably for changing remote information into local one (thus reducing the cost of subsequent access to this information). The user may also use the facility to redistribute matrices or vectors dynamically according to the requirements of his/her application.

2.4 Incremental Optimization of Operators

Our approach to the design of parallel libraries with EPEE fosters an incremental extension of sequential libraries. Each operator of our linear algebra library is originally provided with a sequential implementation, which goes for all representation variants. Once an operator has been given this "default" optimization, optimizing this operator mainly consists in providing one or several optimized variants. For example, the class MATRIX encapsulates a "default" sequential implementation of the *cholesky* factorization method. This implementation goes for all matrices, whatever their internal representation. A highly optimized version of the *cholesky* method is provided, that performs concurrently when applied to an instance of DCOL_MATRIX. In this version, conditional statements are used for restricting the iteration domain of the algorithm (each processor only computes its part of the resulting matrix) and data transfers are reduced to a minimum. However, from the viewpoint of the user, the selection of the most appropriate implementation is fully transparent.

The optimization of the library does not require for all operators to be optimized at once. In a first step, it is sufficient to select and optimize "basic" operators considered as critical for the performance of the library. Once the most critical operators of the library have been optimized, the remaining of the optimization can carry on incrementally, with the optimization of higher level algorithms as and when they come to be needed in application programs. An interesting approach to provide our linear algebra library with a set of efficient basic operators would be to interface it with the BLAS [LHKK89] kernel. This is actually a possible future extension of the library.

3 Conclusion

In this paper we have described our method for designing an easily extensible object oriented parallel linear algebra library. This design is achieved within EPEE [Jez93], an environment that aims at easing the programming of DMPCs, using powerful object-oriented techniques. An interesting point is that our approach makes it possible to reuse already existing Eiffel sequential classes in a parallel context. It therefore fosters an incremental porting of already existing sequential applications onto DMPCs.

The performances of the parallel linear algebra library should be roughly equivalent to those obtained with a hand-written FORTRAN source code. Since the library is in the process of being ported from Eiffel 2 to Eiffel 3, we cannot exhibit benchmarks of the tests performed with Eiffel 3 yet. Interested readers can nevertheless refer to [GJ93] that presents some of the results we obtained with Eiffel 2.

References

[DPW93] J. Dongarra, R. Pozo, and D. W. Walker. LAPACK++: a design overview of object-oriented extensions for high-performance linear algebra. In *Proceedings of SUPERCOMPUTING'93*, 1993.

[For93] High Performance Fortran Forum. *High Performance Fortran Language Specification.* Technical Report Version 1.0, Rice University, May 1993.

[GJ93] F. Guidec and J.-M. Jézéquel. Numeric parallel programming with sequential object oriented languages. In *Proceedings of the First Annual Object-Oriented Numerics Conference (OONSKI'93)*, pages 55–69, April 1993.

[Jez93] J.-M. Jézéquel. EPEE: an Eiffel environment to program distributed memory parallel computers. *Journal of Object Oriented Programming*, 6(2):48–54, May 1993.

[LHKK89] C. Lawson, R. Hanson, D. Kincaid, and F. Krogh. Basic linear algebra subprograms for Fortran. *ACM Transactions on Math. Software*, 14:308–325, 1989.

[Mey92] Bertrand Meyer. *Eiffel: The Language*. Prentice-Hall, 1992.

Programming Environments for Massively Parallel Distributed Systems, Monte Verità, Switzerland

A Library for Coarse Grain Macro-Pipelining in Distributed Memory Architectures

F. Desprez*

Computer Science Department
The University of Tennessee
107 Ayres Hall, Knoxville
TN 37996-1301, USA

Laboratoire LIP
URA 1398 du CNRS
ENS LYON, 46, Allée d'Italie
69364 LYON Cedex 07, France

1 Introduction

The most natural way of programming parallel machines is data-parallelism where programs execute phases of computations and communications on different sets of data and no overlap exists between communications and computations. Moreover, communication phases are synchronous, i.e. every processor executes these phases at the same time and waits until the last processor completes his communication phase. From the perspective of program correctness, these data-parallel programs are much more easier to prove than asynchronous CSP-based parallel programs [Hoa85]. Unfortunately, performances of such programs are bounded by the communications cost. To avoid this problem, the solution is to overlap communications by computations. This is not always possible because of the dependences within the code. If data dependences prevent the use of simple overlap, a solution consists in using a pipelined data parallel algorithm by decreasing the grain of computations, and overlapping communications of previously computed parts by the computation of next parts of the set of data. This is also called coarse grain macro-pipelining [Kin88, Tse93]. The resulting code is then much more efficient but, unfortunately, much more complicated too. Our aim is thus to provide one set of high level routines which implement pipelined data parallel algorithms in the most transparent way to the user of parallel message passing machines.

The LOCCS library (Low Overhead Communication and Computation Subroutines) has been first presented in [DT93] and subsets are now available for the

*This work was supported in part by the National Science Foundation Science and Technology Center Cooperative Agreement No. CCR-8809615, CNRS-NSF grant 950.223/07, PRC C^3, Archipel SA and MRE under grant 974, and the DRET.

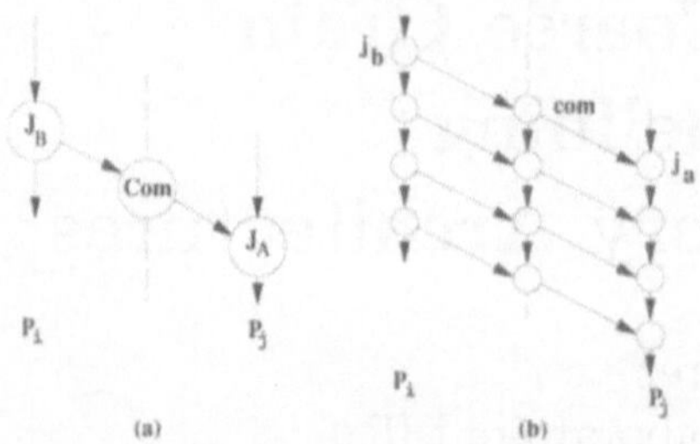

Figure 1: *One dependence graph and the macro-pipeline solution.*

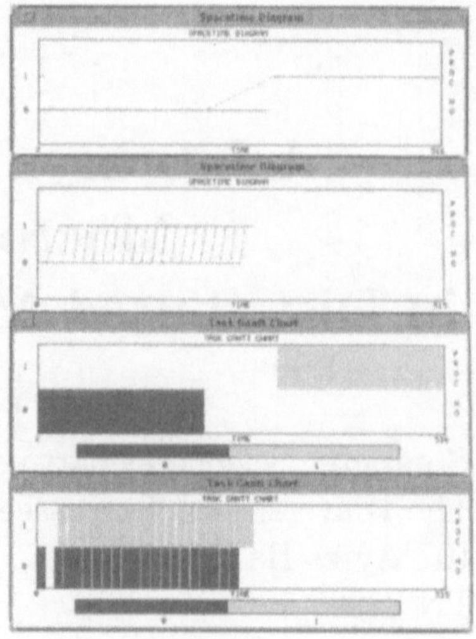

Figure 2: *Execution of a classical macro-pipeline on Intel iPSC/860.*

iPSC/860 and Paragon machines.

The LOCCS library is presented as well as an example of its use. Some experimental results on the iPSC/860 and Paragon machines are then reported and discussed. Finally, we describe the one direct application of macro-pipelining using the LOCCS routines.

2 Statement of the problem and macro-pipelining solution

Because of dependences between computations and between communications and computations, overlap of communications is sometimes difficult to obtain. Consider the dependence graph given on Figure 1a. This is a classical graph for pipelined operations. Processor P_i has to compute J_B before sending the result to processor P_j which in turn executes J_A. Because of the dependences between the computation of J_B, communication and computation of J_A, one may think that no overlap is possible. Using coarse grain pipelining, we are able to solve this problem efficiently. If this is possible, i.e. if no vertical dependences prevent from this operation, a solution consists in decreasing the grain of J_B and sending the results of the small j_b "as soon as possible", i.e. after their computation (Figure 1b). The computation of the next parts of J_B is overlaped by the communication the previously computed ones. One the other side of the macro-pipeline, P_j does exactly the same, breaking J_A in parts (j_a), corresponding to the received data. In such algorithm, we have an overlap of communication and a kind of "load balancing" of computations leading to a more efficient algorithm.

On Alg. 1, initial programs of P_i and P_j are given. D denotes the data which have to be communicated between the two processors after a computation phase on P_i (J_B) and before another computation phase on P_j (J_A). Alg. 2 shows the macro-pipeline version of the program executed by processor P_i.

J_B(D, size_of_D)	receive(D, size_of_D)
send(D, size_of_D, P_j)	J_A(D, size_of_D)

***Alg 1:** Programs of processor P_i and P_j.*

```
jb (0, ν, subblock of D)                           } Initialization
for i=0 to number_of_packets-2
   in // do
      send(subblock i of D, ν, Pj)                 } Normal reg.
      jb (i+1, ν, subblock of D)
   enddo
endfor
send(subblock number_of_packets-1 of D, ν, Pj)     } Termination
```

***Alg 2:** Coarse grain pipelining for processor P_i.*

The trace of the execution of such algorithm on a iPSC/860 with the same tasks before and after the communication is presented on Figure 2 using Paragraph Space Time and Task Gantt views [HE91]. We have a gain of a factor almost equal to 2 that makes the overlap almost optimal. The Gantt views show the tasks and micro-tasks, used in the macro-pipelining execution. The size of the packet ν can be computed theoreticaly and experimentaly. This is the most important factor since it directly affects the performance results. If the number of packets is too large, the cost of the startup times is also too large, leading to poor performance. On the other hand, if the number of packets is too small, the overlap is not complete. Thus, there is an optimal packets size which needs to be carefully determined.

3 The LOCCS library

We have designed and implemented a general library for coarse grain pipelining on different parallel machines. There are 8 routines, corresponding to the classical communication patterns.

For each routine, the communication phase is a call to a non-blocking high-level communication routine on a packet of size ν. This ensures the portability of

Routine	Communication pattern
loccs_oto	One-to-one
loccs_exchange	Exchange between 2 processors
loccs_shift	Shift
loccs_ota	Broadcast
loccs_pota	Scattering
loccs_ato	Gathering
loccs_ata	All-to-all
loccs_pata	Multi-scattering

***Table 1**: LOCCS routines and communication patterns.*

Architecture	Available routines	Environment used
Intel iPSC/860	loccs_oto, loccs_ota, loccs_exchange, loccs_shift	NX/PICL
Intel Paragon	loccs_oto, loccs_ota loccs_exchange, loccs_shift	NX and PVM 3.*
Clusters of workst.	loccs_oto	PVM 3.*

***Table 2**: Different implementations of LOCCS routines.*

the routine. The user, who supplies the code of the tasks, do not have to know the underlying algorithm used for communication.

We now give an example of a routine, `loccs_oto`, which solves the previous problem of a communication between two processors. The two processors involved can have two tasks to perform, one before and one after the communication. A call to the `loccs_oto` routine is realized by:

$$\texttt{loccs\_oto(me, oto, buffer, } \nu\texttt{, size, } job_b\texttt{, } job_a\texttt{)}$$

We have different structures to define environment and buffers. `me` (Id of the caller `loccs_oto`), `oto` (structure giving the id of the two processors), `buffer` (structure for message buffers), ν (packet size), `size` (total size of the message) and job_b, job_a (tasks which will be executed before and after a communication step).

One interest of this library is its portability. We have chosen to implement one subset of the routines on different machines and environments. The first version of the library is written in C but the C++ and Fortran versions are currently under development. Table 2 presents the name of the routines implemented on different machines. For the Intel Paragon, it will be possible to implement the whole set of routines, as soon as we will be able to program the second i860, dedicated to

communications.
We are now going to describe some experiences performed on the Intel iPSC/860 and Paragon machines. The routine tested is `loccs_oto`. The curves obtained give an idea of the executions of the routines of "real" applications and of the computation of the optimal packet size. The tasks use loops of additions and we make them vary to understand the impact of the machine and algorithm parameters on the execution time. On Figure 3, we change the ratio between the two tasks (before and after communication) for the `loccs_oto` on the iPSC/860 and Paragon machine. The total size of computation is 30 units, where one unit is an addition on each element of the current packet. We have executed the routine for the ratios j_b/j_a equal to 10/20, 15/15 and 20/10. For each ratio, we vary the packet size, from one element to the total size of the message. The "hills" on the curves are due to the size of the last packet which size is in the range [1, total size of the message -1]. We can see that the best execution time is obtained with tasks of equal sizes. On the left of the curve, we have only one packet and no overlap. As the packet size decreases, we have more and more overlap until reaching a minimum. After this minimum, the number of packets is too large and we have an extra overhead due to the message latency. The optimal size of packets is always in the same range ([200..500] for a total size of 10000). This size can be computed very accurately using machine parameters and the costs of the different tasks.

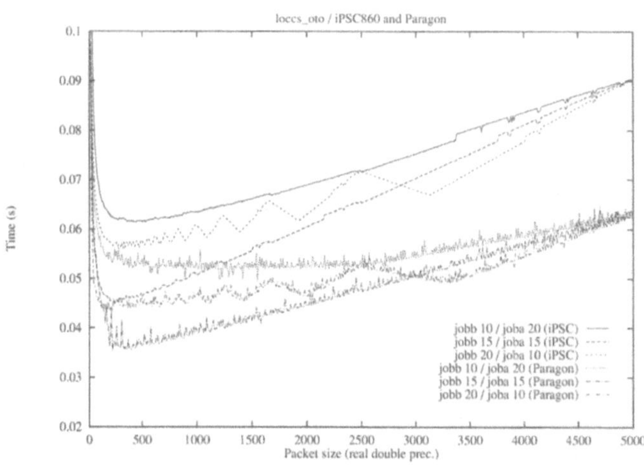

Figure 3: *Some executions of* `loccs_oto` *on Intel iPSC/860 and Paragon machines.*

4 Application example

In this section, we present one example of application of the LOCCS routines, namely the LU factorization of a dense matrix A which transforms this matrix in the product of two triangular matrices L and U, respectively lower (L) and upper (U) triangular. For sake of simplicity, we describe how to improve a row version, described in [GR88]. Although his method does not lead to the bes performances on DMPC, it is one of the simplest to describe. Macro-pipelining methods can also be used with other storages. Alg. 4 presents the classical *broadcast-cube* algorithm on an hypercube.

```
for k=0 to n-1
    root = calc_root(k)
    Determine pivot row
    Update permutation vector
    /* computation part of the algorithm */
    if (me == root) broadcast pivot row
    else receive pivot row
    /* update part of the algorithm */
    for (all rows  i > k that I own)
        l_ik = a_ik / a_k
        for j=k+1 to n-1
            a_ij = a_ij - l_ik * a_kj
        endfor
    endfor
endfor
```

Alg 4: Parallel LU factorization algorithm on hypercube.

The LOCCS routine `loccs_ota` can be directly used for the LU factorization. On Alg. 4, the part of the algorithm corresponding to broadcast of the pivot row and the update of the remaining rows can be replaced by a single call to the `loccs_ota` routine (Alg. 5).

```
for k = 0 to n - 1
    ν = calc_nu_opt(k)
    root = calc_root(k)
    determine pivot row
    update permutation vector
    loccs_ota(me, ota, bufferota, ν, N-j-1, NOJOB, UPDATE)
endfor
```

Alg 5: Parallel LU factorization algorithm using LOCCS routine `loccs_ota`.

Notice that, using this algorithm for he *LU* factorization, there is no j_a. Therefore, `NOJOB` is given as a parameter instead of the routine j_a. `UPDATE` performs the update of all the remaining columns using the received packet of size ν. The resulting code is simpler and more efficient.

5 Conclusion and future work

The use of routines like the LOCCS prevents the developer of a parallel program from the redesign of a complicated pipeline program in order to increase the efficiency. Moreover, the code obtained is much more simpler and efficient. The routines can be optimized for each distributed memory machines and each topology. These routines correspond to the SPMD-like paradigm of execution.

Our current work is to complete the implementation of the set of routines on the Intel Paragon, the ARCHIPEL Volvox IS-860 machines and heterogeneous environment (using PVM) and to propose routines for the computation of ν for some classical algorithms. We investigate the possibility of computing ν during the execution to ensure a better load balance (adaptive ν). Subsets of the routines are available on the two Intel machines. We also study an object oriented interface for this library. The LOCCS routines can also be called by a parallel compiler of FortranD-like programs which knows the parameters of the target machine and the data dependences within the code.

References

[DT93] F. Desprez and B. Tourancheau. LOCCS: Low Overhead Communication and Computation Subroutines. In *High Performance Computing and Networking Conference - Amsterdam.* Elsevier, May 1993.

[GR88] G.A. Geist and C.H. Romine. LU Factorization Algorithms on Distributed Memory Multiprocessor Architectures. *SIAM Journal on Science and Statistical Computing,* 4:639–649, 1988.

[HE91] M.T. Heath and J.A. Etheridge. Visualizing Performances of Parallel Programs. Technical Report ORNL/TM-11813, Oak Ridge National Laboratory, July 1991.

[Hoa85] C.A.R. Hoare. *C.S.P.: Communicating Sequential Processes.* Prentice Hall, 1985.

[Kin88] C.T. King. *Pipelined Data Parallel Algorithm: Concept, Design and Modeling.* PhD thesis, Michigan State University - Department of Computer Science, 1988.

[Tse93] C.W. Tseng. *An Optimizing Fortran D Compiler for MIMD Distributed-Memory Machines.* PhD thesis, Rice University, January 1993.

Notice that using only [illegible] therefore, SOLID is given as a reasonable [illegible] the update of all the [illegible]. The [illegible] is simple and [illegible].

6 Conclusion and future work

The main advantage [illegible] the DOOCS [illegible] the development of a parallel program from the modeling of [illegible] in order to increase the efficiency. Moreover, the [illegible]. The routines can be [illegible] for each [illegible]. These features [illegible] in the SPMD [illegible].

Our current work [illegible] the implementation of [illegible] of routines [illegible] and [illegible] load balancing [illegible] library. The DOOCS [illegible] can also be [illegible] by a [illegible] compiler of [illegible] which [illegible] the data dependencies within the [illegible].

References

[illegible] Elsevier, [illegible] 1993.

[illegible]

Programming Environments for Massively Parallel Distributed Systems, Monte Verità, Switzerland

An Improved Massively Parallel Implementation of Colored Petri-Net Specifications*

François Bréant† breant@masi.ibp.fr

Jean-François Pradat-Peyre‡ peyre@cnam.fr

Abstract

We present a technique to implement massively parallel applications specified by mean of colored Petri-Nets. Such a formalism allows us to concisely describe parallel applications in an architecture independent way. Furthermore, theoretical results issued from this formalism contribute to prove the correctness of a description before its implementation. As colored nets do not impose any process structure, an efficient implementation has to look for structures close to the programming language concepts. We use linear invariants to decompose the model into interacting state machines and to find the mapping solutions of a decomposition on a scalable architecture. We present in this paper an extension of our method that differentiates state machine components and communication flows in a decomposition. Emphasis given to communications leads to an efficient massively parallel implementation.

1 Introduction

Programming of parallel architectures raises many difficult problems from correctness of a specification to its efficient implementation on an arbitrary number of processors. Moreover, diversity of architectures, processors and interconnection networks incites to improve the independence of program about the target architecture. Our contribution consists in developing methods and tools to obtain efficient parallel programs from a formal specification independent of any architecture.

Implementation from validated formal specification appears as the only solution to realize fair parallel programs involving complex communications and syn-

*This work has been supported by the Indo-French Centre for the Promotion of Advanced Research (IFCPAR), Project 302-1

†MASI Laboratory CNRS AU 818, University of Paris 6, 4 Place Jussieu 75252 Paris Cedex 05, France

‡CEDRIC Laboratory, Conservatoire National des Arts et Metiers, 292 rue Saint Martin 75141 Paris Cedex 03

chronizations. Colored Petri nets are well suited for modeling communicating and synchronizing tasks. Their theoretical fundaments allow us to obtain formal proof of behavioral properties [Mur90, Jen81, CHP91, MV86]. Formal validation results (invariant computation, reductions, ...) combined with simulation tools provide a powerful help in debugging the algorithm before the implementation. Moreover, their generic aspect fit specific needs of massively parallel problem specification: local communications, global synchronizations, regular structures, thin grain.

Nevertheless, a high level description provided by a colored net is too difficult to implement straight and efficiently. Furthermore, we aim to obtain a real implementation rather than a classical simulation [BEM90, CSV86].

To achieve this, we have defined a method that decomposes the colored net into a set of interacting components easily translatable into a programming language based on CSP concepts [Hoa85]. Moreover, these components and their mapping are automatically deduced from parametrized invariant computation [BP93]. Such approach allows us to implement efficiently parallel programs on scalable architectures.

Now, this method emphasizes state machine structures to the detriment of the communication structures. We present in this paper an extension of our method that differentiates communication and computation components in a decomposition. New decompositions obtained provide an accurate description of data flows. We define an invariant class that characterize data-flows. Due to the emphasis given to communication characterization, this new method particularly fits massively parallel processing needs.

In section 2, we recall background about colored nets and linear invariants. In section 3, we present briefly the different steps involved in our method and the decomposition by mean of interacting state machines. In section 4, we define invariants that characterize communication structures between state machines. Section 5 presents the new decomposition .

2 Colored Nets and linear invariants

We present briefly some basic definitions of colored Petri-Nets.

Definition 2.1 : *A colored net is a 6-tuple* $< P, T, C, W^+, W^-, M_0 >$ *where* P *is the set of places,* T *the set of transitions,* C *a mapping from* $P \cup T$ *to a set of non empty sets that associates to each place and each transition a color domain,* W^+ *(resp.* W^-*) the forward (resp. backwrad) incidence matrix that associates to each couple* p, t *a mapping from* $Bag(C(p))$ *to* $Bag(C(t))$ [1] *and* M_0 *a marking, a mapping from* P *to* $\cup Bag(C(p))$ *that associates to each place a positive number of colored tokens, with color values in* $C(p)$.

Given a transition t *and a color* $c_t \in C(t)$, t *is fireable from a marking* M *and reaches the marking* M' *defined by* $\forall p \in P, \forall c_p \in C(p), M'(p)(c_p) = M(p)(c_p) -$

[1] if A is a non empty set, then $Bag(A)$ denotes the set of multi-sets over A

$W^-(p,t)(c)(c_p) + W^+(p,t)(c)(c_p)$ *if and only if:* $\forall p \in P, \forall c_p \in C(p), M(p)(c_p) \geq W^-(p,t)(c)(c_p)$.

Color functions are composition of the following basic color functions defined on classes: the identity function (X), the successor function ($X + 1$), and the diffusion function (S), a mapping that associates to a color the set of colors defined upon the class.

To each colored Petri-Net corresponds an incidence matrix $W = W^+ - W^-$ that characterizes transition firing effect (or incidence) on marking. Non negative solutions of $W.X = 0$ constitute a set of invariants called positive-flows. These invariants define subsets of non null weighted places called *Support* of the invariant.

Definition 2.2 : *A positive flow on a color domain D is a vector of places $\mathcal{F} = \sum_{p \in P} f_p.p$ such that $\forall p \in P$, f_p is a mapping from $Bag(C(t))$ to $Bag(D)$ with $\forall t \in T, \sum_{p \in P} f_p \circ W(p,t) = 0_{Bag(C(t)) \to Bag(D)}$*

These flows can be computed by linear programming techniques [CHP91].

3 Implementation by mean of state machines

This section briefly presents the global method and describes the state machines characterisation.

3.1 Overview of the method

One major drawback of specifications involving high level formalism is their difficulty of implementation. It is necessary to structure the model and then, to progressively add new information before obtaining an efficient code generation.

The method presented in this paper involves three main steps. First, the model is decomposed into interacting components. Components interact using *asynchronous interaction* (buffer places) or *synchronous interaction* (shared transitions). Parametrized color sets issued from the colored net provide a generic mapping that does not depend on the size of the problem modelled. As several decompositions may exist for a model, heuristics contribute to determine an efficient one. For instance, a decomposition heuristic may favour rendezvous mechanism rather than asynchronous communication. This step is independent of the target architecture.

Then, when necessary, abstract synchronizations are refined to take in account communication feature of the real architecture [BP93]. This step remains independent of the size of the problem and the architecture. At last, code is generated after having set size parameter values.

The decomposition involves state machine notion, which has two main advantages. First, state machines are easily characterized by algebraic methods such as invariant computation. Second, their implementation involves the widely used sequential process and thread notions.

3.2 State machines characterization

A state machine is a colored subnet, which places model states and transitions constitute the set of actions. Each transition has only one output state place and one input state place. A state is a couple (p, c), where p is a place and c is the color of a token contained in this place. A state machine is instantiated for each token contained in all its state places.

We define the *type 1* linear invariant involved in the current generic decomposition. These invariants are automatically computed on an ordered net [CHP91, CH88]. Colored tokens carried by *type 1* invariants are used to specify a static mapping of each state machine instance.

Definition 3.1 : *Let $\mathcal{F} = \sum_{p \in P} f_p.p$ be a positive flow on D and M a sub domain of D. Then $\mathcal{F}$ is an invariant of type 1 on M if: $\forall p \in P, f_p$ restricted to M is an identity function.*

One can prove that a state machine is structurally characterized by a *type 1* invariant. So, a systematic calculus of invariants allows us to detect all state machine structures.

Type 1 invariants also characterize extended state machines. Such component may contain multiple instances of non-cyclic nested blocks that corresponds to the threads notion.

4 Data flow characterization and interactions

We distinguish two kinds of interactions between components. According firing rules on colored nets, transitions shared between several components define *synchronous interactions* or multi-rendezvous. In the same way, places connected between several components defines simple *asynchronous interactions* [BP93]. Dataflow invariants allow us to include in a decomposition more complex interactions between components. We define *type 2* invariants that characterize asynchronous interactions between components.

Definition 4.1 : *Let $\mathcal{F} = \sum_{p \in P} f_p.p$ be a positive flow on D and M a sub domain of D. Then $\mathcal{F}$ is an invariant of type 2 on M if $\forall p \in P, f_p$ restricted to M is an additive composition of either the identity, diffusion or successor functions.*

A *type 2* invariant defines simple asynchronous interactions modelled by one place, as well as complex interactions involving several places and transitions. Such invariant characterizes a single place (Figure 1.a), data diffusion (Figure 1.b), or

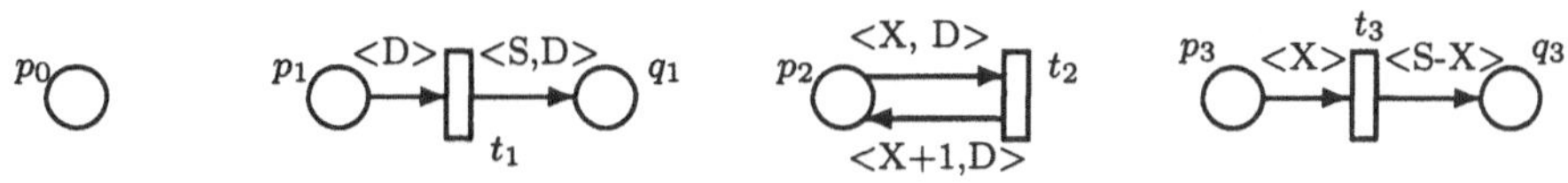

$F = X.P_0$ (a)

$F = S_D.P_1 + < X, S_D > .Q_1$ (b)

$F = < S, S_D > .P_2$ (c)

$F = < S - X > .P_3 + X.Q_3$ (d)

Figure 1: *Some data flow invariants.*

more complex mechanisms like point to point diffusion (Figure 1.c) or a service request to all other instances (Figure 1.d).

Once data-flow invariants are characterized, they can be instantiated and mapped on a topology as well as components. For instance, a decentralized implementation of place p_0 where each instance of p_0 is mapped on different processor will be much more efficient than a centralized one, which has to manage all tokens.

5 Improved decomposition

Our new decomposition method involves two steps. First, the colored net is decomposed into interacting components using *type 1* invariants. Components sharing common transitions are linked by *synchronous interactions*. Simple *asynchronous interactions* consisting of single shared places are also detected [BP93].

Then, once a mapping solution has been determined, we apply a decomposition using invariants *type 2* on the colored net without component subnets. This second step builds the set of possible data flow structures for a given component decomposition and mapping.

Some data flow invariants may characterize abstract structures (Figure 1.b). At this stage, we can apply refinements onto the model that give a more detailed description to fit better architecture features. For instance, data diffusion (Figure 1.b) on a point to point architecture can be refined with a model based on the use of successor function (Figure 1.c).

6 Conclusion

We have shown in this paper how the use of recent results on colored Petri-Nets allow to extend implementation techniques for massively parallel code generation. Modeling using colors to specify mapping increases the code scalability. As the program is automatically obtained from the decomposition of the colored Petri-Net, previous validation of the model ensures fairness of its implementation. Colored invariants allow to distinguish a subset of color classes to map data and computations. From a colored model, we can then propose a set of state machine decomposition and several mapping solutions for each of them. Characterization of data flow using colored invariants improves decomposition and provides accurate information for the code generation step. An important part of our method is independent of the language and architecture. The last steps take advantage of language and hardware characteristics.

We are now studying application of our method on colored nets obtained after translation from a high level language like Ada. Our method would then contribute to improve the parallel implementation of programs which source code remains independent of the architecture.

References

[BEM90] B. Bütler, R. Esser, and R. Mattmann. A distributed simulator for high order petri nets. In *Advances in Petri nets*, Lecture Notes in Computer Science. Springer Verlag, 1990.

[BP93] F. Bréant and J.F. Peyre. Occam prototyping of massively parallel applications from colored petri-nets. In *7th International Parallel Processing Symposium*, pages 842–848. IEEE Computer Society Press, April 1993.

[CH88] J.M. Couvreur and S. Haddad. Towards a general and powerful computation of flows for parametrized coloured nets. In *9th European Workshop on Application and Theory of Petri Nets*, volume II, Venice (Italy), June 1988.

[CHP91] J.M. Couvreur, S. Haddad, and J.F. Peyre. Computation of generative families of semi-flows in two types of colored net. In *proc of the 12th International Conference on Application and Theory of Petri-Net*, Aarhus, Denmark, June 1991.

[CSV86] J.M. Colom, M. Silva, and J.L. Villarroel. On software implementation of petri nets and coloured petri nets using high-level concurrent languages. In *7th Workshop on Application and Theory of Petri nets*, Oxford, June 1986.

[Hoa85] C.A.R. Hoare. *Communicating Sequential Processes.* Prentice-Hall, 1985.

[Jen81] K. Jensen. Coloured petri nets and the invariant method. In *T.C.S.*, volume 14, pages 317–336, 1981.

[Mur90] T. Murata. Petri nets: properties, analysis and applications. In *proceedings of the IEEE Vol 6*, number 1, pages 39–50, January 1990.

[MV86] G. Memmi and J. Vautherin. Analysing nets by the invariant method. In *Petri Nets: Central Model and their Properties*, Lecture Notes in Computer Science. Springer Verlag, 1986.

Programming Environments for Massively Parallel Distributed Systems, Monte Verità, Switzerland

A Tool for Parallel System Configuration and Program Mapping based on Genetic Algorithms *

F. Baiardi D. Ciuffolini A. M. Lomartire D. Montanari
G. Pesce

Abstract

A programming tool based on genetic algorithms aimed at the solution of the mapping problem is discussed. The tool is driven by two genetic algorithms, one of them being involved in the fitness evaluation of the other. Due to the large computational cost of this strategy, a parallel implementation has been devised. A first set of results is presented.

1 Introduction

A mapping of a program defines which processing element, PE, executes a component of the application and the implementation of the communications among components [8]. In the P3M virtual machine [1] for general purpose massively parallel systems, the mapping problem is solved in two steps:

- a configuration that partitions the PEs into two subsets, the processing and the data set, devoted to, respectively, process execution and implementation of nonlocal communications;
- the mapping of the application components onto the processing nodes.

We describe how genetic algorithms, GAs, [5] can be used to define a programming tool that configures a massively parallel system and maps a parallel program on this configuration.

With respect to previous works on GA for program mapping [2, 4, 7], we exploit a hybrid, nested approach, where two GAs and task related heuristics cooperate to solve the complete problem (configuration and mapping).

*Supported by CNR, PFI, Sottoprogetto "Architetture Parallele". F. Baiardi, D. Ciuffolini and A. M. Lomartire are with the Dip. di Informatica, Università di Pisa, Pisa, Italy. D. Montanari is with Tema Spa, Bologna, Italy. G. Pesce is with the Dip. di Ing. Informatica, Università di Tor Vergata, Roma, Italy

This work is organized as follows. Sect. 2 describes the P3M abstract machine and the concept of system configuration and program mapping. Sect.3 outlines our solution based on nested, hybrid GAs. By nested we mean that the fitness of each chromosome of the "outer" GA is computed by another, the "inner", GA. The hybrid features exploits knowledge about the optimal solution. Sect.3 describes the fitness functions of the GAs. A parallel implementation is outlined in Sect. 4 and a first set of results is presented in Sect. 5.

We assume a basic knowledge of the major GA-related concepts [3, 5].

2 System Configuration and Program Mapping

To explain the adoption of a configuration step, we briefly describe the P3M virtual machine [1]. For the sake of simplicity, we assume that applications are developed through message passing languages. We denote by PG the weighted, undirected, graph describing an application. Each node n of PG corresponds to a process P(n) and it is connected to a node m if P(n) and P(m) communicates. Each node n is associated with a weight that estimates the computational load of P(n). The weigth assoicated with an arc (n, m) estimates the amount of data exchanged between P(n) and P(m). We assume that PG thruthfully describes the computation [8]. SG is the undirected graph describing the interconnection structure among the PEs.

While one of the goal of any mapping strategy is to maximise the number of arcs of SG mapped onto one arc of SG, if some arcs of PG cannot be mapped onto one arc of SG, the corresponding communications are emulated through message routing functionalites that exploit the same links used for local communications. To avoid this interference, that can severely degrade the overall performance, P3M configures two interconnection networks at the software level according to the program to be executed.

In P3M, a configuration partitions the PEs into two sets, the processing set PS and the data set DS. The PEs in the PS, processing nodes, execute the processes of the program, those in the DS, data nodes, support nonlocal communications. In turn, the DS can be partitioned into data subsets DS1, ..., DSk as follows: two nodes belongs to the same data subset iff they are connected by a path that crosses nodes in that data subset only. This corresponds to the introduction of a direct interconnection network for local communications, including all the links between two nodes in the PS, and of an indirect one, for non local communications, including all the other links and the PEs in the DS.

To precisely define the conditions to avoid any interference, we define the concept of legal mapping onto a configuration and consider the graph C(SG), that is produced starting from SG and from a configuration (PS, DS = {DS1, ..., DSk}) of SG. Any node c of C(SG) corresponds to a node Q(c) in the PS, two nodes c1 and c2 of C(SG) are connected if Q(c1) is connected to Q(c2) or if both Q(N) and Q(M) are connected to nodes of the same data subset.

A mapping of PG onto C(SG) is legal if it is not a dilation, i.e. after the

mapping distance among processes are not increased. This implies that two connected nodes of PG are mapped either onto the same node c of C(SG) or onto two connected nodes, c1 and c2, of C(SG). If a mapping is legal, any communication can be implemented through only one of the followings
a) the local memory of a processing node;
b) the link between two processing nodes;
c) the PEs in one data subset.

3 The Programming Tool

The inputs of the tool are the graphs PG and SG.

The first, or "outer", GA, searches for an efficient configuration of SG. Its population consists of alternative configurations of SG. If the system includes n PEs, each chromosome is codified as a string of n bits, each codifing an allele. The j-th allele specifies whether the j-th PE belongs to the PS or to the DS. Since any string of n bits is a chromosome that represents a configuration C(SG),this GA can operate at the bit level on chromosomes of a population to produce the next one.

The fitness of a configuration C(SG) is evaluated by another GA, the "inner" GA. Each chromosome considered by this GA codes a mapping m of PG onto C(SG) and its fitness is F(m, PG, C(SG)). This GA computes O(C(SG), PG), the mapping that minimizes F(m, PG, C(SG)). The fitness of C(SG) is F(O(C(SG), PG), PG, C(SG)).

Lack of space prevents a detailed description of how a chromosome codes a mapping. The important point is that a chromosome represents a mapping of spanning tree ST(PG) of PG. All the arcs of ST(PG) are mapped with no dilation. The arcs of PG not belonging to ST(PG) may be dilated. However, since the domain is highly ephistatic [4], even if we assume that any chromosome represents a legal mapping, it is quite complex to define a set of genetic operators that always return chromosomes representing legal mappings only. We have preferred to allow the population to include chromosomes that represents a dilation and the GA operators to work at the bit level. This increases the search space but, as a counterpart, it simplifies the generation of a population.
To allow the GA to deduce information to drive the search even from dilations, the fitness F(m, PG, C(SG)) is defined so that its value for a legal mapping is always lower than the value for a dilation and its value for a dilation is proportional to the number of dilated arcs [5].

3.1 Hybrid Features

If a datasubset is not exploited by Mo(C(SG), PG), then a better resource utilization should be attempted by transforming its nodes into processing nodes. Even if the outer GA can perform the same change through mutation and/or crossover,to improve efficiency we recognize explicitly such an occurrence and act on it directly [3, 4, 6]. Whenever this event occurs, the corresponding bits in the configuration string of C(SG) are changed and the string representing the new configuration C'(SG) is evaluated again. Since each legal mapping of PG onto C(SG) is also a legal mapping of PG onto C'(SG), the initial population to determine Mo(C'(SG), PG) is the final one of the search for Mo(C(SG), PG). This reuses, at least partially, previous work to improve the quality of the solution.

3.2 Fitness of a Mapping

The inputs of fitness function F used by the inner GA are: a program graph p, a configuration C(SG) and a mapping m of PG onto C(SG)

If m is a dilation, F(m, p, C(SG)) is equal to 100 plus the number of arcs of PG that are dilated, i.e. not mapped onto one arc of C(SG).

If m is a legal mapping, F(m, p, C(SG)) describes the various overheads due to m through a linear combination of eight functions, one for each distinct source of overhead:

$$F(m, p, C(SG)) = \sum (j = 1..8) Wj * Fj(m, p, C(SG))$$

The range of each function is 1..100. Each Wj,$0 \leq$ Wj≤ 1, j= 1.. 8, evaluates the relative influence of the corresponding overhead. The following sources of overhead are considered.

- *low utilisation of the processing sets*

F1(m, p, C(SG)) returns 100 if m does not use some nodes of C(SG) and 0 otherwise.

- *low degree of excess parallelism [8]*

An optimal mapping allocates several processes onto a processing node n connected to a data subset DSj. This allows n to execute other processes while one is suspended due to a non local communication. The optimal degree of multiplexing of n is assumed to be proportional to the number of arcs that are both connected to nodes of PG mapped onto n and mapped onto DSj. F2(m, p, C(SG)) returns an overhead proportional to the average difference between this estimate and the number of nodes of p assigned to a processing node connected to a data subset.

- *unbalanced computational load.*

The overhead computed by F3(m, p, C(SG) is proportional to the standard deviation of the computational loads assigned by m to each node of C(SG).

- *low utilisation of program locality*

The overhead computed by F4(m, p, C(SG)) is proportional to the percentage of arcs of p that have been mapped onto a data subset.

- *low parallelism.*

The overhead computed by F5(m, p, C(SG)) is proportional to the number of pair of unconnected nodes of p mapped either onto the same or onto directly connected nodes of C(SG).

- *bad allocation of heaviest communications.*

F6(m, p, C(SG)) takes into account that the heaviest arcs of m should be mapped onto direct connections between two processing nodes. The overhead is proportional to the number of heavy arc of p mapped onto a data subset. Heavy arcs are those whose weight is more than twice the average weight of the arcs of p.

- *unbalanced load on the links.*

If too many arcs of PG are mapped onto the same connection between two processing nodes, conflicts among the corresponding communications slow down the execution. F7(m,p, C(SG)) computes an overhead proportional to the standard deviation among the loads assigned by m to the links between two processing nodes.

- *unbalanced load on the data sets.*

The load imposed on a data set should be balanced among the links to/from the processing nodes from/to that data subset. F8(m, p, C(SG)) computes an overhead proportional to the average overhead of the data subsets. For one subset, the overhead is proportional to the standard deviation of the loads on the links from/to the processing nodes.

4 The Parallel Implementation

Our implementation has been developed for a Meiko Computing Surface where each PE includes a Inmos T800 and one Mbyte of memory. A process MP implements the outer GA an all the other processes, S1, ..., Sn are slaves of MP. Each Si implements the inner GA to compute O(C, PG). After generating a new population of configurations, MP sends a distint configuration to each Si. When MP receives from any Si the fitness of a configuration, it transmits another configuration to Si. After evaluating the current population, MP generates a new population and so on.

A message from MP to a slave codes a configuration, a reply from a slave includes a configuration C, its fitness, and the mapping O(C, PG) corresponding to that fitness. C is included because of the hybrid operator introduced in Sect. 3.2. As a matter of fact, if O(C(SG), PG) does not exploit some data subset, then the slave that has computed O(C(SG), PG) produces C'(SG) and then uses the previous final population to start the search for O(C'(SG), PG).

Both GAs copy a chromosome in the new population a number of times proportional to its relative fitness. Two point crossover and mutation are applied to the new population by working at the bit level.

5 Experimental Results

To tune the various control parameters of the GAs, first experiments have been focused on a 4 x 4 torus of PEs and on isotropic program graphs where the same weight is associated with each arc and each node. In these case the optimal configuration and mapping can be easily determined. The best results have been obtained if the outer GA has a population of 200 chromosomes, a crossover rate of 64% and a mutation rate of 0.1%. The inner GA has a population of 200 chromosomes, a crossover rate of 56% and a mutation rate of 0.1%. Convergence of the outer GA is achieved when 2000 chromosomes have been evaluated. The inner GA converges after the evaluation of 3000 chromosomes.

The following vales are used for the weights of F(m, p, C(SG)): W1=0.44, W2=0.15, W3=0.11, W4=0.1, W5=0.09, W6=0.05, W7=0.04, W8=0.02.

Current experiments consider a system with 64 PEs. The program graphs include from 90 to 100 nodes and differ in the number of arcs of PG not belonging to ST(PG). In these experiments, the optimal configuration and a nearly optimal mapping have been produced. The execution time is strongly dependant on the number of arcs of PG not represented by ST(PG). If the number of slaves is in the range [2..32], the speed up is linear in the number of slaves. The time to compute the various solutions ranges from one to three hours. The hybrid operator is fundamental to speed up the convergence.

References

[1] F.Baiardi, M.Jazayeri, P3M: A Virtual Machine to Support Massively Parallel Computations. Int. Conf. On Parallel Processing, 1993, pp.340-344.

[2] P. Bessière, E.G. Talbi. A Parallel Genetic Algorithm Applied to the Mapping Problem, Siam News, 1991.

[3] L.Davis, Genetic Algorithms and Simulating Annealing. Morgan Kauffmann, Los Altos, CA 1987.

[4] G. C. Fox and N. Mansour. A Hybrid Genetic Algorithm for Task Allocation in Multicomputers, Proc. of Int. Conf. on Genetic Algorithms, 1991.

[5] D. E. Goldberg. Genetic Algorithms in Search, Optimization and Machine Learning, Addison-Wesley, 1989.

[6] J. J. Grefenstette. Incorporating Problem Specific Knowledge into Genetic Algorithms, in L. Davis ed., Genetic Algorithms and Simulated Annealing, Morgan Kaufmann, 1987.

[7] M. R. Leuze, C. C. Pettey, Parallel Placement of Parallel Processes, Proc. 3th Conference Hypercube Concurrent Computers and Applications, 1988.

[8] M.G. Norman, P. Tanish Models of Machines and Computations for Mapping in Multicomputers, ACM Computing Surveys, vol.5, n.3, pp263-302.

Programming Environments for Massively Parallel Distributed Systems, Monte Verità, Switzerland

Emulating a Paragon XP/S on a Network of Workstations

Georg Stellner, Arndt Bode,
Stefan Lamberts and Thomas Ludwig*
Technische Universität München
Institut für Informatik
Lehrstuhl für Rechnertechnik und Rechnerorganisation
D-80290 München
stellner@informatik.tu-muenchen.de

Abstract

Networks of workstations are gaining growing importance in high performance computing. Programming environments like MMK/X [Ste93] or PVM [BDG+91] allow for exploiting the aggregate computational power of coupled workstations. A different approach is to use such local area networks as a development platform for parallel applications which should finally run on multicomputer systems. Therefore an environment on the workstations is required which offers the same programming model as the multicomputer system. The work which is presented here describes the NXLib environment which emulates a Paragon system on a network of workstations.

1 Motivation

In the field of high performance computing multicomputer systems are currently becoming more popular. Mainly due to their better price performance ratio compared to classical supercomputers they are often preferred if a new high performance system should be bought. A decisive drawback of multicomputer systems is the enormous effort which is often required to port existing applications onto these systems. Applications have to be parallelized which leads to frequent test runs producing much additional workload. To withdraw some of this load an environment is needed which allows the implementation of applications for multicomputers on different hardware platforms.

Today, typical environments in universities and companies consist of several workstations all interconnected via Ethernet. The architectural principle behind

*This project was partially funded by a research grant from the Intel Foundation.

multicomputers and coupled workstations is basically the same: independent processing elements with local memory which are interconnected. In difference to the multicomputers' dedicated high performance interconnection network, workstations use a slower interconnect, which has to be shared with other users.

State-of-the-art multicomputer systems like the Paragon currently offer a proprietary message-passing environment. An implementation of that library on coupled workstations would allow for using them as a development platform for applications where the production code should finally run on a multicomputer system.

In the following we will describe the design and implementation of the Paragon communication library for workstations which are interconnected via Ethernet. Therefore we first give a short description of the Paragon and its software environment. Then, we introduce the design of the NXLib package. After that, we provide some performance figures and present a concluding summary in the last chapter.

2 Paragon Multicomputer Systems

The nodes of a Paragon system are interconnected in a two-dimensional mesh topology, which is subdivided into three partitions: the I/O partition, the service partition and the compute partition. Usually the largest partition in a configuration is the compute partition. Parallel user applications are executed on the nodes in this partition and use the Paragon NX library. Apart from synchronous, asynchronous and interrupt-driven communication calls, it provides calls for process management. A more detailed description of the Paragon can be found in [LSBL93]. In contrast to that, interactive processes are executed on the nodes in the service partition. Finally, the nodes in the I/O partition are used to connect I/O devices.

3 Design of NXLib

In the following sections the design of NXLib is introduced. A more detailed presentation can be found in [SLBL93] or [EK93].

3.1 Virtualization of Paragon nodes

A parallel application on a Paragon system consists of two parts. The application processes on the compute partition and the controlling process on one node of the service partition. In the following discussion the term *Paragon node* (PN) will be referred to as the collection of a hardware node, the operating system kernel and a set of application processes running on top of that.

The basic means to model PNs on coupled workstations is virtualization. Consequently, the term *virtual Paragon node* (VPN) describes a PN on a workstation. The hard- and software properties of a PN which are not available on a workstation are virtualized in the following way. A natural approach to model them is to introduce a daemon process which emulates the node hardware and the operating system. The calls of the application processes to NX communication routines are transformed into requests to the daemon.

In such an implementation every system call would require an interprocess communication. To reduce the amount of interprocess communication parts of the operating system's tasks have been moved into the application processes like illustrated in fig. 1.

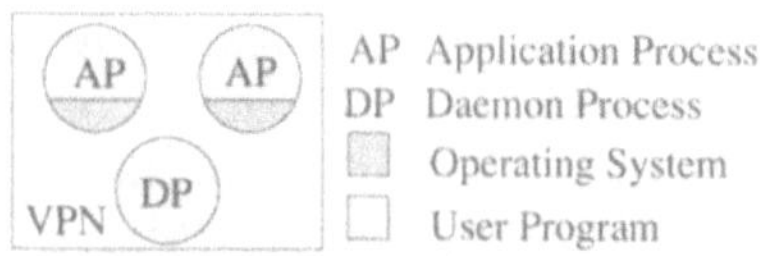

Figure 1: *Processes and the distribution of the operating system on a VPN*

3.2 Modeling Paragon partitions

In addition to the partitions which were introduced before it is also possible to define sub-partitions of the compute partition. In a workstation environment mapping files can be used to emulate such partitions. Within that file a mapping of virtual node numbers to workstations is provided. Thus, the mapping table defines a *virtual compute partition* on a workstation net.

A problem occurs for the service partition. It is not part of the Paragon partition management which is available for the user. Consequently a different means has to be provided to establish a *virtual service partition*. This is simply done by defining the machine where the application has been started as the *virtual service partition*.

3.3 NX message passing calls on workstations

An important issue for message passing libraries is the performance of the communication calls. Both local and remote communication use TCP sockets because this protocol achieves high throughput rates. To reduce the latency it is desirable to use direct paths between communication partners. Every stage in an indirect scheme increases the latency as additional calls have to be performed. On the other hand, on most UNIX systems the number of socket descriptors is limited. A full interconnection of all application processes would therefore drastically reduce the number of participating processes. Establishing and terminating a communication link between two processes for every communication call is not reasonable either as this would introduce much additional effort for every communication.

The basic assumption of our implementation is that typical parallel applications have a regular communication structure in the sense that certain processes regularly communicate with each other. Thus, two processes are either connected and use this link frequently during the computation or they do not communicate at all. Consequently, links need only to be created for those processes that wish to communicate. As the communication structure of an application can not be determined at start time, the interconnection of the processes can certainly not be done during the initialization of the application. So the links between processes are set up on demand during run time. Once established, a connection between two processes is kept until the application terminates. Building up the connections on demand has the advantage that all interacting processes are fully interconnected. So communication latencies can be kept minimal for established links. Finally, as only those processes are interconnected which need to communicate more processes can participate in an application. The only drawback is that the first communication between two processes is more time consuming than the following because the connection has to be set up.

4 Performance Measurements

All results presented in this section were produced either on a Paragon system running OSF/1, version 1.0.3 or on Sun Sparc 10/30 with SunOS 4.1.1, which were the most powerful machines at our disposal. As we only had access to four Sparc 10 we used a four node partition on the Paragon to achieve comparable results. Computations on more machines including some slower Sun SLCs made obvious that the performance is driven by the slowest machine in the configuration. Basically a single PN can achieve a floating point performance which is up to three times better than a single Sparc 10.

4.1 Communication speed, latencies and bandwidth

In order to get a first overview on the communication speed, latency and bandwidth that can be achieved by NXLib calls a simple pingpong measurement has been done (fig. 2).

For messages larger than 1416 Bytes a linear increase of transmission times can be observed with linear increasing message size and remote transfers are slower than local communications. For smaller messages the results are surprising for two reasons. First of all, local transfers need twice the time of remote transfers and second, the transmission times are nearly constant. An explanation for both effects is the buffering mechanism which is used in the TCP protocol implementation for the Sun machines. IP packets which are smaller than the Ethernet packet size of 1514 Bytes are buffered and sent after a timeout of 0.1s. Thus, for messages smaller than the Ethernet packet size the transmission time is nearly constant. For local message exchanges this timeout obviously applies twice: once for the send and once for the receive operation.

The latency and bandwidth values which can be derived from the pingpong

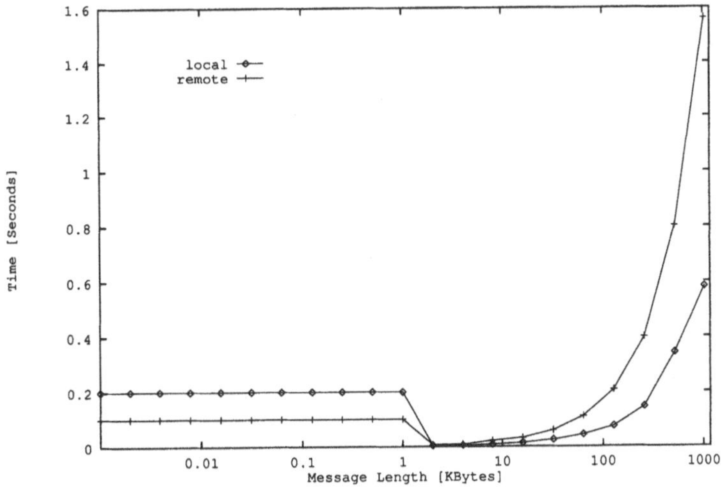

Figure 2: *Local and remote transmission times of messages*

	Latency (0)	Latency (2048)	avg. Bandwidth	max. Bandwidth
local	0.2s	4.17ms	590.2KBytes/s	1761.9KBytes/s
remote	0.1s	6.78ms	242.3KBytes/s	656.1KBytes/s

Table 1: *Latency and bandwidth values of NXLib communication calls*

measurement are summarized in tab. 1. The low average bandwidth values can be explained by the exponential increasing messages sizes which were used for the pingpong measurement. A lot of small messages were used to show the effect of buffering. Small messages on the other hand achieve bad bandwidth values which also leads to bad average values.

4.2 Applications using NXLib

To evaluate the NXLib environment we have used two applications which we have running on Paragon systems: NSFLEX [MMW+93] and MUMUS [SKM93]. In both cases only minor changes to the makefiles were necessary to compile and link the source code. After the compilation the applications can be started like on a Paragon by specifying the name of the executable at a shell prompt. To select a virtual partition the same command line switch like on a Paragon can be used. Instead of the partition name the mapping file has to be specified. In a similar way the number of processes which should be created during the start up can be defined with the appropriate Paragon command line switch.

For each application the same problem was solved on the two different hardware platforms. The computation times which were necessary to solve the given problems on each architecture are summarized in tab. 2.

	MUMUS	NSFLEX
Paragon	13s	3040s
NXLib	24s	8257s

Table 2: *Execution times of MUMUS and NSFLEX on different platforms*

For NSFLEX the Paragon is nearly three times as fast as the workstations. For the computation of the given problem with MUMUS the workstations need about twice the time as the Paragon. Taken into consideration the performance of applications on coupled workstations, using NXLib seems very promising. These results have to be verified on larger clusters and more powerful machines than the Sparc 10.

5 Conclusion and Future Work

The NXLib environment supports using a network of workstations for two main purposes. First, the network of workstations can be used to develop software which should finally run on a Paragon system. Workload can therefore be withdrawn from the multicomputer system. The CPU time which is gained by shifting the development of applications to workstations can be used for production runs of computational intensive problems. Second, instead of using the workstations merely as a development platform they can also be used as a production environment for certain applications. Especially coarse grain applications can achieve good speed-ups on a workstation environment.

NXLib basically offers the same software environment as a Paragon system. Virtualization is the basic means to achieve this. Therefore, source code which has been implemented using NXLib can be ported to a Paragon without any changes.

An important issue for scientific and commercial applications is the support of parallel I/O. Due to the restricted network bandwidth of bus coupled workstations it is not feasible to use a single disk as I/O facility. A more interesting approach would be to use the local disks of the workstations and to set up a virtual Paragon file system on these disks. Concepts for disk and file stripping in such an environment must be examined therefore.

Up to now there is no support for the programmer during the implementation process of an application. Efficient coding is an important issue for software projects. Thus, the support of a tool environment which assists the programmer during all steps in the software life cycle is very desirable. Tools which can be used to visualize or debug parallel applications require the possibility to gather run-time information. This can either be done on-line with a monitoring system or off-line through trace files. In both cases an instrumentation of NXLib is necessary to produce the data.

References

[BDG+91] A. Beguelin, J. Dongarra, A. Geist, R. Manchek, and V. Sunderam. Opening the Door to Heterogeneous Network Supercomputing. *Supercomputing Review*, pages 44–45, September 1991.

[EK93] R. Esser and R. Knecht. Intel Paragon XP/S - Architecture and Software Environment. Technical Report KFA-ZAM-IB-9305, Forschungszentrum Jülich GmbH, Zentralinstitut für An gewandte Mathematik, D-52425 Jülich, April 1993.

[LSBL93] Stefan Lamberts, Georg Stellner, Arndt Bode, and Thomas Ludwig. Paragon parallel programming environment on sun workstations. In *Sun User Group Proceedings* [Sun93], pages 87–98.

[MMW+93] T. Michl, S. Maier, S. Wagner, M. Lenke, and A. Bode. Dataparallel Navier-Stokes Solutions on Different Multiprocessors. In ASE'93, editor, *Applications of Supercomputers in Engineering*, September 1993.

[SKM93] M. Schumann, M. Kiehl, and R. Mehlhorn. Performance Evaluation of NXLib Using Parallel Multiple Shooting. In *Developing Multicomputer Applications on Networks of Workstations Using NXLib* [SSL+93], pages 58–64.

[SLBL93] G. Stellner, S. Lamberts, A. Bode, and T. Ludwig. Design and Implementation of NXLib. In *Developing Multicomputer Applications on Networks of Workstations Using NXLib* [SSL+93], pages 6–17.

[Spi93] Peter Paul Spies, editor. *Euro-ARCH '93*, Informatik aktuell, Berlin, October 1993. Gesellschaft für Informatik e.V., Springer-Verlag.

[SSL+93] G. Stellner, M. Schumann, S. Lamberts, T. Ludwig, A. Bode, M. Kiehl, and R. Mehlhorn. Developing Multicomputer Applications on Networks of Workstations Using NXLib. SFB-Bericht 342/17/93 A, Technische Universität München, 80290 München, December 1993.

[Ste93] Georg Stellner. MMK/X — Using a Network of Workstations as a Supercomputer. In Spies [Spi93], chapter 1, pages 5–21.

[Sun93] Sun User Group. *Sun User Group Proceedings*, December 1993.

Programming Environments for Massively Parallel Distributed Systems, Monte Verità, Switzerland

Evaluating VLIW-in-the-large

B. Bacci, E. Chiti, M. Danelutto & M. Vanneschi
Department of Computer Science
University of Pisa
{bacci,marcod,vannesch}@di.unipi.it

Abstract

Some time ago, we proposed a new computing model, called VLIW-in-the-large, allowing both coarse grain and fine grain parallelism to be exploited in the execution of programs onto the coMP architecture. coMP is an MIMD machine explicitly designed to allow fast inter-processor communications to be performed. These kind of fast, possibly synchronous, interprocessor communications are essential to the realization of the VLIW-in-the-large computing model. In this paper, we present some experimental results that validate both the computing model and the design choices relative to the coMP, massively parallel computing architecture.

1 Introduction

When Fisher firstly introduced "trace compaction" [Fis81], horizontal microarchitectures were going to a pre-mature death due to the scarce amount of fine grain parallelism that could be found in regular sequential programs. By relaxing the basic block limitation inherent to the other compaction algorithms, Fisher opened new perspectives in fine grain parallelism exploitation, that led to the introduction of some new computer architectures, based on VLIW principles, whose main representative has been the Multiflow TRACE computer architecture [Mul87, CNO+88]. After that, despite global compaction techniques and Trace Scheduling itself have been modified and enhanced [GS90, LA83, Lin83], VLIW architectures have disappeared from the scenario of fine grain parallel computing. This has been mainly due to a couple of reasons: on the one hand, the advent of RISC processors (super-scalar and/or super-pipeline) have killed out VLIW processors due to their definitely better cost/performance ratio. On the other hand, the VLIW machines have demonstrated to be very efficient when executing vectorizable code but not in the general case. The consequence is that VLIW architectures have lost the possibility to claim themselves "general-purpose", as they showed either poor efficiency on non-vector code and good performance on vector-code, or high efficiency on non-vector code and poor performance on the vector one.

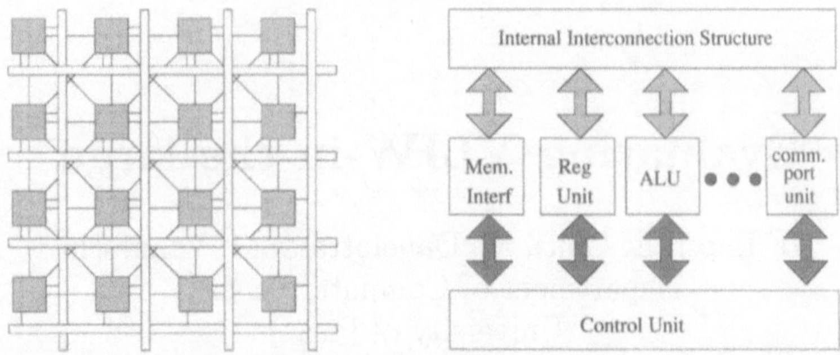

Figure 1: *coMP (left) and coP(right) structure*

Our work began assessing that VLIW can be considered a very interesting way of exploiting fine grain parallelism if and only if it can be "merged" with other, more classical, techniques that can be used to exploit coarse grain parallelism *and* if it can be implemented in such a way that the amount of resources allocated for a program execution depends on the program features, to avoid inefficiencies and bottlenecks. Thus, we designed a new computing model, called VLIW-in-the-large, that combines fine-grain and coarse-grain parallelism exploitation within a uniform framework by means of the coMP MIMD computer architecture. Furthermore, the model allows resources to be dynamically assigned to the execution of a sequential process in such a way that non-vector code can be executed with high efficiency and performance as well as vector code.

In this paper, we first briefly recall the properties of both the coMP hardware (Sec. 2) and the VLIW-in-the-large computing model (Sec. 3), then we give some details of the compiling algorithm used to produce code for the coMP machine according to the VLIW-in-the-large computing model (Sec. 4), and finally we will discuss some experimental results that drove the design process of VLIW-in-the-large, and consequently validated some of our choices (Sec. 5).

2 coMP

coMP [Dan90, DV90] is a MIMD machine, whose name stands for *Communication Oriented Multi Processor*. The machine topology is depicted in Fig. 1 (thin lines represent direct interprocessor links, while the fat lines represent busses), whereas the structure of the PE building block (whose name is coP) is depicted in Fig. 1. The building block processor is a regular RISC processor, but for having a VLIW-like internal structure (i.e. multiple functional units, controlled by means of horizontal microprograms) and for having some register that are both accessible from the processor busses and from the interface lines of the processor. A couple of such registers, one writable from inside the processor and readable from the processor interface lines and another one readable from inside the processor and writable from the processor interface lines, constitutes a coP *communication port*. Each communication port is also supplied with handshake bit registers. Furthermore, each one of the communication ports is supplied with lines that allow the processor clock signal to be propagated to any other processor that is directly (port-to-port) interconnected. Each processor has instructions to start (stop) fetching its clock from a port, as well as instructions to start (stop) broadcasting the clock signal over all the processor communication ports. Each coP processor sports ten communication ports, which are used to interface the processors belonging to the coMP machine to each other: two of such ports are used to link each processor to the *long reach interconnection layer*, i.e. to the row and column busses depicted in Fig. 1, whereas the other eight communication ports are used to connect the coP processors the *local communication layer*, i.e. to their N, NE, E, SE, S, SW, W and NW neighbours. One of the peculiar features of the coMP machine is that a register-size data item can be exchanged within a single clock cycle, between two directly connected coP processors sharing the same clock signal via the lines associated to the communication ports used to achieve the interconnection [DV90]. Overall this structure allows to cut out of the whole machine *pools* of coP processors (tightly coupled and synchronized) that are the entities supporting the VLIW-in-the-large computing model. Each one of these pools, whose size varies according to the features of the program it has to execute, will behave as a single VLIW processor in the VLIW-in-the-large model.

3 VLIW-in-the-large

The VLIW-in-the-large computing model combines the advantages of the VLIW computing model, concerning fine grain parallelism exploitation within sequential code, and the advantages of general purpose, coarse grain parallelism exploitation, concerning the concurrent execution of different processes on different processing elements belonging to the same MIMD architecture.

VLIW-in-the-large uses pools of tightly coupled coP processors (i.e. sharing the same clock signal and directly interconnected by means of their communication ports) to emulate a big VLIW processor. Like in a big VLIW processor different functional units perform independent microoperations belonging to the same microinstruction, in VLIW-in-the-large different coP processors perform different (groups of) independent microoperations belonging to a very (very) long microinstruction. The shared register file of a VLIW processor is emulated by using the communication ports to "distribute" the values of the emulated shared registers to the processors belonging to the pool.

As register values that have to be "consumed" at a microinstruction M_i must be at least be produced during the execution of the microinstruction M_{i-1}, we can exploit the single clock cycle interprocessor communication mechanism provided by the communication ports to perform the register value distribution. Obviously, the set of values needed at time τ_i by a pool processor P_k and produced at time

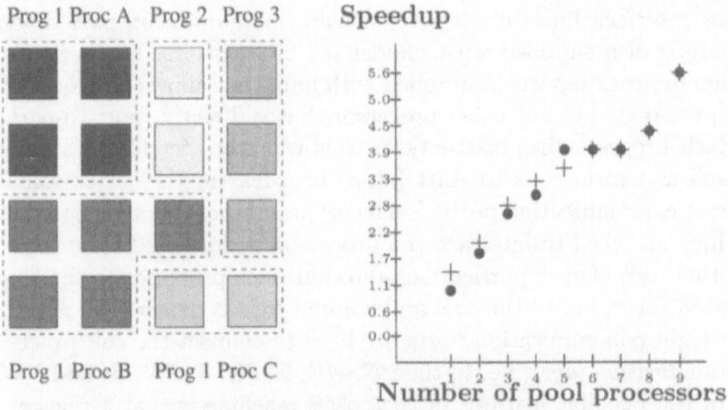

***Figure 2**: Multiprocess execution on coMP (left) and speedups w.r.t. configurations coP$_1^1$ and coP$_1^2$ (right)*

τ_{i-1} on pool processor P_j must be routed to communication ports connecting P_k to P_j at time τ_{i-1}. This is possible because the internal interconnection structure of a coP processor allows any number of data-source to data-drain transfer to be performed in a single clock cycle.

Beyond supporting VLIW-like execution of sequential code on a pool of coP processors, VLIW-in-the-large also supports coarse grain parallel computations by allocating different processor pools to the execution of different coarse grain processes, either coming from the same concurrent program or coming from totally unrelated programs. Communications between pools executing different coarse grain processes can take place using the long reach interconnection layer as well as using the local layer. Such a situation is depicted in Fig. 2 where 5 pools of different sizes are used to execute three different programs. The advantage of VLIW-in-the-large over the VLIW model is twofold: on the one hand, coarse grain parallelism exploitation is possible, by exploiting the MIMD features of the coMP machine; on the other hand, different pool sizes can be chosen to execute sequential processes having different amounts of fine grain parallelism that can be exploited.

4 The coMP compiling tools

Our compiling tools work out a concurrent source program by separately compiling each one of the sequential processes in such a way that it could be executed on a pool of processors behaving like a single VLIW processor. Subsequently, code is inserted to perform inter-pool communications. The compilation of a sequential process proceeds as follows:

1. the code is compiled, using a (almost) regular RISC-like compiler generating coP code. Precautions are taken to avoid to introduce too many data dependencies due to register allocation and other factors.

	LL1	URLL1	LL3	URLL3	LL5	
theor.	2	2.63	3	3	2.6	
measur.	1.77	2.41	2.25	2.5	2.16	
ratio	0.88	0.91	0.75	0.83	0.83	
	URLL5	LL7	URLL7	FUNC	SUM	URSUM
theor	2.55	3	3.75	6	9.75	12.5
measur.	2.3	2.78	3.57	4.75	6.5	10.7
ratio	0.9	0.92	0.95	0.79	0.66	0.85

Figure 3: *Speedup data for a* coP_2^2 *configuration*

2. this code is compacted with an original algorithm we derived from trace scheduling.
3. the code is analyzed, and, by using some heuristic rules, the degree of parallelism possibly leading to the "best" execution of the compacted code is chosen. This value is used to identify the number of PEs to insert in the processor pool emulating the big VLIW processor the code will run on.
4. the RISC instructions coming from the same long instruction of compacted code are distributed in the code of the PEs belonging to the pool. Instructions are inserted to propagate register values within the pool along the communication registers as well as to keep the execution of the programs of the different PEs belonging to the pool synchronized, e.g. by duplicating the proper control flow instructions in the code of all the PEs belonging to the pool.

The details of the distribution process can be found in [Dan90] and in [BCDV93].

5 Evaluating VLIW-in-the-large

With our prototype "compiler", wee performed different experiments aimed at verifying whether the VLIW-in-the-large computing model is better, comparable or worse w.r.t. an ideal VLIW model, and at devising which is the right mix of computation and communication resources that must be included in the coP processor (number of ALUs vs. number of communication ports per neighbour).

The benchmark programs we took into account concerned sequential programs, thus leaving unevaluated the impact of coarse grain parallelism exploitation. Some of the benchmark programs are Livermore Loops while other have been artificially built to stress some particular feature of the VLIW-in-the-large compiling process. In the following, **LLi** denotes Livermore Loop number i, **Up** denotes the "loop-unrolled" version of program p and **FUNC** and **SUM** denote two of the programs we build to stress some of the compiler features (both leading to high degrees of fine grain parallelism).

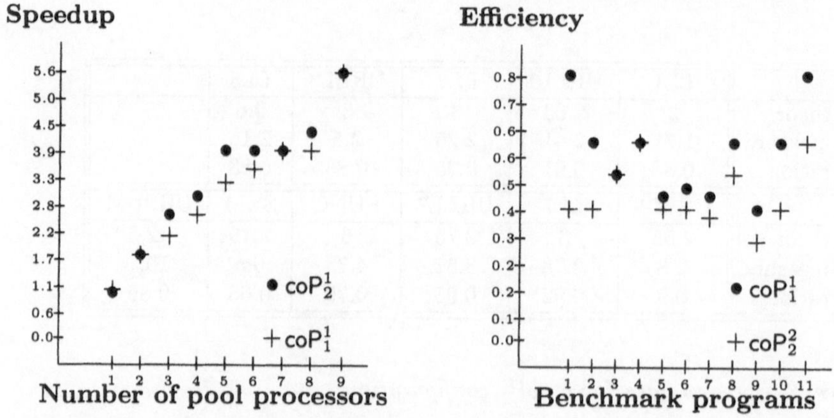

***Figure 4**: Speedup for coP configurations coP$_1^1$ and coP$_2^1$ (left) and relative efficiency of configurations coP$_1^1$ and coP$_2^2$ (right)*

First of all, we measured the efficiency of VLIW-in-the-large with respect to the ideal VLIW model. Table 3 shows the speedups obtained with VLIW-in-the-large with respect to those that can be obtained onto an ideal VLIW architecture. The measured values are very close to the ideal values. This is a very interesting result, expecially concerning the possibility to exploit fine grain parallelism à la VLIW on MIMD machines. Then, we tried to understand which is the correct mix of computation and communication resources that have to be included in a coP processor. We measured the speedups obtained executing the benchmark programs on pools holding processors with different amounts of resources. In particular, we look for the "best" ratio between the number of communication ports per neighbour and the number of internal ALUs (in the following we denote with coP$_m^n$ a coP PE holding n ALUs and m communication ports per-neighbour).

Fig. 2 shows the speedups obtained when a single port is used for communicating with each neighbour and one or two ALUs are included in the processor: 2 ALUs give very small benefits on small pools and no benefits at all on large processor pools. It can be argued that, in order to keep the cost/performance ratio low, the coP$_1^1$ configuration is to be preferred. Fig. 4 shows the speedups obtained on pools of different sizes when the number of ports connecting each neighbour varies between 1 and 2 and the number of ALUs is fixed (1). In that case, we see that the configuration with a smaller number of communication ports behaves worse that the other one. Finally, Fig. 4 compares the efficiency of coP configurations with 1-port and 1-ALU with respect to configurations of 2-ports and 2 ALUs. The graph shows that "finer-grain" processor configuration lead to a better efficiency (efficiency is measured as the ratio between the speedup and the amount of resources (ALUs and ports) used in each processor).

6 Conclusion

We briefly introduced the VLIW-in-the-large computing model and its support architecture coMP. We outlined the properties of VLIW-in-the-large, and finally we discussed some results obtained by means of experiments. The results give two main evidences: on the one hand, VLIW-in-the-large exploits fine grain parallelism in quantities comparable with the classical (and ideal) VLIW model. On the other hand, smaller coP processors, i.e. processors with a minor amount of internal resources (such as ALUs and communication ports) lead to more efficient (and effective) processor pools, thus discouraging the design of VLIW-in-the-large machines having very rich (and more costly) elementary processing elements.

References

[BCDV93] B. Bacci, E. Chiti, M. Danelutto, and M. Vanneschi. Evaluating the VLIW-in-the-large computing model. Technical Report TR-18/93, Department of Computer Science, University of Pisa (Italy), 1993. Available by ftp anonymous at `ftp.di.unipi.it`.

[CNO+88] R. P. Colwell, R. P. Nix, J. J. O'Donnell, D. B. Papworth, and P. H. Rodman. A VLIW Architecture for a Trace Scheduling Compiler. *IEEE Transactions on Computers*, C-37(8), August 1988.

[Dan90] M. Danelutto. *A massively parallel architecture using VLIW for fine grain parallelism exploitation.* PhD thesis, Department of Computer Science, University of Pisa (Italy), 1990. TD05/90.

[DV90] M. Danelutto and M. Vanneschi. VLIW-in-the-large: a model for fine grain parallelism exploitation on distributed memory multiprocessors. In *MICRO-23, The 23rd International Workshop on Microprogramming and Microarchitecture (ACM-IEEE)*, pages 7–16, November 1990.

[Fis81] J. A. Fisher. Trace scheduling: a technique for global microcode compaction. *IEEE Transactions on Computers*, July 1981.

[GS90] R. Gupta and M. L. Soffa. Region Scheduling: an approach for detecting and redistributing parallelism. *IEEE Transactions on Software Engineering*, 16(4), April 1990.

[LA83] J. Lah and D. E. Atkins. TREE compaction of microprograms. In *MICRO-16, The 16rd International Workshop on Microprogramming and Microarchitecture (ACM-IEEE)*, 1983.

[Lin83] J. L. Linn. SRDAG Compaction: a generalization of Trace Scheduling to increase the use of context information. In *MICRO-16, The 16rd International Workshop on Microprogramming and Microarchitecture (ACM-IEEE)*, 1983.

[Mul87] Multiflow. Product bullettin: TRACE computer systems. Multiflow Computer Inc., 1987.

Programming Environments for Massively Parallel Distributed Systems, Monte Verità, Switzerland

Implementing a $\mathcal{N}$-Mixed-Memory Model on a Distributed Memory System*

Vicente Cholvi-Juan　　José M. Bernabéu-Aubán
Departamento de Sistemas Informáticos y Computación
Universidad Politécnica de Valencia, Apartado 22012
46071 Valencia, Spain
{vcholvi,josep}@dsic.upv.es

Abstract

Parallel systems with distributed memory are difficult to program due in part to the complexity of the communication models used for interaction among processes. Memory models of interaction can partially alleviate these problems.

In this paper we present the $\mathcal{N}$-Mixed memory model which is a generalization of the strict and sufficient memory models. This model weakens the strict memory model, but still maintains its simplicity.

The $\mathcal{N}$-Mixed memory model has been implemented on a distributed configuration, showing the performance analisys we have done a good performance, even when reduced to the strict and sufficient memory models.

1 Introduction

Computation in parallel distributed processing systems is carried out by a set of cooperating processes, each one running on a different processor (or node). Cooperation among processes has traditionally been performed using the *Communication Model* [4, 5]: a given process sends a message to another known processes making use of the primitives **send** and **receive**.

However, commonly shared data cannot be easily managed by the communication model [4]. Using this model, each sender process must know the processes which has to receive the data. At the same time, the receiving processes must exist in a state such that they could receive the data. The final picture is that of a difficult system to program.

In part to address the difficulty of programming parallel distributed systems, *Shared Memory Models* are being considered as an alternative to the traditional

*This work has been partially funded by CICYT grants TIC90-0815 and TIC93-0304

communication model in distributed architectural platforms [3, 6, 7, 9]. These models provide a set of shared addresses that the processes can use in the same way they access data locally stored, i.e. using the primitives **`data=read(address)`** and **`write(address,data)`**.

In general, memory models give a simpler view than the communication model in applications where the different processes have to share the same data. This is so because local and remote data is accessed in a transparent manner, hiding the communication mechanisms. This leads to a simplification of the programming task, with a performance which may equal that obtained with the communication model.

In the present paper we propose an implementation of a new memory model on a distributed architecture which can readily be used for providing library and compiler support. The memory model we implement is the $\mathcal{N}$-Mixed memory model[1], which is a generalization of both the *strict* and the *sufficient* models. This model, while being as intuitive as the strict one, permits more parallelism in the execution, presenting, thus a potentially better performance than that obtainable for the strict model.

2 Memory Models

Every algorithm is written based on a set of primitive operations. The properties of such operations determine how they can be combined to obtain a correct algorithm. Memory accesses are among the most widely used operations and their properties and guarantees are very important. Depending on the properties guaranteed by the memory access operations (which can be difficult to maintain due to interleaving of accesses from each process, indetermination of the order of accesses from concurrent process, existing replicas of memory, ...), the algorithms using them will vary in complexity. This is especially true when considering multiprocess shared-memory algorithms.

Thus depending on those properties there are diferent memory models. Maybe the most useful and intuitive memory model is the *Strict*. Roughtly speaking, the strict memory model forces that each read operation to a given address returns the data of the "most recently" write operation at that address [7].

The strict memory model provides strong guarantees for the memory access operations, being efficiently implementable in uniprocessor systems. The implementation of this type of memory in a multiprocessor system may, however, reduce the potential performance gains of the system.

Nevertheless some times the applications do not require such a strong memory for a solution. In those cases it does not make sense to pay the penalties of maintaining the *strong* guarantees, when weaker models can be equally suitable.

Let's consider a two node system with only two shared variables, x and y with initial value 0. We can think of the system as having x and y replicated at each node. Let's further assume that the nodes execute the following program.

- node A: *write(x)1 read(y)*
- node B: *read(x) write(y)1*

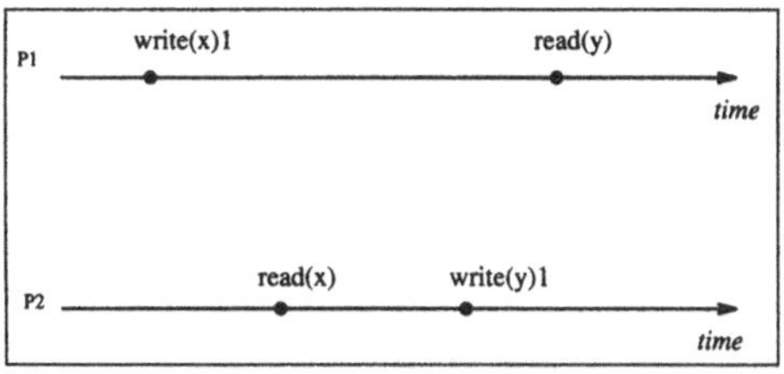

Figure 1:

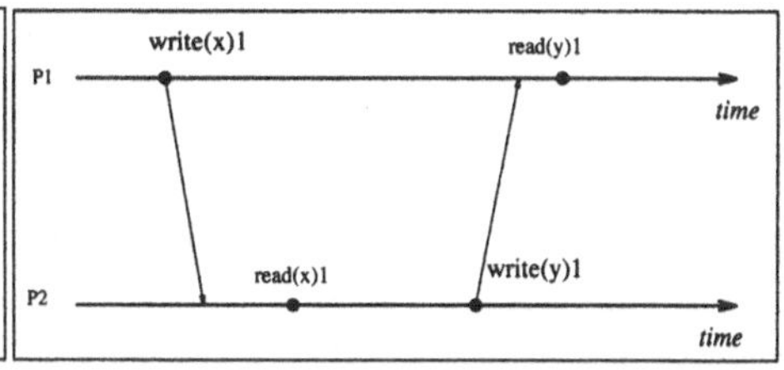

Figure 2:

Considering global time, a possible computation can be the one presented in Figure 1.

It is clear if the computation is subject to an strict memory model, the read values must be both 1. Obviously two messages must be used to communicate the writes (Figure 2). Nevertheless, we have assumed there is a global time observer. But if we don't make that assumption (of course global time is generally not available, and any observation of the copmputations suffers from impredictable notification delays), we may observe different equivalent views [8] of that computation, such as depicted in Figure 3 (we can atribute it to different processor speeds, etc.).

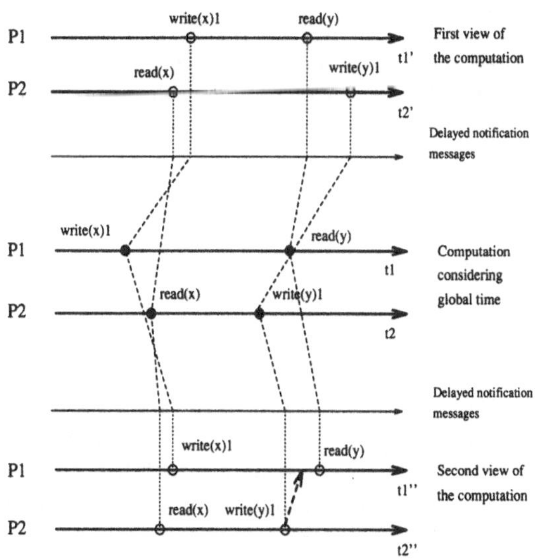

Figure 3: *Different equivalent views of a given computation.*

In order to have those views subject to a strict memory model, some of them will require that messages be used to communicate writes (second view of the computation), but others will not (first view of the computation).

Thus we will introduce the *Sufficient* memory model [1], which doesn't assume the existence of global time, taking care of situations such as the one shown above. This model generalizes the strict memory model potentially needing a lower number of messages to operate, and increasing the parallelism of the system.

Also, the sufficient memory model is similar to the strict model in the sense that both allow only executions having a consistent observation on which all processes agree. As a matter of fact the sufficient memory model is the most general one for which this is true. Thus, to find a memory model weaker than the sufficient one, we would have to lose the existence of a globlal consistent view for all processes.

Finally, we also introduce a new family of memory models that we will call $\mathcal{N}$-Mixed memory models.

They will have all the characteristics of the sufficient memory model, but some variables considered in isolation are forced to have a strict behavior (clearly both the strict and the sufficient memory models are included into the family of mixed memory models).

The $\mathcal{N}$-Mixed memory model, taking advantage of the larger degree of parallelism given by the sufficient memory model, allows at the same time the use of a stricter memory model for a subset of the variables.

3 Implementation of a $\mathcal{N}$-Mixed Memory Model

The memory access operations regulated by a given memory model will eventually translate into lower level operations. The nature of such operations will depend on the architecture of the system on which the memory model is to be implemented (which we will refer to as the *Configuration*).

A configuration gives us only part of the full implementation of the memory model. The part that implements a memory model using a given configuration is called the *Memory Management System*, or *MMS* for short. Thus a MMS will strongly depend on both the memory model it has to implement and the configuration it has to work with.

With a configuration based on a distributed system, a memory model can be provided either at the operating system level or just at the application level, by a set of library functions which aplication programs link with. The second approach has the advantage of not requiring a modification of the operating system, being, thus, much more portable. The main disadvantage of this approach is the need to refer explicitely to the memory access operations as function calls. This, however, can be alleviated with adequate support from the compiler and the operating system.

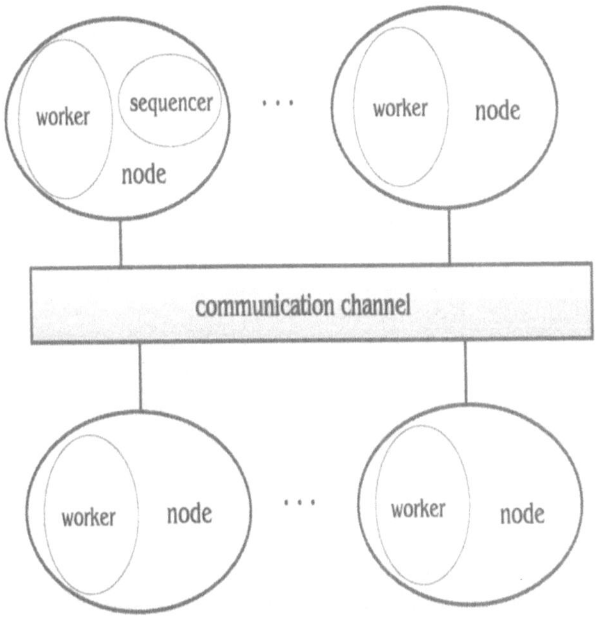

Figure 4: *Location at the used configuration of the modules which compose the MMS.*

Thus, we have implemented a MMS [2] on a distributed system as a set of library functions.

Those are composed by several *worker* modules, each one located at one node and responsible to take care of the application processes memory requests i.e., of requesting shared data to other nodes as well as providing them to other workers modules in the system. Besides at a designated node there is a *sequencer* module, responsible of arbitrate the conflicting request for shared data and ordering them (Figure 4).

This MMS can also be used to implement both a strict and a sufficient memory model. This is so, because both models can be obtain as particular cases of the $\mathcal{N}$-Mixed memory model.

We have also done an analysis of the performance of our proposed MMS, which has showed a performance improvement over one of the most widely known MMS, that proposed by Li & Hudak [7].

4 Concluding Remarks

Memory models of computation can help reduce the complexity of programming parallel systems with distributed memory. In this paper we have proposed a new memory model which has been implemented on a distributed configuration.

Currently we are working on a correctness proof for the proposed MMS using the I/O Automata formalism. We also are investigating in more detail the way in which the $\mathcal{N}$-Mixed memory can be effectively programmed, and the kind of applications that can beneffit of the properties of the $\mathcal{N}$-Mixed memory model.

References

[1] Bernabéu, J.M., Cholvi, V. Memory Access Analysis. *III Jornadas de Concurrencia (Gandía)*, 373-393, May 1993.

[2] Bernabéu, J.M., Cholvi, V. *Implementing a Distributed Compiler Library that Provides a N–Mixed Memory Model*, Technical Report DSIC-II/4/94, Universidad Politécnica de Valencia, 1994.

[3] Carter, J.B., Bennett, J.K., Zwaenepoel, W. Implementation and Performance of Munin. *Operating Systems Review*, 25(5):152-164, October 1991.

[4] Cheriton, D.R. Problem-Oriented Shared Memory: A Decentralized Approach to Distributed System Design. *Proc. Sixth Int'l Conf. Distributed Computer Systems*, 190-197, May 1986.

[5] Gifford, D.K., Glasser, N. Remote Pipes and Procedures for Efficient Distributed Comunication. *ACM Transactions on computer Systems*, 6(3):258-283, August 1988.

[6] Khalidi, M.Y.A. *Hardware Support for Distributed Object-Based Systems.* PhD thesis, School of Information and Computer Science, Georgia Institute of Technology, 1989.

[7] Li, K., Hudak, P. Memory Coherence in Shared Virtual Memory Systems. *ACM Transactions on Computer Systems*, 7(4):321-359, November 1989.

[8] Schwarz, R., Mattern, F. *Detecting Causal Relationship in Distributed Computations: In Search of the Holy Grail.* Technical Report SFB124-15/92, Department of Computer Science, University of Kaiserslautern, Germany, 1992.

[9] Stumm, S., Zhou, S. Algorithms Implementing Distributed Shared Memory. *IEEE Computer*, 23(5):54-64, May 1989.

Working Group Reports

Programming Environments for Massively Parallel Distributed Systems, Monte Verità, Switzerland

Working Group Report: Reducing the Complexity of Parallel Software Development

Jonathan Schaeffer

This working group was to investigate the issues of what it would take to reduce the complexity of parallel software development to that of its sequential counterpart. We all agreed that this would not be achievable in the short term and, indeed, maybe not be in the long term as well.

In our discussions we repeatedly came back to an analogy. The first Fortran compiler took a long time to gain wide-spread acceptance. Computers were expensive and heavily used. Users were unwilling to sacrifice the performance of their hand-coded solutions, even in exchange for large reductions in program development time. 35 years later, we all recognize the advantages of higher-level programming languages. Computers are considerably faster than they were 35 years ago, and the performance loss incurred by using compilers is ignored. Only a few high-performance applications need the speed of assembler code and, even then, only for the time critical parts of their code; the rest is written in a high-level language.

With parallel programming, the same analogy may hold. Parallel computers are still expensive and users are unwilling to sacrifice performance. What happens when the equivalent of a Cray costs the price of a workstation? Will users care so much about performance? Will they be willing to sacrifice performance for the advantages of faster and more reliable software development? It seems as if history may repeat itself.

In our discussions, we emphasized several areas where tool development must proceed to meet the software development and performance demands of the user community. These areas include:

1. **Abstraction**. Hardware details should be completely abstracted from the software development cycle (although, of course, they should be accessible if desired). There is a need for higher-level programming structures/models to further abstract (e.g. producer- consumer structures). Support for abstraction should be part of the programming language(s) used.

2. **Safe language**. Although clearly a contentious issue, we all agreed that the commonly used programming languages for parallel computing need to be

redesigned. In particular, in addition to abstraction described above, we felt it was important to have "clean" semantics that are well defined, and do not allow the user to do "dangerous" things in his code.

3. **Visualization**. Parallel design, execution and examination of the results need to be visualized, both in 2 and 3 dimensions. Sophisticated filters are required to present the information in an easy-to-comprehend format. Unfortunately, it is easy to overwhelm the user with information overload. There is a need to be able to present the user with the "interesting" subset of the information they want.

4. **Complete tool suite**. This includes a variety of tools including knowledgeable debuggers, performance analysis tools, dependency analysis tools, safe transformation tools, etc.

When will parallel programming environments and languages begin to dominate? There are two contributing factors. First, education is important. The notion of parallel computing needs to be introduced earlier in a computer science curriculum, although we were unable to reach consensus as to when would be appropriate and the level of detail that would be involved. Second, attrition will help alleviate the lack of acceptance of these tools. The famous physicist Max Plank perhaps summarized it best:

> An important scientific innovation rarely makes its way by gradually winning over and converting its opponents. What does happen is that its opponents gradually die out and that the growing generation is familiarized with the idea from the beginning.

Programming Environments for Massively Parallel Distributed Systems, Monte Verità, Switzerland

Working Group Report: Usability of Parallel Programming System

Gregory V. Wilson

This session was organized to discuss a set of problems with which to assess the usability of parallel programming systems. The aim would be to find problems which would be simpler, and easier to implement, than the Cowichan suite proposed in Wilson's paper at this workshop. Participating in the session were Alain Fagot, Frederic Guidec, Bruce Irvin, Thomas Kunz, Steve Moyer, Jan Prins, and Julie Vachon.

All of the participants felt that assessing usability was a worthwhile goal, and that it would be possible to begin to do this, albeit to a limited extent, using a set of small problems. To paraphrase Bruce Irvin:

> Most people agree that assessing usability with more rigor than that provided by testimonials is worthwhile. However, people are sick of toy problems. It is easy to understand why people use them (less time to implement, less effort to analyse, less space required to explain them in papers, etc.), but it would be useful if everyone would do it in the same way. If we promote one set of small problems, which can be implemented in 1–2 weeks, everyone will do the same examples, and we'll be able to compare results. No other current method of usability (or other) evaluation is more timely or allows for better comparability of results. So, although I'm sick of toy problems, I don't mind a one week flu, and if everyone gets the same flu, we may build up an immunity to it in the future.

The foremost aim of this set would be to assess the ease with which code can be developed using different systems. Most computer programmers have some intuitive feel for complexity; given examples of problems implemented in several different ways, programmers can evolve some feeling as to which of those ways they would rather use. A set of small problems would complement the full Cowichan suite by being easier to implement (one or a few days per problem instead of four to eight weeks), and amenable to theoretical analysis (so that achieved speedups could be compared to predictions). The criteria arrived at for choosing problems included:

1. Each problem must have one clear objective (but see the comments below on chaining).

2. Each must require no more than one working day to implement in a well-supported serial language such as C or Scheme.
3. Between them, the chosen problems should provide opportunities for using common parallel cliches, such as element-wise operations, reduction and parallel prefix, data-based synchronization, regular structure decomposition, pointer chasing, selection between alternatives, and so on.
4. Problems should be specified according to what is to be accomplished; how that aim is achieved should be left up to the implementor. Thus, if task farming is an appropriate way to solve a problem in one system, while loop splitting is most appropriate in another, implementors should have the freedom to choose.
5. At least some of the problems should not be infinitely scalable. Many (most?) real-world problems are not, and so it is important to see what happens in a system as bottlenecks are hit. This is particularly important if these problems are to be used for the other purposes described in the next point.

Implementations of this problems could also be used:

1. as one- or two-week classroom exercises in a parallel programming course.
2. to provide standard test data (e.g. traces and exectuables) for research on mapping and scheduling, performance visualization, debugging, etc.
3. to test the correctness of new parallel programming languages and tools.

Among the problems listed by the session participants were:

- Either find a single way to place N queens on an $N \times N$ chess board so that none can attack any other, or enumerate all possible ways. (The latter is clearly easier to parallelize.)
- Generate the LU-decomposition of a dense, well-conditioned $N \times N$ matrix.
- Simulate the Game of Life (a cellular automaton) on an $N \times M$ board for G generations.
- Multiply two $N \times N$ matrices (or two sparse matrices, or two skyline matrices, or...).
- Sort N integers (or N' integers, where N' is larger than the number of values that can be held in memory at once).
- Label the connected components in an $N \times M$ binary image.
- Calculate the Mandelbrot Set on a region $[x_0, x_1] \times [y_0, y_1]$ using an $N \times M$ grid.

- Simulate the gravitational interaction of an N-body system in three dimensions for a specified time.
- Find the convex hull of N points.

It was then suggested that a good way to structure the suite would be to require both standalone implementations of these problems, and "chained" implementations, in which the output of one problem is the input to the next. This would help measure how well a system supports software engineering, both by allowing re-use of utilities between problems, and by asking for multiple versions of each problem. It would also produce richer data for use in other research areas, such as performance monitoring.

Programming Environments for Massively Parallel Distributed Systems, Monte Verità, Switzerland

Working Group Report: Skeletons/Templates

Marco Danelutto

1 The discussion theme

The working group on Skeletons/Templates was asked to answer the (provocative) question

> *Are skeleton/templates based approaches to parallel programming a waste of time?*

The question arises especially taking into account the existence of many (real world) problems that seem to behave in a very "irregular" way *and* that the introduction of skeletons/templates *may* introduce inefficiencies by introducing further software layers in the implementation of the applications.

The discussion, from its very beginning, did not deal with the question whether or not the template based approaches were useful. Most of the participants said that they thought they *were* useful, and the discussion moved to the features that skeletons/templates must present in order to be useful.

Thus the discussion moved to the new theme:

> *How can we define/classify the template based approaches in such a way that we could clearly identify true template based approaches, parallel procedure libraries, low and high level implementation techniques suitable for certain classes of problems, all those along with their programming and debugging tools?*

2 What are skeletons/templates?

First of all, we discussed *what skeletons/templates are.* With different names, skeletons, templates, clichés, archetypes, PCFs, algorithmic features (alfs), constructs, assets, pidgets (parallel widgets), all indicate a *way to formulate parallel algorithms in such a way that the target architecture is not taken into account.* The differences between all those different names/concepts lie in the level of abstraction with respect to the target architecture features.

3 Layered view of skeleton/templates

In the perspective of being able to define a sort of *taxonomy* of skeleton/templates, we identified a layered structure, aimed at distinguishing between very high level (with respect to the target architecture), high level and low level features of all the templates we had in mind.

Level 1 Skeletons (algorithmic features). These are the skeletons that have to be used when thinking of the forms of parallelism present in a given application. They are quite abstract and they are not used to actually write the parallel program implementing the application.

Level 2 Abstract Programming Language. This is the language used to specify or describe the parallel program. It's more concrete with respect to to the Skeletons, of course.

Level 3 Application Language + Calls to libraries (e.g. MPI, PVM). Provides the implementation layer. The abstract programming language is compiled to this layer in such a way that the constructs/templates it uses correspond to some application language program, and this program uses the process/communication calls provided by the "parallel" library.

At the very beginning, we also considered another kind of distinction between skeletons (in the sense of the layer classification above): **application oriented skeletons** and **general purpose skeletons**. Application oriented skeletons are those that solve a particular problem, although that problem can be used in the implementation of many different applications. General purpose skeletons do not solve particular problems, but provide "structures" that can be used to implement an application oriented skeleton. As an example, one can have an "application oriented" skeleton computing the Discrete Fourier Transform, and this "application oriented" skeleton can be implemented by using a "general purpose" geometric skeleton.

3.1 Distinction between templates and (parallel/concurrent) libraries

We also tried to identify which are the features that distinguish templates from libraries of "parallel forms", and eventually we came up with three points:

1. **compositionality**, i.e. the possibility to use templates within templates, in such a way that the composition of two templates can be viewed as a new template;
2. **abstraction**, i.e. templates must abstract from data on which they operate, from the code they execute on data and from all of the machine dependent features;

3. **performance calculus**, i.e. something that can be used, once the input data set features are known, to "predict" the performance of a given template;

Templates are compositional, they abstract from target architecture features and should have some performance calculus associated with. It has been pointed out that abstracting from the hardware properties leads to inaccuracies in the performance calculus; still a performance calculus associated with templates seems to be an important property.

4 Template definition and implementation

We also recognized that there is an important distinction between the **definition** of a skeleton and its *implementation.* The definition of a skeleton must be given according to the principles stated above (abstraction from data, code, and target architecture features) in the most abstract way we could give it. Its implementation must take into account the features of the target architecture to achieve the better performance possible with respect to both the architecture and the features of the template.

5 How to define/collect skeletons

Skeletons/templates are useful when the programmer has available a full set of different skeletons to define its parallel application. Thus it is necessary to have a standard way to classify and to store skeletons in libraries. One way to perform this task is to follow the approach of the Basel group:

- define a tuple of "factors" that can be used to characterize a skeleton (such as data decomposition (present, absent, which kind), process structure (independent, not independent, etc.), etc.)
- store skeletons in data structures that hold a data value for each one of the fields of the tuple data structure defining the skeleton.

An alternative way to define skeleton/templates is:

- define a set of rules that specify each template in terms of its control flow and data flow

This is the approach upon which *alfs* are based.

5.1 A list of templates

We also tried to write down a list of (general purpose) templates that should be included in a template based programming language/development-system: **pipeline**, **farm** (same computation over all the data items appearing in a data set, no data

dependencies between any two computations), **produce/consumer**, **divide & conquer**, **geometric construct with stencils** (data distributed over a given topology, each PE performs the same task, possibly gathering data from neighbouring PEs), **iterated geometric construct with state** (like the previous one, plus the possibility to have a local state on PEs, the computation is iterated many times: either n times or until a given condition is satisfied), **unstructured meshes** (geometric with mesh topology and no load balancing strategy known that can be used to partition the data over a real mesh of PEs), **client/server**, **prefix, multiprefix** (tree structured computation with accumulate), **reduce** (tree structured (associative) computations), **map** (forall statement with no data dependencies among the execution of different (concurrent) iterations), **loop** (iteration, either definite or indefinite).
Concerning this list, somebody pointed out that both loop and prefix/reduce templates are somehow "low level" with respect to the other templates of the list.

6 Templates vs. coordination languages

We had a limited discussion on this topic. It was noted that coordination languages are somehow at a lower level with respect to template based programming systems just because the latter ones abstract from some features that coordination languages cope with explicitly (such as data structures). It was also noted that templates do not have the same power of the coordination languages (Gelentner's Linda) just because in that approach coordination is clearly separated from computation. It is an open point whether the efficiency of coordination languages is in general lower than that of template based languages.

7 Tools for template based programming

The discussion there has been quite fast. Everybody agreed that it's useful to have graphic tools that could help the programmer in writing parallel applications using some composition of templates. Many of us recognized that it is very important to have debugging tools available that report errors, performance bottlenecks, etc. relative to the template source code, rather than relative to the application language + library calls.

8 Benchmark applications

We agreed that a set of parallel applications must be defined that could be used as benchmarks to measure the efficiency and the expressive power of different template based systems.

9 Summary of skeleton/template related papers presented at the conference

9.1 Programming languages/ systems based on skeleton/ templates

1. Bacci, Danelutto, Pelagatti *Resource optimization via structured parallel programming.* **P3L**

2. McIntosh-Smith, Brown, Hurley *Intelligent Algorithm Decomposition for Parallelism with Alfer* **alf**

3. Kessler *Symbolic Array Data Flow Analysis and Pattern Recognition in Numerical Codes* **PARAMAT**

4. Fruscione, Flocchini, Giudici, Punzi, Stoffella *Parallel Computational Frames an approach to parallel application development based on message passing systems* **PCF**

5. Decker, Dvorak, Rehmann *A Knowledge-Based Scientific Parallel Programming Environment* **PDE**

6. Burkhart, Gutzwiller *Steps Towards Reusability and Portability in Parallel Programming* **BACS**

7. Szafron, Schaeffer *Experimentally Assessing the Usability of Parallel Programming Systems* **Enterprise**

9.2 Skeleton/templates embedded in existing languages

1. MacDonald, Sekera *The Cray Research MPP Fortran Programming Model* (`data sharing` and `task sharing` directives in HPF)

2. Burgess, Crumpton, Giles *A parallel framework for unstructured grid solvers* (master-slave computations in FORTRAN 77)

3. Clarke, Fletcher, Trewin, Bruce, Smith, Chapple *Reuse, Portability and Parallel Libraries* (PUL project)

9.3 Skeleton/templates and I/O

1. Bordawekar, Choudhary *Language and Compiler Support for Parallel I/O* (directives to support parallel I/O in HPF)

10 Participants of the working group

Name	Institution	Coun.	email
Christoph W. Kessler	U. Saarbrücken	D	kessler@cs.uni-sb.de
Marco Punzi	ACS Milano	I	marcon@ais.it
Robert A. Fletcher	EPCC	GB	bobf@epcc.ed.ac.uk
Guido Haechler	Univ. Basel	CH	haechler@ifi.unibas.ch
Hermann Ilmberger	Siemens AG	D	hermann.Ilmberger@siemens.de
Paul Lu	Univ. Toronto	CAN	paullu@sys.toronto.edu
Peter Ohnacker	Univ. Basel	CH	ohnacker@ifi.unibas.ch
Simon McIntosh-Smith	Univ. Wales	GB	Simon.N.Smith@cm.cf.ac.uk
Marco Danelutto	Univ. Pisa	I	marcod@di.unipi.it
Susanna Pelagatti	Univ. Pisa	I	susanna@di.unipi.it
Helmar Burkhart	Univ. Basel	CH	burkhart@ifi.unibas.ch
Marco Vanneschi	Univ. Pisa	I	vannesch@di.unipi.it
Jiri J. Dvorak	CSCS Manno	CH	dvorak@cscs.ch

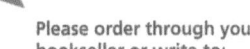

Monte Verità

Centro Stefano Franscini
Ascona – ETH Zürich

Edited by
Konrad Osterwalder, ETH Zürich, Switzerland

The conference center "Stefano Franscini", situated on the Monte Verità above Ascona, was opened in summer 1989, and is under the auspices of the Eidgenössische Technische Hochschule Zürich. International research groups, invited by lecturers of Swiss universities, are given the opportunity to hold seminars on aspects of their respective fields. The meetings cover a great variety of topics and are carefully screened by an international advisory board. Some of the most interesting reports are now being published in our new interdisciplinary series ***Monte Verità*** *and provide excellent accounts of the actual state of the respective research areas. Each volume is unique in that it places particular emphasis on making the connections between the individual contributions explicit and their long-term importance clear.*

Titles previously published in the series:

O. Besomi / C. Caruso: Il Commento ai testi. Atti del Seminario di Ascona, 2–9 ottobre 1989, 1992 (3-7643-2686-7)

O. Besomi / C. Caruso (Eds): L'attribuzione: teoria e pratica. Storia dell'arte • musicologia • letturatura, 1993 (3-7643-2977-7)

W. Czaja (Ed): Synchrotrón Radiation: Selected Experiments in Condensed Matter Physics, 1991 (3-7643-2594-1)

K.M. Decker, / R.M. Rehmann (Eds): Programming Environments for Massively Parallel Distributed Systems. Working Conference of the IFIP WG10.3, April 25-29, 1994, 1994 (3-7643-5090-3)

T. Dracos / A. Tsinober (Eds): New Approaches and Concepts in Turbulence, 1992 (3-7643-2924-6)

W.A. Jury, / K. Roth: Transfer Functions and Solute Movement Through Soil. Theory and Applications, 1990 (3-7643-2509-7)

M. Mansour / W. Truöl / S. Balemi (Eds): Robustness of Dynamic Systems with Parameter Uncertainties, 1992 (3-7643-2791-X)

S. Morgenthaler / E. Ronchetti (Eds): New Directions in Statistical Data Analysis and Robustness, 1992 (3-7643-2923-8)

K. Roth / H. Flühler / W.A. Jury / J.C. Parker (Eds): Field-Scale Water and Solute Flux in Soils, 1990 (3-7643-2510-0)

H. Ruh / H. Seiler (Hrsg.): Gesellschaft – Ethik – Risiko. Ergebnisse des Polyprojekt-Workshops vom 23–25. November 1992, 1993 (3-7643-2955-6)

L.A. Schaller / C. Petitjean: Muonic Atoms and Molecules, 1993 (3-7643-2851-7)

J. Schneider (Hrsg): Risiko und Sicherheit technischer Systeme. Auf der Suche nach neuen Ansätzen, 1991 (3-7643-2608-5)

R. Schulin / A. Desaules / R. Webster / B. von Steiger (Eds): Soil Monitoring. Early Detection and Surveying of Soil Contamination and Degradation, 1993 (3-7643-2956-4)

N. Setter / E.L. Colla: Ferroelectric Ceramics. Tutorial reviews of materials, theory, processing, and applications, 1992 (3-7643-2838-X)